Diving
the World

a guide to
the world's
most popular dive sites

D1305549

Beth & Shaun Tierney

Contents

Introduction ⏵ 5

↘ The authors 6
↘ The hit list 8
↘ Dive travel, where to 9
↘ When and how 10
↘ Costs, fees, small print 12
↘ Planes, bags and kit 14

↘ The hunt for ocean giants inside front cover

Central America ⏵ 56

↘ Essentials 59
↘ Dive brief 60
↘ Dive sites 62
↘ Dive log
Belize 64
Honduras 70
↘ Drying out 76

Galápagos ⏵ 118

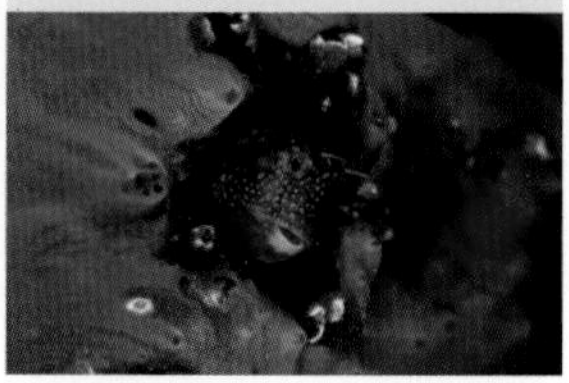

↘ Essentials 121
↘ Dive brief 122
↘ Dive sites 124
↘ Dive log
Central zone 126
Northern zone 128
Western zone 130
↘ Drying out 132

Australia ⏵ 16

↘ Essentials 19
↘ Dive brief 20
↘ Dive sites 22
↘ Dive log
Great Barrier Reef 24
Western Australia 28
↘ Drying out 32

East Africa ⏵ 78

↘ Essentials 81
↘ Dive brief 82
↘ Dive sites 84
↘ Dive log
Kenya 86
Tanzania 88
Mozambique 94
↘ Drying out 99

Indonesia ⏵ 134

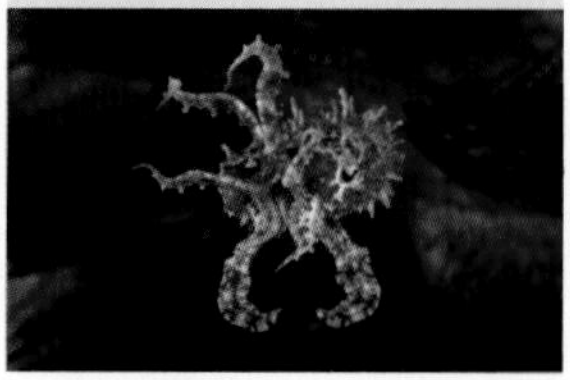

↘ Essentials 137
↘ Dive brief 138
↘ Dive sites 140
↘ Dive log
Bali and Lombok 142
Komodo 145
North Sulawesi 148
West Papua 154
Spice Islands 158
↘ Drying out 161

Caribbean ⏵ 34

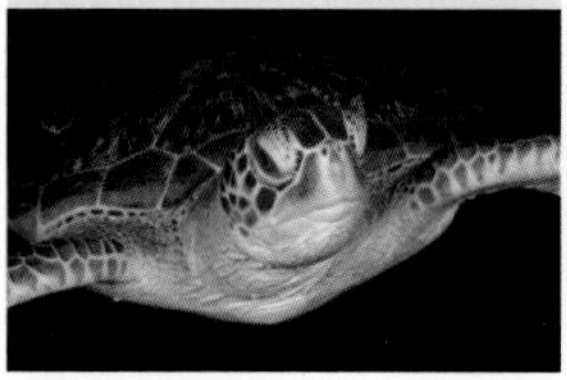

↘ Essentials 37
↘ Dive brief 38
↘ Dive sites 40
↘ Dive log
Leeward Islands 42
Windward Islands 48
↘ Drying out 54

Fiji ⏵ 102

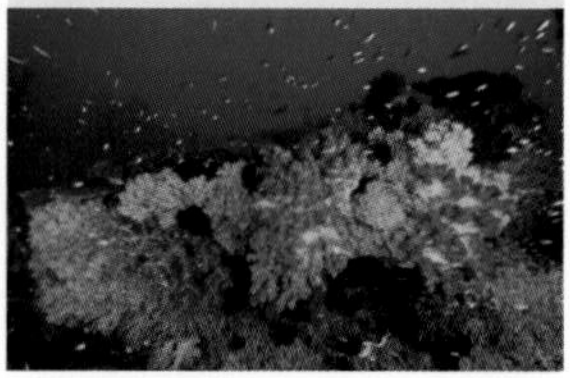

↘ Essentials 105
↘ Dive brief 106
↘ Dive sites 108
↘ Dive log
Viti Levu 110
Vanua Levu 112
Taveuni 114
↘ Drying out 116

Malaysia ▶▶ 164

↘ Essentials	167
↘ Dive brief	168
↘ Dive sites	170
↘ Dive log	
Sabah	172
Peninsular Malaysia	179
↘ Drying out	180

Mexico ▶▶ 200

↘ Essentials	203
↘ Dive brief	204
↘ Dive sites	206
↘ Dive log	
Yucatán Peninsula	208
Isla Guadalupe	214
Islas Revillagigedo	216
↘ Drying out	222

Philippines ▶▶ 262

↘ Essentials	265
↘ Dive brief	266
↘ Dive sites	268
↘ Dive log	
Luzon and Mindoro	270
Palawan	274
The Visayas	278
↘ Drying out	286

Thailand ▶▶ 326

↘ Essentials	329
↘ Dive brief	330
↘ Dive sites	332
↘ Dive log	
Thailand	334
Mergui Archipelago	342
↘ Drying out	344

Maldives ▶▶ 182

↘ Essentials	185
↘ Dive brief	186
↘ Dive sites	188
↘ Dive log	
North Malé	190
South Malé	192
Nilandhoo Atoll	194
Ari Atoll	195
Baa Atoll	196
↘ Drying out	198

Micronesia ▶▶ 224

↘ Essentials	227
↘ Dive brief	228
↘ Dive sites	230
↘ Dive log	
Chuuk	232
Palau	235
Yap	240
↘ Drying out	242

Red Sea ▶▶ 288

↘ Essentials	291
↘ Dive brief	292
↘ Dive sites	294
↘ Dive log	
Egypt	296
Jordan	304
↘ Drying out	307

Resources ▶▶ 346

↘ Marine biodiversity	348
↘ Conservation	350
↘ Diver training	352
↘ Health and first aid	354
↘ Marine nasties	356
↘ Credits	357
↘ Acknowledgements	358
↘ Directory	360
↘ Index	365
↘ Authors' hot-spots	inside back cover

Papua New Guinea ▶▶ 244

↘ Essentials	247
↘ Dive brief	248
↘ Dive sites	250
↘ Dive log	
New Britain	252
Papua New Guinea	256
↘ Drying out	260

Solomons ▶▶ 310

↘ Essentials	313
↘ Dive brief	314
↘ Dive sites	316
↘ Dive log	
Russell Islands	318
Florida Islands	321
Marovo Lagoon	322
↘ Drying out	324

Introduction

We've been here before. It was a decade ago, but as we sink slowly through indigo blue water, we see familiar rocky outcrops dissected by a glaring white channel of sand. The currents are slight, so we settle and wait, the sense of anticipation gnawing at our memories. There is a flicker of grey at the edge of our vision, a rush of metallic silver as a grey reef shark accelerates towards us, does a squealing hand-brake turn and halts right in front. He pauses, watches, shrugs and saunters away. If we could have laughed out loud, we would have. Did he look at us and think, "Oh, just you... you've been here before."

We have many such memories. Deeply ingrained, much treasured and never forgotten; images of stolen moments in an alien world that we have been so privileged to experience: that first ever blue-ringed octopus, a pea-sized boxer crab and a monolithic minke whale, a baby turtle as it took its first steps into the sea.

The underwater realm has been part of our lives for many a year. It's in our blood, a deep addiction that we embrace and manage simply by diving again.

Where have you been? An encounter with an old friend, the grey reef shark, *Carcharhinus amblyrhynchos,* in Palau.
Ulong Channel, Republic of Palau

about
diving the world
the authors

❝❞ Our love of all things underwater first developed whilst snorkelling in Mexico during a round-the-world trip in the late 1980s. By the time we reached Indonesia, we were completely hooked by what we were seeing beneath the surface.

As soon as we returned to London, we got qualified through the BSAC and headed off to do our first open water dives in the Maldives. It was a heart-stopping moment when we came face to face with a whitetip reef shark and the start of a love affair that has influenced our lives ever since. Fast-forward to the 1990s and we went off around the world again as a photo-journalist team, this time specifically to dive. In one incredible year we explored many of the exotic diving destinations that lie between the tropics, plus a few others.

Over the years we have remained involved in the dive industry and have been lucky enough to have revisited, photographed and written about many of the best dive destinations in the world.

❽ Using this book

It's not our intention to claim this is the 'absolute' in dive guides, rather we hope to give divers and divers-to-be enough information to feel secure about choosing and booking that all-important trip.

Everything and everywhere included is based on our personal experiences. Over the years we have dived each and every one of the sites reviewed: some were first done a few years back, but we have been fortunate enough to revisit almost all of them. Many times we would ascend from a new dive thinking we had done it before, so it was a case of working back through old log books to check old descriptions against current site names. Even naming marine species can be confusing as they have conflicting common names, so we have used the names and spelling followed by those who live in the areas we are writing about. When it came to making a decision on which specific sites to include, we asked both sport divers and professionals for their opinions, listening to their often very emotional responses. What remains the most interesting for us though is that, despite our personal preferences, we divers all seem to agree that a stunning dive is just that. However, things change in a heart beat, so regard what we have written as reference and not gospel.

We have done our best to ensure that information is up to date, unbiased and, more importantly, first hand. However, please bear in mind that if you go at a different time of year, chances are that your experiences will be very different to ours. And that, of course, is half the fun of dive travel.

Dive sites These overviews give a general indication of the region, its biodiversity, conditions, the dive styles available and their location. Numbered dives are our favourites and described in the dive log sections. Additional listed dives, marked with an arrow, are ones that were almost as good and worth doing if you can.

Dive logs These are full descriptions of dive sites as we experienced them when we did them. Names for some sites may vary as do the conditions, which change season by season. These logs are not definitive, nor are the descriptions: after all, fish swim away.

⬇8 **Roca Partida – South**	The name of the site when we visited
🌀 **Depth** 39 m	Our depth, not necessarily recommended
◐ **Visibility** good	Visibility on the day, season dependent
🌊 **Currents** moderate but variable	Currents on the day, tide dependent

Maps Dive area maps are a graphic representation of a reviewed dive site's location in relation to the others nearby and to the nearest landmass. Colour changes represent altitudes on land, sea depths and the position of drop-offs to give a loose indication of reef proximity. These maps are not to scale.

Images The photos used in each chapter – and against the dives – are what we saw on the day we were there. We have not taken images in Mexico and used them in the Maldives. If a site is famous for manta rays but we haven't shown one, it's because we missed out. And that, as we all know, is the way of things when you play in the sea.

Drying out At the end of each chapter are ideas for things to do when you are not diving. If time is short, ask your dive centre to help plan some sightseeing so you can explore the local land-based sites.

We have also listed contact details for a few dive centres, resorts, liveaboards and so on. Those with a short description are operations we have first-hand experience of; those with just a name and web address may have been recommended by friends and colleagues, be someone we know who has moved on or perhaps started their own operation. To the best of our knowledge, all diving resorts, operators and liveaboards listed hold BSAC, CMAS, PADI, NAUI, SSI or a similar affiliation, but always check, especially if you are taking a course.

When choosing a resort or liveaboard, remember that what makes us happy may not be to your taste. We target hotels and boats of a 3-star or higher standard as these are more likely to be comfortable, safe for you and secure for all your expensive dive kit. However, star ratings are not consistent or even used in some areas.

Author image © Sean Keen; Chandelier Cave, Palau

Above, green turtle on the reef at Maratua in Indonesia

• Raja Ampat   Komodo •

• Forgotten islands   ...and more •

WWW.DIVE-DAMAI.COM

diving
the world
the hit list

Times change. There is no doubt about it, but even in the sea nothing stays the same for very long. If anything, our oceans are even more unpredictable in this era where climate change is the topic on so many people's minds.

As the world adapts, so does the dive travel industry. A destination that was *the* hot place one year, quietly takes a back seat the next when somewhere new hits the diver radar. And nothing could be truer when the world's economic fortunes ebb and flow as often as the ocean's tides. Yet these changes are what makes being a travelling diver so incredibly exciting: there will always be an unexplored area jostling for position on the top of our hit-lits and there will always be adventurers who continue to push the boundaries, opening up new diving realms for us to visit and see what lies below.

The diver's hit list

For the first edition of *Diving the World* we sent questionnaires to as many people as we could, asking which destinations they had been to and where they wanted to go for their next diving holiday. The results became a list of worldwide where-to-dive destinations. When our second edition came along, naturally we bothered all those dive buddies – and a quite a few more – once again to get any new opinions. In the interim we also received many emails from complete strangers explaining the error of our ways for leaving out their personal favourites. After a bit more research, we dived some of those areas and slid them in as well. And here we are with version three...

We have found that our big, wide dive world has stabilized somewhat. A few old favourites have come back to the fore and, as ever, a few new dive destinations are opening up. The Asian countries still top everyone's lists but there has been a move towards countries where you can dive with specific creatures: Mexico for Great white sharks or the Maldives for manta rays, for example. The work of marine conservation bodies can be held responsible for that fantastic trend. There will always be those who want to push the boundaries just that tiny bit further. Well done to the intrepid divers who take the plunge to ensure the rest of us always have a new challenge to consider.

Looking at our planet from outer space, the first signs of life are coral reefs. Once these incredible structures were seen simply as a hazard by those who explored our vast oceans. Now we know that, like rainforests, they are vital to our survival...

dive travel
where to go

Every diver has their own hit list of must-dive destinations and, usually, it's a very long list. So how do you decide which one to visit first – the absolute number one priority – and which dream will have to wait for yet another year?

This guide aims to cover the places that are consistently the most popular with travelling divers, the ones they dream about and aspire to reach. Inspiration for the ultimate dive trip can come from this book, television, magazine articles or tales from friends. Wherever you plan to go, specific details of getting there and what to do once you've arrived are covered in the respective chapters. However, before you rush into booking, take a look at the bigger picture. Does your chosen dive destination have all the elements that you're looking for? It's not enough to know that someone else had fun when they were there – if you don't get what you personally want, you will be disappointed.

To solve this, define your requirements before you start the booking process. Think about what time of year you can go and the prevailing weather conditions at that time; how much you can afford, including the cost of the trip itself plus the cost of any extras; and, most importantly, what type of diving you want to do and what you want to see.

The world is a small place these days, and the seas cover most of it. Explore, dream, discover.

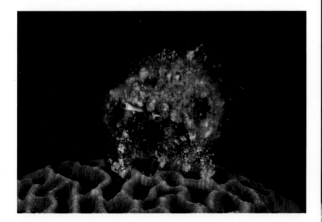

AUSTRALIA
GREAT BARRIER REEF • CORAL SEA
& REMOTE FAR NORTHERN REEFS

> Dive remote region Great Barrier Reef

> Coral Sea shark dive & 3000ft walls

> Australia's premier liveaboard

SPIRIT OF freedom
CAIRNS • AUSTRALIA

spiritoffreedom.com.au

dive travel when and how

Once you have decided which place ranks first on your personal hit list, ask yourself, do you want to be on a liveaboard or on land? Being on land is perfect for people who are happy with fewer dives, have a non-diver or family with them or want to enjoy the local culture. There's more flexibility to go where you want when you want but there is usually a limit to the number of dives you can do. In some countries, two dives will be crammed together into a single morning trip; in others, dives will be spread over a relaxing whole day, but that leaves no time for other activities. Liveaboards, by comparison, are perfect for serious divers who like to do as many dives as possible in their time away, or for those who just like floating about in an idyllic location with no need to do more than eat, sleep and dive. You will have access to more remote, uncrowded areas with fewer divers and often better reefs.

Next, and possibly the most important, consideration is the weather and the season. Are you going at the best time of year or the cheapest? If you go in low season to save some money, don't be surprised if it rains or the seas are choppy. That's why it's the low season. Marine life is seasonal too: be aware that even if a destination is promoted as year round, its most famous attraction may not be. Pelagic species in particular move great distances and can often only be seen for a few months. Also consider if you want to combine diving with land-based attractions. A cultural experience or rainforest trek may be ruined by rain while, underwater it's not such an issue.

The checklist

Land-based diving
» Is the hotel near a beach, restaurants, bars and shops?
» Is the dive centre on site or will you need to travel there each day; if so, will they pick you up?
» Is the dive centre BSAC, CMAS, PADI, NAUI or SSI affiliated?
» Distance to the dive sites – is it shore or day boat diving?
» How many divers and guides will be on the boat?
» Can you dive just with your buddy or are you expected to remain with your group? If so, will you have to abort your dives if others run out of air?
» What courses are available? Do you need nitrox?
» Are there camera facilities on the boat?
» Are there other activities for the kids, a non-diving partner and things to do on drying out days?

Liveaboard diving
» Do the cabins have en suite or shared bathrooms, air-con or fan?
» Meals are always included but can special diets be catered for and what drinks are included?
» What is the maximum number of passengers?
» How many dives in a day?
» Are nitrox and courses available if you want them?
» What is the boat policy on buddy pairs, solo or group diving?
» Are land visits scheduled?
» If you are travelling with a non-diver, are sites suitable for snorkelling and are there other activities available?
» Are there camera and computer facilities, battery charging stations, specific rinse tanks for non-dive equipment
» On bad weather days can the boat shelter or be re-routed?
» Boats rarely accept children but you may want to check.

Dive holiday options: a dedicated resort, liveaboard or day trip diving.

Booking

Although this is probably the first thing on your mind, it should be the last thing you do. Once you are confident that you know what you want, you can either contact a specialist dive travel agent or book the trip yourself.

DIY Becoming ever more popular as the internet continues to spread its web, booking your own trip can have advantages: you might find a product that is not available in your home country, and direct rates are sometimes discounted. However, if you book direct you assume complete responsibility for your own trip. You have to ask all the right questions, ensure you have all the right papers and coordinate every aspect involved: accommodation, visas, flights, transfers, diving, meals, sightseeing. It can be a hefty job, but if you like a sense of adventure it can also give you the flexibility to make on-the-spot changes.

Agents With access to information and systems not available to the public, agents can be a mine of information. A dedicated dive travel specialist will not only understand divers' needs but also be incredibly knowledgeable about the regions they promote. They will have suggestions, up-to-date information on local situations and often first-hand experience. They will also take the flack if things go wrong – very important these days – rearrange flights when schedules change or re-book you to another destination if there is a political or natural disaster. In some countries, they are also bonded or registered with government-backed bodies. This may not always be a failsafe, but it really can help.

There are many specialist dive travel agents around the world. Everyone will have their favourites, just as we do.

- ▸ **Dive Advice Travel**, diveadvice.com. Based in Valbonne, France.
- ▸ **Dive Discovery**, divediscovery.com. In San Francisco, along with Africa Discovery, africa-discovery.com, for safaris.
- ▸ **Dive-the-world**, dive-the-world.com. Offices mainly in SE Asia.
- ▸ **Dive Worldwide**, diveworldwide.com. Based in Hampshire, UK
- ▸ **Ultima Frontera**, ultima-frontera.com. Located in Madrid, Spain.

dive travel costs, fees and the small print

There is no doubt about it, diving is an expensive sport, especially if you are travelling to a foreign country. It is a generalization, but the cost of living at your destination will define the cost of your trip. Holidays to wealthier countries like Australia or American-run Micronesia will cost far more than going to less prosperous ones such as Egypt or much of Southeast Asia.

This becomes particularly obvious when it comes to working out how much you might need for extras. What might be more surprising, though, is that even less developed countries can be pricier than you thought if, for example, you are obliged to buy items such as drinking water which you usually take for granted. Buying bottled water or soft drinks can add a lot to overall costs.

When you are budgeting, look at all the angles to see if you are getting good value. Many people reject a liveaboard as the initial price can seem prohibitive, yet many boats include nitrox or unlimited diving, plus extras like mineral water, soft drinks or even beer, so the cost in real terms may not be as high as it first seems. To work out a value-for-money comparison, try looking at

Indonesia mid-range liveaboard for 10 nights	
Up to 38 dives, all meals, soft drinks and beer	US$3,225.00
Cost per dive (3,225 ÷ 38 dives)	*US$84.86*
Indonesia 3-star resort for 10 nights	
Up to 27 dives, 3 meals, no drinks	US$2362.00
Cost per dive (2,112 ÷ 27 dives)	*US$87.48*

the cost per dive. Add the cost of your accommodation, flights, dives and any extras you can think of (nitrox, marine park fees or visas) together and divide by the potential number of dives. Use this as a benchmark to see if your trip is good value. The simple comparison below indicates that the liveaboard gives far more dives and some extras in the time you have. Of course, this scenario won't always come down in favour of a liveaboard, as much depends on flights, the time of year and what you want out of your holiday.

Fees, taxes and surcharges

When you are planning and budgeting for your trip, allow a 'slush fund' for all those little extras you never quite know about until you arrive. These can be marine park fees, diver taxes that are ostensibly intended to support local recompression chambers or rescue services. Fuel surcharges are becoming ever more common. Individually, these costs are quite low but they can add up.

Currency

It is a worldwide standard for US dollars to be the currency of choice with dive operators, although more and more are quoting and accepting Euros. When it comes to currencies, US dollars are easy to exchange and many resorts accept them as well as (and often rather than) the local currency. Depending on current world politics, it might be advantageous to have a little cash in a second currency as well. Hotels charge a premium to change money, so it pays to know the going rate in advance. Check rates inside your arrival airport. These may be slightly lower than a local exchange office, but the airport is more secure and less hassle.

Fortunately, there are few destinations without cash machines these days so always bring a debit (cash) card with you and a credit card just in case. You may get charged a nominal fee for using the service but, in the end, you cannot beat having a credit card with you. A few countries add ridiculous surcharges for using them, but they are a good safety net and give you automatic insurance on purchases from flight tickets to souvenirs.

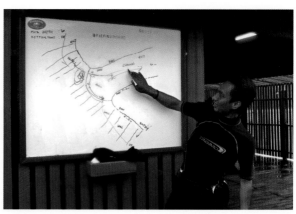

Exploring Adiamu in West Papua; briefing from the divemaster.

Insurance

Dive travel insurance is an absolute necessity. Don't ever consider trying to save a few bucks by not covering yourself properly. You need a policy that will cover flight delays, cancellations, bags and diving equipment, money, cameras, iPads and similar valuables. Make sure you read the small print, as some policies can have surprising exclusions, for example an airline closing down.

More importantly, ensure you are fully covered for all medical emergencies – both diving and non-diving related – including repatriation home or to the closest recompression chamber. DAN (The Divers Alert Network) has thorough dive accident insurance, but they do not automatically cover travel-related issues. Other insurers offer policies that may suit personal needs better, so check in your home country for specialist suppliers. A special note is to also check other insurance you may have; some life insurance policies, for example, specifically exclude scuba diving as a high-risk sport.

Paperwork and disclaimers

There you are, just arrived and settling in when along comes a raft of paperwork. You feel like you are signing your life away: first, acknowledge that your operator is in no way liable for any harm that might come your way. Next, promise that if something does go wrong, you won't take action against them, then accept that even if there is a complete blunder, you will only ever blame yourself. Finally, sign the papers regardless, as you know, deep down, there is no choice. And in reality there isn't.

If you question a disclaimer, or refuse to sign it, it's likely you won't be able to dive. Where disclaimers may once have been a declaration of fitness and training levels, they have since become a reflection of a society inclined to sue at the drop of a hat. There is nothing the average diver can do about this, except ensure you choose reputable operations that will take all the necessary precautions to guarantee your safety.

😵 Tipping

The question we get asked most – always – is how much should the crew get tipped. This is such a sensitive subject. Individual attitudes to tipping depend very much on where you grew up. In America it's an accepted way of life to tip generously for every service, as staff rely on their tips to make a living wage. In Europe the attitude is more likely to be a considered sum for good service (and nothing for bad!), while in Australia and Singapore people tip less, if at all, as these countries have much higher minimum wage structures. Bear in mind, too, that over-tipping in certain countries can be an insult, so where that is the case, a gift for or just spending a little time with the crew will be more appreciated than cash.

There is no magic formula when it comes to tipping your dive crew, but consider how much work they do behind the scenes, whether their actions ensured your trip went smoothly – or better than smoothly – and what their likely wage is. Although they will have been paid in line with local standards, a tip will reward those who often work very long hours for meagre salaries. Liveaboard crews, in particular, are often on call 24 hours a day to cater to your every whim. And always remember that these are the people who ensure you come back safely from every dive.

There is a growing trend among higher-end operations to formally request that guests leave 10% of the trip cost as a tip. Although this may well be appropriate, many divers find the approach offensive, regarding it as an extra charge. Don't feel obliged to do this if it isn't what you personally believe in, but always remember that all the hard work was worth something and being generous is a good thing.

In the end, only you can decide what the service was worth. If you need advice, ask your cruise director or resort manager.

Kitting up on the shore at Medjumbe; the hardworking crew on Dive Damai.

dive travel planes, bags and all that kit

The saying 'getting there is half the fun' was obviously coined by someone who had never spent 18 hours in the rear economy class cabin of a jumbo – with two screaming kids behind and the seat in front resting on their nose. Nothing will ever convince most people that flying is a good way to spend time, but it is a means to an end. The trick is to minimize the discomforts.

Airlines

A law unto themselves, some airlines still treat their passengers as honoured guests, while others bring a new meaning to the term 'cattle class'. Some are so much better than others that paying a little extra really can make the difference between a miserable long-haul flight and a pleasant one. Ask yourself if you really want to save a few dollars on a 14-hour flight and not have seat-back TVs with on-tap entertainment and free drinks?

The ever-expanding number of low-cost carriers makes this comparison even more obvious. Try booking a cheap flight with one. Half way through the booking process you realise that the bargain of the year has just skyrocketed: order a meal (click, $20 extra) or book a seat with your partner (click, $20). Do you want to check your bags? Click. Are you overweight? *Excuse me?* Click. The only positive result is at least it is clear what you are paying for. Until you get on board and it's, 'Headphones?' $10. Plus the plane is freezing, so you ask for a blanket, and guess what?

If you are booking your own flight and can choose between airlines, go to **skytrax.com** for reviews then look at **seatguru.com** for advice on which seats are best.

Luggage

All divers bemoan their lot when it comes to included baggage allowances, but the good news is that most scheduled airlines will waive a couple of kilos. But that does mean a couple, not ten or twelve! Heightened security means hand luggage is also coming under more frequent scrutiny and it is now common for those bags to be weighed as you check in.

Be sure to check your included allowance before you head to the airport. In general, the majority of scheduled airlines allow 20 kilos in economy, while US airlines will sometimes allow two bags of up to 23 kilos each. However, even if you do get a higher allowance, many internal flights on small, local airlines still only allow the lesser amount so be careful. (In some countries, they will even weigh the passengers!) If you know you will be over, call the airline to see what they will do but, if you exceed their limit, be prepared to be charged. If you are faced with having to pay at check-in, keep cool and try to negotiate based on being a diver. However, bear in mind that the standard complaint that 'golfers can take clubs for free' is rarely true and, if you use this type of strategy at the desk, you are likely to get less sympathy. They have heard it all before.

Another item of note: always lock your bags. There is a trend of not doing so because 'if security wants to check, they'll break the lock.' This is true, but it is better than having a stranger sneak a look at the contents of your bags. There have been several high profile cases of people being arrested for drugs offences after leaving unlocked bags in hotel foyers and airports. Always carry spare miniature padlocks or use plastic cable ties to secure your luggage if you are not with it.

Waiting for the flight at London Heathrow; Checking in the bags at Manila.

" " On our last research trip to Africa we decided not to take our own trusted dive equipment and instead, rented from four different operations. Three of them had fantastic kit that was almost new. At one, things were a little less than perfect but still completely usable after a few swaps were made. It was a reminder to ensure we double-checked everything we were given.

Equipment

We are taught how important it is to be familiar with our dive kit and are encouraged to buy our own. This is a valid standpoint until you want to travel abroad with it.

The problem for most divers is that dive kit is not very travel-friendly. Few of us consider the weight of an item before buying it but if you do a lot of travelling, you should. A full set – BCD, fins, mask, regulator with octopus, wetsuit and dive computer – can weigh 12 or 15 kilos, around 65% of your total allowance. When you buy items, compare the weights of different brands while you think about what you need them to do. A second, travel-friendly set of equipment will cost less than excess charges at check-in, which can be as much as 1½% of a full economy fare.

There is another solution – consider renting one or two heavy items. For some people this simply won't work: if you are really tall or really small, it's less likely you will find appropriate sizes. However, it may be worth renting fins, which can be up to two kilos a pair, or a regulator, which may be two to three kilos. Email in advance to find out what is available. Many dive operators offer complete kit packages purely for this reason. On the same note, never take spares of bulky items like regulators with you. If you trust this operator to find you floating in an ocean after a dive, chances are they can supply you with a good regulator.

Well-maintained rental kit in Carriacou.

⊗ Packing

It has taken us many years of constant packing, unpacking and repacking, to keep our bags beneath the European 20 kilo limit and we know it's not easy! Every time you add an extra snorkel/sarong/sandal, the balance changes and you have to chuck something else out. Here are some tips:

▸▸ Reduce the weight of your actual bag. A hard case can weigh as much as five kilos more than a soft bag.

▸▸ Reduce the weight of your kit by investing in travel BCD's, lighter regulators and fins.

▸▸ Buy a safety sausage rather than a reeled SMB and invest in small, lightweight torches and dive knives.

▸▸ Do not take scuba toys – or other toys – away with you unless they serve a purpose.

▸▸ Do not take doubles of major items. Any dive centre that's worth diving with will have a spare if yours breaks down.

▸▸ Take a small repair kit for minor repairs. Include duct tape, superglue, strong cord, cable ties and a spare mask strap.

▸▸ Get out the clothes you think you need and halve them. Then halve it all again. Really, no one cares what you wear.

▸▸ Reduce toiletries by getting mini-bottles, take medicines out of packets and write instructions down.

▸▸ Get rechargeable batteries – they are much better for the environment – and aim to get all one battery type if you can so that you only need one recharger.

Power tools

Is there anyone out there that doesn't have an iPad these days? On our last group trip, out of 16 guests there were 10 iPads and six laptops. It's a good thing, as you can download all your equipment and camera manuals plus some reading matter to those and save a few kilos. There are even iPad Minis that fit in your pocket. (And, yes, other brands too...) However, you will need to ensure you have the right power adaptors for these, as well as camera equipment, rechargers and any other electrical items: common plug types are in the table below and referenced in the Fact files at the beginning of each chapter.

Type A   Type B   Type C   Type D   Type E

Australia

19
↘ **Essentials**

20
↘ **Dive brief**

22
↘ **Dive sites**

24
↘ **Dive log**

Great Barrier Reef
24 Inner Reefs
25 Ribbon Reefs
27 Coral Sea

Western Australia
28 Rowley Shoals
29 Cocos (Keeling)
30 Christmas Island

32
↘ **Drying out**
32 Great Barrier Reef
33 Western Australia

Beware the dragon: needle-sharp teeth and devilish horns define the reclusive dragon moray eel, *Enchelycore pardalis*.
Kelana's Mooring, Christmas Island

INDONESIA

Java

Bali

PAPUA NEW GUINEA

🌏 Christmas Island ▶▶ p30

Timor Sea

● Darwin

Coral Sea

🌏 Cocos (Keeling) ▶▶ p29

🌐 Great Barrier Reef ▶▶ p2

🌀 Rowley Shoals ▶▶ p28

● Broome ✈

Cairns ●

PACIFIC OCEAN

AUSTRALIA

INDIAN OCEAN

● Exmouth

▲ Uluru

Brisbane ● ✈

destination
Australia

Sydney ● ✈

Tasman Se

Geographically isolated from the rest of the planet, Australia is a place of timeless beauty. From sun-warmed cityscapes to dense tropical rainforests, cool southern beaches to roasting barren deserts, the mind-boggling list of natural attractions is, for many, the biggest drawcard of this island continent.

'Big' is an adjective often used in conjunction with Australia. Its sheer size can be overwhelming, and visitors rarely realize just how enormous the place is. For divers, there is the biggest reef system on the planet – the Great Barrier Reef. Stretching over vast tracts of sea, it has distinct geographic zones but the most coveted is the far north, where you can even snorkel with one of the ocean's goliaths, the dwarf minke whale.

The Reef isn't the only diving in Australia's tropical waters. Those continually searching for the next frontier will find distant and unspoiled islands and atolls off the western coast. Isolated and barely visited, these are a far cry from the mainland, both physically and culturally.

On land, there are more sights than you could ever hope to see. Major cities share a love of art and culture, sport and the great outdoors – sail past the Sydney Opera House or climb the Harbour Bridge; fly over Uluru; tour the wineries; camp with kangaroos or trek in the Kimberley. Just don't hope to do it all in one trip.

Essentials

Most major airlines fly to Australia, so there are no problems getting there. However, reaching any major dive region will mean an extra internal flight, so consider breaking your journey either en route or at your entry point. For the Great Barrier Reef, fly to Cairns and break the trip in Brisbane or Sydney, both great cities for a stopover. For the islands off Western Australia, the only way to get there is via Perth. The internal carriers are Virgin Blue, Qantas and Jetstar so always check their connecting schedules before committing to the long-haul flight.

Local laws and customs

Australia and etiquette? Aussies would be the first to laugh at that idea. Things are informal here. People generally live an outdoor life with an easy-going attitude. The national motto has got to be 'no worries, mate'. There are few pretensions, though places such as Sydney and Port Douglas have trendy establishments where smarter clothes for evenings out are a good idea. Beyond that, it would be hard to insult most Aussies – unless you pinch their drink!

Health and safety

When it comes to medicine and health care, Australia is a world leader. Should you be unfortunate enough to get ill, you will be extremely well looked after. The sun can be very strong so a high factor sunscreen is a must. The Aussie saying is 'slip, slap, slop': slip on a shirt, slop on sunscreen, slap on a hat. It's good advice.

Australia's sheer size coupled with a small population means that even the biggest cities can feel like small towns to travellers from London, New York or Paris. The upside is that the crime rate is relatively low and personal safety, even in the capitals, is no serious cause for concern. Dive regions are traveller-friendly but anywhere can attract a small-time thief.

Costs

Australia's cost of living is comparable to other western countries; the larger cities and tourist regions are as happy to relieve you of your cash as anywhere in Europe or the USA. There are restaurants to suit every budget, with major cities boasting some world-class eateries. Based on the fusion food concept, they can be pricey but will have some of the most interesting food you will ever try. At the other end of the scale, you can eat quite cheaply in a tavern or pub. Similarly, a bottle of wine in a store can be just a few dollars while one in a restaurant will require a credit card.

Australia is very much a destination where you get what you pay for. Hotels work along much the same lines: cheap will mean basic or a little run down but usually clean; higher rates bring corresponding standards. Tipping is not the norm: Aussies rarely tip as the minimum wage is comparatively high and strictly adhered to. You should only feel obliged to tip if someone has given excellent service and then it's mostly 10% or less.

Fact file

Australia

Location	27°00's, 133°00'E
Capital	Canberra
Flights	American, BA, Cathay, Emirates, Malaysian, Qantas, Singapore to Brisbane, Perth or Sydney
Internal flights	Virgin Blue
Land transport	Countrywide buses, trains and car hire
Departure tax	Usually included in ticket
Entry	Everyone except New Zealanders needs a visa. Most airlines issue an electronic travel authority with their ticket. There may be a small fee
Money	Australian dollars (AUD)
Language	English
Electricity	240v, plug type E (page 15)
Time zone	GMT +8 Perth, GMT +10 Sydney
Religion	Christian
Communications	Country code +61; IDD code 0011; Police 999 Internet access is freely available.
Tourist information	Christmas Island: christmas.net.au; Cocos (Keeling): cocos-tourism.cc; Queensland: tq.com.au; Western Australia: westernaustralia.com
Travel advisories	gov.uk/foreign-travel-advice; state.gov/travel

dive brief

Diving

What makes Australia fascinating for divers is that it has over 25,000 kilometres of coastline spanning several distinct climate zones. The tip of northern Queensland is just 10 degrees short of the Equator, while Tasmania in the far south has weather a bit like northern England. This vast expanse is also bordered by two of the world's largest oceans and many different seas, adding up to the most varied diving on the planet.

Although you could pick up a tank and dive almost anywhere, there are two main destinations. The one that lures most, divers and non-divers alike, is the Great Barrier Reef in Queensland. A few years back it was even voted second in a major survey of 'top things to do before you die'. This sizable natural phenomenon consists of nearly 3000 individual reefs with 1500 species of fish, 4000 molluscs and over 400 corals. It is also a World Heritage Site, but that's not to say it's pristine along its entire length. The GBR is an active, working, continually changing resource, where divers co-exist with fishermen, tropical cyclones and exotic marine fauna, such as the devastating crown of thorns starfish.

Across the continent, Western Australia is the biggest of the country's five states and almost half her landmass. It's an empty, impressive wilderness, and, with so much coastline you'd be forgiven for thinking it would be a magnet for dive operations, but it's not. There's some cool water diving near Perth, but the only tropical diving centres around Ningaloo Reef. The reason why? Well, distances are enormous, local populations are small and diving is highly seasonal. However, there is access to a set of isolated Indian Ocean islands that are perfect for adventurous divers or those who might feel they've done everything else.

Snorkelling

On the GBR, the best diving tends to be a long way from shore, while snorkelling is better nearer the coast. Day trips to closer reefs are mostly on cruise-style boats to designated tourist zones with a plethora of commercial services attached. On the west coast, there are organized whale shark snorkelling tours at famed Ningaloo Reef, but these are expensive and, again, very commercial. Christmas Island's shoreline is great for snorkelling, but get advice on the daily currents and tides.

Australia is my birthplace, and even after three decades, I still wish for just a single dollar for every time I'm asked why I left. Apart from marrying a Brit, the answers would fill a whole book! Even though I don't live there now, I will always say that it is one of the world's most beautiful countries – unique wildlife, remarkable landscapes, colours so rich and seas so varied you can't believe they are real. Even if you only go once, you must go.

Whip corals on Perpendicular Wall, Christmas Island.

Marine life

Australia's two tropical diving areas sit just below the Coral Triangle countries. They may be in different oceans, but they both have high biodiversity with similar small reef creatures. The differences are revealed by the bigger animals: you are more likely to see whales along the eastern seaboard and larger populations of reef sharks on the isolated atolls.

Making the big decision

As this is the single longest haul you are ever likely to make, there is absolutely no point in travelling so far to do just one thing. On the other hand, Australia is so vast it's also impossible to do it all. Australian tourism is set up to work in short, sharp bursts, so choose the one dive destination you fancy most and build a trip around that. Bear in mind, too, that many really experienced divers find that the most accessible diving isn't challenging enough, so push the limits on where you decide to go. All the same, in a three-week trip you can dive, visit a rainforest or desert, see a major city and still return home without feeling you already need another holiday.

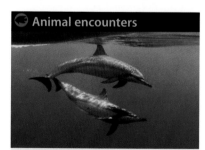

🌐 Animal encounters

The Great Barrier Reef: there are plenty of unusual and colourful small fish to spot, but somehow every trip turns into a big animal one, with Minke whales, tiger sharks and Napoleon wrasse.

Indian Ocean islands: with almost as many big animal encounters, including whale sharks in season and spinner dolphins (above), the offshore territories are also havens for some smaller creatures like the rare dragon moray.

dive sites

The enormous Australian continent sits firmly between two of the planet's most important oceans – 71% of the earth is covered by water and, of that, the Indian and Pacific claim around 44%. To the east, the Great Barrier Reef wanders down the coast until it disappears above the Tropic of Capricorn. This enormous landmark is Australia's most aspirational scuba diving destination. Beyond it, the Coral Sea is dotted with open water atolls. The dives are rather more adventurous, with large pelagics and amazing visibility.

Taking the adventure concept further, you could head for the Indian Ocean to three barely-known Aussie offshoots. The flat atolls of the Rowley Shoals surround shallow lagoons with near-vertical walls rising from very deep water. Further west, rainforest-clad Christmas Island is bursting with endemic creatures including the famed red crab migration. Spectacular dives include steep walls, schooling fish and easily accessible cave diving. And, last but not least, are the two Cocos (Keeling) atolls with extensive fringing reefs surrounding a horseshoe-shaped lagoon.

Barrier Reef and Coral Sea ▶▶ p24

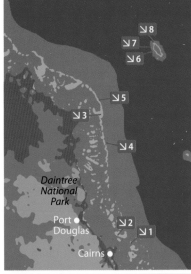

Christmas Island Wet 'n' Dry Adventures

Conditions
Tropical regions only

Seasons	December to February can be uncomfortably hot and humid; June to August has pleasant air temperatures but comparatively cool water.
Visibility	5 m inshore to 40 m+ in open water
Currents	Lightning speed fun at the Rowley Shoals
Temperatures	Air 30-34°C; water 25-30°C
Wet suit	3 mm full body suit; 5 mm for GBR in winter
Training	Courses available everywhere: look for PADI, NAUI or SSI training agencies
Nitrox	Available in Queensland. Most liveaboards also carry, but quantities may be limited so pre-booking is advised
Deco chambers	Brisbane, Freemantle, Sydney, Townsville

Diversity

reef area 48,960 km²	
HARD CORALS	360
FISH SPECIES	4,668
ENDEMIC FISH SPECIES	522
FISH UNDER THREAT	113

All diversity figures are approximate

Log Book

↘1 Double Bommie, Thetford Reef
↘2 Tongue Reef

→ **Mackay Bommies:** shallow lagoon and critter dive near Cape Tribulation
→ **Phil's Reef:** an array of hard corals on the inner side of Agincourt Reef

↘3 Pixie Pinnacle
↘4 Steve's Bommie
↘5 The Cod Hole

→ **Lighthouse Pinnacle:** chimney-shaped pinnacle ringed by striped snappers
→ **Tracey's Wonderland:** colourful reef wall with lettuce corals and cuttlefish

↘6 Half Way Wall
↘7 North Horn
↘8 The Entrance

→ **Round the Bend:** caves and overhangs on a submerged promontory
→ **North Horn Wall:** unbelievably steep wall coated in bright yellow soft corals

Rowley Shoals ▶▶ p28

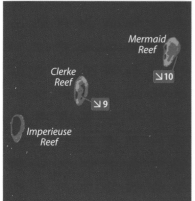

Mermaid Reef

Clerke Reef

↘10

↘9

Imperieuse Reef

ⓘ Log Book

↘9 **The Channel, Clerke Reef**
↘10 **Cod Hole, Mermaid Reef**

→ **Blue Lagoon, Clerke Reef:** shallow lagoon with coral clad swim-throughs
→ **Western Pinnacles:** bumphead parrots around three hard coral pinnacles at Clerke Reef
→ **Jimmy goes to China:** a promontory that catches conflicting currents

Cocos (Keeling) ▶▶ p29

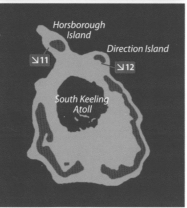

Horsborough Island

Direction Island

↘11

↘12

South Keeling Atoll

ⓘ Log Book

↘11 **Cologne Gardens**
↘12 **Cat's Cables, Direction Island**

→ **Clare's Corner:** pyramid butterflies and angels hiding in ridges and gullies
→ **Ripper:** fantastic hard corals along the outer reef wall at Prison Island
→ **The Canons:** undulating reef ridges and canyons that might reveal a manta ray

Christmas Island ▶▶ p30

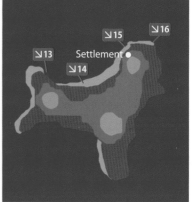

↘15   ↘16

↘13   Settlement ●

↘14

ⓘ Log Book

↘13 **Perpendicular Wall**
↘14 **Thundercliff**
↘15 **Flying Fish Cove**
↘16 **Coconut Point**

→ **West White Beach:** cave system with three entries divided by rock buttresses
→ **Chicken Farm:** unbelievably rich hard corals and the rare dragon moray eel
→ **Norwegian Wreck:** a completely broken wreck of a freighter from WWII

⊗ Endangered oceans

Australia is very protective of its natural resources and rightly so. Much of what you will see is unique, both in geological formation and position. You will be constantly reminded of this, especially in national parks where much is being done to eradicate non-native species. What is bizarre, though, is the contradictory nature of so many environmental policies; it makes you wonder how the policy-makers make their decisions. This country is home to the world's largest coral reef system yet the authorities not only allow people to walk on it, they actively encourage it. There are designated usage zones right down the length of the GBR – some are for recreation and sports, some for research, but most are for fishing. There is no way for these zones to be effectively policed. On top of all that, approval was recently given for a section of the reef to be dredged, creating better facilities for coal shipping. This policy is threatening the reef's status as a World Heritage Site. All that, along with the natural effects of tides and weather, means that you will not see the best of the GBR unless you take an extended trek away from the coast.

dive log

Great Barrier Reef: Inner Reefs

It's easy to get the impression that diving the Great Barrier Reef is straightforward but, in fact, much of this enormous natural phenomenon is a substantial sail offshore, only nearing the coast in the far north. Its geography creates three distinct sectors, with the Inner Reefs sitting on the lagoon created by the reef edge and the coast.

A couple of hours' sail from shore, these reefs can be reached in a day trip so are often used by snorkellers as well as for training. The dives are usually under 20 metres deep and season dependent. Visibility is OK in the summer, but in winter the water is murky. However, the sea remains calm, while more distant reefs are exposed to incoming winds.

⛵1 Double Bommie, Thetford Reef	
🕐 Depth	12 m
◐ Visibility	poor to good
🌊 Currents	mild

⛵2 Tongue Reef	
🕐 Depth	15 m
◐ Visibility	poor to good
🌊 Currents	slight to medium

Due east from Cairns, Thetford Reef takes just an hour or so to reach. The complex of coral outcrops has several different dive sites dotted around it. Double Bommie is a nice, easy dive. The coral species are not all that colourful, but the reef's character is built on lots of small cut-throughs and tunnels. The outer edge attracts a bit more fish life: moorish idols and sea perch are quite common. Thetford also makes a great night dive, as the tunnel walls are covered in shrimp and small crabs.

This oval-shaped reef is a short sail from Port Douglas and, although the dive isn't particularly challenging, there are a lot of bigger animals, including a resident turtle and Napoleon – or Maori – wrasse. The scenery is principally made up of staghorn corals, which guard plenty of smaller reef fish like butterflies and wrasse, sweetlips and coral trout. At certain times you can spot barramundi cod along with their spectacular juveniles, which flutter about like hyperactive butterflies.

Chromodoris nudibranchs and cuttlefish are both typical of the inner reefs.

dive log
Great Barrier Reef: Ribbon Reefs

The Ribbon Reefs mark the outer edge of the Great Barrier before it drops to the continental shelf and down to the deep-water Queensland Trench. The open ocean conditions mean that the diving is far more exciting, but reaching even the closest of the Ribbon Reefs from Cairns is a liveaboard-only scenario.

It is worth it, though, as there are dramatic pinnacles and sloping reef walls formed by centuries of wave and tidal action. Visibility improves dramatically, but the currents can be stiffer, attracting larger pelagic species: dive the famous Cod Hole and, between June and August, you can snorkel with pods of migrating dwarf minke whales.

⬛3 Pixie Pinnacle	
🕓 **Depth**	28 m
◐ **Visibility**	good
〰 **Currents**	mild to strong

⬛4 Steve's Bommie	
🕓 **Depth**	40 m
◐ **Visibility**	good
〰 **Currents**	can be strong

This small pinnacle rises from the seabed to just below the surface. A slope near the base has nice soft corals and fans. Red and purple anthias dart around a small cave, with tiny pipefish keeping them company. Around the pinnacle there is good macro life, including the flame fire shell, which has an electric current lighting up its bright red tentacles. It nestles in crevices, while nearby white leaffish hide amongst plate corals. Out in the blue are chevron barracuda, trevally and midnight snappers.

Typical of the Ribbon Reefs, Steve's is a pinnacle but one with a flat, sloping base. The lee side shows some damage but fin around into the current and the pace picks up. Schooling jacks hover in small groups and surgeonfish display courtship protocol with a male/female colour-change dance. A few tuna often pass by, surrounded by rainbow runners. The wall has tubastrea coral trees and, if you are lucky, you can spot the tasselled wobbegong – a very pretty, native shark. The area around Steve's

is also known for pods of dwarf minke whales that, curiously, come to play with dive boats. This behaviour was first noted when scientists realized these minkes were different from both Antarctic and 'true' minkes, which are only seen in the northern hemisphere. The GBR visitors are two metres shorter than their Antarctic cousins and have different skin colours and patterns. At up to eight metres long and weighing five or six tonnes, these are one of the biggest creatures you'll ever get close to in the water.

66 99 We waited for days before seeing the minkes for the first time – they simply weren't where we were. When we finally met and could snorkel above them, I was amazed by the sensation of having this whale looking at me from just a metre away. But we saw them better from the deck, and my best memory was watching a mother herding her baby gently towards the boat.
Sue Laing, managing director, Sydney, Australia

the
cod
hole

↘ 5

🔽 **Depth**	28 m	
🔘 **Visibility**	good	
🌀 **Currents**	mild to strong	

In the early 1970s, famous Australian biologists and adventurers Ron and Valerie Taylor discovered a patch of reef consisting of three parallel coral ridges and gullies with a depression, or hole, to one end. This reef topography created a protected haven for several large marine species, in particular giant potato cod and whitetip sharks. The word got out and, not long afterwards, dive operators started feeding the fish to ensure their continual

presence for divers. Ecologically this is a practice now regarded as unsound and is discouraged. Yet the cod have remained and, as you enter the water, they come to greet visiting divers just as they always did.

The giant potato cod is a curious chap and will hover close by as long as someone is in the water. Likewise, small Napoleon wrasse and large schools of red snapper will do the same. Leaving the hole to explore the ridges and gullies, you'll see that the hard corals are beautiful and in good condition. In fact, the entire site is very pretty. As you work your way up and down the reef you are likely to meet other cod being cleaned in a crevice, a polka-dot patterned barramundi cod or a small turtle resting on a bommie. Whitetip sharks sit on the sandy seabed but take off as soon as divers approach, no doubt feeling that the narrow spaces are just not big enough for everyone. There is also an enormous clam – well over a metre long – nestling in the top of one of the ridges.

" " The main attraction on the Great Barrier Reef has to be that most famous of dives, the Cod Hole. In all truth, we weren't looking forward to revisiting it. We'd dived there 10 years previously and it had been trashed: too many divers, too many feeding sessions. Now, ecotourism has kicked in and dive operators are more responsible. Some still feed the cod (mentioning no names), but the practice is fading away. The hard corals have regenerated well yet all the animals remain.

dive log

Great Barrier Reef: Coral Sea

The Coral Sea reefs are a solid 12 hours' sail offshore. Technically outside the Great Barrier Reef, these are located in open ocean, with virtually no land in sight, and are by far the most challenging diving you can do in this area.

In 1803, when this group of isolated atolls was discovered, the only inhabitants were a large population of seabirds. It's still the same, as there are no land masses, just exposed reef tops. Below the waterline the reefs are in pristine condition, as they are only ever visited by liveaboard dive boats. The reef that attracts the most dive visitors is Osprey, a 21 kilometre-long oval with a shallow inner lagoon ringed by sharp fringing walls.

6 Half Way Wall

Depth	25 m
Visibility	good to excellent
Currents	slight to strong

This steep wall has sharp cut-backs along its face. The mooring line drops to a round hump that masks an overhang full of whip corals that grow, rather unusually, both up and down and create a curtain across the front. At the base of the wall, a sandy area is home to plenty of damselfish and blue flagtails that flit towards you then away in a strange game of chase. There is a large patch of lacy fire coral that protects well-camouflaged stonefish and puffers. There are some lesser-known small fish such as bluestreaked gobies and midas blennies, as well as longsnout butterflies, whip coral gobies and a stream of whitetip sharks.

7 North Horn

Depth	40 m
Visibility	good to excellent
Currents	slight to strong

North Horn is on the northwestern tip of Osprey and is subject to enough current to always attract schooling sharks. From the second you drop in, the clear visibility ensures a good view of the resident grey whaler sharks. Large barracuda hang off the wall, which drops to a ridge of soft coral trees and fan corals. A horn-shaped coral head juts upwards from about 20 metres and the resident whitetip sharks circle it constantly. Smaller animals include coral trout, gobies and various hawkfish. Safety stops back on the shot line are ever entertaining as the whalers perform belly rolls below. This dive is quite a rush.

8 The Entrance

Depth	25 m
Visibility	good to excellent
Currents	slight to strong

A group of hard coral bommies surround a narrow channel that leads to the inner lagoon. The sandy seabed harbours critters suchs as imperial shrimp on cucumbers and commensal shrimp and goby pairs. The dive takes you around the bommies, where there are clownfish living in carpet anemones, different types of hawkfish and blennies. Between two of the pinnacles, and just under the mooring line, is a very small, double-ended cave. You can swim through carefully and, midway, see a decaying anchor embedded in the coral. No one knows where it came from but it's thought to date from either the late 19th or early 20th century.

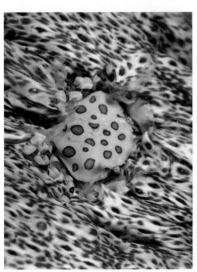

Swimming crab on a sea cucumber; diving at North Horn; whitetip reef shark at The Entrance.

dive log

Western Australia: Rowley Shoals

On the northern coast of Western Australia, the town of Broome is a multicultural little place that feels somewhat like the Wild West. Its past is based around the early 1900's pearl industry. Broome is also the closest access point to the Rowley Shoals.

This small group of atolls is 260 kilometres offshore and reaching it involves a rough 12-hour crossing, which can only be made from September to November as conditions are too difficult at other times. However, once there, there is some outstanding diving in crystal-clear water, so there's no risk of missing whatever pelagic life passes by.

↘9 The Channel, Clerke Reef	
🌀 **Depth**	20 m
💧 **Visibility**	good to excellent
🌊 **Currents**	mild to ripping

A sharp-sided, narrow channel cuts from the outer edge of this circular reef to the inner lagoon and transports water in and out during tidal changes. It's a thrilling drift dive that takes a little nerve, as the flow of water propels you faster through the tight, confined space than you could ever go on your own. Passing the walls and outcrops, reef fish and corals, the current finally deposits you at the end of the ride into complete calm in the sea. On the outer wall, away from the rush, large schools of jacks hang about in clusters, as do bronze whalers and, quite frequently, tiger sharks.

↘10 Cod Hole, Mermaid Reef	
🌀 **Depth**	30 m
💧 **Visibility**	fair to good
🌊 **Currents**	mild

Not unlike its more famous Queensland counterpart, this Cod Hole is a maze of small bommies, crevices and cut-throughs in the reef. Three resident potato cod are always around at the start of the dive to greet visiting divers. One is 1.5 metres long and very curious and is accompanied by another about a metre long. A third has distinctive pale skin. All three come very close, even nudging divers for attention. The rest of the dive reveals schooling fish like trevally, jacks and snappers and can be good for spotting bigger predators like sharks, which seem indicative of this region.

ROWLEY SHOALS EXPERIENCE PASS
ROWLEY SHOALS MARINE PARK
MERMAID REEF MARINE NATIONAL NATURE RESERVE

❝❞ Strange as it may sound, we discovered extreme snorkelling at Clerke Reef. One day, we were told to grab fins and masks quickly, then jump into the tender. We motored over the inner lagoon to a submerged channel leading to the ocean. Poised to roll in, we awaited the 'go' signal then flipped over backwards. With hardly a second to turn the right way up, were grabbed by a raging current and sent flying through the narrow cut in the reef at an incredible speed. There was no time to see a thing; it was all we could do to steer away from the sides until the current spat us into the Pacific, where the water was – unbelievably – perfectly still. The tender came to take us back to the main boat, but we were on such a high that we insisted on doing it again.

Soft corals at Blue Lagoon and one of the residents of Mermaid Reef's Cod Hole.

The two Cocos atolls lie far closer to Java than to Australia. But, as the Australians had a military presence on the islands during both world wars, it was to this country that the local Malay population turned for economic and political support in 1955.

Afterwards the islands reverted to being as sleepy as ever and, with just two flights a week and only 600 residents, this may be one of the quietest places you will ever visit – until you get under the water. Diving takes place mostly around South Keeling, a horseshoe-shaped atoll dotted with a ring of islands around a central lagoon.

Western Australia:
Cocos (Keeling)

Ⅺ11 Cologne Gardens	
Depth	35 m
Visibility	fair to great
Currents	mild to strong

Horsborough Island's reefs are smothered in hard corals: the leather corals are most impressive, and at depth, the fan corals are patrolled by highly inquisitive young whitetip sharks. At the top of the wall are clownfish in anemones and masses of pyramid butterflyfish. The channel beside the island is also a haunt for bottlenose dolphins, which are attracted by the sound of the dive boat approaching. They wait impatiently for new playmates to drop into the water with mask and snorkel then instigate a frantic game of chase. No prizes for guessing who gets tired first!

Ⅺ12 Cat's Cables, Direction Island	
Depth	22 m
Visibility	fair to good
Currents	mild to strong

Inside the lagoon, the sandy seabed is affectionately known as 'diving the desert.' At first glance, it seems quite barren but the flat sand is peppered with rocky ridges and small patches of hard coral where you see giant green morays and tiny pipefish. There is a small wreck, the remains of a fibreglass refugee boat: the engines and some of the skeletal structure are still intact but the hull is slowly disintegrating as are the unused Second World War telecommunications cables that stretch across the seabed. If you are really lucky, you might see Cat, the resident dugong.

Rainbow runners sweeping past Clare's Corner; beneath Cologne Gardens.

dive log

Western Australia: Christmas Island

> **❝❞** Something unexpected always happens here. I have seen mola-mola three times, a rare seahorse just once but hammerheads about 20 times. And then there was the day we saw humpback whales... there were two passing through just metres from shore.
> *Linda Cash, marketing manager, Christmas Island, Australia*

Even closer to Java than Cocos, Christmas Island often hits the headlines for all the wrong reasons – as the site of a refugee station. However, covered in dense rainforest, the island is also referred to as the Galápagos of Australia due to the exceptional number of endemic species.

The wildlife is beyond impressive, with native birds, a unique fruit bat and – the island's biggest claim to fame – the annual red crab migration when millions of bright crustaceans scuttle out of the rainforest then down to the coast to spawn. The underwater realm is equally special. The island is the tip of an ancient volcanic mountain that rises from the Java Trench. Reefs are smothered in unbelievable hard corals; pods of spinner dolphins come to play with the dive boat and pelagic species patrol the outer reef edges. Late in the year they are joined by whale sharks who are attracted to these waters – no one quite knows why. Critter life is less evident, but the rare dragon moray eel is seen regularly, and several coastal cave systems can be safely explored.

⌖13 Perpendicular Wall	
🧭 **Depth**	35 m
◐ **Visibility**	excellent
〰 **Currents**	none to strong

Before arriving at this spectacular site you may encounter the resident bronze whaler sharks who are attracted by the boat's engine noise. You can snorkel with them, as they are inquisitive yet have never been known to be aggressive in this situation. When you do reach the dive site, you find an overhang full of parallel fans growing to catch the sunlight like solar panels. After you fin around the bend in the wall where the view is breathtaking, there are masses of gigantic gorgonians hanging off the wall and some even bigger ones in a cave. Out in the blue are grey reef sharks, a school of jacks and midnight snappers.

▶14 Thundercliff

◉ **Depth**	8 m	
◑ **Visibility**	fair to stunning	
≋ **Currents**	none to mild	

A dive, a swim and a walk: this is probably one of the most unusual experiences you will ever have. Entering over a shallow section of reef, you swim down into a sandy channel, under an overhang and into a wide-mouthed cave. A short fin takes you past a rock that juts almost to the surface and has hundreds of silvery fish swarming it. Continuing on through a narrow tunnel, you reach a dark cavern where you can surface inside to admire the stalagmites before descending into a second tight passage that leads to a much bigger cave. Surfacing again, you find it is decorated by impressive limestone structures. Next, you swim up to a rocky beach and exit onto the rocks, before dekitting for a walk through the cave system to a small pool of brackish water. Inside the pool is a rare red shrimp (as yet unnamed) that is attracted to torch beams, plus a surprise that no one knows about until they've been.

▶15 Flying Fish Cove/Kelana's Mooring

◉ **Depth**	35 m	
◑ **Visibility**	excellent	
≋ **Currents**	none	

This small, pretty bay is the island's only year-round mooring point but it's awash with marine life. There are at least two dives. You can start by being dropped at Kelana's Mooring then swim back to shore, or start from shore to dive between the main jetty and the ruins of the collapsed original one. There's even the wreck of a Second World War-era supply ship. The mooring is the favoured site for finding the spectacular dragon moray. At 25 metres a substantial stand of corals is filled with morays (at least five different types are tucked inside, along with Debelius shrimp). It takes some hunting but a shy dragon is always there. Further up in the shallows, there is less coral but plenty of marine life: octopus, mating pufferfish, huge hawkfish and lots of nudibranchs. At night, and closer to shore or around the old wreck, it's easy to spot critters such as pink leaffish, lionfish, crustaceans and sleeping parrotfish.

▶16 Coconut Point

◉ **Depth**	38 m	
◑ **Visibility**	excellent	
≋ **Currents**	none to mild	

A three-in-one dive site, Coconut Point starts at a small sand gully under the cliff. It is surrounded by a flat reef that is completely covered in small hard corals interspersed with critters such as rare gold spot scorpions. Swimming over this area, you reach a sheer wall that drops past 60 metres and you can see all the way to the bottom. Indian Ocean triggers and pyramid butterflies mob you as you descend. At 40 metres there are masses of huge gorgonian fans, while grey reef sharks, dogtooth tuna and trevally patrol the depths. Returning to the gully, a channel leads into a huge cavern with openings to the cliff face on two sides. The light inside has an eerie glow. At the back of the cave you can crab-crawl through the surge over beautifully rounded rocks until the light fades. If you turn on your torch, you spy an incredible number of huge lobsters nestled into virtually every crevice.

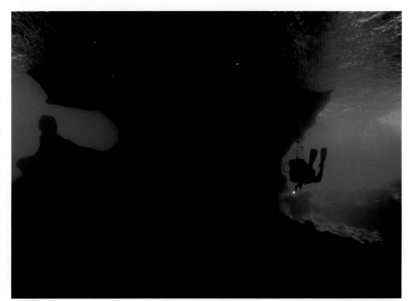

Bubble coral shrimp peaking from the bubbles; the double entrance to Coconut Point.

drying out
Great Barrier Reef

The heart of the Great Barrier Reef dive industry lies in the city of Cairns whose airport is just 15 minutes from the centre of town. This bustling city has everything you could ever need, from hotel rooms to car hire. Ultra-trendy Port Douglas is an hour's drive north and has good facilities as well. It is also a far more user-friendly and stylish town.

Cairns
Diving
Pro Dive, prodive-cairns.com.au
Tusa Dive, tusadive.com
Sleeping
Coral Tree Inn, coraltreeinn.com.au Small and neat hotel in the city centre.
Rydges Tradewinds, rydges.com Modern hotel on the Cairns waterfront.

Liveaboards
Mike Ball/Spoilsport, mikeball.com. Large, modern vessel. Trips from 3-7 nights.
Spirit of Freedom, spiritoffreedom.com.au. Top-class liveaboard with great crew and facilities. Cruises range from 3-10 nights.

Port Douglas
Diving
Port Douglas Dive, portdouglasdive.com.au
Poseidon Cruises, poseidon-cruises.com.au
Sleeping
Hibiscus Gardens Spa Resort, mid-range resort, hibiscusportdouglas.com.au.
Peninsula Boutique, peninsulahotel.com.au. Stylish apart-hotel with fabulous views.
Liveaboards
Eye to Eye Marine Encounters, marineencounters.com.au. Cruises with an education and research bias.

Days out

Touring in the tropical north is a DIY affair. Hire a 4WD and explore at your own pace.

Cairns The town centre borders a stylish waterfront. It's a small but lively city with a few square blocks of shops, restaurants, travel and tour agents and car hire agencies. Dive shops are everywhere.

Port Douglas Life centres on Macrossan Street, a row of classy restaurants, shops and galleries that links the jetty and small town beach with the beautiful stretch of Four Mile Beach. Daydream at the marina.

Daintree Rainforest This World Heritage Site is regarded as the world's most vital lowland rainforest. You will need a 4WD vehicle to negotiate the river crossings. There are nature trails, aerial walkways and, inside designated work zones, small cottage industries and tropical fruit farms.

Cape Tribulation About two thirds of the way through the Daintree, this Cape was named by Captain Cook as the Endeavour went aground near here. It's the point where the GBR comes closest to the coast. Take care – saltwater crocodiles inhabit nearby creeks.

City stopovers

Brisbane If you arrive via this northern capital, take a break and a quick look around. Nestled on the winding Brisbane River, this is an outdoors-orientated city with a touch of colonial history.

Sydney Not exactly on the diver trail, Sydney is the biggest, most cosmopolitan city in the country, yet it is also a compact one. A short stopover will give a taste of the Aussie way of life. Do a tour in just a few hours or spend a couple of days seeing a little more. Landmarks like the Opera House and Harbour Bridge speak for themselves.

The cuddly Australian koala – and no, it's not a bear; Cairns city waterfront; fording the Daintree river in a 4WD car.

drying out
Western Australia

In contrast to the easily accessed facilities way across country, Western Australia's offshore territories are a long way apart but great for those who like to get off the beaten track without giving up life's little luxuries. You could land in Perth then fly straight out again, but the city is a pleasant place to get past the jetlag. Alternatively, there are some amazing areas to explore if you can build in some extra holiday time.

Broome (for the Rowley Shoals)
Sleeping
Cable Beach Club, cablebeachclub.com
Sea Shells Resort, seashells.com.au
Liveaboards
MV Great Escape, greatescape.net.au
Classy operation with seasonal departures for diving the Rowley Shoals.

Cocos (Keeling)
Diving
Cocos Dive, cocosdive.com. The only dive centre on the island and also agent for all hotel bookings.
Sleeping
Cocos Castaway, cocoscastaway.com
Cocos Seaview, cocosseaview.com

Christmas Island
Diving
Wet'n'Dry Adventures, the lone dive operator is at divingchristmas.com.
Sleeping
The Cabin, Captain's Lookout and The Retreat are indicative of the many small and charming accommodation options. Contact Christmas Island Visitors Centre for availability, christmas.net.au.

Days out

From the centre of Perth, you can visit the botanic gardens where the city views are superb. The Swan Bell Tower is home to the original 14th-century bells from St Martin-in-the-Fields in London. To the north is Aquarium of Western Australia. A little south of Perth is the oldest city in the country, the port of Fremantle. A bit further on, is the underwater observatory at Bussleton Jetty and the Margaret River, an award-winning wine region.

Heading further afield, Monkey Mia beach resort attracts visitors wanting to swim with resident bottlenose dolphins. Interaction is highly controlled. On the north coast, Broome was founded by Chinese and Indonesian settlers who created a pearl industry in the early 1900s. The trade has declined leaving the eerie atmosphere of a post-boom frontier town. The never-ending, pink sands of Cable Beach are stunning.

Northwest of Broome, the Kimberley National Park has landscapes carved by ancient forces. Caves, rivers and rock formations rival Ayers Rock. Speaking of which, Uluru can be found the middle of Australia – and the middle of nowhere. You can walk to the top of this sacred aboriginal site and should stay at least one night to see how the rock changes during the day as light moves across it.

Christmas Island

With its huge number of endemic wildlife species, Christmas is the natural world at its most accessible. It takes less than an hour to drive from one end of the island to the other, so you can see every unique feature, both above the waterline and below. Walk through virgin rainforest to see the 16 indigenous land crabs or watch blowholes on the prehistoric south coast. Explore caves dressed by stalagmites and stalactites; discover beaches occupied by nesting turtles, and rare, endemic birds in the treetops. If you are there during the annual; red crab migration, you'll never see anything like it ever again: bright red bodies cover every available surface en route to the ocean to spawn.

Beach on Cocos (Keeling); endemic Christmas Island creatures: a red crab and the CI Goshawk.

Caribbean

37
↘ **Essentials**

38
↘ **Dive brief**

40
↘ **Dive sites**

42
↘ **Dive log**

Leeward Islands
42 Saba
45 St Kitts

Windward Islands
48 Carriacou
51 Grenada

54
↘ **Drying out**
54 Leeward Islands
55 Windward Islands

Is this my best side: a green turtle, *Chelonia mydas*, pauses to provide the best possible pose for the camera.
Torrens Point, Saba

Devise a daydream that includes a remote island idyll... think white sandy beaches, rustling coconut palms, cool breezes and soothing warm waters. Add a few sprinkles of nutmeg, cinnamon, chocolate or rum, then the rhythm of a steel band and you have arrived on a quintessential Caribbean island.

destination
Caribbean

Fast forward to the modern day and figure in all the elements that the 21st century must deliver. This destination can be a relaxing haven or an assault on the senses, especially if you spend some time beneath the waves. Each island and every reef has its own range of creatures and colours, but the appeal for many divers is the multitude of wrecks that rest in this shallow sea. Tales from the past may have been romanticized but the history of these sunken vessels stands the test of time.

Diving features like these may be manmade additions to the marine realm but they are rare and unusual treats, surrounded by the gentle coral reefs that are so typical of the Caribbean Sea and which create a muted backdrop to the past that rests within them.

Back on dry land, terrestrial and marine vistas are complemented by rich history and vibrant culture. Local towns, festivals and markets are unmissable and easily justify time spent away from the sea.

Puerto Rico

St Maarten

Saba ▶▶ p42

Antigua

Basseterre

St Kitts ▶▶ p45

Nevis

ATLANTIC OCEAN

CARIBBEAN SEA

Guadaloupe

Dominica

Martinique

St Lucia

St Vincent

Barbados

Carriacou ▶▶ p48

St George's

Grenada ▶▶ p51

Trinidad
and Tobago

VENEZUELA

Essentials

There can hardly be a Caribbean island without an airport, whether it's a large and modern one or the world's smallest on Saba. Direct intercontinental flights go to a few of the bigger airports – including Grenada and St Kitts – and, from those, there are several daily connections to the others. Hotel transfers are rarely included, unless you have booked a package through a tour operator, but hotels and dive centres will arrange a taxi to be waiting for you, simply email in advance. Travelling around and between islands is straightforward, with inter-island ferries and networks of mini-buses. Taxis are comparatively costly so car hire can be a good option if you want to spend some time seeing more of the interior of these beautiful islands.

Local laws and customs

Customs in the Caribbean islands tend to reflect their colonial past, but all are fairly religious with a plethora of Christian churches, so be respectful. Courteous standards of behaviour and neat dress codes are a good idea. Homosexuality is illegal in Grenada and St Kitts, while Saba, with its Dutch roots, has legalized gay marriages. Female travellers may be amused (or amazed) by some of the chauvinistic views from local men. Note that there are severe penalties for any drug-related offences, even minor ones.

Health and safety

Curiously, many Caribbean islands have world-renowned health-related education facilities. Should you get ill, it really won't be a problem getting help, although expats say that local services are a little behind the times. On the surface, the islands seem friendly and easy-going, but there are issues wherever tourism is more developed. Both Saba and Carriacou are fairly untainted, as they are small and feel rather village-like. Everyone knows everyone, so any hint of trouble will get noticed. On the other hand, Grenada and St Kitts are busy and developing rapidly, which encourages unrest and negativity. In busy areas, especially at night, be aware of what is around you, get a taxi and don't display valuables.

Costs

With many local economies linked to the USA, travellers may find these islands expensive. When thinking about budgets, regard costs as being similar to London, Sydney or San Francisco. You may not spend quite that much, but at least you will have enough cash with you. Soft drinks and bottled water are pricey but the local beers are reasonable value, as are wines imported from South America. Hotel rooms usually have a fridge, so you can stock up for sunset drinks on the balcony. There are service charges on bills, so while tipping is not expected, in smaller establishments, it is much appreciated. Many operations ask that you leave crew tips with the shop to be divided equally.

Fact file

Saba	
Location	17°63'N, 63°23'W
Capital	The Bottom
St Kitts	
Location	17°20'N, 62°45'W
Capital	Basseterre
Grenada	
Location	12°007'N, 61°40'W
Capital	St George's
Flights	Air Canada, , British Airways, Delta, US Airlines, Virgin Atlantic
Internal flights	LIAT, SVG Air, Win Air
Land transport	Taxis, inter-island ferries, mini-buses
Departure tax	Grenada – $20, St Kitts – included in your ticket
Entry	Visas are not usually required
Money	US dollars (USD) and Caribbean dollars (XCD)
Language	English
Electricity	220-240v, plug types A and B (see page 15)
Time zone	GMT -4
Religion	All Christian religions are represented
Communications	Country codes: St Kitts +1 869; Saba +5994; Grenada +1 473; IDD code 11; Police 911 Internet access is good
Tourist information	sabatourism.com; stkittstourism.kn; grenadagrenadines.com
Travel advisories	gov.uk/foreign-travel-advice; state.gov/travel

dive brief

It seems to us that diving in the Caribbean is a bit two-sided. As soon as you think you have a grip on it, it throws a curve ball. One day you are finning along a sandy channel, then you stumble upon a solitary man working at his typewriter. Bizarre... Classic reef dives display angelfish and butterflies, then a Pacific lionfish appears; an anchor embedded in the reef is revealed as 300 years old but the bulldozer just beside it is this century. Unusual can't describe it; eccentric is getting closer. These dives may be unorthodox at times but they are surprisingly good fun.

Diving

Although it formed millions of years ago, the Caribbean Sea is regarded as one of the youngest on the planet. Enclosed on three sides by the American continents, its eastern edge is denoted by a moon-shaped arc of islands. These are the tips of a once gigantic mountain range that separated a basin of land from the developing Atlantic Ocean. As sea levels rose, the area flooded, forming a warm and shallow sea. Officially, this chain is known as the Lesser Antilles: from Puerto Rico to Dominica they are the Leeward Islands and from Martinique going south, the Windward Islands.

The islands' eastern coastlines face the Atlantic and are rugged: reefs are battered by the surf and rarely in good condition, although larger animals can be seen when conditions allow. On the other hand, cross to the western side of the islands and you would hardly know you were in the same place. Marine topography varies according to where you are, but there is a mixture of sloping walls and patch reefs divided by sandy-bottomed gullies.

Saba and St Kitts sit on the northeast corner of the chain and, despite being near neighbours, are very different propositions. Saba is steeply volcanic, while St Kitts has rolling green hills. Strong oceanic currents and winds approach from the southern Atlantic but weaken by the time they reach this point, so diving is rarely difficult. And if, at one site, it's windy you simply move until you find a peaceful one.

Grenada and Carriacou sit at the very bottom of the chain, divided from South America by the deep Grenada Channel. Currents and winds force their way into the Caribbean basin by passing through this channel, creating more challenging diving conditions.

North or south, what makes the Lesser Antilles a diving treat are the wrecks and artificial reefs. Grenada is promoted as the Caribbean's wreck capital, due mainly to its most famous ship, the *Bianca C*. There are others to explore around all the islands: ancient cargo ships, sailing yachts, tugboats, buses, bulldozers and even sculptures. Saba is the exception to the rule, with no wrecks at all. However, the marine topography here is uniquely dramatic, which gives the island its own edge.

Snorkelling

Plenty of shallow reefs are ideal for surface huggers – even for divers – as very little of anything is beyond 25 metres. Beachside snorkelling reveals plenty of life, and the Grenada sculpture park is unmissable. The only caution is not to go snorkeling off the Atlantic coasts, as currents and surge can be difficult to say the least.

Marine life

Having formed in isolation from other seas and oceans, the quantity of marine species in the Caribbean is far lower than in the Indo-Pacific. However, the currents come into play, ensuring that a continual supply of plankton feeds these young reefs and the animals that live on them. Although the reefs may not seem as lush, what is there is healthy.

Typically of these waters, large schools of creole wrasse are a given; turtles are about but always small and you are virtually guaranteed an encounter with a great barracuda. Nurse sharks and southern stingrays are seen at times and there are a few unusual critters for those who take the time to hunt in nooks and crannies.

Making the big decision

Many of the Caribbean islands can be regarded as similar in a lot of ways. They are all pretty and ringed by lovely, warm turquoise water with hidden coral reefs. Access is fairly straightforward; land-based facilities are usually good and there are dive centres everywhere. From island to island, the marine life will be much of a muchness as well and that might make you think that a single destination would cover all the diving options. However, to absorb the different cultures and lifestyles of the islands, it is worth combining two that are close together. Grenada and Carriacou are an obvious choice, as they are part of the same country and only a short ferry ride apart. Saba and St Kitts are a short sail apart but only connected by flights or a liveaboard, an option which comes highly recommended.

Animal encounters

All islands: underwater residents may seem the same from island to island but there are some unusual small critters. In St Kitts, look for the blue-throat pike blenny (right) and sun anemone shrimp; Saba has whitespotted filefish (above) and web burrfish; Carriacou and Grenada have lots of seahorses and quillfin blennies.

dive sites

The islands of the Lesser Antilles may well have been born of ancient volcanic activity but the marine realm as seen by modern day divers tends to be fairly flat. Scatterings of submerged rocky pinnacles display evidence of the volcanic origins, as do the mountainous interiors, but the Caribbean is a shallow sea so dives are close to shore and are rarely beyond sport diving limits.

The long and very colourful maritime history creates the perfect foil for these shallow reefs, each island is encompassed by an abundance of dive sites tucked into coves and bays that are – principally – away from the rougher Atlantic coast. And although the Caribbean doesn't have the highest species diversity rankings in the tropics, the wealth of sunken ships and other artifical reefs adds excitement to the variety of dive sites and styles.

Saba is the most blatantly volcanic with steep shorelines that extend beneath the sea. A few dives are deeper but, in general, the island has the most interesting topography in the group. St Kitts, just a short distance away, is quite different, with hardly a dive beyond 20 metres, making it an ideal destination for less experienced divers. Carriacou, although a long way south, is surprisingly similar while larger Grenada next door has dive sites tucked inside and around the deep moon-shape of Grand Anse Bay. The dives are mostly ideal for all levels of diver but around on the south coast, the reefs are subject to strong ocean currents from the Atlantic.

Saba ⏩ p42

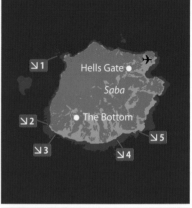

↘1

Hells Gate ●

✈

Saba

● The Bottom

↘2

↘5

↘3

↘4

Log Book

↘1 **Torrens Point**
↘2 **Tedran Reef and Wall**
↘3 **Tent Wall and Reef**
↘4 **Big Rock Market**
↘5 **Dave's drop off**

→ **Eye of the Needle:** steep reef wall with lots of small caverns and lively currents.
→ **Custom House:** loaf-shaped reef with Caribbean reef sharks and nudibranchs
→ **Ladder Labyrinth:** nurse sharks and web burrfish patrolling sandy gullies

Conditions

Seasons	The rainy (or hurricane) season runs from June to December when humidity rises. Storms are more frequent, but an actual hurricane is less likely. The dry season is from January to May.	
Visibility	Varies according to location and season: from 5 to 25 metres with an average of 20 metres.	
Currents	Generally fairly easy	
Temperatures	Air 24-34°C; water 25-30°C	
Wet suit	3 mm full body suit, 5 mm in winter for Grenada	
Training	Courses available everywhere	
Nitrox	Available in most dive centres	
Deco chamber	Barbados, Saba, Trinidad	

Diversity

combined reef area
350 km²

	Leeward Islands	Windwards Islands
HARD CORAL	40	33
FISH SPECIES	462	495
ENDEMIC FISH SPECIES	0	0
FISH UNDER THREAT	20	21

All diversity figures are approximate

St Kitts ▶▶ p45

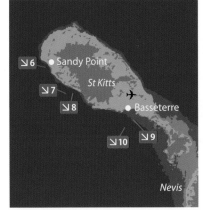

Log Book

- ↘6 **Anchors Aweigh**
- ↘7 **Paradise Reef**
- ↘8 **Old Road Bay**
- ↘9 **Wreck of the Corinthian**
- ↘10 **River Taw Wreck**

→ **Bedroom Bay:** shallow site inside Shitten Bay that is an ideal night dive

→ **Brimstone Shallows:** actually a deeper wall dive reaching to around 30 metres

Carriacou ▶▶ p48

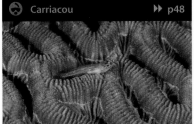

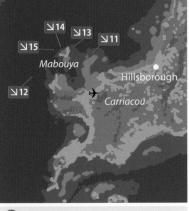

Log Book

- ↘11 **Divers Surprise, Lighthouse**
- ↘12 **Sister Rocks**
- ↘13 **Twin Tugs**
- ↘14 **Magic Garden**
- ↘15 **Sharky's Hideaway**

→ **Sandy Island:** gentle drift dive with overhangs that hide nurse sharks.

→ **The Rose:** wreck on a small sailing yacht resting on sand and seagrass

Grenada ▶▶ p51

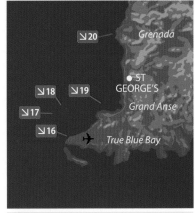

Log Book

- ↘16 **Blackforest**
- ↘17 **Bianca C**
- ↘18 **Purple Rain**
- ↘19 **Shakem**
- ↘20 **Molinere Bay**

→ **Happy Valley:** small drop-offs and winding walls inside the protected zone

→ **Veronica:** wreck of a coastal freighter covered in small cup and soft corals

→ **Fishermen's Paradise:** a long shallow reef leads to the sailing boat, *Kapsis*

Endangered oceans

Lionfish – elegant, whimsical and much admired – are now on the menu in the Caribbean. And in a lot of ways that is heartbreaking. But this glamorous fish has broken the rules by crossing borders without leave to do so. It was about 20 years ago that this Indo-Pacific native was first spotted in Atlantic waters. Initially, this was thought to be a freak incident but, as time went on, the hardy creature took hold and was soon seen from New York City right down to the Caribbean. No one knows quite how it happened – ideas such as being flushed down the loo from home aquariums or expelled in bilge water from tankers coming from Asia were bandied about. But, regardless, lionfish are interlopers and causing damage to local reefs as they have no known predator. Many marine parks have adopted the policy of killing them, and fishermen are encouraged to bring them up to be sold as food. Don't be surprised if you see them on the menu. You might prefer to see them under the waves but, sadly, they need to go from these waters.

dive log

Leeward Islands: Saba

Exploding skywards from the ocean depths, the island of Saba was born of a volcanic eruption that left sharp, craggy cliff faces that hide rainforest-clad hills and often misty valleys.

Flat could never be used to describe this island, where villages cling to steep hills and have names like The Bottom and Hell's Gate to reflect their locations. Even the miniscule airport needs pilots to be specially trained before they can land there.

Saba also has marine topography that is unique to the area; it is not a reef-ringed island, so rocky shores replace the sandy beaches typical of the Caribbean. Despite that, it has some of the most diverse diving in the region, as the sheer cliffs extend beneath the water to meet tall pinnacles and tumbled boulders. The Saba National Marine Park was set up in 1987, so all the dives here are inside a protected zone.

66 99 Saba is our yardstick against which all others dive destinations are compared. Saba, with its magnificent sea mounts and walls, means diving without disappointment. The turtles and nurse sharks are particularly approachable and plentiful. With a uniquely enchanting island as a backdrop to the diving, words like "magic" are insufficient.
Brenda Kirkby, professor, Grenada

⏱	Torrens Point	
⏱	**Depth**	12 m
◐	**Visibility**	good
≋	**Currents**	none

This shallow dive is a tour around the fallen boulders and outcrops that lie beneath a cluster of rocky pinnacles off the top of the island. Surfaces are covered by a light dusting of algae, seaweeds and corals. There are tiny fish feeding everywhere – juvenile boxfish, gobies and blennies. At the shallowest point of the dive, a tunnel leads beneath the rocks creating a short swim-through and, at the exit, there is an area of football-size boulders covered with incredible numbers of frilly lettuce leaf slugs. Oversized lobsters wave their long antennas from their caverns attracting attention. Both flamingo tongue shells and spotted cyphomas can be seen living on small fans that are attached to the rocks. Ascending to the boat, several two-metre long tarpon come in to meet divers.

⏱	Tedran Reef and Wall	
⏱	**Depth**	26 m
◐	**Visibility**	excellent
≋	**Currents**	none

Dropping to this site through the clearest of water leads to a deep sandy slope that is broken by a series of gullies and raised coral outcrops. Along the sides of the coral 'fingers', the steep walls are clad in a thick covering of long, crawling brown tube sponges that look just like gigantic octopus tentacles – each arm of the sponge is dotted with extended tubes that mimic the octopus suckers. There are many other sponge types too, in a range of colours that make Tedran one of the most colourful dives in the area. Hidden around the reef there are also a few old anchors, but they are well disguised by the rich reef growth. Plenty of smaller fish and moray eels hide in the cracks and crevices along the wall, while snappers and jacks swim about in the blue.

Juvenile smooth trunkfish are a mere 10 millimetres long.

N3 Tent Wall and Reef

Depth	21 m
Visibility	good
Currents	none to some

So called because of a triangular red rock on the cliff face above, this beautifully decorated small wall is almost reminiscent of ones in other oceans, as there is so much colour from the sponges and small fans. Dropping in, adult lobsters poke their heads out to see the interlopers, as do the moray eels, then, as you go along the wall there are coral banded shrimps in almost every hole you look in. The juvenile of a spotted drum and one in teenage stage are both in residence. Masses of sergeant majors dart about madly trying to protect their eggs from hungry goatfish, several types of angelfish and some nosy creolefish. At the end of the wall, a flat shelf shimmers in tones of yellow, with sponges and fans jostling for space. This area seems to be a home for young turtles, with six making an appearance in less than five minutes. There can be current across this reef top, but if not, there is a swim-through on the other side of the plateau.

N4 Big Rock Market

Depth	23 m
Visibility	good
Currents	none

Named after the main supermarket on the island (really!) this dive site is a bowl-shaped depression that is ringed by slightly raised reefs and interspersed with small coral outcrops. It is a very easy and pretty dive amongst a garden of pastel-toned sea plumes and a variety of large sponges. There are also a few trespassing lionfish – these are just gorgeous but, of course, shouldn't be here. However, other fish that should be include anthias, angelfish, creole and butterflies. There are spinyhead blennies on all the rocks and several nudibranchs. At the end of the dive, and under the boat, there are clusters of jacks.

Clockwise: Tent Reef – any colour as long as it's yellow; lettuce leaf sea slug; and every colour available on Tedran Wall.

Dave's drop off

Depth	24 m	
Visibility	great	
Currents	slight	

Located on the windier and potentially rougher south side of the island, this dive leads right up under the cliff wall to where the surf crashes against the rocks. However, the dive starts away from the coast and follows a bed of boulders down to about 24 metres. They cover a wide swathe of the seabed and are broken by dense hard coral outcrops. The topography is really very impressive, as it is coated in gigantic sponges and soft coral plumes displaying far more life than you might have expected. When you come back up into the shallow areas, there are some substantial – and now rare – stands of elkhorn corals that glow a mustard colour in the sunlight and are surrounded by lots of small yellow or white fans and lots of yellow sponges.

From here you can swim up under the wall to investigate two inlets – turtles hide in these, chomping around the rocks for food. There might be a little surge but there are also flutemouths attempting to hide on fans and lizardfish skittering about. This dive can be done again, in the other direction, where there are more channels occupied by angels, porcupinefish, mating trunkfish and a nosy giant barracuda that follows divers around for a lot of the dive.

dive log
Leeward Islands: St Kitts

St Kitts is just half of the small nation of St Kitts and Nevis. You can stare across The Narrows – the strait that separates these two sister islands – from the capital Basseterre or, if you are standing on the southern tip, you could almost swim across the three-kilometre gap.

Yet, it is St Kitts that attracts the majority of divers and that has a lot to do with the past history of the island. Christopher Columbus discovered it in 1493 and claimed it for Spain but, as is typical of colonial expansion at the time, the French and British soon muscled in. They fought with the local Carib Indian tribe and each other until the 18th century, at the end of which it became British.

This historical outline also outlines much of the diving nature. The foreign powers were attracted to the calm and protected bays on the western side of St Kitts, which allowed them safe anchorage. The reefs that gave the vessels protection now provide shallow and easy conditions for divers. There is always a surprise or two to be had, with ancient anchors evidence of the galleons of the past. Some wrecks, though, are far more recent and in good shape, unlike the colonial ones, which have long since rotted away. These dives have very little in the way of strong currents although the tidal movement means visibility is good if not as crystal clear as in neighbouring Saba.

⬇6 Anchors Aweigh	
🧭 **Depth**	18 m
◐ **Visibility**	OK
≋ **Currents**	none

The furthest dive to the north of St Kitts, and close to Sandy Point, Anchors Aweigh is part of the National Marine Park. It is a shallow, flat area of sandy seabed that is divided by a series of raised reefs. These create channels that can be explored. While you are swimming through each one, watch out for one of the old anchors used for mooring in times gone by. Even the mooring for dive boats is a huge anchor from the 18th century. These anchors can be hard to spot as they are encrusted in small fan corals and sponges, as are the small walls that rise vertically from the sandy seabed. As you travel around the site, you meet morays eels and young nurse sharks. There are web pufferfish, some big crabs and the spotted drum in its juvenile, teenage and adult phases. Turtles can often be seen in a small cave to the east. This dive is also a known haunt for frogfish, but you will be lucky to spot one. They are small, and a red so dark they are almost black, plus they choose to nestle on an equally dark sponge. There are plenty of pelagic fish with mackerel and jacks swimming overhead and an enormous school of yellow tailed jacks hover under the dive boats until a lone barracuda chases them off.

One of the many anchors found in the National Marine Park; spinyhead blenny.

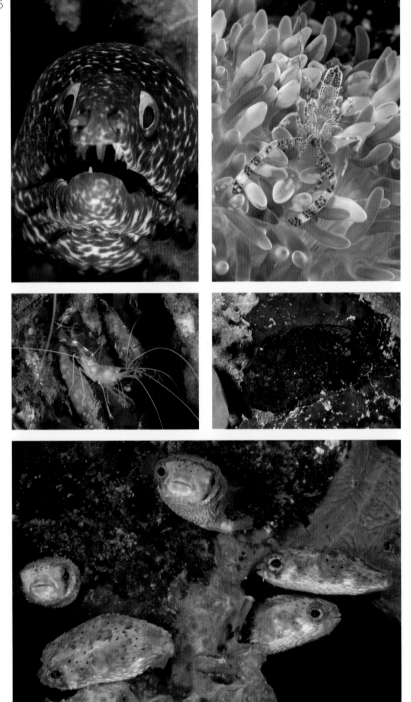

Critters in St Kitts: spotted moray eel; sun anemone shrimp; frogfish being a sponge; a cluster of baby balloonfish, aka pufferfish; the golden coral shrimp.

⌄7 Paradise Reef	
🜛 **Depth**	18 m
◑ **Visibility**	good
🌀 **Currents**	none

Many boats took shelter behind Paradise Reef and, like Sandy Bay a short distance away, it saw battles between the various colonial powers of past centuries. There are masses of anchors embedded in the reef, which consists of raised strips broken by gullies. The oldest anchors have no wooden cross at the top; newer ones are metal but they are all well encrusted. Animal life includes moray eels, big crabs, tiny blennies and a turtle ot two. Another rarity here is the pike blenny, who can be coaxed out of his sandy den by standing a mirror nearby. Next thing you know, he is out and trying to find the critter in the mirror. Chances are you will see fishing cages on the seabed, as local people are allowed to fish here using traditional methods even though it's a marine park.

⌄8 Old Road Bay	
🜛 **Depth**	18 m
◑ **Visibility**	good
🌀 **Currents**	usually mild

Still inside the park zone, but closer to shore than Paradise Reef, this dive is in very shallow water. Finning inshore and across a bed of seagrass, you see two old, rotting logs smothered in coral banded shrimp, Pederson cleaner shrimp and gorgeous golden coral shrimp. There are even juvenile lobsters hiding beneath. Above one log a small fan has countless juvenile fish on it, including a lone slender filefish. Further along there are arrow crabs as well as some juvenile angels at just a centimetre or so long. Off in the seagrass, you can spot tiny scorpionfish, lime green sea hares and several teensy filefish. As you ascend, a few pelagics make an appearance, including giant barracudas.

⚓9 MV Corinthian Wreck

🕐 **Depth**	21 m
◑ **Visibility**	fair
🌊 **Currents**	none

⚓10 MV River Taw Wreck

🕐 **Depth**	14 m
◑ **Visibility**	fair
🌊 **Currents**	slight

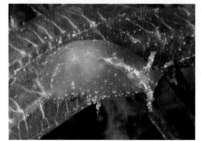

The Corinthian is the wreck of a small tug boat that is sitting totally upright on the seabed. She is a lonely sentinel with no topographic features immediately around her. However, she is pretty much intact and home to a lot of small fish, especially around the wheelhouse. After investigating this and around the hull, you can follow a chain that leads to a small wall where a crane is resting, before swimming over to where there is the chassis of a some sort of vehicle. All the mechanical items are showing signs of healthy coral growth. As this site is closer to Basseterre harbour and the port, the visibility tends to be lower than dives around the coast.

Although there are varying opinions as to how and when the *River Taw* first went down, she is known to have been on the seabed in 1985. For many years she sat there completely upright, then, in 1989, Hurricane Hugo came along and broke the boat into two parts, turning the stern a full 180 degrees before settling again. Originally 144 feet long, the Taw operated as an inter-island freighter. Descending over the bow, you see the remains are now painted by tunicates and small fan corals. There are schools of snappers and anthias hovering around and feeding on the surfaces until some small gangs of jacks dart through the others at speed.

Descending to the sea floor then across to the stern, you swim through the cracked hull, passing fish, arrow crabs and shrimp before emerging above the holds. The surrounding seabed is equally interesting, with jawfish popping up and down to feed and a large stingray pausing to rest. A short distance from the wreck itself is the decaying chassis of a truck or van plus a submerged bulldozer.

The River Taw wreck and (above) a sea hare at Old Road Bay.

Caribbean Dive log Leeward Islands: St Kitts

dive log

Windward Islands: Carriacou

Carriacou sits 90 minutes by fast ferry north of its sister, Grenada. The pair are divided by an open channel dotted with a handful of smaller volcanic islands.

Far quieter than her neighbour, Carriacou is a step back in time: gentle rolling hills drop to almost deserted bays, with tiny wooden cottages scattered amongst the trees. The main town of Hillsborough is little more than a main road that leads to other points, yet it has a surprisingly good range of facilities. But come nine o'clock at night, the island is pretty much asleep.

Carriacou means 'land of reefs' and you only have to look from shore to see these hovering beneath the surface. The water is classic turquoise and the marine realm is very healthy with areas of huge tumbled boulders, gaping caverns and even some volcanic gases escaping like champagne bubbles from the seabed. To top it all off, there are even a few new wreck dives.

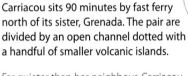

ⓧ11	**Divers Surprise, Lighthouse**	
🕐	**Depth**	18 m
◑	**Visibility**	good
🌊	**Currents**	none

A few minutes from shore is flat Sandy Island and this reef starts near the metal light beacon – more usually a perch for pelicans. There are rows of channels and gullies between the reefs which are coated in crusting corals and young hard corals. A small turtle is jammed under a ledge, and if you are really lucky you may spot a tiny opistobranch: the lettuce sea slug is an elegant and frilly little chap. There are said to be seahorses here too, but if you don't spot one of those there will be endless slender filefish hiding on the fronds of the seaplumes, some hermit crabs, lots of creole wrasse, the Shy hamlet and at least one golden moray.

ⓧ12	**Sister Rocks**	
🕐	**Depth**	24 m
◑	**Visibility**	good
🌊	**Currents**	mild to medium

Two sharp-sided craggy pinnacles break the surface to the south of Hillsborough. Both are home to seabirds and below them is, without doubt, the most dramatic dive here. There are several routes you can take to navigate around them. The western side is completely covered in fans and corals. There are a lot of fish species feeding in the current including a resident school of barracuda. It's unusual to see, but look out for white 'snow' in and around some of the barrel sponges. This means they are spawning. Nurse sharks often take refuge under the rocks closer to the base of the pinnacles where the terrain changes to bigger boulders and crevices which reflect the land above. Other animals shelter too, like pufferfish and moray eels and there are many schools of small fish in the surge that washes the gaps between the islands then out to the east side.

Soft corals on Sister Rocks; slender filefish at Divers Surprise.

▶13 Twin Tugs	
🧭 **Depth**	28 m
◐ **Visibility**	good
〰 **Currents**	usually mild

Two tug boats sit on the seabed north of Mabouya. Both were sunk deliberately to create dives. The slightly deeper one is the *Westsider*, which is sitting at 28 metres and is about 30 metres long. She was sunk in September 2004 but, shortly afterwards, Hurricane Ivan hit – the current was so strong it moved her 180 degrees around and sat her back down again. The intact propellor is inside a circular guard, with the blades and surrounding hull carpeted in small pink and white soft corals.

Heading up the side of the tug, the hull is also well coated in corals and dotted with small sponges. You can penetrate her to investigate the intact engine room, then swim back out through a hatch to the deck. Above are swirling schools of baitfish and a solitary giant barracuda.

Next, it's over to the *Boris*, just a short fin away. This tug also sits upright on the sand. She was sunk in September 2007 and isn't as well covered in corals yet but is still impressive. The decks are starting to show signs of growth and you can carefully slide inside the cabin – the entry doors are very narrow – and go inside the engine room. This one is smaller and quite cramped, so best just to look from outside.

66 99 The *Westsider* is proof that artificial reefs really do work... all around her hull is barren seabed, but the life she has attracted in just a few years is prolific.

◥14 Magic Garden

🕐 **Depth**	24 m	
🌓 **Visibility**	good	
〰 **Currents**	slight	

◥15 Sharky's Hideaway

🕐 **Depth**	23 m	
🌓 **Visibility**	good	
〰 **Currents**	slight	

To the north of Mabouya island, this wreck of a small tug boat lies in the sand at 20 metres or so. She hasn't been down for very long so, as yet, there is only a minimal amount of coral and sponge growth on the outside of the hull. However, growth inside the small wheelhouse is richer and swamped with fish – the numbers are phenomenal. The wheel is coated in pretty pink sponges but you can hardly see it for the swarms of snappers and goatfish that are sheltering there. After a short time, it's up the nearby slope and over the reef until you reach a shallow gully where streams of volcanic gases escape as bubbles from the sea floor. The dive ends around some big boulders at the base of the island, but not before you meet up with a large school of southern sennets, which are a type of barracuda.

This reef also starts just to the north of tiny Mabouya and continues along its western side with the potential for several dives. From the main entry point, it's down a slope to 23 metres. The coral growth is good, with a lot of crusting hard corals. Animals living in this area include juvenile drums, coral groupers, lobsters, parrot and squirrelfish, morays, coral banded shrimp and masses of tiny sharknose gobies that sit on just about every surface. The most unusual fish is a quillfin benny – unusual in that this one displays different colours and patterns to those seen in other parts of the Caribbean. A bit further along, the dive focuses on exploring around a series of large boulders that have created small caverns. Inside are copper sweepers, both reef and spiny lobsters and lots of small fish. At the end of the section of boulders

a natural bowl in the reef heaves with waves of baitfish. Gangs of chubbs swoop in to chase them through the surge.

Finally, there is a series of gullies and raised reefs where slipper lobsters, a turtle and squid compete for attention but get ignored in favour of a southern stingray, which is about two metres long, and over a metre wide. To round off the dive, in the next gully it's an encounter with an adult nurse shark.

dive log

Windward Islands: Grenada

An island of contrasts, Grenada swaps from being an ultra-modern young nation to a laid-back location, from a lush tropical paradise to rugged and weather-worn terrain, and all without blinking an eyelid. It all depends on what side of the island you are on.

The majority of tourist facilities are based around the toe of land that extends from the southwestern corner. This is where you find all the main landmarks of note: the capital, St George's; the most famous beach on the island, Grand Anse, and the international airport. Known as the tourist belt, this is by no means an indication of the incredibly beautiful mountainous interior but it is where all the dives sites are. Jutting into both the Atlantic and the Caribbean, the reefs are shallow and healthy. There are many wrecks and some of them sit at depth, but here 'deep' is easily within sport diving limits. As they say on the island, if you wanted to go any deeper you would need a shovel.

↘16 Blackforest	
Depth	26 m
Visibility	fair
Currents	slight

One of the most indicative reefs on the outer edge of the Grand Anse Bay region, Blackforest is a long, gently sloping drop that is covered in a variety of sponges, seaplumes and, of course, many black fan corals. These stand proud of the reef in rows like small trees in a young forest. It's all pretty enough and a very calm dive until you get near to the end. At about 14 metres one small area suddenly comes alive as a huge lobster runs about waving its antennae and several curious, free-swimming spotted moray eels make an appearance. The local divemasters know the location of a gigantic seahorse. It is a real beauty (aren't they always?) and often seen when heavily pregnant.

↘17 Bianca C	
Depth	38 m
Visibility	poor
Currents	slight

Grenada's most famous wreck dive has to be on this luxury cruise liner. It is referred to as Grenada's *Titanic*, as she had cruised into port with a full complement of guests when fire broke out in the boiler room. Her history is quite something – built in France in 1939, she was sunk by the Germans in 1944, raised and refitted then sent off to Japan. Next she was used as a hospital ship but in the late '50s she became a cruise liner again. You have to wonder if all her past incarnations made her jinxed.

After the fire, the *Bianca C* was towed away from port and eventually sank slowly to her current depth, so you won't see all that much of the ship. As time has gone on, the vessel continues to suffer. Even sitting on the seabed, a recent storm twisted her bow, which broke away from the rest of the hull. You are also warned not to penetrate any part as she is highly unstable, with the centre of the ship now collapsing into itself. As you descend, you are taken straight into the swimming pool, which is actually quite hard to recognize. There are a few tiles not covered in silt and a couple of hand rails. It's then back up to deck level, finning along the side, which is covered in dark fans and whip corals before heading up to the fore-mast.

molinere
↘18 **bay**

Depth	24 m
Visibility	poor to fair
Currents	slight

A few minutes by speedboat to the west of St George's is Grenada's most unique dive site, an underwater sculpture park. This very unusual dive is a surprise to many, perhaps because it is so unexpected, or maybe as it's something so completely different.

London-born sculptor Jason de Caires Taylor created and installed the sculptures in 2006, designing each one both to create artificial reefs and to relate tales that are relevant to the environment, conservation and local folklore. Much of the park can be explored by snorkellers, as some sculptures are as shallow as five metres. The most noted is *Vicissitudes*, a ring of children from diverse ethnic backgrounds. Dive boats moor up beside this so it's very easy to see. Beyond, there is a series of long outcrops and sandy channels where more of the sculptures are hidden.

For divers, the plan is to descend to 24 metres where there is the wreck of a small sailing boat, the *Buccaneer*. She is about 20 metres long and lying on her side on a slope. There is little left of her but lots of fish shelter inside and all the surfaces are sprouting soft and black corals. It's then time to head back up the slope and into the various sandy channels where you encounter more of the sculptures. There are 65 in total but the most emotive has to be *Sienna*, kneeling on the sand..

↘19 Purple Rain

⬡ Depth	28 m
◐ Visibility	poor to fair
≋ Currents	slight

Named after the ever-present schools of creole wrasse, this pretty, gently sloping reef also gets a bit of current. Dropping down to the bottom of the slope and onto the sandy seabed, you often find a couple of small turtles and then a small barracuda. Looking around, you see he has a few mates and, as the current lifts, they start zipping through the balls of baitfish that move in. Ascending up the slope, a slipper lobster appears from a tiny cave – unusual in the daytime – then a huge spiny lobster wanders out of his hiding place. There are lots of angel and boxfish and the very shy redspot hawkfish.

↘20 Shakem

⬡ Depth	32 m
◐ Visibility	fair to good
≋ Currents	slight

This is one of the most popular dives in the area as the *Shakem* is comparatively shallow and can be easily and thoroughly explored. The story goes that, in 2001, a local strike meant that cement had to be shipped in from Trinidad. The vessel was overloaded, her cargo shifted and she started to take in water, later sinking to an upright position on the seabed. Below the bow, the anchor is sitting on the sand with a good cover of crusting corals. The propeller is at the deepest point and is perfectly intact. Rising up the side of the hull there are young fans and soft corals coating all the surfaces, while below deck you can see all the bags of cement tied up in stacks. There are a lot of sergeant majors inside the hold and they follow divers about, almost leading them over to the crane. Stairs then lead up to the cabin and along a gangway to the stern where all the surfaces are covered in tiny white soft corals.

" Grenada... Spice Island... not a first choice for a diving destination. It was an impulse holiday: booked one week and on Grand Anse beach the next. The *Bianca C*, is the signature dive. But, for me, the highlight was the *Shakem*. Now, before I go on, I should point out I'm not a wreck girl, much preferring coral gardens and watching the fish go by. But there was something about the *Shakem* that touched my sense of mystery. She doesn't have a romantic tale to tell – she sank simply by being overloaded. However, she was home to a seahorse. We were less than optimistic about our chances of seeing her but luck was on our side.

I sometimes wonder what happened to her. Did she leave the security of the *Shakem* in search of a mate? Who knows, but she was the first seahorse I'd ever seen and, for that reason alone, Grenada holds a special place in my heart.

Jackie Hutchings, founder, Scubadviser.com

The *Shakem* wreck; a shy hamlet; a redspot hawkfish.

drying out
Leeward Islands

Saba is small and compact, while St Kitts is large and well-supplied. These islands are a good contrast to each other; they have a good range of hotel options but neither is overwhelmed with diving operators. The good news is that the Leeward Islands do have the option to take a liveaboard and do it all.

Liveaboard
Caribbean Explorer II, Explorer Ventures, explorerventures.com. Few liveboards sail the Caribbean, but this modern vessel has weekly trips departing from St Maarten and ending in St Kitts. Or vice versa. Dives are scheduled for Saba and St Kitts. A very comfortable ship with a route that covers the best diving in this region.

Saba
Diving
Saba Deep Dive Center, sabadeep.com
Saba Divers, sabadivers.com
Sea Saba, seasaba.com
Sleeping
Juliana's Hotel, julianas-hotel.com
Scout's Place, scoutsplace.com
The Cottage Club, cottage-club.com

St Kitts
Diving
Dive St. Kitts, divestkitts.com
Kenneth's Diving, kennethdivecenter.com
Pro Divers, prodiversstkitts.com
Sleeping
Ocean Terrace Inn, oceanterraceinn.com.

Saba

Unlike most Caribbean islands, Saba was not found and claimed by Christopher Columbus – on seeing the imposing rock walls, he sailed away. For two centuries, the colonial powers went to and fro over Saba, until the Dutch came out on top. Local taxi drivers conduct tours to the main sites, starting at the port and at the beginning of "the road that couldn't be built." After being told it would be impossible, a resident took a correspondence course in civil engineering and built one. Heading up this vital landmark you arrive in The Bottom, the lowest of the three towns, where there is a church and the government buildings. Next uphill is pretty Windwardside, with the tourist office, hotels, shops and restaurants, before you finally reach Hell's Gate. From each town you can divert up trails through the rain and cloud forests or go down to the lowland forests and coast. The landscapes and fauna are impressive – there are 60 bird species, and endemic animals include Saban anole lizards, green iguanas and red-bellied racer snakes.

St Kitts

While Christopher Columbus turned his back on Saba, he took one look at St Kitts and was quickly ashore, claiming the island for Spain. France and Britain soon moved in, keen to have a stake in the island's productive soil. Sugar became the principal crop. Centuries of fighting followed, with local tribes annihilated, before the British finally gained full control. The battles are reflected in the number of war memorials and forts on the island. The most prominent was and is Brimstone Hill Fortress now a UNESCO World Heritage Site and the largest ever built in the Eastern Caribbean. With amazing views over the island, you can see the rich and fertile landscape and understand a little of why St Kitts was so fought over.

The capital is Basseterre, an amalgamation of the original colonial town and a very busy cruise ship terminal with modern shopping malls. However, wandering through the older streets will reveal some lovely colonial houses, many churches, memorials and a tiny museum.

Wingfield Estate is on the west coast. It was owned by Sam Jefferson, ancestor to Thomas Jefferson who became the third US president. The estate produced sugar and rum, and you can see the original workings and distillery. Romney Manor is next door. Jefferson sold the manor to the Earl of Romney who is renowned for being the first land owner to declare his slaves free men. The manor is now a fantastic botanic garden and produces traditional batiks.

To the north is Bloody Point, the tragic site where more than 2,000 Carib Indians were massacred. Black Rocks, on the northeast shore, is where the surf has sculpted huge lava deposits into unusual shapes.

Saba's rocky shores and cliffs; The Bottom, Saba; Brimstone Hill Fortress on St Kitts and St George's Church in Basseterre.

drying out
Windward Islands

Grenada has countless hotels in styles to suit all budgets but as there are just a few dive operations, it make sense to stay and dive with the same one. They are all in southwest of the island and minutes from the airport. On Carriacou, standards are more rustic so a good option is a local guesthouses. Choose one near one of the three dive centres.

Grenada
Diving and sleeping

Aquanauts and True Blue Bay Resort, aquanautsgrenada.com/truebluebay.com. On the Atlantic coast overlooking the bay. Spacious dive boats and great crew.

Dive Grenada and the Flamboyant Hotel, divegrenada.com/flamboyant.com. On the hill above Grand Anse beach. Good value package deals and small dive boats.

Carriacou
Diving

Arawak Divers.com, arawakdivers.com
Deefer Diving, deeferdiving.com. A few minutes from the jetty in Hillsborough.
Lumbadive.com, lumbadive.com. These two operations are both in Tyrrels Bay.

Sleeping

Ade's Dream, adesdream.com
Grand View, carriacougrandview.com

For a more laid-back, island feel, ask the dive centres to recommend a small self-catering cottage. The supermarkets on Carriacou are very good.

Grenada

A tour of Grenada is at its best once you head away from the southern corner, but start in the capital city of St George's, where churches, forts and markets tumble down steep roads to the horseshoe-shaped harbour. Much of the town's history dates to French colonization in the 1650s but by the mid-1800s the British were in control.

Heading north along the coast road, you pass through a time warp. Gone are all signs of modern development and you discover the real Grenada: hills thick with spice trees and rainforest plants are interspersed with pretty pastel houses and small towns. The coastal village of Gouyave is known for Fish Friday – a weekly festival all about eating the local catch. On the north tip of the island is Sauteurs Bay where the last remaining Carib Indian natives jumped to their deaths in 1651 rather than be conquered by the French. There is a touching and an impressive monument to them.

Turning south, a stop is made at one of the island's most beautiful spice plantations, Belmont Estate. Now a thriving commercial concern, this estate was established in the late 1600s. Spices and chocolate are still cultivated using age-old methods. Afterwards it's down to a rum distillery: another curious time warp, River Rum Estate has firmly refused to be dragged into the 21st century and is still distilling with exactly the same methods – and equipment – used in the 1700s. Taste the

product and beware – this stuff is strong. After the over-indulgent assault on your senses with rum, food and spices, it's time to pass through the cooling rainforest below Mt St Catherine, stopping for a moment at the idyllic Grand Etang Lake.

Carriacou

With a good mini-bus system, getting around Carriacou is easy but a tour with a local guide will fill you in on the island's past and present.

Start in Hillsborough, with its banks, shops and tiny museum before driving to Belair, with great views from the Princess Royal Hospital. In front are some age-old cannons said to be left from the days when the French were repelling the British.

On the east coast, facing Petit Martinique, the village of Windward is where a group of Scottish boat builders settled in the 19th century. Even now, the boats are built in the traditional way and may take up to a year to complete. Launching one is a celebration for the whole community. Driving through the hills and back towards Hillsborough, you pass ruins of old plantation houses and windmills. Limes and sugar were once the mainstay of the island economy. To the south is nigh-on deserted Paradise Beach – the name says it all – and around Point Cistern is Tyrrel Bay, a delightful natural harbour and marina.

Belmont Estate plantation; River Rum distillery; Hillsborough Carriacou; the view from Belair.

59
↘ **Essentials**

60
↘ **Dive brief**

62
↘ **Dive sites**

64
↘ **Dive log**

Belize
64   Inner Barrier Reef
65   Turneffe Atoll
67   Lighthouse Reef

Honduras
70   Roatán
73   Utila

76
↘ **Drying out**
76   Belize
77   Honduras

Central America

All that glitters: an explosion of tiny silversides, *Hypoatherina barnesi*, proves that gold is not the most precious metal in the sea.
Tarpon Cave, Lighthouse Reef

Shaped by the ice age, the small sea now known as the Caribbean developed in isolation from the world's other oceans. It's almost as if it was at the back of the queue and missed out on its fair share of marine species. However, it did inherit the world's second largest barrier reef, which defines the eastern coastlines of Central American Belize and Honduras.

Like elsewhere in the region, diving from these countries is not a mind-numbing assault on the senses, but rather a far more subtle underwater experience. Pastel-toned soft corals and neutral-toned hard corals create a delicate backdrop for a marine realm that never screams for attention but waits patiently for observant divers to appreciate its unique features. That isn't to say there aren't some truly unusual diving experiences, including one of the world's most famous, the Blue Hole in Belize. Or, if you simply want to go critter hunting, you can do that on a quiet and laid-back Honduran island.

Edging the western side of the Caribbean, these countries feel more Latin American, their histories shaped first by the Maya, then by colonial invaders and later pirate exploits. There are some cultural diversions but, in reality, their landside charms lie with the many gifts from nature.

Ambergris Caye

Inner Reefs ▶▶ p64

Caye Caulker

BELIZE CITY ●

Lighthouse Reef ▶▶ p67

Turneffe Atoll ▶▶ p65

BELIZE

Dangriga ●

destination
Central America

Guanaja

West End ● Roatán ▶▶ p70

Caribbean Sea

Utila Town ● Utila ▶▶ p73

Cayos Cochinos

● Puerto Barrios

GUATEMALA

San Pedro Sula ✈

✈ ● La Ceiba

HONDURAS

▲
Pico Bonito

Essentials

At a time when air travel couldn't be easier, it seems bizarre to find a region that is so tricky to reach; unless you are in the US, you are likely to need several flights to get to either Belize or Honduras. Because Belize doesn't have a national carrier, and has just a lone international airport at Belize City, you need to fly via the USA and then connect to a shorter flight with another airline. Honduras is strangely similar despite having three major airports. Divers can fly direct to the international terminal on Roatán but only from Houston or Miami. Several small airlines then link Roatán to the Bay Islands via La Ceiba on the mainland coast.

Local laws and customs

A rather informal place, Belize has a laid-back lifestyle with serious Caribbean island overtones. There are traces of ancient cultures, but about half the population is Catholic and the remainder is a mix of other Christian religions. Honduras is principally Catholic although a few indigenous religions are still practised. The people here can be somewhat more reserved, but you may only notice that if you head across to the mainland.

Health and safety

The appearance of things in Belize might make you think that medical standards are low, but the country has a good health record with clinics in most villages. In Honduras, medical facilities are a mixed bag. On the islands English-speaking doctors are easy to find, less so on the mainland. Generally, though, health risks are low. However, on the insect front there is one noteworthy nuisance: the no-see-um. These biting midges live in the sand and, although they don't spread disease they do cause plenty of discomfort. Always use a repellant. Personal safety in either country is as expected – bigger cities require caution; islands are generally safe and easy-going. However, drug use is illegal so be careful to not get drawn into that relaxed Caribbean lifestyle.

Costs

These countries can be as expensive or cheap as you want them to be. You can easily find a decent guesthouse and eat in local restaurants. Honduras is possibly a little cheaper than Belize and Utila is one of the most economical places on the planet to learn to dive. Costs in most resort-style hotels don't necessarily reflect the cost of living in the country, as many are US-run with US or European staff. There are even upmarket eco-lodges owned by the rich and famous (Francis Ford Coppola owns two in Belize). Seafood is good, unless you go in conch season when it's conch curry, conch burgers and conch and chips. Service charges are added to some bills but, if not, then tipping is at your discretion – but 10-15% is the done thing.

Fact file

Belize

Location	17°15'N, 88°45'W
Capital	Belmopan
International flights	American, BA, Delta, KLM, TACA, Virgin,
Internal flights	Maya Island Air and Tropic Air
Land transport	Countrywide buses, taxis, water taxis
Departure tax	US$35, but usually included in ticket
Entry	Visa not required for EU, USA, Canada, Australia and NZ. Other countries' citizens should check.
Money	Belize dollars (BZD)
Language	English officially, Spanish is common
Electricity	110v, plug type A/B (see page 15)
Time zone	GMT -6
Religion	Christian
Communications	Country code +501; IDD code 0; Police 916 Internet access is minimal and expensive
Tourist information	travelbelize.org

Honduras

Location	15°00'N, 86°30'W
Capital	Tegucigalpa
International flights	American, BA, Delta, KLM, TACA
Internal flights	Atlantic, Isleña, SOSA, TACA,
Land transport	Countrywide buses, island buses, taxis
Departure tax	US$30 in cash only
Entry	30 days entry for most nationalities
Money	Lempira (HNL)
Language	English and Spanish
Electricity	110/220v, plug type A (see page 15)
Time zone	GMT -6
Religion	Christian
Communications	Country code +504; IDD code 00; Police 119 Internet access is good countrywide
Tourist information	roatanonline.com and aboututila.com
Travel advisories	gov.uk/foreign-travel-advice; state.gov/travel

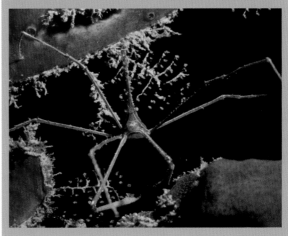

dive brief

Diving

The planet's second largest barrier reef runs for nearly 1,000 kilometres through the Caribbean Sea along Mexico's Yucatán coast, south through Belize and on to Honduras. Known as the Mesoamerican Barrier Reef – to distinguish it from that other more famous one – this extensive system is a UNESCO World Heritage site.

The Caribbean Sea developed in isolation from the others on the planet so it has far lower biodiversity levels than those in Asia or the Pacific. You might think this means the diving isn't so hot – and comparing diversity figures, you will see that the area does lag behind – yet this reef has the highest levels of marine life in the region. Of all the fish species found in the Caribbean Sea most can be found in Belize or Honduras.

The geographic structures that define the barrier reef have been carved by a variety of current patterns and these give each country special features both on land and underwater. Mexico's segment of the reef is influenced heavily by strong currents but, as you travel down towards Belize, they lose their aggression. Diving the small cayes just off the coast is always easy-going. Heading east and further out to sea, Belize has two impressive atolls: Turneffe is closest to shore, then next is Lighthouse Reef, regarded as the best in Belize and location of the famous Blue Hole. Dive sites are, in the main, a mix of gentle, open mounds and steep drop-offs, with sharp channels that cut through the reef rim.

Further south in Honduras, levels of marine diversity are at their highest, due to its location at the very base of the reef and the influences of Central America's volcanic geography. Divers target the Bay Islands, which sit 30 or so miles offshore. Roatán and Utila are the most attractive while Guanaja and the Hog Islands (Cayos Cochinos) have some good diving but are less visited. Conditions are fairly easy, with consistent water temperatures and fewer notable currents.

Marine life

Reefs consist of a rocky strata covered by layers of soft corals, known as sea plumes. These look like twiggy trees until currents bring out polyps to feed, creating soft and furry feathers. Statuesque sponges add scale and colour. Hard coral species are far

We first travelled to Central America as trekkers, not divers, and always enjoyed the pace of life in these countries. It's odd how they are so close, with so many similarities, yet also have some features that set them apart. No matter which you choose, though, you will feel completely immersed in that distinctive style of island life: hammocks under palms, rum cocktail in hand, the sun setting fiery red over cool turquoise...

The diamond blenny is just six centimetres long; Great barracuda on Lighthouse Reef.

less prolific than in other oceans but you seem to see more pelagic life. Strange but true... Bigger animals include eagle rays, turtles and the most enormous tarpon. Not that these outdo smaller creatures: the indigo hamlets, indigenous bluebell tunicates and some very sexy seahorses.

Snorkelling

Those who prefer not to submerge will find some great places to snorkel. In the Bay Islands there are many artificial reefs, including some small boat wrecks that sit close to shore. And, if you are in Utila at the right time, there are excursions to find migrating whale sharks. Belize's shallow seagrass beds attract many large bottom feeders, while reefs around the outer atolls come in close to shore so it's easy to see the 'big stuff'.

Making the big decision

First, choose either Honduras or Belize; combining these neighbouring countries is hard because transport links are minimal. Serious divers go for a Belize liveaboard to get easy access to the Blue Hole, famously lauded by Jacques Cousteau as one of the world's 'must-dives'. Sailing to Lighthouse Reef is also more comfortable and you can dive along the way. There are also plenty of resorts on the islands for those who prefer to be land-based. Honduras, however, has the advantage of being the most diverse marine region within the Caribbean Sea. The hardest decision will be where to go, as each of the Bay Islands has its own personality – at least they are all close enough together to organize a multi-island trip.

◯ Animal encounters

Belize: there seems to be a smiling Great barracuda in the vicinity on most dives, while small critters include quillfin blennies and delicate painted tunicates.
Honduras: look for bluebell tunicates, the cryptic teardrop crab and the delightful longsnout seahorse, which vies for attention with spotted eagle rays.

And in both countries, look for graceful grey reef sharks like these at the Blue Hole.

dive sites

Belize lies at the heart of the substantial Mesoamerican Barrier Reef system. The coastal reefs may be shallow, but dives along the inner barrier reef, which parallels the coast, are known for some surprisingly active dives. Further offshore, Turneffe Atoll is a gently shelving, oval-shaped reef and is dotted with 200 or so cayes that provide shelter for a range of marine animals, as well as for birds and land-based creatures. The most distant reef is, of course, famed Lighthouse Reef. At only 30 miles long and eight miles wide, this is where you'll find the best diving in Belize.

To the south and at the very bottom of the reef, the Bay Islands in Honduras play host to the highest regional levels of marine diversity in the entire Caribbean Sea. Roatán is the best known and busiest destination, with an international airport, top-notch dive facilities and a certain level of sophistication. Close to Roatán but a long way apart in terms of atmosphere, Utila is a chilled-out little island with an air of casual chaos that is reminiscent of the Caribbean of the past. Both islands are ringed by small walls and sloping reefs, plus a few curious and fun wreck dives.

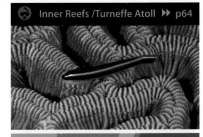

Inner Reefs /Turneffe Atoll ▶▶ p64

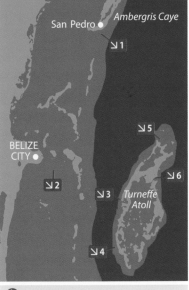

San Pedro ● Ambergris Caye
↘ 1
↘ 5
BELIZE CITY ●
↘ 6
↘ 2
↘ 3 Turneffe Atoll
↘ 4

Conditions

Seasons	In Belize, the driest months are February and March. It gets windy in September. Honduras is wetter from October to January with the chance of hurricanes from August to October.
Visibility	10 m inshore to 40 m+ in open water.
Currents	Generally mild
Temperatures	Air 20-34°C; water 24-30°C
Wet suit	3 mm shorty or full suit, 5 mm+ for the cenotes
Training	Available everywhere. Cheapest on Utila but look for accredited training agencies
Nitrox	Available in resorts, but quantities may be limited, pre-booking advised
Deco chambers	Ambergris Caye, Roatán and Utila

Diversity

combined reef area 2,540 km²

	Belize	Honduras
HARD CORAL	51	54
FISH SPECIES	596	955
ENDEMIC FISH SPECIES	2	2
FISH UNDER THREAT	27	26

All diversity figures are approximate

Log Book

↘1 **Hol Chan Marine Reserve**
↘2 **Canyons II**

→ **Eagle Ray Canyons:** just south of the marine reserve, the name says it all.
→ **Cyprus Gardens:** a variety of hard corals across a shallow reef.
→ **Spanish Bay Wall:** a pinnacle off the sheer wall attracts passing pelagics

↘3 **Sandslope**
↘4 **Sayonara Wreck**
↘5 **Rendezvous Point**
↘6 **Tubular Barrels**

→ **Wonderland:** known for its patrolling pod of bottlenose dolphins
→ **The Terrace:** a series of ledges reveal a forest of black corals
→ **Elbow:** fun drift dive around the southern point of Turneffe Atoll

Lighthouse Reef ▶▶ p67

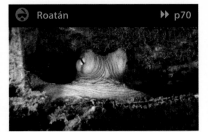
Roatán ▶▶ p70

Utila ▶▶ p73

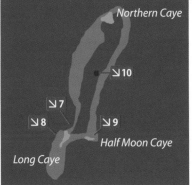
Northern Caye
↘10
↘7
↘8   ↘9
Half Moon Caye
Long Caye

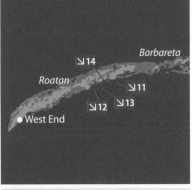
Barbareta
↘14
Roatan
↘11
↘12 ↘13
● *West End*

↘15   ↘16
Utila Town ●
Roatan
↘17 ↘18

Log Book

Log Book

Log Book

↘7	**The Aquarium**
↘8	**Cathedral**
↘9	**Tarpon Cave**
↘10	**The Blue Hole**

↘11	**Calvin's Crack**
↘12	**Valley of the Kings**
↘13	**Forty Foot Point**
↘14	**CocoView Bay**

↘15	**Great Wall (Duppy Waters)**
↘16	**Aquarium I & II**
↘17	**Halliburton Wreck**
↘18	**Ted's Point**

→ **Long Caye Wall:** pastel soft corals coat an underwater promontory

→ **East Cut:** enormous barrel sponges lined upon the wall

→ **Uno Coco:** green morays compete with lobsters to live in the crevices

→ **Missing Link:** cracks and crevices washed by rays of sunlight

→ **Wreck of the Captain G:** critters hiding in the remains of a shrimping boat.

→ **Carib Point:** night dive for gorgonians and mitrax crabs waving their claws

→ **Reef Resort:** bluebell tunicates hide in the soft corals

→ **Rocky Point:** vase sponges, whip and hard corals across a lovely sloping wall

→ **Jack Neal Point:** an ID list of small fish, from gobies to angels to spotted drums

🌐 Endangered oceans

With a plethora of marine parks tripping down the Belize section of the Mesoamerican Barrier Reef and then around the bend to the Bay Islands in Honduras, this region certainly appears to be taking care of its marine ecosystems. Conservation projects in Belize rescue, care for then tag hawksbill and loggerhead turtles and are now monitoring the Olive Ridley after one was found caught in fishing lines. This proves they are, at least, living in the region. Another new resident is the alien lionfish, which is invading the entire Caribbean. Education projects are encouraging overfishing – and eating – of this non-native population. A constant watch is kept on vital seagrass beds to ensure that several small populations of dugongs are safe. These shallow environments also act as nursery grounds for many reef species.

Meanwhile, down in Honduras, the Bay Islands were declared a marine park a few years back. Busy Roatán now has a co-ordinated series of coastal zones – some give the reefs complete protection, others are buffer zones that intend to set up and maintain a series of sustainable purposes for areas around the island. A huge step forward was made when the Cordelia Banks were protected. This small reef is squeezed between two cruise ship docks on Roatán's southwest coast yet is a rare section of reef that still includes staghorn corals, a species that is listed as critically endangered by the IUCN. Neighbouring Utila is very active in protecting shark populations amongst other things. The island was declared a shark protection zone specifically to ensure the safety of Caribbean reef sharks but, more famously, the island is also known to be a whale shark highway. These magnificent gentle giants migrate through these waters and are photographed and tagged whenever they pass through.

dive log
Belize: Inner Reefs

The inner barrier reef is less than an hour from Belize City and close to the islands of Ambergris Caye and Caye Caulker. South of these, smaller cayes have evocative names like Drowned Caye and Spanish Lookout Caye, a reflection of their illustrious pasts.

A deep marine trench separates the inner reef cayes and lagoons from Turneffe Atoll and Lighthouse Reef to the east. Shallow and well protected, there's relaxed diving and snorkelling in the marine parks where fishing is restricted. The ecosystems are varied and include coral reefs, seagrass beds and mangroves: the mangrove trees are well-used habitats for seabirds while many species of fish, shellfish and other marine organisms begin life protected by their roots.

⊾1 Hol Chan Marine Reserve

🕐 **Depth**	12 m
◑ **Visibility**	fair
≋ **Currents**	unlikely

This small marine reserve lies off Ambergris Caye and is a favourite destination for both divers and snorkellers. It's not particularly challenging and it can get crowded, but it is a good example of an inner Belizean reef. The structure runs east-west, creating a long, winding ridge with cuts, fan corals and hard coral outcrops. There are a lot of pelagic fish such as barracuda and grouper as this is a no fishing zone. Spending some time up in the shallow seagrass beds is worthwhile, as even snorkellers might encounter gentle nurse sharks, rays and morays, and often in waist-deep water.

⊾2 Canyons II

🕐 **Depth**	25 m
◑ **Visibility**	fair
≋ **Currents**	can be strong

Spanish Lookout Caye may be close to Belize City, but it has to be one of the more interesting dives in the inner reef area. Within seconds of hitting the water you are likely to see eagle rays, groupers and lobsters. Smaller animals nestle into cracks and crevices and include cleaner shrimp, arrow crabs and morays. Off over the edge of the wall there are barracuda and tuna watching curiously. An area of mangrove swamp is a fantastic nursery ground for lobster and molluscs and, if you are lucky, you may see one of the manatees feeding on the seagrass beds.

dive log
Belize: Turneffe Atoll

Sailing east from Belize City, then over the inner barrier reef, you encounter a series of atolls divided by deep water marine trenches. Turneffe Atoll is the first and sits on the shallower, of two submarine ridges.

There are small islands dotted right across this scenic atoll and many are covered in dense mangroves which act as breeding and nursery grounds for many creatures. The water is shallow inside the central lagoon, but there are dive sites all the way around the atoll perimeter. Tides and winds distribute nutrients around so fish populations are fairly substantial even though differing sets of weather conditions mean that the north and west can be choppy.

S3	Sandslope	
Depth		36 m
Visibility		fair to good
Currents		none to medium

This oval-shaped reef consists of lots of small bommies with coral patches dotted around them. There is good coverage of seaplumes, rods and whips and even some fan corals that are several feet high. These thrive in the currents created by the atoll's tidal flow. The very pretty indigo hamlet is a resident, as is his cousin, the shy hamlet. These small skittish fish are easy to miss, unlike the lobsters that settle on anything they find comfortable, sometimes even inside the really tall vase sponges. As the atoll is so far away from the coast, you are likely to see some of the more unusual Caribbean fish, such as the white sargassum triggerfish and highly patterned diamond and quillfin blennies – check the male's dorsal fin. There are also arrow crabs on almost every sponge, plenty of cleaner shrimp residing in corkscrew anemones and spinyhead blennies squatting in holes made by tube worms. Spotted morays poke noses up from the reef and jawfish live in burrows in the sand.

S4	Sayonara Wreck	
Depth		33 m
Visibility		good
Currents		none to mild

Off the southwest of Turneffe Atoll, this long, sloping wall drops to over 40 metres and has a pure white sandy seabed with seaplumes and barrel sponges scattered across it. Finning along the reef ridge you find a series of cuts and gullies, creating nice swim-throughs for divers and shelters for the fish. Mackerel pass overhead in small groups and always appear to be followed by a solitary oceanic triggerfish, a fish that never seems to have a mate. Heading back towards the mooring, you come to the wreck of the *Sayonara*, a cargo boat that was deliberately sunk in 1985. There's nothing much left of its wooden hull save for a few planks and a lot of mechanical detritus, but there is an incredible number of indigo hamlets and just as many spotted trunkfish. The rare toadfish is known to live on this reef so if you want to see this elusive creature stick closely to your dive guide!

The indigo hamlet (left); a red hind grouper and the not-so-common male quillfin blenny.

↘5 Rendezvous Point

🕙 **Depth**	21 m
◐ **Visibility**	good
🌊 **Currents**	mild to strong

Sitting on the northwestern side of central Turneffe atoll, this dive marks the edge of one of the few safe entries to the inner lagoon. The wall begins at 15 metres and slopes down to a series of undulating canyons. The marine topography is quite gentle in this area with far fewer tunnels than are found in the south of the atoll. All the same, this series of shallow grooves that divide the reef are always full of life, with swarms of glassfish, masses of small neon gobies and arrow crabs sheltering inside. The sloping wall has a variety of sponges and plenty of schooling fish, plus you may catch a glimpse of a blacktip reef shark, eagle ray or turtle.

↘6 Tubular Barrels

🕙 **Depth**	22 m
◐ **Visibility**	good
🌊 **Currents**	mild to medium

Another charming and relaxing dive, but on the eastern side of the atoll. The wall is shallow but covered in an amazing array of sponges – yellow tube sponges, azure vase sponges and huge burgundy-toned barrel sponges that stand proud of the surrounding pastel-toned soft corals that clad the reef surfaces. All the protruding items are ringed by small shoals of flitting fish and provide homes for plenty of small flamingo tongue shells and, as always, masses of arrow crabs. There are a few cleaning stations and a surprising number of boxfish. Bottlenose dolphins are regular visitors here and can also be seen at Wonderland a little way north.

❝❞ The smell of a street corner BBQ; the gritty road that leads away from the noisy, clogged city; reminders that dreams are usually not this real. The colour of the skittish sargassum triggerfish with its blue hue, patch of white above the eyes and small, dark, choco-like sprinkles. Playing hide and seek at Turneffe with the waving beard of the endemic whitespotted toadfish. The contrast between the been-there-done-that diver's disdain for the Blue Hole and the face of a new and hesitant diver at 115 feet, as imposing stalactite formations come into sight. Learning to appreciate every site for what it kindly offers and being rewarded with the capacity to see things I was once blind to, like the many decorator crabs, diamond, quillfin, and spinyhead blennies... All of these things are my images of Belize and what kept me there – smiling – as an instructor for over a year.

Vladimir Soto, PADI master instructor,
Mexico City and Torino, Italy

dive log Belize: Lighthouse Reef

The reason most people give when asked why they want to dive Belize is to witness the spectacle made famous over 30 years ago by one Jacques-Yves Cousteau: the Blue Hole at Lighthouse Reef.

This National Monument has definitely entered diver folklore, and there's no doubt that, as a dive, this is a serious adrenaline rush. It's all to do with the perfectly vertical drop to depth and, probably, the excitement building up to the dive as much as actually doing it.

There are many other great dive sites around Lighthouse Reef, which sits on the second of Belize's submarine ridges and is divided from Turneffe Atoll by another, deeper marine trench. Dives around Half Moon and Long Cayes at the southern tip all display a fairly similar profile – sharp walls are cut by deep grooves and interspersed with small caverns. Some are backed by sandy shelves leading to seagrass beds.

Diving is subject to prevailing weather conditions but, even when the winds pick up from one direction, the boat can simply move to the opposite coast. What's more, the Blue Hole is smack-bang in the middle of it all so you'll never miss out on diving that.

↘7	The Aquarium	
🕐	**Depth**	20 m
◐	**Visibility**	great
🌀	**Currents**	slight to medium

Like so many of the dive sites along the western side of the atoll, this is a very pretty wall that drops all the way down to about 60 metres. There are lots of twists and turns along the reef edge, which is coated with large fans, soft corals and some very big sponges surrounded by clusters of fish. Just over the edge of the reef rim, a resident and very friendly giant barracuda hovers, keeping completely still, while watching the divers. Also seen on the wall are two well-known midnight parrotfish – these guys are the largest in the parrot family and grow up to 75 centimetres long! Angels, boxfish, porkfish, butterflies and damsels flit among the prolific corals and sponges. If you're watching the blue, you may spot eagle rays as they rush by below and, heading back to the boat, you'll see the ever-present swarms of jacks, snapper and chubb shadowing the hull.

↘8	Cathedral	
🕐	**Depth**	35 m
◐	**Visibility**	excellent
🌀	**Currents**	slight

Although this wall is nowhere near as pretty as some of the others at Lighthouse Reef, the topography is some of the most interesting, with lots of cut-backs and gullies in the reef to swim through. At the bottom of the wall large lobsters hide in the crevices and, at certain times of year, you'll notice that the females are heavily pregnant. Coming back up the wall and swimming through the cuts, you are often met head on by large mackerel trying to swim out. Back on the upper section of the reef lots of tiny roughhead blennies poke their heads up from their holes in the rocks, flamingo tongue shells sit on sea plumes and inside miniature caves are pairs of banded coral shrimp. The bigger pelagic fish – chubbs, snapper, jacks, creole wrasse and inquisitive great barracuda – are still hanging out under the boat, but this time, they are joined by a tarpon. Great to watch on a safety stop.

Lobster and tarpon on Lighthouse Reef.

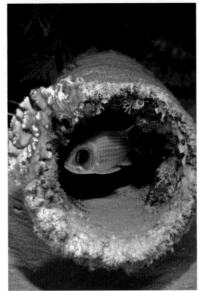

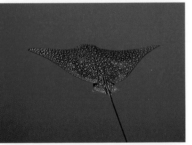

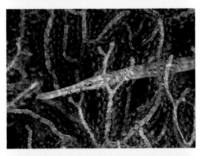

	9	Tarpon Cave	
	Depth	40 m
	Visibility	excellent
	Currents	slight

This dive, which lies on the eastern side of Lighthouse Reef, has some fabulous topography that is fun to explore. Entry is over a level seagrass bed at eight metres, which then leads across an area of sand covered in conch that are crawling in every direction and leaving scribbled trails in the sand. The plan is to swim down to about 20 metres where you face a barrier formation that rises up again creating a hump at 15 metres. Tunnels cut through this barrier to the reef rim then leading on to the outer wall. The water here drops to depths well over 60 metres.

Swimming into one of the tunnels, you are bound to meet at least one five-foot long tarpon. His scales are metallic silver and highly reflective, and it seems that he is just waiting to have his photo taken. Another smaller cave further along the reef is dark with silversides, and you can watch barracuda swoop in to feed on them. Swimming along the outer wall, an eagle ray passes by below then, a few seconds later, you might see a turtle or two heading up to the surface for a gulp of air. Back up on the reef top, schools of black and blue tangs go crazy feeding in the algae. The seagrass area is a good place to stop at the end of the dive and spend time watching the stingrays as they fluff up the sand, looking for food.

Clockwise from top: juvenile French angelfish, tiny rabbitfish in a pipe, flutemouth on fan, Queen angelfish, painted tunicates, eagle ray.

the blue hole

🌀	**Depth**	45 m
🔆	**Visibility**	fair to good
〰	**Currents**	none

The Blue Hole gained celebrity status after Jacques Cousteau's *Calypso* expedition in 1972. Sitting at the midpoint of Lighthouse Reef, it was believed to be a cave whose roof collapsed at the end of the Ice Age. Now, the deep blue, circular opening is over 300 metres across and drops to about 150 metres. At about 40 metres an overhanging shelf is marked by ancient stalactites. As limestone can't form beneath water, and stalactites are created when fresh water drips through limestone rock, these are evidence that the cave was once above sea level.

This unique dive is an exhilarating experience for novices who have rarely, if ever, been to such depths. After a thorough briefing in which guides emphasize the depth and say things like "there's more cameras on the bottom of the Hole than in all Belize", divers are led in a vertical line down to see the stalactites. The water temperature drops substantially by the time you reach 45 metres, and you only get a few moments to admire the stalactites and an occasional grouper before being told it's time to ascend again.

Apart from a few fish, the dive is rather lifeless; however, operators have picked up on the fact that the area is visited by a group of grey reef sharks and now use bait to attract them. These beautiful animals circle divers during the safety stop, hoping for further handouts.

Some divers can get disoriented by the depth, so no matter how seasoned you are, stick with your buddy and use a carabiner (or d-clip) for your cameras and torches.

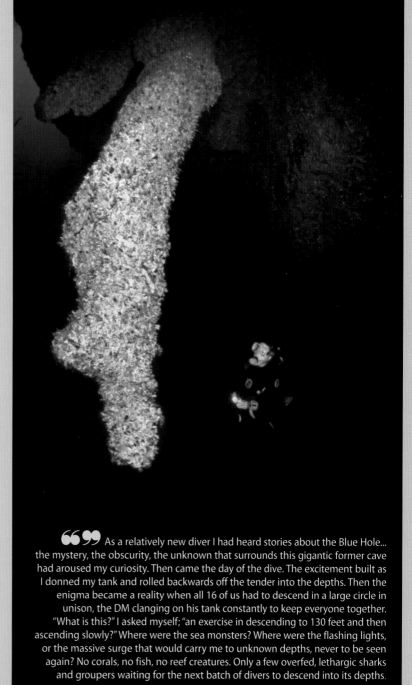

❝❞ As a relatively new diver I had heard stories about the Blue Hole... the mystery, the obscurity, the unknown that surrounds this gigantic former cave had aroused my curiosity. Then came the day of the dive. The excitement built as I donned my tank and rolled backwards off the tender into the depths. Then the enigma became a reality when all 16 of us had to descend in a large circle in unison, the DM clanging on his tank constantly to keep everyone together. "What is this?" I asked myself; "an exercise in descending to 130 feet and then ascending slowly?" Where were the sea monsters? Where were the flashing lights, or the massive surge that would carry me to unknown depths, never to be seen again? No corals, no fish, no reef creatures. Only a few overfed, lethargic sharks and groupers waiting for the next batch of divers to descend into its depths.

Phil Tobin, diamond broker, Portland, USA

dive log

Honduras: Roatán

The largest of the Bay Islands at 58 kilometres long but less than eight wide, Roatán is jungle-bound, with hills falling steeply to the sea. The coast is ringed by palm-clad sandy beaches, riddled with tiny cayes and studded by deep water inlets called blights.

It was these that gave birth to the island's notorious history. A safe haven for boats, the blights were used by huge numbers of pirate ships during the 16th century, and it wasn't until the 1740s that a combined Spanish army and navy offensive removed them. The blights are also notable in the Roatán diving scene. A barrier reef, which sits just below the surface, rings the entire island a short way offshore. Inside this reef a protected lagoon has calm and comfortable diving, while outside, especially in the south, there are steep walls, fissures, overhangs and ledges. Northern coastal sites tend to be gentler with sloping walls and reefs, but right around the island conditions are similar.

N11 Calvin's Crack	
Depth	30 m
Visibility	good
Currents	mild

Rather like a game of follow the leader, this dive involves a quick drop down to the reef top plateau at about 15 metres before descending into a sharp crack in the reef. The divemaster then shepherds his group together, pauses by the reef rim and waves to an enormous green moray who is watching the morning's divers. Suddenly the leader simply drops out of sight. Divers file after him in turn, swimming through the dimly lit, narrow passageway and past gigantic, metre-wide king crabs, which huddle into the cracks. A few lobsters wave a claw at the passing intruders until everyone exits from the tunnel at 27 metres. A slight current runs on the wall, so you drift with it and admire the huge fan corals, which are displaying their fluffy feeding tentacles.

N12 Valley of the Kings	
Depth	32 m
Visibility	good
Currents	mild

This is one of the more impressive walls along the south coast as it seems to have some of the biggest corals and sponges in the area. Fan corals wave over the top of overhangs, competing for attention with azure vase sponges and amazingly long red and pink rope sponges. There are also some small black coral bushes. Winding their way through them are black-and-white spotted morays and a lot of the reef fish that are typical of these waters. French angelfish and boxfish are common and tend to follow divers. The relatively rare sargassam triggerfish can be seen on occasion and there are striped snapper everywhere you look. The top of the reef here rises up to five metres in places, so this can be a good snorkelling site as long as there is no current.

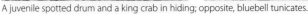
A juvenile spotted drum and a king crab in hiding; opposite, bluebell tunicates.

N13 Forty Foot Point

Depth	22 m
Visibility	good
Currents	mild

Not very imaginatively named, this reef dive drops from around 25 feet to – you guessed it – 40 feet. The outer wall has a good covering of sponges and soft corals with passing schools of jacks, snapper and spadefish. The visibility is excellent and, with little or no current, this is a very calm and relaxing dive. However, the pace starts to change back up on the top of the reef as the big attraction can be found hiding in the patches of coralline algae covering the more level areas – disguised amongst the bright green carpet are longsnout seahorses. These beautiful animals are not easy to spot, despite being bright colours, because they are so tiny. There are also jacks, lobster, crabs and goodness knows what else, but who cares when you have just encountered one of these most beautiful of endangered creatures.

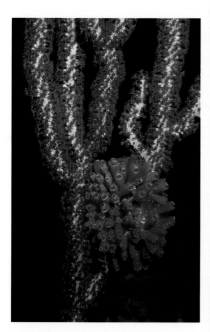

COCO view
bay

↘14

🌀 **Depth**	32 m
🌀 **Visibility**	poor to good
🌀 **Currents**	none to slight

CocoView Resort sits on a tiny private caye that nestles in a shallow lagoon. A channel leads from the beach to beyond the outer reef. The protected inner lagoon has been turned into a diving theme park of sorts – but don't be put off by that. This is a great dive and snorkelling location. Just off the beach is a partly submerged kitting-up table, where you can haul on your fins and then drop to your knees to follow a heavy chain that leads away from the table, past jawfish, shrimp and upside-down jellyfish to the wreck of the *Prince Albert*. This 47-metre long island freighter is upright and pretty much intact. You can swim through the open holds and around the decks. When visibility is good you can see her entire length and, as one end is just seven metres deep, snorkellers can too.

Heading off to one side, another chain leads from the bow to the fuselage of a DC3 aeroplane with octopus and pufferfish huddling in its remains. There are also two diveable walls on either side of the channel. These attract schooling fish plus colourful rabbitfish, parrotfish and rock beauties. As you head back to shore, keep your eyes down on the seagrass beds for flounder.

❝❞ The first time we dived the *Prince Albert*, the boat was newly scuttled and completely naked. A decade later and she has developed into a princess, dressed to impress with a colourful coat of corals, sponges and tunicates.

dive log
Honduras: Utila

From the moment you set foot on the airstrip on Utila – no terminal, no check-in desks, no luggage handler – you see why this island is a favourite with hikers and long-term travellers. The small town is a rather haphazard affair with just one main road sweeping around the bay and connecting restaurants, shops, small hotels and more dive centres than you could possibly wave your kit bag at.

Only 30 nautical miles from Roatán, Utila is as flat as her neighbour is hilly. The island sits on the edge of the continental shelf, so the diving is a little different too. On the south, the dives are shallow, but there are lots of interesting cracks and crevices along the reef walls. These create overhangs, swim-throughs and sand channels to investigate. While the marine species are naturally similar, there seems to be far more critter life. On the north side of the island, the reefs are more dramatic, with steep walls and drop-offs. However, this side is affected by weather conditions, so you may not get up there as much as you would like. It is also recognized as a whale shark highway, with regular sightings in the dry season.

⌖15 Great Wall (Duppy Waters)	
🜁 **Depth**	36 m
◐ **Visibility**	very good
🜨 **Currents**	none to medium

Just outside Turtle Harbour on the north of the island is one the most spectacular dives on Utila. A sharp slope descends quickly to a wall that feels like it drops off into infinity. You certainly can't see the bottom. The slope is covered in corals and sponges, with many moray eels residing amongst them. Over the reef lip there are huge fan corals and giant barrel sponges reaching out into the sea. Fish hovering in the blue include jacks, creole wrasse, great barracuda and occasional turtles. Back up on the top of the reef there are plenty of juvenile fish plus grey angels, Townsend angels and damsels, plus scorpionfish hiding under the soft corals. As the boats head back to the south coast they are often accompanied by a pod of dolphins.

UTILA LODGE
Phone: 011-504-45-3143
Fax: 011-504-45-3506
Honduras Bay Islands

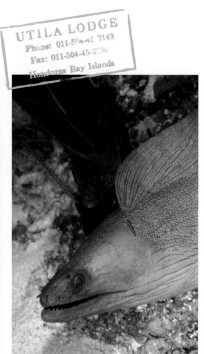

Juvenile slender filefish hiding on a whip coral; moray eels coming to see the divers.

⬔16 Aquarium I & II

⏱ **Depth**	16 m
◑ **Visibility**	fair to good
≋ **Currents**	mild

The coastal landscape on Utila's eastern end has jagged volcanic rock formations, which can be seen both above and below the waterline. The two Aquarium sites are quite shallow and great for exploring these unusual formations. Caves and overhangs have been carved by centuries of crashing waves, leaving chimneys and blowholes in the coastal strip above. Sitting in relatively calm water, you can watch the powerful wave action continuing its work. Inside the caves, if you look down, are some very interesting creatures like mantis shrimp, trunkfish and the greater soapfish. A little deeper are large garden beds of pastel-hued swaying soft corals, whips and sea plumes. Hiding amongst their fronds are flutemouths and parrotfish, banded jawfish and peacock flounders.

⬔17 Halliburton Wreck

⏱ **Depth**	30 m
◑ **Visibility**	poor to good
≋ **Currents**	mild to medium

This 30-metre-long cargo ship was sunk in May 1998 to create an artificial reef. She sits upright on the seabed near the lighthouse at the edge of East Harbour and catches the tides and murk from the bay. Visibility is low, but the flow of nutrients is aiding coral growth. The wreck is marked by two buoys – one is attached to the bow at 20 metres, which is a good place to start. As you descend you see new corals decorating the hold while a few large grouper hang below the bow. You can then swim around the hull or through a few openings until you reach the wheelhouse. A bicycle is locked to the rail outside and snappers hover inside unless disturbed. A giant green moray often slithers around. Finally, ascend up the second mooring line for a safety stop.

⊠18 Ted's Point

🕐 **Depth**	23 m
◑ **Visibility**	good
🌊 **Currents**	mild

Ted's is just outside East Harbour on the south coast. Typically, this site is a bit so-so during daylight hours but, as soon as the sun sets, it comes alive.

Using a torch at night is a great way to find and focus on smaller reef creatures, some of which you would never see otherwise as their camouflage is simply too good to spot them during the day. A sloping sand patch leads down to the remains of a small sailboat that is covered in sponges and tunicates. If you know what you're looking for you may find the very tiny, nocturnal cryptic teardrop crab sitting on a sponge. They are always there but take some spotting, so this is definitely the time to keep an eye on your dive guide.

There are other critters on the remains of the wreck including nudibranchs and neon gobies resting on the tiny sponges. Across the sand there are flamingo tongue shells feeding on the small clusters of soft corals and, beneath them, are Pederson cleaner shrimp living on their corkscrew anemone hosts. Plenty of other night crustaceans start to emerge from their lairs, including another curious find, the swollen claw mantis, a tiny chap just five or six centimetres long.

At just 12-18 millimetres wide, the delightful cryptic teardrop crab is a decorator crab that uses tiny ruby red sponges on its carapace; the lettuce sea slug is one of the region's most unusual nudibranchs as it mimics algaes; the colours of the swollen claw mantis allow it to merge with the neutral tones of a variety of corals.

drying out

Belize

Belize City
Sleeping
Radisson Fort George Hotel, radisson.com
Villa Boscardi, villaboscardi.com

Inner Reefs
Sleeping and diving
Hugh Parkey's Belize Adventures, dive centre on Ambergris Caye and a full service resort at Spanish Lookout Caye, spanishbayresort.com. Transfers about 1-hr.

Turneffe Atoll
Sleeping and diving
About 1.5-hrs from Belize City, full-service dive resorts are located at:
Blackbird Caye, blackbirdresort.com
Turneffe Flats Lodge, tflats.com

Lighthouse Reef
Liveaboard
Sun Dancer II, dancerfleet.com

Sun Dancer liveaboard; Half Moon Caye; the view from the Swing Bridge in Belize City.

Days out

Although slightly overshadowed by the Maya and Aztec sites and land attractions in neighbouring Mexico and Honduras, Belize still has plenty of interesting things to do and see.

Belize City The former capital is divided in two by Haulover Creek: the halves are connected by the Swing Bridge, the only manually swung bridge in the world still in operation. The Fort George area includes the City Museum, the National Handicrafts centre, the Maritime Museum and Memorial Park. Cross south over the bridge to the commercial centre, St John's Cathedral – the oldest Anglican church in Central America – and the Baron Bliss Institute (the cultural centre).

Caye Caulker Even if you're not staying here, this extremely laid-back island is worth a visit. The town is just one main road and lots of sandy lanes with cafés and shops in pretty clapboard houses. In the north, there are mangroves and forests, with walking trails and good birdwatching.

Ambergris Caye Bigger and brasher than Caye Caulker, this much more developed island has a museum and cultural centre, lots of hotels, restaurants and bars (and even more dive centres). There are some Maya remains dotted around but they can be hard to find so take a tour. There are eco-tours to visit Little Iguana and Rosario Cayes for birdwatching, or go to San Pedro Lagoon where you might spot racoons or crocodiles. For nightowls, or those who like to do more than just dive, this is a good island to be based on.

Half Moon Caye National Monument
You are only likely to see the amazing birdlife on this protected island if you are on a liveaboard. The caye is protected as one of only two Caribbean nesting areas for the red-footed booby: there are said to be 4,000 here, along with frigates and around 90 other bird species, plus iguanas, lizards and loggerhead turtles. You can wander the beaches or head along the narrow nature trail to a bird-viewing platform.

Cockscomb Basin Wildlife Sanctuary
About two hours south of Belize City, in the shadow of the Maya Mountains, 100,000 acres of tropical forest rise from sea level to the summit of Victoria Peak. Originally established in 1984 to protect a large jaguar population, it shelters plenty of birds and beautiful flora but the chances of seeing a jaguar or any other local wild cat is slim.

Altún Ha Just an hour north of Belize City, this Maya city (Altún Ha means 'Rockstone Pond') dates from around 250 BC and was a major ceremonial and trading centre. An impressive carved jade head representing the sun god, Kinich Ahau, was found here.

Tikal Regarded as the most important of all the Maya archaeological sites, Tikal is just over the border in Guatemala and deep in the Petén jungle. There are dozens of stone temples and palaces, some dating from 300 BC, though the main buildings were built between AD 500 and AD 900. You can arrange a tour from Belize City or fly to Santa Elena and stay overnight in Tikal's twin town of Flores, perched on a tiny island in Lake Petén Itzá. Note that you will probably need a visa to do this tour.

drying out
Honduras

Roatán
Sleeping and diving
Anthony's Key Resort, anthonyskey.com.
On the northwest coast. 15-min transfer.
CocoView Resort, cocoviewresort.com.
Private caye half way along the south coast.
Airport ransfers take 25-mins.
Reef House Resort, reefhouseresort.com.
On the south coast near Oak Ridge village,
about 40-mins transfer.

Utila
Sleeping and diving
Laguna Beach, lagunabeachresort.info
Utila Lodge, utilalodge.com. Located right
on the bay in town; 5-mins transfer.

La Ceiba
Sleeping
The Lodge at Pico Bonito, 20-mins from
La Ceiba airport; picobonito.com.

Days out

The Bay Islands are not renowned for
cultural attractions despite their colourful
pirate past. However, one of the most
spectacular of all Maya sites lies at Copán,
near the border with Guatemala.

Copán Ruinas One of the least known of
the Maya sites, yet one of the best to visit,
Copán has many exquisitely carved 'stellae',
which tell tales from Maya history, and some
well-preserved temples. Archaeologists are
constantly discovering new sections, one of
the latest being some hidden tombs. You
can walk through the tunnels beneath the
impressive ruins and visit the new museum
where some of the more fragile finds have
been displayed. Copán town is also pretty
with cobbled streets, restaurants and shops.

Pico Bonito Cloud Forest Across from the
Bay Islands, near La Ceiba on the Honduran
coast, are the Nombre de Dios mountains.
Rising to 2700 metres, they are nearly always
swathed in clouds, created when cool
mountain air meets warmer temperatures
at the coast. Spend some time exploring
the forest and spot one of the 325 known
bird species. Hike through the park and, if
you are lucky, see a jaguar or puma, tapir,
deer or white-faced and spider monkeys.
The lodge was converted from an old
chocolate plantation – cocoa pods hang
over your door – and they say that big cats
have been known to sit on guests' terraces.

Roatán The island has a notorious history,
steeped in tales of the infamous pirates of
the Caribbean including the Briton Henry
Morgan (but no Johnny Depp, sadly). The
pirates were incredibly well organized and

built sophisticated fortifications, but in the
1740s a Spanish offensive removed them.
The British legacy remains in place and is
evident in both the use of English and in
the names of the island's towns. Many cruise
ships dock here, so there are organized
activities such as horseriding or white-water
rafting or you can visit an iguana or butterfly
farm. The Carambola Nature Reserve has
hiking trails to see orchids and spices. West
End, the main town, is ideal for a bit of retail
therapy or a meal, or go to Oak Ridge, a
true Caribbean fishing village, where you
can imagine what life might have been like
back in the pirate days.

Utila There's not a huge amount to do on
Utila, although there are organized hikes to
see the rock formations at Iron Bound or up
through the small patch of forest at Pumpkin
Hill. There's an iguana breeding station,
some horseback riding and seasonal whale
shark spotting. Apart from that, wander
along the only road for drinks at a sunset bar
or investigate the excellent handicraft shops.

The other Bay Islands East from Roatán is
Guanaja, which is mountainous and highly
undeveloped. The island bore the full brunt
of 1998's Hurricane Mitch and the reefs on
the south took a battering. Business never
quite recovered and resorts closed down.
If you like adventures, watch for new resorts
opening – we dived Guanaja in the past
and it was good. The two islands and 13
cayes that make up the Cayos Cochinos
are closer to the mainland and a marine
reserve. The shallow reef surrounding them
is said to be the macro capital of the area.
A new and tempting dive eco-resort has
opened, turtlebayecoresort.com.

Honduran parrot; stela at Copan; looking over
the lagoon at Oak Ridge.

East Africa

81
↘ **Essentials**

82
↘ **Dive brief**

84
↘ **Dive sites**

86
↘ **Dive log**

Kenya
86   Kenya coast

Tanzania
88   Pemba island
90   Zanzibar

Mozambique
94   Pemba
97   Medjumbe

99
↘ **Drying out**
99   Kenya
100   Tanzania
101   Mozambique

Jackfish Spot: a solitary coral-clad arch lures divers downwards to see jackfish schools in the deep.
Mnemba Atoll, Zanzibar

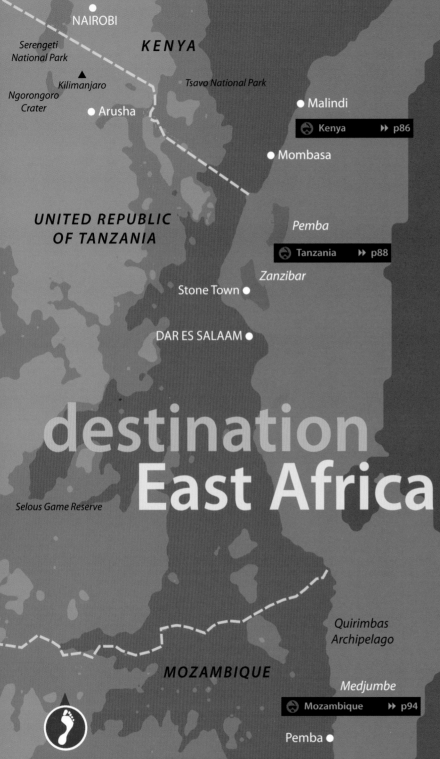

NAIROBI

KENYA

Serengeti
National Park

Kilimanjaro ▲

Tsavo National Park

Ngorongoro
Crater

● Arusha

● Malindi

👣 Kenya ▶▶ p86

● Mombasa

**UNITED REPUBLIC
OF TANZANIA**

Pemba

👣 Tanzania ▶▶ p88

Zanzibar

Stone Town ●

DAR ES SALAAM ●

destination
East Africa

Selous Game Reserve

*Quirimbas
Archipelago*

MOZAMBIQUE

Medjumbe

👣 Mozambique ▶▶ p94

Pemba ●

Wide open plains baking in the African sun, ancient tribes facing up to the realities of modern life, herds of exotic animals roaming wild and free... At least once in your life you have to come face to face with the big five. It's a heart-stopping, spine-tingling moment when a male lion walks straight up to you – just inches from your open Land Rover – and looks deep into your eyes.

If you're a diver, however, it might seem hard to give up peaceful days floating in warm waters for a close encounter with nature on dry land. But you don't have to. East Africa is an alluring dive destination simply because you can do it all.

While inland landscapes are baked to exquisite shades of gold and terracotta, the coastal waters are cooler tones of deep indigo and pale turquoise. Sitting on the fringe of the Indian Ocean, the world's warmest, the vista changes to one that is lush with coconut palms, spice trees and mangroves. Under perfect blue skies, tiny dhows float over little-known fringing reefs which meander gently along the shoreline. They protect the flat coastal regions that lie behind while creating nursery grounds for rainbow-hued reef fish. And although larger animals are mostly to be found on land, the marine life is still exciting enough to justify a visit.

Essentials

For Europeans, getting to the eastern coast of Africa is a cinch. But if you're coming from any other continent, you will probably need to route through a European hub or, most likely, fly via the Middle East. Nairobi is the easiest capital to get to with plenty of onward connections. There is also the international airport at Dar es Salaam and one at Kilimanjaro, should you feel the need to climb a mountain before submerging.

If you intend going on a safari, it makes a lot of sense to do that first: a substantial network of small airlines connect the cities, national parks and coastal areas.

Local laws and customs

The people of both Kenya and Tanzania are an almost equal mix of Christian, Muslim and tribal religions, while in Mozambique about half the population are Catholic and about 20% are Muslim. Be sensitive to local practices. Common sense goes a long way – don't walk around half dressed in a Muslim coastal town, for instance – but generally the people in all of these countries are friendly and outgoing.

Health and safety

East Africa requires most of the standard jabs and malaria is a risk but these potential dangers are easy to protect against. Health facilities are not great, so if you do get ill, chances are you will be airlifted to Johannesburg or straight home. It has to be stressed that HIV is a problem right across Africa.

Travellers should be cautious in the major cities (Nairobi's nickname is 'Nai-robbery') and, although most crime is petty, it's best to catch a cab at night and carry as little as possible. Lone female travellers should be cautious even in smaller towns. Now that the bad news is over, here's the good news: dive regions tend to be well away from troubled city centres; safari parks are well policed; hotels employ security guards, and locals just love tourists, who they see as generous and friendly.

Costs

It must be said that East Africa is not a cheap destination. Most coastal resorts and island hotels are self-contained complexes where your package will include – at least – breakfast and dinner. Kenya is perhaps the least costly for accommodation as there is more competition, while Mozambique has fewer choices and standards are high. However, drinks and extras can be pricey everywhere. It's unusual to be able to walk somewhere else for a snack unless it's to the hotel next door. Tipping is the done thing for all services. However, value for money almost becomes irrelevant once you've spent a day sitting beside a new--born zebra or sharing a patch of reef with an equally young turtle.

Fact file

Kenya	
Location	1°00'N 38°00'E
Capital	Nairobi
Tanzania	
Location	6°00's, 35°00'E
Capital	Dar es Salaam
Mozambique	
Location	15°00'N, 86°30'W
Capital	Maputo
Flights	Kenya and Tanzania: Emirates, Kenya Air, Qatar Mozambique: Linhas Aéreas de Moçambique
Internal flights	Kenya Airlines, Precision Air, ZanAir
Land transport	Countrywide bus connections
Departure tax	US$30, if not included in your ticket
Entry	Visas are required for Tanzania, US$50 and Mozambique, US$30
Money	Kenyan shillings (KES), Tanzania shillings (TZS) and Mozambique meticals (MZM)
Language	Swahili officially but English is common
Electricity	220-240v, plug types B,C,D (see page 15)
Time zone	GMT +3
Religion	Christian, Muslim, animist and tribal variations
Communications	Country codes: Kenya +254; Tanzania +255; Mozambique +258; IDD code 00; Police 0 Internet access is patchy but improving
Tourist information	magicalkenya.com; tanzaniatouristboard.com; mozambiquehc.org.uk/tourism
Travel advisories	gov.uk/foreign-travel-advice; state.gov/travel

dive brief

66 99

When we first started travelling, an African safari was right at the top of our must-do list and we were not disappointed. The Masai Mara, the Serengeti... these places are burnt into our memories and, every now and then, remind us that there is more to life than diving. While East Africa's warm waters and the rainbow tones of her marine realm are delightful, the quality and variety of diving may not be quite enough for hardened tank-suckers. However, put this together with a safari and it becomes a holiday that simply can't be rivalled.

Diving

While seeing animals on land in East Africa is a given, life in the marine realm is less well known. The defining geography both on land and underwater is the incredibly flat topography. The continental shelf is generally less than 20 kilometres wide from the centre of Kenya to the top of Mozambique. Even the islands that emerge from it are small and equally flat.

The mainland and island coastlines are bordered by long fringing reefs which are often completely exposed at low tide. These protect the shorelines but take a pounding from constant wave action and the effects of the sun when the tide is out. Every day as the sea recedes, the reef tops are revealed and the lagoons behind them become so shallow that snorkelling and even swimming are often out of the question. Diving is restricted to times when there is enough water for boats to navigate over the reef.

Another set of conditions is created by the constant movement of water over the shallow seabed, which, combined with several massive river deltas and mangrove regions, means that visibility in most areas is less than you would like for substantial

periods of the year. The Indian Ocean has consistently warm sea temperatures and this means that hard corals – especially in the shallower sections – are not as prolific as in other oceans. All the same, once you are out over the reef edge or off one of the nearby islands, and get below about 10 metres, the marine life can be lively.

Snorkelling

Conditions for snorkellers are better than the above comments would lead you to believe. Floating over a very shallow reef at low tide is less of an issue without a tank on your back to hold you down. Most hotels run snorkelling trips to just outside the reef, but watch the time – at extreme low tide you may have to walk back over the fragile exposed reef, which won't do it any good at all.

Marine life

Although the reef structures and corals along the Indian Ocean coast are not particularly lush, there are plenty of small fish and crustaceans, and animals like turtles and morays are frequently seen. The migratory patterns for both manta rays and whale sharks traverse this stretch

Giant frogfish blending into the reef background; swimming crab on a sea pen.

of coast. They are occasionally spotted by divers, especially in Kenya, but sadly less often than the diving operators would care to have you think. If you get out in the blue, there are plenty of pelagic fish.

Making the big decision

Your choice of dive destination in East Africa will be dictated by where else in the region you want to go, if anywhere.

If you simply want a relaxing break, with a couple of morning dives and a few afternoons out, the Kenya coast is for you. The diving will be pleasant and you will have easy access to the country's famed game parks. If you want to get a bit further off the beaten track, Tanzania's islands are the place to head for. The life in their surrounding waters is a little more prolific and influenced by the open Indian Ocean beyond the continental shelf. Tanzania's safari regions are also bigger and wilder. However, for lovers of simple luxuries and blissful island destinations, there can be no better choice than the comparatively new tourist destination of Mozambique. The islands of the Quirimbas Archipelago are idyllic, but bear in mind that diving this coast is equally affected by the daily tides and seasonal conditions.

Animal encounters

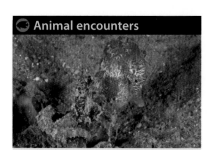

Kenya: all fingers crossed for an encounter with the ocean's most gentle giant, the whale shark.

Tanzania: watch out for the huge Djibouti Spanish Dancer, which is seen in daylight, and the rarer psychedelic Dragon moray eel.

Mozambique: one of the few places you will see the delightful Reunion seahorse, apart from Reunion.

dive sites

Although the marine geography is similar all along this Indian Ocean coast, each country has its own unique features. In Kenya, the many resort hotels lining the beaches have easy access to both the reefs and nearby wildlife parks. However, due to tidal conditions, the best dives are in the deeper waters of Watamu Marine Park on the north coast and, in the south, from Diani Beach to the Kisite-Mpunguti Park.

Tanzania's best sites are around the offshore islands. Pemba is less well known and less developed, with deep dives off the east coast contrasting with calmer waters facing the mainland. Zanzibar is livelier and more of an all-round holiday island. The reefs are a little less varied, as the sloping seabed rarely drops beyond 40 metres deep.

Further south is Mozambique. This calm, post civil-war country is a long way from being a major holiday destination. And that is the great joy of it, with just a couple of top hotels and a few small ones. In the north, there is reef and muck diving around Pemba bay, and a short distance away, the tiny islands of the Quirimbas Archipelago dot the Indian Ocean.

Kenya   ▶▶ p86

Malindi ●
Turtle Bay ● ↘1
↘2
Mombasa ●
Shimoni ●
↘3
↘4
Pemba

Conditions

Seasons	Rainy seasons vary but are between December and May depending on location. Islands may be affected by wind patterns from April to May.
Visibility	10-40 m but can be reduced due to river run-off in rainy periods.
Currents	Generally easy
Temperatures	Air 25-34°C; water 25-29°C
Wet suit	3 mm shorty or full body suit
Training	Courses available in most hotels, standards vary; look for PADI/SSI schools
Nitrox	Not easily available
Deco chambers	Mombasa, Zanzibar, Durban

Diversity
combined reef area 6,070 km²

	Kenya	Tanzania	Mozambique
HARD CORAL	237	314	314
FISH SPECIES	752	984	1,586
ENDEMIC FISH SPECIES	11	55	15
FISH UNDER THREAT	102	182	78

All diversity figures are approximate

Log Book

↘1 **The Canyon**
↘2 **Red Firefish Reef**
↘3 **Nyuli Reef**
↘4 **Coral Gardens**

→ **Turtle Reef, Turtle Bay:** a deeper dive with, unsurprisingly, a few turtles
→ **Deep Place, Turtle Bay:** a wall along the outer reef and a fun drift dive
→ **Galu, Diani Beach:** easy morning conditions make this a regular site
→ **Kinondo, Diani Beach:** large rays and schools of fish with some current
→ **Kisite Island, Shimoni:** a shallow dive on a sloping wall clad in hard corals
→ **Hassan Reef, Shimoni:** colourful soft corals and masses of fairy basslets

Pemba island, Tanzania ▶▶ p88

Zanzibar, Tanzania ▶▶ p90

Mozambique ▶▶ p94

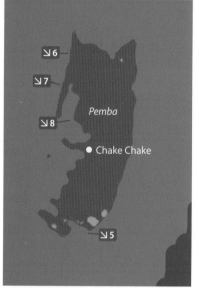

↘6

↘7

↘8

Pemba

● Chake Chake

↘5

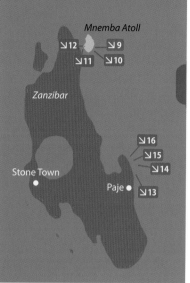

Mnemba Atoll

↘12 ↘9

↘11 ↘10

Zanzibar

↘16

↘15

↘14

Stone Town

●

Paje ● ↘13

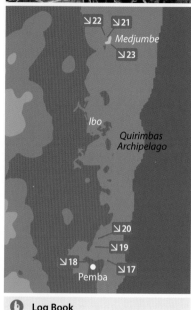

↘22 ↘21

Medjumbe

↘23

Ibo

Quirimbas Archipelago

↘20

↘19

↘18 ↘17

Pemba

⏱ Log Book

↘5	**Mtangani**
↘6	**Manta Point**
↘7	**Shimba Hills**
↘8	**Uvinje Gap**

→ **Fundu Gap:** steep reef wall with lots of small caverns and lively currents

→ **Njao Gap:** extends from the main reef wall with pipefish and nudibranchs

→ **Ras Upembe:** slope leading to small drop off haunted by lobsters

⏱ Log Book

↘9	**Jackfish Spot**
↘10	**Coral Gardens**
↘11	**Kichwani**
↘12	**Aquarium to Grouper Rock**

→ **Sandbanks:** coral outcrops with several resident giant frogfish

→ **West Bank:** current-washed dive on the that occasionally attracts sharks

→ **Big Wall:** 50-metre dive for advanced divers hunting the big stuff

↘13	**Shindano**
↘14	**Ukwele**
↘15	**Point 8**
↘16	**Cave 20**

→ **Mkanda:** plateau dive with Napoleon wrasse, jacks and barracuda

→ **Ciupis Garden:** multi-level reef known for octopus and commensal shrimp

→ **The Lagoon:** a shallow protected site with seagrass, pipefish and lobsters

---

⏱ Log Book

↘17	**The Gap**
↘18	**The Ranch**
↘19	**Playground**
↘20	**Sailfish Tree**

→ **Rivermouth:** juvenile fish from the nearby mangroves at the Tari River delta

→ **Ponta Saide Ali:** a valley with massive numbers of anemones and clownfish

→ **Garden of Eden:** enormous fan corals hang on the edge of a steep wall

↘21	**Edge of Reason**
↘22	**Sambi-Sambi**
↘23	**Joe's Ridge**

→ **Laura's Leap:** a deep channel with a vertical wall and overhangs

→ **The Restaurant:** flat plateau covered with table corals, hence the name

→ **Rocha Rocks:** sloping rocky reef with plenty of small fish

dive log Kenya

The coast that stretches north and south from Mombasa is paralleled by low-lying coral reefs. Its basic structure is of hard corals that form small drop-offs and gentle sloping banks. The corals tend to be slower-growing, hardier varieties that can survive the pounding Indian Ocean swells.

Due to the substantial tidal range all along the coast, diving is only possible for part of the day. Currents can be strong, although rarely unbearable, and visibility is never crystal clear – the area surrounding Mombasa town suffers from its industrialized nature and Malindi, to the north, can be affected by the run-off from the Sabiki River.

However, all is not lost as better all-round conditions can be found where there are natural bays and deeper water. On the northern coast, very pretty Turtle Bay sits inside Watamu Marine Park and although the area is still tidal the formation of the bay means it is possible to swim and dive for longer periods of the day. On the other side of Mombasa, the conditions improve as you head further south, with the best diving in the Kisite-Mpunguti Marine National Park. Almost on the Tanzania border, the park edges the deeper waters of the Pemba Channel so the diving is a little more adventurous and less limited by tidal changes.

⛴ The Canyon, Turtle Bay	
🌀 **Depth**	20 m
◐ **Visibility**	fair
🌊 **Currents**	can be strong

This classic Kenyan dive site is just a short boat ride away outside the main reef in the marine park, then a descent to the reef top at about 10 metres. The reef structure is principally hard corals with some small soft corals for colour. Swimming over the edge leads to an archway where you can sometimes find resting turtles. If the current is running, and it often is along this section of reef, whitetips will spin past in the blue. The divemasters say this is one of the best places to spot passing whale sharks, but these are occasional sightings and you are more likely to spot lobsters, lionfish, angels and butterflies plus plenty of nudibranchs.

Nudibranch in Turtle Bay; Regal angelfish and Napoleon wrasse (above right).

Coral Gardens, Shimoni

Depth	12 m	
Visibility	fair	
Currents	mild to strong	

This site is typical of the reefs ringing the small islands inside the Kisite-Mpunguti Marine Park. Conditions are usually fairly easy with very little current. As the top of the reef is shallow, this is a good spot for snorkelling as well. Unlike some of outer reefs, which are subject to the effects of the currents, the hard corals here are in good condition and interspersed with some pretty and colourful soft corals. The reef backdrop supports a wide array of small fish, including coral trout and butterflyfish, prolific anthias, blue-green chromis and regal angelfish. It's even possible to see juvenile angels tucked into the cracks and crevices of the hard corals. There are quite a few large fish species – sweetlips and striped snappers are prolific. Some say you will even see reef sharks here, but that means looking away from the reef, which really holds your attention.

Red Firefish Reef, Turtle Bay

Depth	20 m	
Visibility	good	
Currents	can be strong	

Heading out past the inner reef for about 15 minutes brings you to this sloping site. The corals are quite pretty but sparse and patchy, which makes for lots of hidey-holes for the marine life. A resident grey stingray usually makes an appearance fairly soon after divers enter the water. There are also blue-spotted rays on the sand, lobsters in small caverns and some sweetlips hanging on the mini-wall. Smaller fish include clowns in anemones and fire dart gobies.

Nyuli Reef, Shimoni

Depth	20 m	
Visibility	good	
Currents	mild to strong	

Nyuli Reef is just outside the marine park and is known for its strong currents. The corals have suffered damage in the past, both from natural and man-made causes, but the deeper waters attract schools of fish and some pelagics. The reef top starts at about 20 metres then drops sharply to over 40. Shoals of fish such as barracuda and snapper are seen regularly and reef sharks are common visitors, although you are unlikely to get close.

66 99 We descended on Verena as a large Napoleon wrasse watched our approach; a whitetip shark swam lazily towards a small outcrop and, as we approached it, a manta ray, as large as my living room, appeared from behind us. It looped up towards the surface and back down, its left wing passing right over my head. We finished the dive and climbed back on the boat, thinking to ourselves 'what could be better?' when our dive leader shouted, 'whale shark!'
Roy Calverley, IT specialist, Redhill, UK

dive log

Tanzania: Pemba island

The Tanzanian island of Pemba is so close to the Kenyan coast that the conditions reflect what is found on the mainland opposite. The underwater geography is just as liable to the vagaries of time and tide: the fringing reefs are only a short distance from shore and the inner lagoons behind them are extremely shallow.

All the same, this is classic reef diving, with walls, sloping reefs and a surprising number of unusual critters. Currents are an every-dive occurrence, although they are not as strong on the western side of Pemba where there are many small islands to shelter behind. For more adventurous sites, the east is exposed to the open Indian Ocean and the diving here is mostly big blue. Rough seas and strong currents can sometimes bring in schools of sharks; hammerhead sightings are said to be common, but even if they were, the sharks are generally deeper than sport diving depth limits will allow.

⑤ Mtangani

🕐 **Depth**	35 m	
🌓 **Visibility**	excellent	
🌊 **Currents**	ripping at times	

When they say the currents that run off Pemba's east coast can be strong, it's no exaggeration. This water races, and less experienced divers may find the challenge hardly worthwhile unless, of course, the hammerheads come past. The issue is that when they do, they are often deeper than you can sensibly go to see them. Instead, dives are spent pretending to fly through unbelievably clear water watching out for them, whitetips or even some Napoleon wrasse. It's still quite an adrenaline rush.

⑥ Manta Point

🕐 **Depth**	22 m	
🌓 **Visibility**	fair	
🌊 **Currents**	slight to medium	

As soon as someone sees a manta on a dive site, it gets named in honour of the event. So what are the chances of actually seeing a manta at Manta Point? Opinion varies – and the operators do tend to wax lyrical – but this is still a very good reef dive. Tucked in amongst the protective islands off the west coast, currents are less aggressive and there are plenty of animals. Snapper and turtles often pass by and, of course, the mantas – if you are lucky. Otherwise, it's angels and triggerfish.

Barracuda passing through Uvinje gap.

↘7 Shimba Hills

Depth	20 m
Visibility	fair
Currents	slight to medium

Many of the shallower reefs in this region are affected by their position. The warm, shallow waters make it difficult for hard corals: they struggle to survive, especially as the reefs are exposed at low tide. This reef off the north of the island shows a fair bit of damage because of this and also due to the constant wave action. Despite all that, it somehow manages to be a very interesting dive. A gentle wall drops down to a rubble-strewn sea bed. The reef is dotted with some olive green tubastrea coral trees. Each one has a cloud of anthias flitting around it. Further along the wall, a series of caverns and overhangs protect angelfish, snappers and coral grouper. It's worth taking some time to inspect the smaller cracks and crevices, as they reveal all sorts of interesting animals. These include many types of shrimp, several different coloured leaffish and even a couple of small lobsters.

↘8 Uvinje Gap

Depth	22 m
Visibility	fair
Currents	slight to medium

The string of small islands along Pemba's west coast separate it from the channel and distant mainland. At the bottom of the chain are Uvinje and Kokota islands with a series of good dives, including a surprising one in the gap between the two.

The walls on the outer sides of Uvinje Gap drop to as much as 40 metres deep, but dives are mostly at 25 metres. Along the walls caverns and overhangs are full of masses of shiny glassfish. The hard corals are in pretty good condition, with the currents feeding the table, lettuce, and tubastrea species. There are nudibranchs, morays and all the usual fish. This is also a very good site for spotting turtles and – very occasionally – passing by in the blue are schools of barracuda.

A second dive involves dropping right between the two islands to a really good critter-hunt location with the type of life that is reminiscent of far distant countries. There is plenty to see in daylight, with swimming crabs and tiny imperial shrimp on sea cucumbers, shrimps in anemones and the seagrass ghost pipefish. At night, the dive is even more exciting with masses of decorator crabs, octopus, cowries and mantis shrimp, which seem to appear from nowhere. The sandy seabed comes alive with sprouting seapens, each one revealing their resident porcelain crabs.

Mantis shrimp, striped snapper, seagrass ghost pipefish, slipper lobsters and the ornate ghost pipefish are all easy to spot around Pemba.

dive log

Tanzania: Zanzibar

Zanzibar is just south of Pemba and has a unique mix of history, culture and natural beauty. The marine life is similar to Pemba although, due to the shallow reef system, the water is rarely gin clear.

The majority of divers head to Mnemba Atoll, off the northern point, or to the east coast beaches. These two areas attract quite different sorts of visitors. The village of Matemwe opposite Mnemba has traditionally catered for backpackers and travellers who have been up Kilimanjaro or across the Serengeti. Mnemba is a pear-shaped atoll with gentle sloping reefs and coral outcrops. The atoll is regarded as a conservation zone and while some would question that (see page 351), there is no doubt it is a charming spot with some impressive marine life, but it does get busy.

Divers in search of a quieter location go southwards to the coastal area near the village of Paje. Because these reefs are only easily accessible to those staying nearby, it's unlikely you will meet any other divers apart from your buddies. The underwater terrain is almost perfectly flat, with a shelf that extends for some way at 15 metres or so before a sudden drop over a short wall. This leads down to another flat reef at 25-28 metres, which again descends almost imperceptibly until it finally crashes to great depths from about 50 metres.

Leaffish hiding on a sponge at Aquarium; batfish in their hundreds at Jackfish Spot.

◷9 Jackfish Spot	
Depth	36 m
Visibility	good
Currents	can be strong

This dive site lies on the eastern side of Mnemba island where the wall comes in closest to the lagoon area. Descent is into the blue and you drop down rapidly to over 30 metres to find a sharp, perfectly vertical wall. This then drops down around another 10 metres or so and leads to an even deeper plateau. There are caverns along its front that are full of colourful corals and fish, but you don't get time to look into them before the most stupendous school of batfish starts buzzing you. There must be hundreds that whizz in quickly, around and up, off then back. They don't stay long but it's quite an overwhelming sight. Next, as you ascend, you pass through schools of snapper and the jacks. The shallows are perfect for gassing off, but the anemones, imperial angelfish, puffers and scorpionfish somehow seem less interesting after the huge schools.

◷10 Coral Gardens	
Depth	20 m
Visibility	good
Currents	slight

One of Mnemba's signature dives, Coral Gardens is also on the eastern edge of the lagoon but in shallow water. Lots of hard coral bommies are dotted about a lovely white sand seabed. Divers can hop from one to the next, hunting out the resident creatures. Discovering all the small animals is a non-stop adventure: one minute it's a giant puffer, the next an unusual zebra moray. Beneath another coral head are clusters of lionfish, then passing by them, you stumble over an enormous Spanish Dancer, the *Hexabranchus Djibouti*, which is the largest known nudibranch. Usually nocturnal, these are wandering across the sand in broad daylight. They measure up to 60 centimetres long and often have imperial shrimp hiding in their gills. When it's time to ascend into the shallower hard coral gardens, you find there are loads of small and colourful fish.

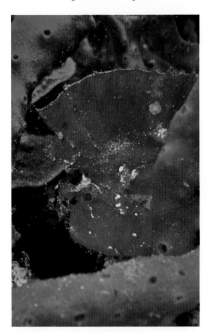

⑪ Kichwani

Depth	20 m
Visibility	good
Currents	can be very strong

⑫ Aquarium to Grouper Rock

Depth	20 m
Visibility	good
Currents	none to mild

A little further west around the bottom of Mnemba, Kichwani can be done as a very deep drift dive, but the divemasters bypass that idea by casually mentioning a resident dragon moray eel, who lives in just four metres of water on a hard coral bommie. These rarely seen morays must be the most beautiful in the species group with their bizarre patterns, colours and horns. The local chap is living just where expected, nestled in a hole between the hard corals with a tiny brown moray companion. After investigating the shallow bommie, which reveals plenty of other morays but just this one dragon, the dive moves down a slope to a small drop-off, which is mobbed by loads of schooling fish. The water appears golden as there are so many yellow-toned species including the ever-present striped snappers, fiesty sergeant majors guarding their eggs and prolific moorish idols.

The section of reef closest to Mnemba island is where most newcomers get taken for their first dive, yet there are so many levels to explore that you end up wanting to go back time and again. Entry is over a slope covered in powdery white sand and interspersed with small outcrops of rock. These would have once been coral: it died back in the past but is regenerating with healthy regrowth showing clearly. Travelling along Aquarium towards Grouper Rock – these are close enough together that you can do them on the same dive – there are stands of thick lettuce leaf corals and many fish hover above: rabbitfish, rainbow runners, moorish idols, sweetlips and angels. Jacks hang off the reef edge and several really big grouper lurk about but will never let divers get close.

Down on the sand though is where the real action is. It's a non-stop treasure hunt with playful mantis shrimp, pink, beige and white leaffish, lionfish and blue-spotted rays who nestle in every nook and cranny. Scorpionfish sit inside matching sponges pretending to be non-existent.

At the bottom of the sloping wall near the drop-off, an encounter with a turtle is almost guaranteed. By the time you head back to the shallows you will have seen five or six. They are quite small and curious with beautifully patterned clean shells.

Mnemba's rarer creatures: the Djibouti Spanish Dancer and the dragon moray with friend; bluefin trevally joining the divers.

↘13 Shindano

Depth	25 m
Visibility	good
Currents	mild

Travelling south and down the east coast of Zanzibar, the dive sites start to take on a different slant: long, straight fringing reefs parallel the shore, creating, at low tide, a shallow inner lagoon. Beyond these inner areas, the underwater topography is reminiscent of a series of rice terraces. The level seabed is clad in low-lying corals that extend out towards the ocean then suddenly drop a few metres in a short, perfectly vertical wall. Broken by mini caves, these small walls end on another terrace, which then extends further and drops again. On Shindano, one tiny ledge of about a metre deep is full of glassfish and all around are leaffish and scorpions. There are cleaning stations and even a titan triggerfish sits inside a hole to be spruced up. There are shrimp everywhere: hingebeak, coral banded, Durban dancing shrimps and a Saron shrimp.

↘14 Ukwele

Depth	34 m
Visibility	good
Currents	mild

Dives on the deeper, outer sections of this stretch of reef require a blue-water entry. The boat waits above the reef rim for divers to roll in then descend through the dark blue water until the top of the reef appears. It sits at about 25 metres or so and can drop to unfathomable depths. Depending on the time of the month, there can be some current along these outer edges, which can attract some pelagics. Even when there is no current, you can be lucky and drop straight into a massive school of chevron barracuda. This isn't a common occurrence, so even the divemasters are surprised when it happens. Down on the reef rim, there is another small wall that hides a tiny cavern which is full to bursting with copper-coloured glassfish. Investigating inside, there are white leaffish and marbled dragonets that skitter around the sand.

↘15 Point 8

Depth	18 m
Visibility	good
Currents	can be very strong

Although Point 8 is found on one of the flatter sections of reef, the terrain here is a little more interesting than on some of the terraces. The sloping reef drops gradually from around eight metres down to about 20, but it's unlikely you will get beyond the shallow section as you keep stopping to investigate the life in the coral mounds that rise up from the flat seabed. It seems that everywhere you pause you find another creature. Blue ribbon eels are the stars of the dive, lurching up from their tunnels to demand attention if you stop near one to look at something else. There are nudibranchs and whitemouth morays then, hidden deep in porites coral, are gold spot scorpionfish and tiny coral crab. Another mound is host to the prolific glassfish found on almost every dive, plus copper sweepers, juvenile tobies and fluttering, juvenile oriental sweetlips.

Coral banded shrimp on almost every dive; lagoon damselfish at Shindano; blue ribbon eel on Point 8.

cave20

Depth	42 m	
Visibility	good	
Currents	none	

For more experienced divers, this is quite probably the best site in the area. Most divers enjoy it so much they ask to go straight back. Entry is past the reef edge and down through blue water until you land on a flat section of seabed at about 25 metres that drops gradually, leading past an area thick with garden eels. The next patch of sand is covered by masses of blue-spotted rays who are disturbed by the passing divers and take off rapidly.

Eventually you reach a small lip in the reef where there are a few caverns and the most enormous numbers of fish. There is a cobia on the sand: a torpedo-shaped fish with a long, depressed head and small eyes that, from a distance, can be mistaken for a reef shark. It takes off just as quickly too, revealing the tail of a huge marbled ray hiding inside a cavern. The ray is almost impossible to see, as the cave is masked by phenomenal numbers of glassfish. All over the reef rim above are schools of striped snapper, small pink cardinals, untold numbers of rabbitfish and some unicornfish that have commensal remoras. In the blue are jacks and striped trevally.

❝❞ The surface was like glass; the viz was so good I could see the reef below from the boat and I was about to dive my favourite site, Cave 20. Pink whip rays, garden eels and ribbon eels, cobia and groupers... once again the dive didn't disappoint. And people have to ask why I chose this as my profession!

Gabriel Frankel, dive instructor, Johannesburg

dive log
Mozambique: Pemba

Once a Portuguese colony, Mozambique has only recently started to appear on the diver radar. For many years, the southern coastal reefs were dived by South Africans, who could hop over the border to dive along the neighbouring shores, while the northern and central coasts remained delightfully unexplored. The whole region is now attracting adventurous divers from around the world.

Pemba is the most northern coastal city and is located on the world's third largest bay. It is a fairly neat town despite being the major port for the region. The diving can only be described as unexpected – prolific hard coral reefs run around the outer edges of the massive bay and are backed by lush mangroves and beautiful white-sand beaches. Most dives are shallow, but there are a variety of sites and marine life, including some incredible muck diving. However, the visibility tends to be quite low, especially in the rainy season as several rivers dump freshwater and sediment into the bay. The rainy season runs from November to April, but this is also the best dive season. After that, the winds pick up and can make being out on a boat unpleasant.

☒17 The Gap	
⚉ **Depth**	40 m
◑ **Visibility**	fair
☰ **Currents**	mild

One of the few deep dives in the area, the Gap is a short distance from Wimbe Beach heading towards Ponta Maunhane, the point on the southern side of the bay. This is where the continental shelf comes closest to shore. Entry is over a plateau of hard corals at around 15 metres which then leads to an almost sheer drop that ends at over well over 100 metres. The visibility isn't great here, especially if there has been an overnight storm, so the dive takes on dark and mysterious overtones. A small tunnel opens up beneath a shelf at about 35 metres and then exits on the other side of the wall at 40. Just beneath and around the cave mouth are clusters of big fans. There are plenty of fish, including a small gang of batfish.

The cave at The Gap; current-swept anemone at Playground.

⬛18 The Ranch

🕐 **Depth**	12 m
◑ **Visibility**	poor to fair
〰 **Currents**	slight

Inside Pemba Bay, past the shipping docks is an area of pea green water. It's hard to believe this is going to be an outstanding dive although the water clears a little once you are past the jetties. Briefed not to kick up the silt, you drop down to see there are almost no landmarks, not even any bits of rubbish, yet every tiny hollow or dip in the sand has a critter inside it. These include prolific numbers of seahorses, which are thought to be the Reunion Seahorse, lots of urchins with tiny cardinalfish sheltering in the spines, sand dollars (spiny critters that are related to urchins), filefish, dwarf zebra lions, cuttlefish, small moray eels hiding in holes and octopus in shells.

⬛19 Playground

🕐 **Depth**	15
◑ **Visibility**	fair
〰 **Currents**	mild

On the opposite side of Pemba Bay, the winding coastal wall is defined by short rocky cliffs with sharp undercuts created by wave and surge action. Dropping down to the base of the small wall, the seabed is covered with hard corals and swathes of anemones, most with fantastic orange-coloured skirts and each hosting masses of damselfish with their tiny black juveniles. Outcrops of rock are plastered with razor clams and vase sponges often hiding leaffish (called paperfish here), lionfish, juvenile sweetlips, anthias and tobies. Critter life includes commensal shrimp and goby pairs, starfish and flatworms.

Residents of The Ranch, clockwise: a scrawled filefish; Reunion seahorse; an unusual nudibranch; juvenile flying gurnard; cuttlefish on a rope; octopus in hiding; juvenile cardinals living an urchin; a minute dwarf lionfish.

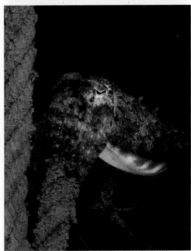

Depth	22 m	
Visibility	fair	
Currents	mild	

Heading from Wimbe Beach across to the opposite side of the bay, then north along the coastline, you eventually reach the delta from the Tari River. A little way past the river mouth, a solitary casuarina tree stands sentinel over a deserted white beach. Known as Sailfish Tree, this marks the entry to another shallow wall. No doubt because it is on the Indian Ocean coast, this stretch of reef is far more impressive than the ones in the bay: the hard corals are in amazing condition, spreading across the seabed and walls to create lovely gardens. The short wall drops from about two metres below the surface and is interspersed with overhangs and shallow caverns. Large fan corals and black coral bushes grow outwards into the currents that run between the wall and some rocky outcrops off to the ocean side. These are also well coated with low-lying hard corals and attract many schools of fish. There are snappers and sweetlips and masses of different coloured anthias. Larger fish are not seen very often, but there are occasional pufferfish and even bigger groupers. Despite fringing the open ocean, visibility is still low and reduces even more on a second dive at Rivermouth, which is actually an extension of the first site.

While gassing off between these dives, you can usually snorkel in the mangrove forests that sit just inside the river mouth. The water is fairly clear and you will see young cardinalfish, moray eels and a variety of nudibranchs.

dive
log
Mozambique:
Medjumbe

Running north from Pemba are 32 tiny coral islands. They stretch up as far as the Rovuma River which forms the border with Tanzania. Collectively known as the Quirimbas Archipelago, these islands are sandwiched between the coast and the Mozambique Channel, which is said to drop to over 400 metres deep.

Along with a vast area of mainland forest, the 11 most southerly of these coral islands form the Quirimbas National Park. This entire area is incredibly remote. Flying overhead in a small aircraft reveals that there is virtually no human habitation, yet the marine realm is a well-populated, but very much unexplored, region.

Dives here are conducted around the whims of the daily tides. The broad lagoon that encompasses tiny Medjumbe is a breathtakingly beautiful sight, but it does extend for quite some way, restricting the movement of boats. At certain times, you literally have to wait for the sea to return so you can travel to the fringing reef. This also means that the sand is moving constantly and visibility can be low. Some days you will be forced to sit and admire the view and the seabirds, but that's no great hardship.

⋈21 Edge of Reason	
🧭 **Depth**	45 m
◐ **Visibility**	fair
🌊 **Currents**	mild

Definitely the most spectacular dive near Medjumbe's shores, this sheer wall drops vertically from the lagoon top. Enormous fan and whip corals jut out from a series of soft-coral-clad ledges and caverns. Each one has a sandy bottom that harbours big schools of fish: silver sweetlips mix with surgeonfish and often mask a giant grouper. At nearly two metres long this might be a goliath grouper, which then bolts out from the back of the cave, taking his 50 or so pilot fish with him. The flat reef top lies at 15 metres and is covered in thick patches of seagrass (much of which is swept over the wall to disturb the visibility). In between are hundreds of triggerfish nests – and just as many triggerfish, who fortunately are not aggressive. During a safety stop, you might spot huge turtles on the sand.

Coral-clad cavern and a goliath grouper on the Edge of Reason.

⬇22 Sambi-Sambi

🧭	**Depth**	30 m
🌓	**Visibility**	fair
〰	**Currents**	mild

North of Medjumbe and just beyond the lagoon, this gently sloping wall has a thick covering of hard corals. These are mostly gardens of lettuce leaf coral that are so prolific you can't see the seabed. The first part of the dive takes you east, where the bottom of this reef drops down as far as 80 metres. Looking to greater depths you can see a lot of big fans below the hard corals while back up on the reef top, at less than 10 metres, this changes to huge swathes of staghorn corals. As this area is both protected and undived, all the corals are very healthy, although the fish are not so numerous. On a second dive along this reef, you can head west, which is shallower but the corals are equally prolific and pristine. Occasionally, a giant barracuda will be hovering.

⬇23 Joe's Ridge

🧭	**Depth**	18 m
🌓	**Visibility**	poor
〰	**Currents**	mild

The flat reef at Joe's Ridge lies off the southern side of the island on the edge of the lagoon. The visibility can be low due to tidal changes, but the seabed is covered in small, low-lying outcrops of hard and soft corals. These harbour a variety of juvenile fish: tiny angelfish and butterflies, a baby bicolour parrotfish and a brushtail tang juvenile with its huge, startled eyes. There are a few small nudibranchs and some twin-tailed slugs, whip coral gobies, anemones and their clownfish and the rarely seen leopard blenny hiding in the hard corals.

Medjumbe marine life: impressive fan corals, a juvenile brushtail tang and a whip coral goby.

66 99 **The Edge of Reason is the closest you can come to the sensation of flying... the feeling of falling slowly over a cliff with no visible bottom is quite exquisite.** *Lindy Bucceri, divemaster, Medjumbe*

Hotels and resorts stretch all the way along the Kenyan coast almost from the border with Somalia to the border with Tanzania. They vary in size and cost but all tend to be enclosed complexes. Few are 100% diver focussed but many have either a dive shop on the premises or work with one nearby. Costs vary from budget to 3-star to 5-star but those in the mid-range tend to be good value.

Nairobi

Stanley Hotel: sarovahotels.com. A colonial legend and the haunt of the likes of Ernest Hemingway. Ideal if you need a stopover.

North coast

Ocean Sports, Watamu: oceansports.net and diveinkenya.com. Transfers take 2 hrs by road from Mombasa airport.
Turtle Bay Beach Club: turtlebay.co.ke. Diving on site. 2-hr transfer to Watamu.

South coast

Papillon Lagoon Reef: Rexresorts.com. Dive centre on site, 80-mins from airport.
Southern Palms Resort: southernpalmskenya.com and divingthecrab.com. 90-mins from airport
Shimoni Lodge: shimonireeflodge.com. Diving on site. 2-hr transfer from airport.

Days out

Malindi Just beyond Watamu, Malindi was first made famous because Vasco de Gama stopped here in 1498. This small but historic town now looks rather frayed but gives an insight into life on the coast.
Mombasa One of the oldest cities in East Africa, the original town dates back some 700 years. Now manic, noisy and bustling, the city sprawls up and down the coast and is a curious combination of old and new, with many markets and bazaars.

Safaris

Start from the coast and finish in Nairobi, or start from Nairobi and finish on the coast. Whichever way you go, the choices of safari are endless with various routes, styles and number of days. If you have time, target the more remote, inland parks as they have the most substantial animal populations. If time is limited, it's possible to do a day trip safari from the coast. These are a good taster, but they can't compete with a more extensive inland safari.
Samburu Head north of Nairobi to the Rift Valley, where landscapes are classic Africa: deep-red soil lush with acacia trees. All three big cats can be seen and unusual animals include the long-necked gerunuk, Grevy's zebra and the reticulated giraffe.

Lake Nakuru A change of pace will take you to this endless – and pink – body of water. The population of flamingos is so enormous that from a distance the water looks rose tinted, especially at dusk when the sun sets across millions of pink feathers.
The Masai Mara National Park This is where you are likely to see all of the big five – lion, African elephant, African buffalo, rhino and leopard. You can also stop and visit ancient tribes who still adhere to their traditional way of life. There are no TVs out in the mud huts but old film canisters are regarded as one of the better earlobe-stretching devices. Meanwhile, baboons eat wild figs, which ferment in their tummies until, rather inebriated, they fall out of the trees. Quite amusing when it happens around your luxury tented campsite!
Shimba Hills National Reserve About 50 km south of Mombasa, this small game reserve includes a coastal rainforest. You can see elephant, giraffe and several monkey species. Unique to the reserve is the sable antelope.
Tsavo East One of the largest reserves in Kenya, the eastern section is close enough to the coast to allow a day trip. However, it will take 3-4 hours to get there and you won't get very far inside. You might see elephants and lions, but buffalo, giraffe and various deer species are far more likely.

Kenyan Beach; elephant walkabout; cheetah resting; watching the wildlife.

drying out

Tanzania

These two Tanzanian islands contrast quite strongly when it comes to choices of where to stay and who to dive with. Pemba is a small place with just two main resorts, both with dive centres, plus some backpacker-style places in Chake Chake. Zanzibar, however, has more resort hotels that you can count, but many are aimed at sun-worshipping holiday makers.

Pemba island

Fundu Lagoon, fundulagoon.com. Flight from Dar es Salaam and transfer in 2.5 hrs.
Manta Reef Lodge, themantaresort.com. Dive 360 on site. 2-hrs from Dar es Salaam.

Zanzibar

Mnemba Island Lodge, mnemba-island.com. Luxury option with dives included. 1.5-hrs from Zanzibar aiport.
One Ocean, zanzibaroneocean.com. At Matemwe Beach Village and other Zanzibar locations. 1-hr from airport.
Rising Sun Dive Centre, Paje, risingsun-zanzibar.com. At Breezes Beach Club and Baraza Resort. 45-mins from the airport.

Dar es Salaam

Protea Hotel Oysterbay, proteahotels.com. Great stopover hotel with a restaurant and pool; airport transfers can be arranged.

Stone Town; Masai Warriors; zebras in the Ngorongoro Crater; camping in the Serengeti.

Days out

Pemba island The islands main town is Chake Chake with shops, banks, ruins of an 18th-century fort, a small dhow port and a fish market. About 10 km south at Pujini are the ruins of a 15th-century fortified palace, while the Ngezi Forest is the last remaining tract of indigenous forest and home to the Pemba flying fox, an endemic bat.

Zanzibar Stone Town is the cultural heart of Zanzibar and now a World Heritage site. Built in the 19th century, the town is a maze of winding alleys, bustling bazaars, mosques and grand Arab houses with ornately carved wooden doors and enclosed verandas. The two most visited buildings are Beit-El-Ajaib, (aka the House of Wonders) a museum of sorts, and the 18th century Arab Fort, which has an amphitheatre and artisan stalls. The town was a major centre for the slave trade and the Anglican Cathedral is built on the site of a former slave market. It was also a base for explorers like David Livingstone but the island's most famous 'son' is singer Freddie Mercury. One of his homes on Kenyatta Street is now the Zanzibar Gallery.

Spice tours The history of Zanzibar is one of spices: nutmeg, cinnamon and pepper brought the Sultans of Oman to the island, initiating the slave trade. Plantation tours demonstrate using spices in cooking, cosmetics and for many ailments.

Jozani Forest In the east central region of Zanzibar, this is home to red colobus monkeys. These roam freely beside Sykes monkeys, small bucks and bushpigs.

Safaris

There are countless pre-organized safari options, but a fabulous route is to start from Arusha, near Mount Kilimanjaro. Flying over that is quite a sight and if you fancy the climb, there are several treks – some are regarded as gentle at five days up and one day to get back down. Many others would loudly disagree with the word 'gentle'.

Alternatively, enjoy some mountain air at a lodge before setting off for the amazing Ngorongoro Crater. This ancient gorge is occupied by elephants, giraffe, lions, rhino, zebra and cheetahs. It is an intense experience as the animals are concentrated in a small space. At sunset you can sip an icy beer on the rim of the crater with the monkeys and giraffe just feet away. Next, explore the wide open Serengeti. Days are long, hot and grubby but the rewards are high. All the big cats live here, the great wildebeest migration is beyond spectacular, as is watching a pride of cheetahs. Evenings are spent around the campfire after cleaning up in a hot bush shower. Sleep under canvas listening to the sounds of nocturnal animals on the prowl. No need to panic, there are armed guards.

drying out
Mozambique

Tourism in the north of Mozambique is still quite a new affair, although there are a fair selection of hotels and resorts on both the coast and the nearby islands. The number of facilities in Pemba town have grown since the discovery of oil nearby, with the entire area becoming far more business-orientated. The island resorts remain as lovely as ever. Better known hotels tend to sit at either end of the cost scale, with some truly glorious, and all inclusive, island resorts. However, to balance things up, there are both top-end hotels and a few budget-priced ones on Wimbe Beach. Most will have a dive operation.

Avani Pemba Beach Hotel & Spa, pembabeachresort.com. International style hotel right on Wimbe Beach with an on-site dive centre. 20-mins transfer.

Pemba Dive and Bush Camp, pembadivecamp.com. Simple nature resort on Pemba Bay with dive centre.

Anantara Medjumbe Island Resort & Spa, medjumbe.com. 45-mins private flight from Pemba to this stylish and romantic resort island. Dive centre on site.

Days out

Pemba Originally named Porto Amelia after a Portuguese queen, this small city is a bit run down, but compared to many an African centre, it is really quite tidy. Colonial architecture rubs shoulders with fishing villages made of wooden huts. The centre has a sense of faded grandeur and a souk that stretches for 2km. Silver and local crafts are available, but avoid anything that might be made of ivory as selling this is illegal. Wimbe Beach, where the dive centres are based is becoming popular with tourists.

Ibo Island Once the Mozambique capital, Ibo dates back to the times of Vasca de Gama. It was colonized by the Portuguese in the early 1600s, its economy thriving due to the slave trade, pirate commerce and ivory trading. Many of the colonial houses have been abandoned and walking about feels like stepping back 200 years. Day trips visit the Catholic Church and the old fort of St Jao Baptista where silversmiths melt down old nickel coins and recraft them as pendants and bracelets.

Quirimbas National Park Stretching along the northeast coast, the park was formed in 2002 to protect forests and mangroves, as well as the southernmost 11 islands of the Quirimbas Archipelago. A few of these are principally resorts but there are day tours that include the islands and forest, snippets of colonial history and old plantations.

Medjumbe Island A 45-min flight over the archipelago delivers you to a tiny haven of peace and tranquility. Circumnavigating the island on foot takes about half an hour, depending on how long you stop to wade in rock pools, watch the diverse populations of seabirds or sit beneath the old lighthouse. The only entertainment is at sunset, when the tide retreats and the sand spit that stretches back towards the coast changes into a sea of terns.

Safaris

With tourism being so new, following the long civil war, wildlife safaris are still rare in Mozambique. The quantity of big animals is lower than elsewhere, but as research continues, the numbers and species appear to be more diverse than was once thought. The Niassa National Reserve in the north of the country is known to have 370 birds, including the rare Angola Pitta and Pel's Fishing Owl, and three recently discovered endemic species: the Niassa Wildebeest, Boehm's Zebra and Johnston's Impala. The Lugenda Wilderness Camp is the lone facility for viewing animals and is said to be best for those who have a pioneering spirit (lugenda.com). For a more guaranteed safari experience, Mozambique borders the Selous Reserve in Tanzania, it may be better to head back there, especially if you are flying via Dar es Salaam.

Flying over the Quirimbas; Medjumbe's lagoon; rooms with a view; Indian Ocean moonrise.

105
↘ **Essentials**

106
↘ **Dive brief**

108
↘ **Dive sites**

110
↘ **Dive log**

110 Viti Levu
112 Vanua Levu
114 Taveuni

116
↘ **Drying out**

Painting a rainbow: the marine realm in Fiji glistens with colours like light shining through falling raindrops above.
Rainbow Reef, Taveuni

Yasawas

Koro Sea

Somosomo Strait

🔅 Vanua Levu　▶▶ p112

✈ ● Savusavu

🔅 Taveuni　▶▶ p114

destination

Fiji

Mamanucas

✈ ● Nadi

▲ Mt Victoria

Ovalau

🔅 Viti Levu　▶▶ p110

✈ SUVA ●

Beqa

Kadavu

PACIFIC OCEAN

Lying across the 180 degree meridian, Fiji is where the dawn of each new day occurs, the rays of a rising sun lighting up over 300 scenic spits of land hovering over the world's deepest ocean.

These tiny Melanesian islands sit just outside the Coral Triangle in the southwestern Pacific Ocean, and along their northern edge lies the third longest barrier reef in the world: the Great Sea Reef. This volcanic archipelago is both reliant on and influenced by her maritime position.

For divers, what sets these reefs apart from other favourite tropical destinations is their colour. Nicknamed the soft coral capital of the world, the marine realm displays enough hues and tones to put an artist's paintbox to shame. Intensity of colour is only outdone by the profuse marine life that lives in these waters. No matter where else you have been, you won't have seen anything quite like this.

On land, the peaceful islands disguise an eventful but shadowy past: Fiji was once known to wary outsiders as the 'Cannibal Islands', yet this has since become one of the friendliest nations you could ever wish to visit.

Essentials

While the Americans and Aussies have it easy, there is nowhere that is quite so far away from Europe as Fiji, sitting right on the international date line. The shortest route from Europe is via Korea, but options are better if you fly via the US, especially if you can connect with Air Pacific, Fiji's national carrier. The main airport is at Nadi, and flights land there rather than at Suva, the capital. Once you have arrived, travelling between the islands is a breeze. Fiji Airlines, small aircraft ensure a scenic ride to all the best diving areas.

Local laws and customs

Fiji's population consists of around 50% indigenous people, who are Christians, and 45% who are the descendants of indentured Indian workers: a mix of Hindu, Muslim and Sikh. All Fijians are incredibly friendly and the usual courtesies will go a long way. However, if you visit a local village, take note that sunglasses and hats are thought to indicate disrespect for the chief; shoes should not be worn indoors, and both sexes should cover shoulders and knees. When visiting a village, it is customary to take a gift of kava root. Be cautious with praise – if you admire something too much, the owner will feel obliged to give it to you. Bear in mind that homosexuality is illegal, and drugs offences carry severe penalties.

Health and safety

Fiji carries few health risks for visitors other than the usual issues of too much sun and not enough water leading to dehydration. However, mosquitoes are active during the day, so use plenty of repellent. Medical facilities are of a reasonable standard but most, including the main recompression chamber, are on Viti Levu. The islands are generally crime free but there is some small-time petty theft and occasional muggings in the city centres. In a country which virtually shuts down on a Sunday – the day of rest – this upsets the older generation, who are saddened by what they see as a lack of respect amongst Fijian youth.

Costs

Value for money is a given in Fiji. There is a wide selection of hotels, from dirt cheap to expensive, and most offer combined diving and accommodation packages. Of course, if you don't want to be limited to staying, diving and eating in the same place, you can always use the closest resort's dive centre. Local restaurants are simple and cheap, but there won't be a huge choice. Chinese food is common on the smaller islands, Indian food on Viti Levu. Getting traditional Fijian food is more difficult, but resorts will do a 'lovo night', when a meal is cooked over hot stones. Likewise, apart from in Nadi and Suva, there won't be a huge selection of shops. Tipping isn't customary in Fiji, although you may find it's expected in the more expensive resorts, while some will have a special staff fund.

Fact file

Location	18°00'S, 175°00'E
Capital	Suva
Flights	Air New Zealand, Air Pacific, Korean, Qantas
Internal flights	Fiji Airlines (a.k.a Pacific Sun)
Land transport	Taxis, buses and ferries
Departure tax	FJD$30
Entry	EU, US and Commonwealth – valid passport required for stays of up to 4 months
Money	Fijian dollars (FJD)
Language	English
Electricity	220v, plug type E (see page 15)
Time zone	GMT +7
Religion	Christian, Hindu, Muslim, Sikh
Communications	Country code +679; IDD code 00; Police 911 Internet access available in better hotels
Tourist information	bulafiji.com
Travel advisories	gov.uk/foreign-travel-advice; state.gov/travel

dive brief

Diving

Fiji's reefs have earned more elaborate, flowery descriptions than appears logical to most divers– until you get there. Terms like underwater rainbows, technicolour wonderlands and kaleidoscopic colours are used and over-used to exhaustion.

Despite that, when it comes to the soft corals, this tiny country deserves every fancy description that comes its way. Yes, divers and writers do tend to over-enthuse, but it will only take one dive amongst this most incredible array of rainbow-hued soft corals and you will understand. It's not just that the colours seem extraordinarily bright in the clear waters, it's the sheer range of colours that often clash with each other. Sometimes gaudy might be a better tag.

But it's not only about the colourful corals. Like much of the South Pacific, Fiji has diving sites that are varied and exciting, with both shallow reefs and sheer walls. There are narrow tunnels, overhangs and small caves to explore. Small schooling fish paint the reefs with ever more colour, and pelagic life is plentiful. Yet, somehow, it still all comes back to the soft corals, which can be found all over the country, from huge fans near the surface to fragile black corals that are well below normal diving limits. All this is possible thanks to the 30 metre-plus visibility, which keeps the depths well lit. Plankton blooms during April and May or November and December can reduce the visibility a little, but they also bring in filter-feeders and pelagics. Conditions are fairly easy: there can be some strong currents, but drift diving is straightforward and water temperatures are consistent.

Snorkelling

Protected lagoons and gently shelving beaches around many of the islands mean that snorkelling can be very rewarding. However, these spots are not always in the same places as the best diving. Taveuni would be one of the better exceptions to that, as would the tiny, sandy islands of the Yasawa Group, off Nadi. Viti Levu has fewer easily accessible snorkelling areas, but resorts arrange trips to offshore reefs where the snorkelling is much better.

We discovered Fiji while crossing the Pacific on a round-the-world flight. What a contrast to the stops one either side – Hawaii and Australia! There are so few places in the world these days that manage to live in the 21st century yet still remain 'unspoilt'. Of course, everyone's idea of unspoilt varies, but there is little in Fiji to taint the experience. It's calm, it's quiet, it has welcoming people and amazing diving. And yes, we will go back one day.

Camouflaged and motionless, the ever-patient leaf scorpionfish.

Marine life

Did anyone mention the mass of incredible technicolour soft corals? All reef species are well represented here – perhaps not in such great numbers as in the countries of the Coral Triangle – but there is everything from reef sharks to crustaceans to crinoids.

Making the big decision

Once known to wary outsiders as the Cannibal Islands, this is now one of the friendliest nations you could ever visit. However, the biggest issue for many is the distance to Fiji. At 2,700 kilometres east of Cairns and around 10 hours flying time from the west coast of America, it cannot be denied that this country is a little out of the way for most, and flights could not be regarded as cheap. However, what is far too tempting to ignore, is the quality of what you will see underwater. This small part of the Pacific Ocean also seems a little removed from many of the problems facing our planet's seas. There is tourism, and marine tourism, but it doesn't engulf the country or its personality. There is a fishing industry, but it isn't overwhelming. You may only go to Fiji once, but it will be a once-in-a-lifetime experience.

◔ Animal encounters

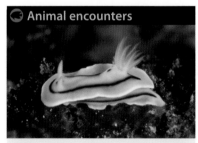

Countrywide: as marine creatures in Fiji are fairly consistent from island to island, you don't need to choose a destination based on seeing a specific animal. However, wherever you go, the iridescent rainbows of soft corals tend to mask the many smaller creatures found living around them. Equally colourful are the blue ribbon eels, red hawkfish, orange clownfish and snowy white nudibranchs (above).

dive sites

Way out in the South Pacific Ocean and lying right on the 180 degree meridian where the dawn of each new day occurs are the 300 or so islands that make up this small country. Each one emerges as the epitome of a South Pacific idyll. Only a 100 or so are inhabited – the rest are left as pristine nature reserves – and almost all are ringed by coral reefs. These are as exciting and varied as you would expect anywhere in the tropical belt, but the most compelling reason for diving in Fiji is, and will always be, the wide range of colours of the corals. It really isn't hard to see where the much-used nicknames came from.

Viti Levu is Fiji's principal island and is the location of both the capital, Suva, and the international airport at Nadi. It is ringed by many smaller islands, each one with a range of reefs and dive sites. The Mamanuca and Yasawa island groups off the west coast are easy to reach, their exotic names reflecting the exotic location. However, proximity to the airport means these attract more general holidaymakers, while most dedicated and serious divers tend to bypass this area to head straight to the two world-renowned destinations in the northeast.

The two islands that really draw people to Fiji are Vanua Levu, the second largest, and just eastwards, smaller Taveuni. Both sit on the edge of the famed Somosomo Straits, where the continual and often fast flow of water ensures that the soft corals are pristine, prolific and almost always out feeding, revealing multiple colours, tones and hues that have no rival. This rare environment attracts plenty of small fish too, while larger pelagics hover over the deep blue channels.

Vanua Levu borders the top edge of the Straits. Drift dives can be challenging at times and contrast strongly with the more sheltered sites inside Savusavu Bay. Hugging the bottom edge of the Straits, Taveuni dive sites were the ones that first spawned the 'soft coral capital of the world' title. The conditions are much the same as those around Vanua Levu but travelling times to the most famous dive sites are a little shorter, and local dives off the coast a little shallower.

There are many other island groups in Fiji that are rarely seen by divers. If you have done the rest, you might think about travelling to the Kadavu group to the south of Viti Levu. This marks the position of the world's fourth largest barrier reef, the Great Astrolabe Reef, which is said to have some incredible hard corals. Although the islands are only 35 minutes by plane from Nadi, they are remarkably remote, with a minimal infrastructure. This is in part because weather conditions mean flights get cancelled, and also because there are no roads – Vunisea, the main town, has just a few but, apart from these, it's walking trails and boats.

Conditions
Tropical regions only

Seasons	Summer, between November and April, is the wet season and subject to occasional cyclones. Winter, from May to October, is the dry season.
Visibility	20 m in summer to 50 m in winter
Currents	Generally mild except on well-known current dives like the Great White Wall.
Temperatures	Air 20-31°C; water 25-30° C
Wet suit	3 mm full body suit; 5 mm in cooler months
Training	Available on the islands; look for PADI or NAUI affiliated schools
Nitrox	Generally available
Deco chambers	Suva

Diversity

reef area 10,020 km²

HARD CORALS	398
FISH SPECIES	1231
ENDEMIC FISH SPECIES	4
FISH UNDER THREAT	33

All diversity figures are approximate

Viti Levu ▶▶ p110

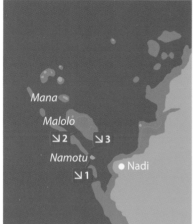

Vanua Levu ▶▶ p112

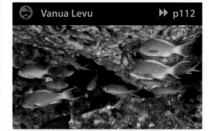

Taveuni ▶▶ p114

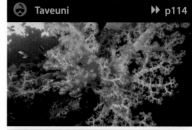

Log Book

- **↘1 Namotu Wall**
- **↘2 Wilke's Passage**
- **↘3 Plantation Pinnacles**

→ **North Reef:** a cluster of coral bommies sculpted by staghorn and hard corals

→ **Castaway Passage:** the currents escort divers into a lagoon to see what arrives

→ **Magic Reef:** shallow but very pretty coral gardens above Namotu Wall

Log Book

- **↘4 Nuggets**
- **↘5 Goldilocks**
- **↘6 Alice in Wonderland**
- **↘7 Mystery Reef**

→ **The Pinnacle:** clownfish and anemone-clad pinnacle in the Somosomo Straits

→ **Lighthouse:** deep dive on the point of the bay with schooling snappers

→ **Dream House:** pelagic fish overload and lots of sharks on the right day

Log Book

- **↘8 The Corner**
- **↘9 Blue Ribbon Eel Reef**
- **↘10 The Great White Wall**

→ **The Ledge:** an isolated pinnacle with moorish idols, butterflies and damsels.

→ **Fish Factory:** juveniles of all the bigger fish you see on the reefs

→ **Rainbow's End:** everything from nudibranchs to whitetip reef sharks

☻ Endangered oceans

The Fijian islands, like many in the South Pacific, pay more than a little lip-service to caring for their coral reefs. It has long been part of the culture to respect the natural realm and, today, even the constitution refers to protecting the natural world for future generations. However, despite such deeply-held beliefs, the surrounding seas are threatened.

The increased need for modern resources to support a growing population has led to substantially more pressure on marine resources. It is said that Fiji can no longer meet its own food needs from currently established coastal fisheries.

To address this and rather than create havoc with such a precious resource, the government and many local communities have established their own marine protected areas. Even the people living in distant island groups enforce their own conservation zones with strict management rules. This means that the migratory paths of four critically endangered turtles are respected; sharks are not fished, and exotic fish that are heavily exploited elsewhere – like Napoleon wrasse – are thriving here.

dive log Viti Levu

Although most serious divers head away from Viti Levu, targetting one of the more distant island groups to find the best diving in the country, there are many coral reefs and tiny islands that are just perfect for a few days of relaxed and easy diving.

Just off Nadi's shoreline are two chains of classically pretty cays. The Yasawas are further north, so slightly less accessible, but the Mamanuca islands are less than an hour away and riddled with small resorts and dive centres. Some of the sites along the outer barrier reef can be really quite exciting and are worth seeing. Many of these resorts are targeted at budget travellers, so courses are good value, too.

There is a lot more diving off Viti Levu, including the southern stretch also known as the Coral Coast. Over 10 miles across, Beqa Lagoon is actually the crater of an extinct volcano. There is a very popular shark feed dive at Shark Reef, where you have a good chance of coming face-to-face with grey reef, bull and tiger sharks.

Conditions around Viti Levu are good but less so than around the outlying islands as this area is prone to cyclones. Visibility is about 30 metres at best, as all that lovely, white sand does cloud the water when the winds are up. At the same time, surface conditions can be rocky, and while reef conditions are pretty good, they are nowhere near as impressive as elsewhere.

⛴1 Namotu Wall	
🔻 **Depth**	20 m
◐ **Visibility**	fair to great
🌊 **Currents**	mild

Magic Island, more properly known as Namotu, is little more than a small cay ringed by sand. Next door is Tavarua island and diving the passage between them can be highly exhilarating at times. The coral formations take second place to the incredible numbers of fish seen as you get closer to the wall. You are more than likely to encounter some schooling barracuda, a couple of turtles and perhaps a whitetip shark or two. Depending where you enter the site you can also offgas in the shallows above or make that a separate dive. The top levels of the reef are packed full of small colourful fish including lionfish and butterflies. Curious black and white banded sea snakes are sometimes seen feeding around the small hard corals.

Underwater rainbows, technicolour wonderlands, kaleidoscopic colour: Fijian soft corals.

Wilke's Passage, Mamanuca

Depth	22 m	
Visibility	very good	
Currents	mild to strong	

It's unusual for an open water dive site to be good for snorkelling, but this one is. It's also a favourite for surfers. Northwest of Magic Island, Wilke's Passage cuts through the outer edge of the barrier reef. The flow of water on the outside creates decent waves for the surfers, and there are frequent dolphin sightings too. The inner lagoon is good for snorkelling, while below the water, these conditions create an interesting drift dive. The currents can be strong but not so fierce as to make dives difficult, and they attract schools of barracuda and trevally. Corals flourish in the nutrient-rich waters.

Plantation Pinnacles

Depth	24 m	
Visibility	good	
Currents	can be strong	

A little further north is Mamanuca Lagoon, where three pinnacles protrude from the seabed. Conditions here are usually easy – you can do several circuits, some swim-throughs then slowly ascend up the sides. At the base there are black coral trees with resident longnose hawkfish, and small fans and soft corals coat the sides. At the top, the macro life is particularly interesting, with nudibranchs and starfish, masses of anemones and clowns, leaffish and morays.

Clown triggerfish with wacky skin patterns.

dive log Vanua Levu

Fiji's second largest island is incredibly undeveloped, except around the capital, Savusavu. Yet for divers, this island, along with neighbouring Taveuni, is possibly the biggest attraction in the country. And it's all because the fantastic Somosomo Straits run between them.

Even discounting the Straits, Savusavu Bay has steep walls for drifting over, pinnacles to circumnavigate and caves to explore; the fish life is varied, and pelagic species are reasonably common. One of the area's best features is it's capacity to provide dives for everyone. There are sheltered sites inside the bay, lively coastal dives and the exhilarating Somosomo Straits are still close enough to enjoy in a day.

↘6 Nuggets	
🕙 **Depth**	18 m
◐ **Visibility**	excellent
≈ **Currents**	medium

On the southern edge of Savusavu Bay, the Nuggets are two towering coral heads. Rising from 18 metres deep to just below the surface, the main pinnacle measures about 50 metres around at its base. It's a tiny area but a whole world resides there. Myriad soft corals are surrounded by schools of fairy basslets, from the tiniest babes to adults. Masked bannerfish and damsels flutter about the steep walls, and young angels seem to pop out of tiny caves every few seconds. Leaffish are spotted nestling in crevices, and occasional jacks circle above. On the surrounding sandy seafloor titan triggers nest, they can be very aggressive while guarding their eggs so it's best to watch from the safety of the pinnacle. The second, smaller bommie is covered in golden soft corals with lionfish, scorpions and moray eels poking about; longnose hawkfish hide on a fan while giant pufferfish hover nearby.

↘7 Goldilocks	
🕙 **Depth**	20 m
◐ **Visibility**	good to stunning
≈ **Currents**	mild to strong

Heading south and around the outer edge of Vanua Levu, but still only half an hour or so from the centre of Savusavu town, you reach the Koro Sea. Away from the protection of the curved bay, currents are stronger and, consequently, the coral growth is thicker and lusher. As you descend over the reef, the first thing you encounter is a vast carpet of hard corals. There seems to be a substantial variety crammed into a very small area. Finning round the edge of the reef, a bommie appears. It is thronged by tropical fish, while beneath it are several small rays. Further on, a second bommie is completely smothered in bright yellow soft corals, hence the name of the dive site. Bright yellow plumes seem to drip from every crack and crevice. Of course, there are plenty of other corals, plus nudibranchs, unicornfish and many damselfish couples guarding their eggs.

Diving in Savusavu Bay: starfish on the reef; a yellow crinoid.

N4 Alice in Wonderland

⏱	**Depth**	22 m
◐	**Visibility**	good to stunning
〰	**Currents**	mild

N5 Mystery Reef

⏱	**Depth**	20 m
◐	**Visibility**	good
〰	**Currents**	medium

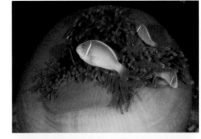

Located towards the outer reaches of Savusavu Bay, the story goes that this dive was named after the huge mushroom-shaped coral heads that cover the wide swathe of patchy reef. The area is exposed to currents flowing from the south and east, so there are lots of schooling fish. Small whitetips cruise in to feed and lurk about beneath the 'mushrooms' of hard coral, all of which are in impeccable condition. There is some interesting macro life, with plenty of cleaner shrimp hopping around tube anemones and coral banded shrimp under sponges.

Half an hour or so from shore and just a little past Alice, the seafloor at Mystery Reef is also scattered with hard coral heads, but these are painted with a huge number of multi-coloured soft corals, a feature that is typical to this area. There are plenty of fish too, as the whole reef seems to be a breeding ground. There are clownfish with their babies, moorish idols chasing each other in mating games, while newborn damselfish hide behind their parents. Even tiny scorpionfish sit on the seabed. Coral trout, Spanish mackerel, angels and parrotfish are also in residence.

66 99 We steamed to the Namena Marine Protected Area, southeast of Savusavu. This region can only be reached by liveaboard and is generally regarded as having some of the best sites in Fiji. It certainly did not disappoint. The pinnacles and ridges are all covered in a glorious blanket of soft corals (among other things) with plenty of fish life and the occasional shark too. The colour and sheer health of the reefs were breathtaking and it really helped to hit home that some of these sites are truly world class.
Gavin Macaulay, director, dive-the-world.com

Leopard shark resting on the seabed.

dive log
Taveuni

Fiji is big on nick-names and two of its most profound originated here. Taveuni lies opposite Vanua Levu and is a small but perfectly formed island. Its steep hills are shrouded in the riotous flora that earned it the title of 'Garden Island.' However, that title and the beauty that spawned it pales beside the underwater glory of the 'soft coral capital, the Somosomo Straits.

The stretch of water separating Taveuni from Vanua Levu is a narrow channel that funnels water from south to north and back again, supplying nutrients, stimulating growth and ensuring the health of reef-building animals. The currents are constant, not always strong but ever-present.

⤡8 The Corner, Rainbow Reef	
🐟 **Depth**	18 m
◐ **Visibility**	good
🌊 **Currents**	medium to strong

Rainbow Reef was obviously named after the immense profusion of multi-coloured soft corals that envelope this entire reef. The topography is highly varied, with walls, caves and swim-throughs. The Corner is a popular dive, with shallow coral gardens on the inner edge of the reef interspersed with sandy channels. There are young whitetip sharks hiding under table corals living alongside groups of giant clams. Bommies that grow upwards towards the surface are covered in masses of anemones; anthias dance in the soft and hard corals and it's a great site for spotting nudibranchs.

⤡9 Blue Ribbon Eel Reef	
🐟 **Depth**	20 m
◐ **Visibility**	fair to good
🌊 **Currents**	slight to strong

This drift dive is just a few minutes' boat ride from shore. As you drop over the reef, you are met by patches of purple soft corals that almost make it easy to bypass the main attraction – the blue ribbon eel. This is one of those sites where they are almost guaranteed, although few people spot them first time round. These elusive creatures retreat rapidly into their holes in the sand as soon as they feel threatened. However, the dive guides know where they are, and waiting for a few minutes nearby means they usually pop their heads out again. Although these eels can grow to as much as a metre long, you mostly only see about a hand's length, which is enough to admire the vivid bands of blue and yellow on a young male. All yellow ribbon eels are female and adult, while black ones are the juveniles. The males change to female on maturity. Of course, there are plenty of fish too, with angels and moorish idols swarming around the corals.

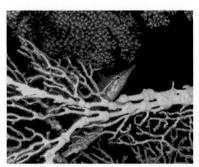

Longnose hawkfish and regal angelfish living on Taveuni reefs.

↘10 the great white wall

Depth	31 m
Visibility	stunning
Currents	medium to strong

Arguably Fiji's most famous site, diving on the Great White Wall means diving with a current; if, for some reason, that has dropped off completely, there is really no point in going.

This dive involves a descent over the reef edge then swimming down through a tunnel which has two exits. The first exit is at 10 metres and you might find a moray here, but the more exciting exit is at 30 metres. Emerging onto a sheer wall that plunges down to unfathomable depths, you then find yourself surrounded by a fantastic swathe of pure white. The water that moves constantly over the wall encourages all the soft corals tentacles out to feed. The effect is luminescent, almost like snow on a hill which glows when the sun's rays bounce off it. There are huge quantities of these small soft corals carpeting the reef surfaces and, if you shine a torch on them, you can see they are actually a pale pink or mauve.

A few whip corals and fans sprout from the wall into the current, so you might spot some gobies or a longnose hawkfish sheltering in them.

Meanwhile, off the wall, several large humphead wrasse swim along in tandem with the divers, and reef sharks are often seen hanging around in the shallows, but their attraction pales in comparison to the overall effect of the landscape.

❝❞ The vision of these pale, same-coloured corals after several days of gaudy, multi-toned reefs is really quite breathtaking. The light they reflect back from the reef is a little ghostly, definitely a bit other-world.

drying out

One of the great pleasures of travelling and diving in Fiji is the wide selection of resorts on all the islands. They vary in standard and hence price, so for those on a limited budget, it is possible to stay in a small hotel – perhaps closer to town with access to local facilities – and dive with an affiliated company.

Coastal and offshore island resorts on the western side of Viti Levu are less than an hour from Nadi's international airport, while transfers to Beqa Lagoon and the Coral Coast take around two hours. To both Vanua Levu and Taveuni, scenic flights in small aircraft take about an hour, while the hop between these two takes 15 minutes.

Viti Levu

Diving
Subsurface Fiji, fijidiving.com. Dive centres located in a dozen or so resorts around Nadi and the Mamanuca Islands.

Sleeping
First Landing Resort, firstlandingfiji.com
Malolo Island Resort, maloloisland.com.
Beqa Lagoon, beqalagoonresort.com. Dive centre on site. 2-hr airport transfer.

Vanua Levu

Diving and sleeping
Jean Michel Cousteau Fiji Islands Resort, fijiresort.com. L'Aventure Divers are on site.
Daku Resort, dakuresort.com. Diving arranged through local dive centres.

Taveuni

Diving and sleeping
Garden Island Resort, aquatrek.com. About 20-mins from the airstrip and moments from the Meridian line.
Paradise Taveuni, T+679 888 0125 paradiseinfiji.com. Dive centre on site. Airport transfers take 1-hr.

Liveaboards
MY Nai'A, naia.com.fj. Nai'A sails around the central Fijian area. Expensive but this is the boat with 'the' reputation.
SY Fiji Siren, sirenfleet.com. One of the Siren Fleet, which uses Indonesian phinisi schooners so is somewhat unique in Fiji.

Viti Levu

Nadi Not a very pretty place but there is some decent shopping. Day tours that include the centre also take in the Vatukoula Gold Mines near the market town of Tavua and Viseisei Village, which is regarded as the 'foundation village' of Fijian heritage and culture.

Koroyanitu National Park Located 10 km east of Lautoka, the park has beautiful bush walks, waterfalls, archaeological sites and lush native rainforest.

Ba and Rakiraki Ba is an Indian town known for its mosque and colourful bazaar. Rakiraki is the home of Ratu Udre, Fiji's last known cannibal. His tomb at the town junction is ringed by 999 stones to represent the number of people he ate.

Sigatoka A small town on a river mouth with markets and access to archaeological sites on the south coast sand dunes. Digs have uncovered skeletons and artefacts dating back to 15 BC.

Suva The political capital has markets, shopping and nightlife, a few museums, some colonial architecture and the main governmental buildings. Like Nadi, there is little to hold you here for more than a day or perhaps two.

Ovalau Island Northeast of Suva, this tiny island is home to Levuka, Fiji's first capital, and most historic location. This national heritage site is well worth a visit to see its gloriously faded main street.

Vanua Levu

Downtown Savusavu With the feel of a Wild West staging post, there's just one road with banks, ATMs, a post office and a few shops. There are two marinas: the older one is the Copra Shed, a converted warehouse that has some tourist and craft shops and a café. A bit further along is Waitui Marina, where you can chill out on the decks overlooking the bay.

Salt Lake Kayaking Drive up the Hibiscus Highway to a salt water river that leads to a salty lake, the island's largest.

Waisali Rainforest Reserve A gentle walk through dense rainforest with the cooling spray of the waterfall at the end.

Tunuloa Peninsula Said to be the island's best birdwatching spot, including the chance to see a rare silk-tail.

Waivunia Village Take an excursion to see the village, homes and church. The villagers display local arts and crafts.

Taveuni

Bouma Falls In the National Park, these three waterfalls are in a remote area but are fairly easy walks. And you can swim beneath them to cool off once you arrive.

Lavena Village A picturesque, traditional village where you can meet some of the villagers. The spectacular beach is a great snorkelling spot.

Lake Tagimoucia This old crater lake, which is filled with floating plant life, is just below Des Voeux Peak. The hike is strenuous, up to 4 hours each way, but the views are amazing. You may spot Fiji's most famous flower, the tagimoucia, subject of local legend. Birdwatching is said to be excellent.

Kava ceremonies It's a great honour to be invited to join a kava ceremony, the ritualized drinking of a bowl of muddy brown water, with the village elders. Kava is a root from the pepper family and, when ground and soaked in water, has a very faint narcotic effect. Expect numb lips at least. Ceremonies are held constantly to celebrate all sorts of events, even a local sports day. It's generally a male preserve but female tourists are happily tolerated. If you are invited to attend make sure you do; it's bad form not to.

Wairiki Mission This old Catholic mission overlooks the site where local warriors once defeated thousands of Tongans then celebrated their victory by cooking them in a lovo oven and eating them with breadfruit! The priest who advised the warriors was 'rewarded' for his help by the building of the large mission.

Left: Nadi sunset and a break from diving on Taveuni. Right: landing at Taveuni; Kava ceremony; view over Savusavu Bay; Levuka high street.

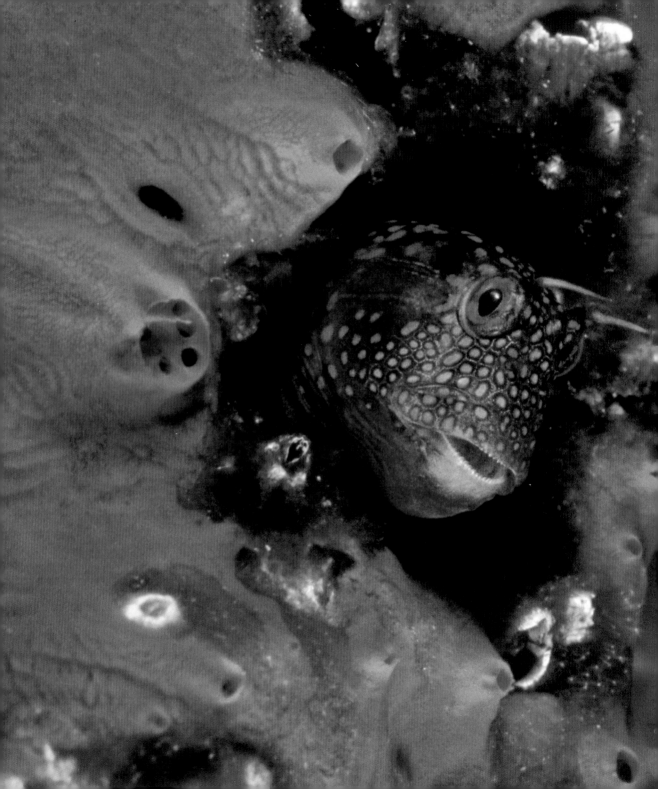

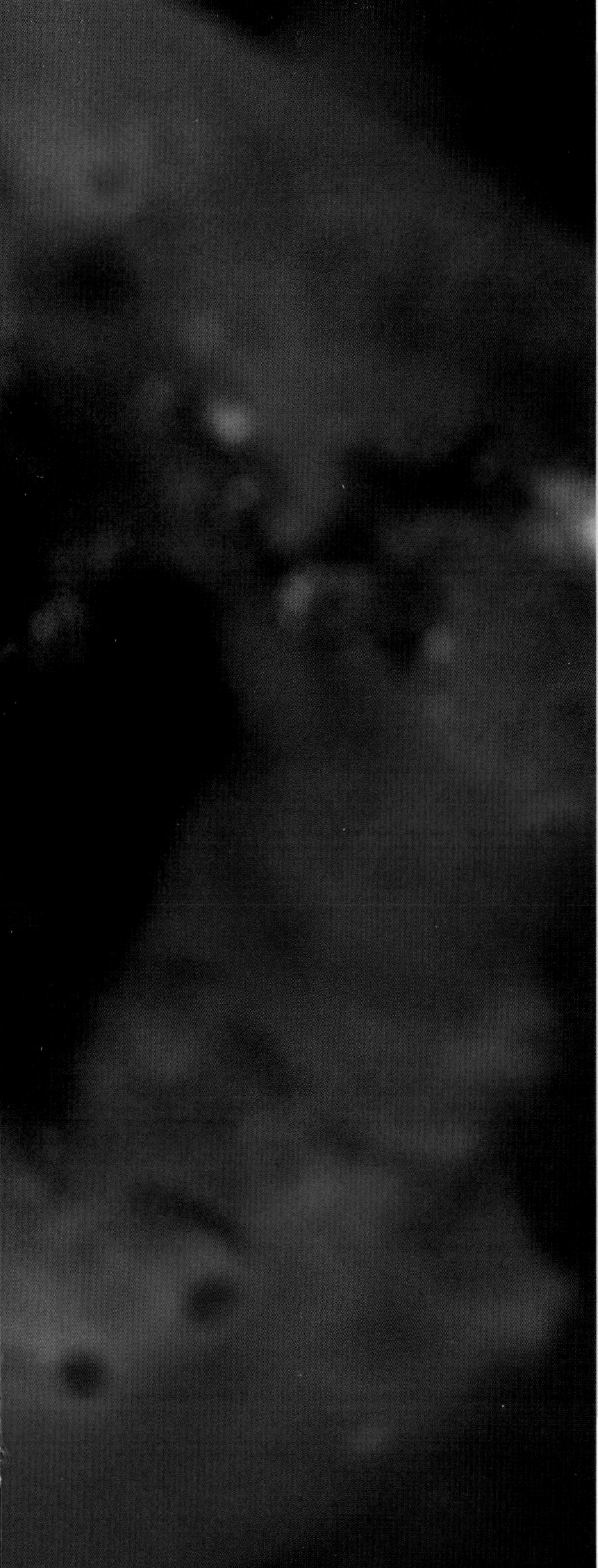

Galápagos

121
↘ **Essentials**

122
↘ **Dive brief**

124
↘ **Dive sites**

126
↘ **Dive log**

126   Central zone
128   Northern zone
130   Western zone

132
↘ **Drying out**

Peek-a-boo: the Barnacle Bill blenny, *Hypsoblennius brevipinnis*, is rarely seen, even in the Galápagos.
Gordon Rocks, Santa Cruz

destination Galápagos

Darwin

🌐 Northern zone ⏩ p128

Wolf

🌐 Western zone ⏩ p130

🌐 Central zone ⏩ p126

PACIFIC OCEAN

Esmeraldas ●

QUITO ✈

ECUADOR

Isabela

✈ *Santa Cruz*

✈ *San Cristóbal*

The Galápagos

Guayaquil ● ✈

● Piura

PERU

The Galápagos Islands are home to some of the most intriguing and unique wildlife on earth. Lying right on the equator, this ancient archipelago of harsh volcanic landscapes is ruled by animals, and human visitors are reduced to the role of voyeur. Both above and below the water, sit back, wait patiently and allow the animals to come to you. They nearly always do.

Biodiversity figures are not as high as in some other countries, yet the number of endemic species is unparalleled. Beneath the incessant waves, there are – still – vast numbers of sharks: from the sleek silky to gentle whale sharks; you'd have to be asleep not to see half a dozen

different species. Huge schools of hammerheads are the most common, yet they can also appear solo, sitting by your shoulder.

On land, immerse yourself in another world. Sit beside newborn sea lion pups and their parents will simply lift their heads and give you a cursory glance. Marine iguanas bask by your toes, while birds pause on their backs doing daily clean-up duty.

Despite their relative isolation and the cost of getting there, these islands are-ever popular. A steady stream of people flies in daily, passing along well-trodden routes to witness the spectacular wildlife show.

Essentials

Finding a flight to Ecuador is easy but if you are further away than the US, try to get one that will take you in a modicum of comfort, as routes via major US hub cities can be tortuous – at least there are daily connections to the capital, Quito. Most flights arrive either early in the day or very late at night, so you might as well stop over, especially as the city is fascinating. Getting around is easy too, but avoid unlicensed 'taxi amigos', which will cost extra. After a couple of days, take a connecting flight to either San Cristóbal or Baltra for the Galápagos. It is probably best to ask an agent to organise all this, as everything to do with these islands is highly regulated.

Local laws and customs

Ecuador is overwhelmingly Catholic. with just a small minority following alternative forms of Christianity. Some indigenous Ecuadoreans have adapted their version of Catholicism to incorporate traditional beliefs. Dress modestly and behave with courtesy and respect especially inside Quito's historic churches. Losing your temper in public is regarded as very bad form.

Health and safety

If you are going to get sick, it's only likely to be a bit of altitude sickness in Quito. The city is 2,800 metres up and the air is thin. Most visitors feel a little more tired than usual and perhaps a bit breathless. Some people also report stomach upsets and sinus problems. Down at sea level, mosquitoes can be a problem at dusk and, depending on the time of year, the sun can be very strong (remember you're sitting on the Equator). There is no malaria in or around Quito or in the Galápagos. Ecuadoreans are very friendly and helpful people but common sense should prevail, especially if you go out at night.

Costs

Regardless of the price of diving there, going to the Galápagos is costly. But worth it. Added to the basic travel costs, there is also a hefty US$100 per person National Park tax, which is collected at the airport on arrival. That aside, if you go on a liveaboard, there is little extra to pay for except the odd souvenir and drinks. If you want to spend a few days on land, there are plenty of hotels and restaurants at all budget levels. And while the islands can seem expensive, mainland Ecuador is particularly good value. There are hotels at all levels, though standards are variable. Eating out in Quito is an absolute pleasure, with trendy fusion-style restaurants, traditional bistros and snack bars that are cheap and ubiquitous. There is a 10% service charge on bills, but adding a bit extra is usual. Cab drivers and porters appreciate a small tip.

Fact file

Location	2°00'S, 77°30'W
Capital	Quito
Flights	American, British Airways, Delta or Virgin to Miami; American or Taca to Quito
Internal flights	AeroGal or TAME for the Galápagos
Land transport	Countrywide bus and train routes
Departure tax	US$25
Entry	EU, US and Commonwealth – valid passport required for stays of up to 90 days
Money	The US dollar is the official currency
Language	Spanish
Electricity	110/220v, plug type A (see page 15)
Time zone	GMT -5
Religion	Catholic
Communications	Country code +593; IDD code 00; Police in Quito 911; Police elsewhere 101. Internet access available in most hotels.
Tourist information	vivecuador.com; ecuadortouristboard.com; galapagospark.org
Travel advisories	gov.uk/foreign-travel-advice; state.gov/travel

dive brief

Diving

Created some five million years ago by a series of volcanic eruptions, the Galápagos straddle the equator 1000 kilometres west of the South American coast. Still one of the world's most active volcanic regions, the islands are also at the crossroads of seven major ocean currents. The main influences are the Equatorial (Cromwell) current, which sweeps in cold water from due west, the warmer Panama current coming from the northeast and the cold Peru (Humboldt) from the south. Each of these brings in its own species, resulting in a rare mixture of tropical, subtropical and temperate sea animals. And this is what makes it such a special diving destination.

More than almost any other destination, a dive trip to the Galápagos requires a high level of understanding of local conditions. If you are used to cold water diving, these conditions will not be news, but this is not diving for the faint-hearted: the water can be icy; it's rarely dead calm and currents or surges are an every-dive occurrence. At certain times, entries are in huge swells, so getting back on the RIB then onto your boat is no fun. Underwater, currents can be so strong you have to grab hold of the nearest rock with two hands – bring gloves! There are substantial seasonal differences from summer to winter as well and hugely varying sea current patterns. And, lastly, you have to add in the fact that each island has its own microclimate.

Now that the warnings are done, the best time for the biggest animals is winter as they are attracted by cool water. Whale sharks start to appear at the end of May as the water temperature drops to 15°C or so. When it warms up again, the chances of seeing mantas improves. No matter what time of year it is, thermoclines can be an issue. One minute you can be 25°C then, in seconds, it will drop to 14°C. No joke!

Generally speaking, though, the most favourable periods are those around the change of seasons, meaning from April to June then November and December. December to May are warmest, when the weather could be regarded as sub-tropical to tropical in the north. June to December is cold and sees some unusual anomalies like banks of mist around Roca Redonda.

Snorkelling

There are shallow bays with good marine life around Santa Cruz and the potential to get close to the sea lions. Liveaboards and day boats tend to go to more challenging dive sites around submerged pinnacles where the surge is rough. If you only want to snorkel, ensure you book onto a wildlife or naturalist trip, not a diving one.

> 66 99
>
> **Darwin said: "It is not the strongest of the species that survive, nor the most intelligent, but the one most responsive to change." That hits the nail right on the head for diving in the Galápagos. This is a place where you can't even hope to predict accurately what conditions you will find or the animals you will see. We thought we would see mantas and whalesharks but got hammerheads and whales; we were told it was the warm season and we got ice-cold thermoclines. Everyone on our boat said the same thing... expectations were not always met, but often exceeded. Go with an open mind, adapt to the conditions and you will enjoy it.**

Pacific spotted scorpionfish; guineafowl pufferfish; playing with a sea lion.

Marine life

The marine life here is big with a capital B. If big pelagics are your thing, you will not leave disappointed. Dive with hundreds of hammerhead sharks, or do your safety stop surrounded by 20 – or more – silky sharks. Galápagos and whitetip sharks are common companions, and hammerheads are seen on almost every dive. Turtles, eagle rays and marble rays are everywhere as, of course, are curious and playful sea lions. Mantas and whale sharks are seasonal and seen less often. There are small creatures too – moray eels, seahorses and even tiny nudibranchs. Many fish may seem familiar, but may have regional differences, plus some are endemic to the islands. There is, however, very little in the way of corals, so the reefs are not classically pretty like somewhere in the tropics.

Making the big decision

The Galápagos Islands are on almost every diver's hit-list, but before rushing out to book a trip, consider a couple of things: are you experienced – and adaptable – enough to cope with unpredictable and frequently rough surface water conditions and the equally unusual ones below? Are you picking the right boat? Changes in local governments policies have left very few liveaboards with valid diving permits. Those currently running are professional and 100% diver-focussed but that means you will probably want to organize some extra time on land to see other animals the islands and the mainland.

Although this is an extraordinary diving experience, it is not an easy or cheap one, so plan your trip carefully to get the most out of your time.

Animal encounters

Countrywide: the big animals are always the big attraction for most divers, but make sure you look down sometimes or you will miss some of the rarer species: giant hawkfish, the King angelfish (above) and the cute Barnacle Bill blenny. But back to the big animals: spend some time on deck between dives as it's also likely you will see several types of whales – Bryde's, Killer and Pilot whales – passing by on their migratory paths.

Galápagos Dive brief

dive sites

The most populated Galápagos islands, by humans at least, are Santa Cruz and San Cristobal, and one of these is likely to be where your dive journey commences, the other where it ends. Loosely referred to as the central zone, the underwater realm is calmer and warmer than more distant regions, as it is protected from the harshest currents and conditions by seahorse-shaped (how perfect is that!) Isabela Island to the west. It is ideal for less experienced divers or simply to acclimatize.

A long way north and totally exposed to all the elements Mother Nature throws at them are isolated outposts Wolf and Darwin. This is a rock-your-dive-boots-off experience, with countless eagle rays and more hammerheads. The Humboldt current has a lesser effect but, even when the surface temperature reaches 28°C, thermoclines at depth can still be icy.

Around the nose of Isabela's seahorse, the Western zone is totally open to the wide Pacific Ocean and heavily influenced by every one of the seven major ocean currents. This is an area of wildly varying conditions, often with icy water, yet some of the most unusual dive sites are found beneath the volcanic landscapes.

Choosing a time to visit and dive the Galápagos should be based on what you want to see most. For example, July to November is the peak season for whale sharks off Wolf and Darwin Islands, while the following three months see the arrival of manta rays. The sharks and sea lions will be there regardless.

Endangered oceans

Until the early 1500s, the Galápagos islands had never seen a human; the lands and wildlife developing in complete isolation from any predatory forces. It was this that made them so completely unique, with many species never seen anywhere else. However, it all changed dramatically once whalers arrived in the 1800s, and then, in the 20th century, many tuna fishing boats arrived to exploit the region.

The government formed a management plan in the 1970s and, by 1998, a special law formalized the Galápagos Marine Reserve. This extends some 40 nautical miles from land and is the second largest marine reserve in the world. Despite this, the lucrative fishing markets for sea cucumbers, along with illegal shark finning has had a devastating effect. Both sea cucumber and lobster populations have been seriously depleted and there is intense pressure to expand fishing rights.

Research is ongoing but, as yet, there is limited data on how these changes put pressure on migratory marine species, such as whales and whale sharks, and equally important is how this impacts the land-based species – marine iguanas, the indigenous Galápagos penguin and even the Galápagos hawk (below) are all also reliant on the sea. More information is at galapagospark.org and darwinfoundation.org

Conditions		
Seasons	Weather patterns are less relevant than the seasons in which specific animal species can be seen. The water is cold all year round.	
Visibility	10-40 m	
Currents	Unpredictable and can be strong	
Temperatures	Air 30-34°C; water 13-28°C	
Wet suit	5 mm full body suit minimum in summer 7 mm semi-dry minimum in winter	
Training	On land	
Nitrox	Can be pre-booked	
Deco chambers	Puerto Ayora; there are no airlift facilities	

Diversity	
reef area 50 km²	
HARD CORALS	25
FISH SPECIES	493
ENDEMIC FISH SPECIES	35
FISH UNDER THREAT	46

All diversity figures are approximate

Galápagos Dive sites

| Central zone ▶▶ p126 | Northern zone ▶▶ p128 | Western zone ▶▶ p130 |

 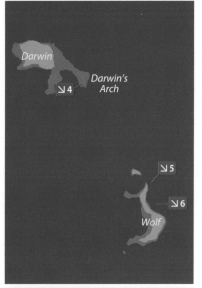 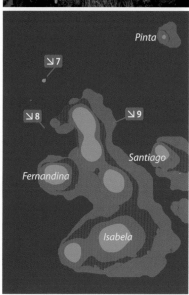

Log Book

↘1	**Gordon Rocks**
↘2	**Cousins Rock**
↘3	**Bartolomé**

→ **Isla Lobos:** gentle dive site occupied by gangs of playful juvenile sea lions

→ **North Seymour:** garden eels in the sand, eagle rays above

→ **Bartholomew Point:** rocky formations sculpted around ancient lava flows

---

Log Book

↘4	**The Arch, Darwin**
↘5	**The Caves, Wolf**
↘6	**Rockslide, Wolf**

→ **Shark Bay, Wolf:** true to name, there are hammerheads in the blue

→ **The Channel, Darwin:** swift currents that attract dolphins, tuna and, in season, whale sharks.
The Tower, Darwin: west of the arch with ever more sharks and schools of pelagic fish

---

Log Book

↘7	**Roca Rodonda**
↘8	**Punta Vicente Roda**
↘9	**Cape Marshal**

→ **Punta Albermarle:** marbled rays settle on the sand beneath vertical cliffs

→ **Puerto Egas:** valleys between sharp walls and, if you're lucky, a mola-mola

→ **Garcia Point:** turtles and harlequin wrasse brave the cool currents

dive
log
Central zone

San Cristóbal island on the eastern side of the archipelago is where you get your first taste of the amazing Galápagos marine wildlife. The dock is surrounded by masses of tiny boats, each one with gangs of sea lions sitting on every available surface.

The Galápagos' second entry point, Puerto Ayora on Santa Cruz is just 30 minutes flight away. This rather pretty port town is also the economic hub of the islands and will probably be your last stop if you are on a liveaboard.

Both islands sit in the centre of the Galápagos, the best place to start diving as it will allow you to acclimatize to local conditions. The waters here are some of the easiest, a little shallower and a little warmer than elsewhere, plus dive sites tend to be in protected coastal bays. The best aspect of this region though is that, post diving, you can take trips ashore to see the landscape and wildlife as the islands have 'pedestrian access'.

↘1 Gordon Rocks	
🧭 **Depth**	19 m
🕐 **Visibility**	good
〰 **Currents**	medium to strong

Not far from Santa Cruz, two large rocks protrude from the water, indicating the remains of an ancient volcano. The sunken caldera is marked by half-moon-shaped rocky masses, with the top level open to currents. Three large pinnacles divide the space; the central pinnacle is thought to be the point of eruption. You can dive right around the site, but beware – the

dive is also known as 'La Lavadora' (the washing machine), as currents can be fearsome. Schools of eagle rays fly past, along with a green turtle or two. If you head out through one of the channels, the currents attract schools of king angelfish and, on the outside edge, hammerheads. The outer walls are absolutely sheer and full of bubble-shaped holes – erosion, evidently – and each is inhabited by a pencil urchin or fish, while gangs of young sea lions race up and down the walls playing with each other. These walls are also good locations for spotting bright red Barnacle Bill blennies and giant hawkfish.

Razor surgeonfish by the hundreds; the tiny, indigenous Galápagos penguin.

66 99 Suddenly, from nowhere. a pair of big eyes appeared in front of me. After playfully staring me out for a second or two, the sea lion blew a huge bubble and then shot off to join his friends on the surface. Moments later he came hurtling towards me again, performing a somersault with elegant ease. *Amy Wheeler, freelance business journalist, Southampton, UK*

⌄2 Cousins Rock

🌀 **Depth**	19 m	
🔅 **Visibility**	good	
🌊 **Currents**	medium to strong	

North of Bartolomé, this exposed rock is home to passing sea birds and masses of playful sea lions. The sea lions slide down the walls when they see divers enter the water and then swim away again, leading you over a series of terraces that are smothered in black coral bushes in tones of gold. Longnose hawkfish and the giant Galápagos seahorse can be spotted among the corals, along with the unusual blue-eyed damselfish. Sandy-bottomed ledges house impressive starfish and gangs of whitetip sharks. Descending to the base of the wall, a tongue of land pokes out into the current, where several types of ray are surfing along with a school of pelican barracuda. Meanwhile, the sea lions are still darting around divers as they chase schools of tiny snapper, their favourite food.

⌄3 Bartolomé

🌀 **Depth**	19 m	
🔅 **Visibility**	good	
🌊 **Currents**	medium to strong	

No, it's not a dive; it's a snorkel in the bay, but it is worth it – even for hardened tank-suckers – as you get to see one of the few remaining colonies of Galápagos penguins. Sadly, their numbers are in decline. At just about a foot tall, they zip past underwater at the speed of light. You are more likely to see them sunning on the rocks, where they stand proudly over the much inferior snorkellers. The penguins also stand a way apart from each other as they have a strong sense of personal space. Other marine life includes massive starfish, blennies and small schools of butterflyfish. Snorkellers slip into the water beside a pointed rocky pinnacle that soars into the sky and neatly divides the island.

dive log
Northern zone

⬊4 The Arch, Darwin	
Depth	35 m
Visibility	poor to fair
Currents	ripping

⬊5 The Caves, Wolf	
Depth	28 m
Visibility	poor to good
Currents	slight to ripping

There's very little point in going all the way to the Galápagos and not seeing Wolf and Darwin islands. Only reached by liveaboard boats, they are regarded as the ultimate in diving in this archipelago.

These sheer-sided, rocky landmasses are home to birds such as red-footed boobies and frigates, but little else. You cannot make landfall nor, for that matter, can the other animals. Even the sea lions struggle to find resting spots. Underwater, there is one big attraction: hammerhead sharks. No matter when you come, these two outposts are famous for attracting vast schools of them. At certain times there are whale sharks too, but most divers come to immerse themselves amongst these strange, prehistoric-looking sharks.

One of the archipelago's most impressive landmarks is Darwin's Arch. The eroded remains of a long-forgotten eruption mark an oval-shaped reef that drops away to great depths. A gradual slope is covered in enormous boulders, and currents sweep upwards from who knows where to hit the rocky reef broad side before veering off in all directions. No matter where you enter the water, you seem to catch both surge and current, so it's a case of dragging yourself down over the boulders – admire the morays and lobsters as you go – then making your way to the sandy channel. Moving forward, you slowly become aware of the silent wave of hammerheads above. Some are curious and move in closer, and others watch from a distance but are hard to see. Visibility over the channel is not always good, as the currents lift the sand. However, your reward for peering into the blue may be a bottlenose dolphin – a frequent visitor – and, it is said, whale sharks in the winter months.

Kitting up on deck at the base of Wolf island's sheer cliffs, you look across at the sea and know that the currents are going to be absolutely fearsome – the clue can be seen in the swirling surface movements. Once you are down though, the site is a marvellous wall interspersed with caves and surrounded by boulders. You drift quickly along to a swim-through, although it might be better described as a suck through as the currents are as strong as expected. The caves are protected by the boulders at the front, creating a break for butterflyfish, snappers and divers. Hover in the calmer water to watch a few whitetip sharks then it's back out on the wall as a Galápagos shark swims by. Some are over two metres long and swim in front of a hammerhead while marble rays flit along the sea bed. At the end of the wall you can divert to a nearby underwater pinnacle but at this point you are likely to encounter some fierce washing machine currents so it may be safer to ascend.

Sheephead wrasse; giant hawkfish.

rock slide
wolf island

↘6

🕐 **Depth**	35 m
◐ **Visibility**	fair to good
〰 **Currents**	slight to ripping

Sometimes known as Landslide, this site is on the east of Wolf Island. Way back when, violent geological activity resulted in a rockslide that, in turn, formed a gently falling slope. Starting just beneath the surface at the base of Wolf's steep walls, there are masses of enormous boulders that have been shaped and smoothed by centuries of surge. Traversing these often requires a crab walk, hand-over-hand, to take you down to the open channel. This is a dive where currents are all important, not only for safety reasons but also because no current means no animals. However, when the currents are running, the pelagic life is incredible.

Stopping at 20 metres, you can watch the schooling hammerheads come in. There are at least 30 in the blue, often very many more. It's worth descending a little further to watch them hover above your head, but be aware that the deeper water can be like ice. Glancing back up the slope, the resident school of eagle rays pass by. They pause and take a look at the divers, dropping a little to let the exhaust bubbles caress their tummies. Up in the

shallows, Galápagos sharks cruise by and large green turtles hide in the crevices. The ascent to the surface is through a school of pompano so numerous they block out the sun-rays. As you glance back down during your safety stop, you realize there are a lot of silky sharks approaching. These beautiful creatures disperse the pompano but hang around to admire your fins, as long as you stay to gas off.

❝❞ **It was our first dive at Wolf. Mike and I chose our spots on the edge of the wall, and within minutes a steady stream of hammerheads arrived. As we were watching them swim from right to left, some of them veered off and cut up between us, almost within arm's reach, cruising around behind us and back down again. This pattern continued for the entire dive. I caught Mike's eye through the passing sharks and our thoughts were clearly the same: "Awesome!!" I could have stayed there until we hit zero psi!** *Carol Metz, veterinary practice manager, Raleigh, USA*

Galápagos Dive log Northern zone: Rockslide, Wolf Island

dive log

Western zone

Isabela is the largest island in the group and creates a barrier between the open Pacific Ocean and the remainder of the Galápagos archipelago. She is shaped a bit like a seahorse – which is appropriate as the islands have their own indigenous version – and most diving takes place around the seahorse's head.

Isabela's other claim to fame is that her position divides current patterns in such a way that diving in her waters can be like stepping into a tub of ice water. The cold Cromwell current sweeps in from the west, hits Isabela and Fernandina and then is directed north to Cape Marshall and on to Roca Rodonda. This, along with the fact that the region's volcanoes are highly active, creates yet another mini-ecosystem.

🟦7 Roca Rodonda	
🕙 **Depth**	35 m
◑ **Visibility**	poor to fair
〰 **Currents**	slight to strong

Heading south from Wolf, the first real land mass you come to is Roca Rodonda, the tip of a still active volcano. Descending over a landscape of barnacle-covered boulders, you notice gangs of small fish hunkering down in cracks and crevices. Actually, they are basking in water that has been warmed by streams of hot volcanic gases fizzing up through the seabed. You would think they were bubbles in a glass of champagne except for a hint of sulphur. Thermoclines here are extremely uncomfortable due to the contrast with the naturally warmed water. There are also some serious down currents on this site, so dives can be called off or aborted, which is a shame as the life is impressive and includes hammerheads, king angels and schooling surgeonfish.

⬛8 Punta Vicente Roca

🧭 **Depth**	35 m
◑ **Visibility**	fair to good
🌊 **Currents**	medium to strong

Just west of the seahorse's nose, this dive lies beneath a pretty cove which is itself beneath the eroded remains of a volcanic cone. The geography of the dive mirrors the landscape above, with hills and gullies, walls and lots of tumbled boulders. There is a lot of coral; the mola-mola, or oceanic sunfish, is seen occasionally, and green turtles are common. An unusual fish is the harlequin wrasse which is consistently inconsistent in appearance and comes in various shades of orange, white or black. It's a colourful dive, but the water can be breathtakingly cold so it's a relief to ascend into warmer shallows where there are schools of native salema, a small member of the grunt family and the favourite diet of fur seals and sea lions.

⬛9 Cape Marshall

🧭 **Depth**	35 m
◑ **Visibility**	poor to fair
🌊 **Currents**	ripping

This long sharp wall sits almost exactly on the Equator. It's covered in tiny yellow gorgonian corals, which are rarely more than about 20-25 centimetres long, their growth stunted by the surge and currents. The effect is very pretty, though, looking like heather on the rocks. As you enter the water, you see quite a lot of life out in the blue – couple of turtles, hammerheads or a few golden cow rays. There are unusual puffers such as the yellow spotted burrfish and guinea fowl puffer. Thermoclines can lower the temperature down to 15°C, and the visibility drops as you pass through them. If you make it around the point and into the nearby bay, some interesting smaller fish are seen, especially at night.

Schools of barberfish (left) and coral-clad walls at Cape Marshall.

drying out

There really is no better way to see – and dive – the Galápagos than from a boat, but if you prefer a land-based trip, then the town of Puerto Ayora on Santa Cruz has a delightful mix of facilities all in walking distance from each other. This is also the location of the Charles Darwin Research Station.

Liveaboards

Permits are restricted (see Undercurrents, below) but the following operations had valid ones at the time of publication:

Galápagos Master, masterliveaboards.com
Galápagos Sky, galapagossky.com
Humboldt Explorer, explorerventures.com

Santa Cruz

Diving

Nauti Diving, nautidiving.com
Scuba Iguana, scubaiguana.com

Sleeping

Finch Bay Eco-hotel, finchbayhotel.com
Silberstein, hotelsilberstein.com. Small, charming, hotel with their own dive centre.

Quito

Sleeping

Grand Hotel Mercure Alameda, accorhotels.com. International standard in the New City; free internet access.
La Cartuja, hotelacartuja.com. Colonial style in the old British Embassy.

Touring

Quasar Expeditions, quasarex.com. One of the biggest tour organizers in Ecuador; specialist boats with diving, naturalist and land tours.
Safari Tours, safari.com.ec. Diverse day trips and activity tours – cycling, mountain climbing, rafting, trekking and jungle trips.

Undercurrents

Politics and diving shouldn't be mixed but too often they are. A political stance may change the way dive, cruise and fishing operations work in national parks or at World Heritage sites. In some countries fishermen are encouraged to swap their permits for dive ones. The idea is to help protect an already fragile ecosystem by re-employing them in the tourist industry.

In the Galápagos a few years back, this strategy seems to have happened in reverse and quite a few dive boats lost their permits, ostensibly to fishermen. This confusing situation developed out of concerns over the growth in tourism and a desire to ensure that operators were kept in check. Some were applying for one permit then doing something completely different. From a diving point of view, it didn't quite make sense; the situation has settled but liveaboards permits are restricted to just a handful of vessels. Before booking any liveaboard dive cruise check that the operator has the correct permits.

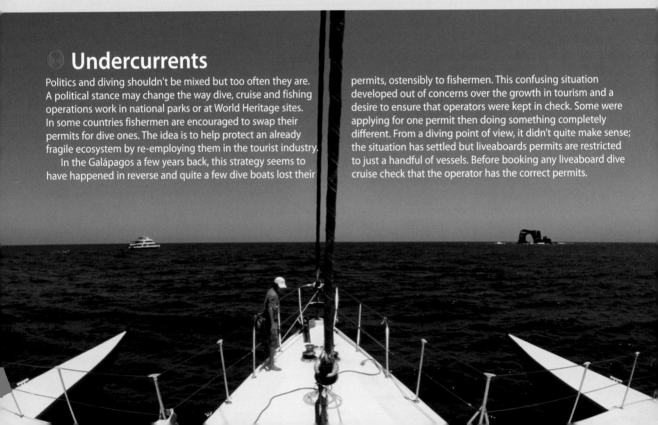

Days out

Isla Lobos A short sail from San Cristóbal, this island makes a fantastic afternoon stroll. Walk across the sandy beach within inches of blue-footed boobies; get an evil look from a marine iguana who is definitely not moving from your path, and admire a herd of sea lions snoozing under a tree. Don't disturb the mums with new pups, but it would be hard to compete with the noise of those babes suckling.

Puerto Egas This well-trodden nature trail on Santiago is the highlight of many a trip. The large natural bay requires a wet landing (jumping into the surf from your tender) but after that the walk around the coast is easy. Fur seals and sea lions live in rocky, lava-ringed pools and are curious enough about their human visitors to approach them. Marine iguanas bring their body temperatures back up to normal after a hard day's fishing by wiggling into sun-warmed crevices and, if you are lucky, you might spot the endemic Galápagos hawk guarding a kill. Native mockingbirds peck at berries on scrappy Palo Santo trees; herons stalk the rocks, and lava lizards run away at the slightest footfall.

Puerto Ayora The capital of Santa Cruz is a lively small town with a cosmopolitan feel. There are hotels with restaurants, restaurants with dive centres attached and a healthy selection of cafés, bars and dive facilities. And of course, this is the location of the Charles Darwin Research Station, where you can see several age-old Galápagos tortoises.

Quito

The capital of Ecuador was declared a World Heritage site in 1978 and is worthy of the title. Much of the colonial Old City dates from the early 1500s although there were settlements long before. Sadly, the colonists wiped all traces of the Inca past.

Take a taxi to the Plaza Grande in the Old City and admire the four sides of the square. The Cathedral on the west was consecrated in 1572; the Archbishop's Palace is opposite. The 18th-century Government Palace is north and the modern Municipal Palace is on the south side. Get a walking tour map (from the Cathedral) and head down the Street of the Seven Crosses, where every building holds something of interest: churches, galleries and museums – even one that explains the history of currency in the region, from Inca times to the present.

Next, divert to the Plaza San Francisco, a few minutes away. This colourful square was built over an indigenous trading market. The open-air restaurants are a perfect spot for people-watching with an icy beer and some lunch. Later, view the overwhelming interior of the Franciscan church, convent and museum and then continue exploring more of the Old City's cobbled streets. Many attractions are free, while a few want just a dollar or two.

Otavalo

If you are in Quito on a Saturday, book a day trip to see the Otavalo markets. This town is a haven for all sorts of artisans, plus a day tour will also give you a taste of the Ecuadorean countryside. Tours drive north from Quito, then through the Andes past several points of natural beauty. Stops are made at the San Pablo lake, Imbabura volcano and in the valley of Guallabamba, where the major industry is flower-growing. Stops are also made at several local cottage industries that are hidden away in small towns you wouldn't know existed. There is really no pressure to purchase anything; this is just about displaying local talent and traditions.

Otavalo itself is both a shopaholic's and a photographer's dream. Indigenous handicrafts jostle for space with fresh fruit, vegetables and local spices. The local artists and craftspeople sell their work at very reasonable prices. It is all amazingly colourful and lively.

The return route to Quito goes via the nature reserve at Cotacachi-Cayapas, which surrounds a sunken caldera and is backed by the volcano itself – though it's often hidden in the cloud layer.

The Galápagos tortoise; Plaza Grande in Quito; marine iguana; Plaza San Francisco in Quito; local handicrafts at Otavalo.

Indonesia

137
↘ **Essentials**

138
↘ **Dive brief**

140
↘ **Dive sites**

142
↘ **Dive log**
   142 Bali and Lombok
   145 Komodo

   North Sulawesi
   148 Manado
   151 Lembeh Straits

   West Papua
   154 Raja Ampat
   156 Triton Bay

   Spice Islands
   158 Ambon
   160 Banda

161
↘ **Drying out**
   161 Bali and Lombok
   162 Komodo, North Sulawesi,
         West Papua, Spice Islands

Don't even think about it, big guy! Serious attitude emanating from a four-centimetre long crinoid cuttlefish, *Sepia species*.
Rhino City, Ambon

destination
Indonesia

PACIFIC OCEAN

• Manado

◎ Sulawesi ▶▶ p148

• Balikpapan

Kalimantan

Celebes Sea

Sulawesi

• Sorong

Raja Ampat

◎ West Papua ▶▶ p154

Ambon

◎ Spice Islands ▶▶ p158

Banda

Banda Sea

Java Sea

◎ Bali and Lombok ▶▶ p142

Java

Denpasar ●

Flores

◎ Komodo ▶▶ p145

Timor

Timor Sea

INDIAN OCEAN

Indonesia is the largest archipelago on the planet, an extensive arc of islands that form the southern edge of the Coral Triangle, reach up past Malaysian Borneo and border the Melanesian nations to the east.

Not only is this a physically immense country, Indonesia is also where the world's marine diversity rankings are at their highest, with greater numbers of marine species than anywhere else on the planet. Every inch of water has the potential for mesmerizing diving: some is up-tempo and adventurous, some just as relaxed as you could wish for. Marine animals regarded as rare elsewhere are common here. No matter what it is you are looking for, chances are you will find it.

Despite the massive changes the country has seen in recent years, Indonesia faithfully retains a sense of tradition. On land there are almost as many religions, arts cultures and cuisines as there are islands – diversity is not confined to Indonesia's realm beneath the seas. From peace-loving Bali to the outer reaches of West Papua, this water-bound land is one of the world's most fascinating places.

Essentials

Travelling to Indonesia is simplicity itself, with flights from just about everywhere. There are also endless internal flights that connect distant islands with major hubs. If you need one, ask your dive operator to handle this for you and don't worry if they book you on an unknown airline: new ones appear almost by the minute. What won't work by the minute though, are schedules, as planes run rather like buses, hopping from island to island, so delays can have a knock-on effect. Airport to hotel transfers are almost always included and taxis are reasonably priced. If you fancy a day or two to explore land-based sights, ask your hotel or dive centre to arrange a driver and car to escort you around.

Local laws and customs

Right across Indonesia there are substantial Muslim, Buddhist, Christian, Hindu and Animist communities, with each one strongly influencing the others. That makes it hard to define a behavioural pattern for tourists except to say that anywhere divers are likely to go will be 'tourist tolerant'. The religion most people encounter is Balinese Agama Hinduism, which is not the same as Indian Hinduism. Its calming presence is strongly felt in day-to-day life.

Safety

Indonesia has had its fair share of trouble and strife, with terrorist actions, natural disasters and racial tensions in out-of-the-way regions over the years. Despite all that, crimes against tourists are rare and divers travelling to a suitable resort and using private transport are unlikely to encounter any trouble. If you are out at night, take only what you need and keep valuables concealed.

Health

Malaria and other mosquito-borne diseases occur in some areas. It depends on who you talk to as to how much of a risk this is, but it makes sense to always use repellents. There are plenty of medical facilities, but these vary depending on the relative wealth of a particular area. A trip to the doctor is just a few dollars and, for minor illnesses, local doctors are well-trained and know their stuff.

Costs

Of all Southeast Asia's destinations Indonesia consistently provides the best value for money. You could spend a fortune on an all-singing, all-dancing villa with a private pool and maid, but it will still be only half of what it would cost elsewhere. The variety of accommodation is incredible, from ultra-modern to traditional and simple. In areas where you are limited to a lone dive resort, it will be of a good standard and this will be reflected in the price. Food is much the same: a delightful meal in a small, local restaurant may be just a few dollars or visit an ultra-trendy affair a mile along the bay and pay much more. The local brews are cheap too, while imported wines are pricey due to import duties. Tipping is the done thing.

Fact file

Location	5°00'S, 120°00'E
Capital	Jakarta
Flights	Air Asia, Eva, Jetstar, Malaysian, Qantas, Qatar, Singapore Airlines/Silk Air, Thai, United
Internal flights	Garuda, Lion Air, Merpati
Land transport	Plenty but use private rather than public
Departure tax	International 200,000 IDR; Domestic 20,000 IDR
Entry	Visas required for most nationalities, US$25
Money	Indonesian rupiah (IDR)
Language	Bahasa Indonesia, English is widely spoken
Electricity	220v/110v, plug types A/C (see page 15)
Time zone	GMT + 8 (Bali/Manado), GMT + 9 (West Papua)
Religion	Muslim, Hindu, Christian, Animist
Communications	Country code +62; IDD code 001; Police 110 Internet access widely available
Tourist information	my-indonesia.info; indonesia-tourism.com; balitourismboard.org; komodonationalpark.org; diverajaampat.org; divenorthsulawesi.com

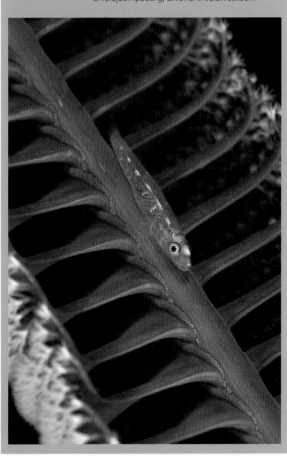

dive brief

Diving

Indonesia is the largest of Southeast Asia's countries, with an estimated 18,000 islands that stretch east to west for over 5,000 kilometres. Compare that to continental America at only 4,400 kilometres wide and realize just how big this archipelago is. Her myriad land masses sit surrounded by six different seas and two oceans and include around 18% of the world's coral reefs. You can take it for granted that the diving will be impressive. What's more, Indonesia's southern islands mark the edge of the Pacific Ring of Fire and the country falls completely within the Coral Triangle, the most diverse marine region on the planet. There are also many localized features that go even further to ensuring that no matter where you choose to dive, there will be a fantastic ecosystem to explore.

Another feature that makes Indonesia so special is the recognition that the marine realm is also a vital business. Areas that are easy to get to have many professional dive operations catering for all budgets and tastes, while for those with an adventurous spirit, distant areas that can be reached only by liveaboard are continually being explored and opened up to dive tourism.

Conditions and dive styles vary region by region and sea by sea, according to the prevailing monsoon. Surprisingly, this is good news, as you are not restricted to visiting in specific months as in some countries. Simply choose a destination according to when you can go. However, bear in mind that, at times, conditions can be challenging. Indonesia is the 'through-route' for waters that travel between the Pacific and Indian Oceans. This major current influences all weather patterns across Southeast Asia, as well as creating some spiky drift dives.

Snorkelling

With so many coral reefs, the options for snorkelling are endless. On Bali reefs reach right into shallow bays; at Bunaken Island off Manado, you can hover over the top of steep walls. More adventurous regions have fewer options, as currents can be strong, but that should not put non-divers off. Good liveaboards always ensure the dive tender stays nearby if someone is in the water. And what could be more alluring than snorkelling over a reef in Raja Ampat that is so remote that the closest island doesn't even have a name?

> **If there was only one country in the world we could dive, this would be it. We have seen it develop and change; we have been there both in peaceful and troubled times and we still love it the most. The marine realm is superb, and there is something about the people and their incredible integrity that keeps it at the centre of our affections. On the dive side, every season promises something fresh – a new area opens up as an old one goes out of favour, only to bounce back a few years later.**

A recently discovered pygmy seahorse, *Hippocampus Pontohi*; sweetlips on Tatawa Besar.

Marine life

It is important to recognize that Indonesia is regarded as the world's most biodiverse marine environment. Research studies have found more species in Indonesian waters than anywhere else. Big animals are less frequently seen than you might expect, but that has a lot to do with dive styles that focus on reef-building species; new fish and coral species are discovered all the time. The government has passed legislation that makes the whole country a manta ray sanctuary. The Komodo National Park is a World Heritage Site while Raja Ampat, Bunaken National Park, Banda and the Derawan Islands have been placed on the tentative list for World Heritage status. All this makes it impossible to list exactly what you will see, but you will see plenty.

Making the big decision

It isn't easy to recommend one area over another as they all have exciting dives in an incredible marine realm. An idea would be to decide what else you want to do. Bali is by far the most developed island, with everything you would expect from a major destination, including fascinating land attractions. In comparison, a liveaboard to West Papua won't suit if you like to have all the mod cons (no mobile phones or TV way out there), while Manado would sit somewhere between the two. Or choose an area by dive style: big open waters with pelagics and massive schools of fish in West Papua or the ultimate in muck diving in the Lembeh Straits. Whichever way you look at it, there will aways be somewhere exciting to go.

⚙ Animal encounters

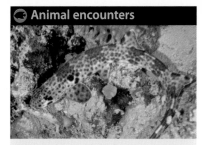

Countrywide: without a doubt, the marine residents that attract most divers are the small and wacky ones: from weird frond-covered Ambon scorpionfish and unbearably cute picturesque mandarinfish to almost any critter you can think of having a bad-hair day... hairy frogfish, hairy pipefish, hairy octopus. And then there are the recently discovered critters such as the Psychedelic frogfish, miniature Pontohi seahorse and the headline-grabbing epaulette shark that walks on his fins.

Indonesia Dive brief

dive sites

Big stuff, small stuff, wrecks and reefs; an occasional cave dive, a lot of drift diving, deep dives, shallow dives: it's all there.

Bali and Lombok are the first stop for many, simply because access is so easy. These two islands sit on either side of the biologically important Lombok Channel. This marks the Wallace Line, as first noted by naturalist Alfred Wallace. To the west the flora and fauna are Asiatic, while the eastern side is more in tune with Australia. The differences are obvious both on land and underwater. To the east is Komodo, where the channels between islands sit in the Indonesian Throughflow, which creates adrenaline-rush currents as water travels from the Pacific to the Indian Ocean.

The tortuous North Sulawesi coastlines are the location of two of Indonesia's most popular dive regions. The reputation of the coral reefs around the world-famous Bunaken Marine Park is well-deserved. An hour away are the much-loved Lembeh Straits, where rich volcanic nutrients gave birth to the muck diving destination that surpasses them all.

To the far east are Indonesia's frontier regions, although these are becoming ever more popular as flights increase. With the Halmahera Sea and Pacific Ocean lapping the northern edges and the Ceram Sea to the south, this is an incredibly diverse area and, while many other regions promote high diversity, there is no doubt that West Papua has something of an edge. Diving conditions are variable, like anywhere in Indonesia, but never difficult enough to be off-putting even for novice divers.

Bali ▶▶ p142

Log Book

- ↘1 **Anker Wreck**
- ↘2 **Puri Jati**
- ↘3 **The Liberty Wreck**
- ↘4 **Sekolah Desar**

→ **Gili Biaha:** coral-clad caverns that house leaffish and baby sharks
→ **Seraya Secrets:** night dive or muck dive, this is a renowned critter hunt
→ **Manta Point:** manta rays and mola-mola, but only if you're lucky

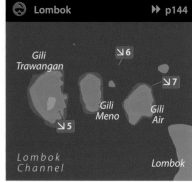

Lombok ▶▶ p144

Log Book

- ↘5 **Stingray**
- ↘6 **Simon's Reef**
- ↘7 **Hans**

→ **Manta Point:** not true to name, a site for reef sharks
→ **Deep Turbo:** interesting topography painted with whip and fan corals
→ **Gili Meno Wall:** an incredible night dive with turtles and nudibranchs

Raja Ampat ▶▶ p154

Log Book

- ↘22 **Manta Reef**
- ↘23 **Melissa's Garden**
- ↘24 **Kawe Castle and the Keep**
- ↘25 **Nampele Mangroves**

→ **P47 Wreck:** the remains of an American fighter plane, sitting upside down
→ **Cape Kri:** dense schools of fish accompany divers on a drift dive
→ **Three Windows, Boo Island:** windows through a pinnacle thronged by fish

Triton Bay ▶▶ p156

Log Book

- ↘26 **Black Forest**
- ↘27 **Little Komodo**
- ↘28 **Larry's Heaven**

→ **Giant Trevally Rock:** wobbegong and white tip sharks hiding under pinnacles
→ **Mangkawu:** night dive with seagrass and ornate ghost pipefish
→ **Batu Cave:** corals, fish, corals, fish and giant groupers hiding in crevices

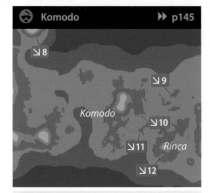

Komodo → p145

Log Book

⊿8 Mentjeng Wall
⊿9 Crystal Rock
⊿10 Cannibal Rock
⊿11 Manta Alley
⊿12 Tatawa Besar

→ **Copy Cat Copy Cat:** a superlative muck dive outside Bima Harbour
→ **Batu Bolong:** gorgeous current-washed site but often done at screech speed
→ **Pantai Merah:** aka Valerie's Rock, this pinnacle dive has a bit of everything

Manado → p148

Log Book

⊿13 Molas Wreck
⊿14 Lekuan I, II & III
⊿15 Siladen
⊿16 Mandolin
⊿17 Sahaong

→ **Fukui:** rare for Bunaken, a gentle slope, where turtles feed and giant clams reside
→ **Buwalo:** where dormant Manado Tua drops to unimaginable ocean depths

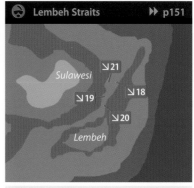

Lembeh Straits → p151

Log Book

⊿18 Angel's Window
⊿19 Jahir
⊿20 Pantai Parigi
⊿21 Hairball

→ **Police Pier:** seahorses and frogfish, frogfish and seahorses
→ **Nudi Falls:** lots of nudibranchs and, even better, the rhinopias frondosa
  Mawali Wreck: intact WWII-era cargo ship sitting in the channel

Spice Islands → p158

Log Book

⊿29 Tanjung Lain, Pulau Tiga
⊿30 Laha I, II & III
⊿31 Amet, Nusa Laut
⊿32 Karang Hatta
⊿33 Mandarin City

→ **Pertamina Wreck:** small cargo ship that sank beside the oil refinery
→ **Rhino City:** more fascinating tiny critters including resident rhinopias
→ **Lava Flow:** rejuvenating reef on the slopes beneath active Gunung Api

Conditions

Seasons	Generally, the dry and cooler months are May to September, while from November to March, it is wet and humid. Seasons depend on the arrival of the monsoons.
Visibility	5 m inshore to infinity in open water
Currents	None or, sometimes, at rip-your-mask-off levels
Temperatures	Air 19-36°C; water 23-32°C
Wet suit	3 mm full body suit, 2 mm extra for Komodo
Training	Look for PADI 5-star (or equivalent) agencies
Nitrox	Available on land and on better liveaboards
Deco chamber	Bali, Manado, Jakarta, Singapore

Diversity

reef area 51,020 km²	
HARD CORALS	602
FISH SPECIES	3,593
ENDEMIC FISH SPECIES	125
FISH UNDER THREAT	146

All diversity figures are approximate

Indonesia Dive sites

dive log Bali and Lombok

Two of Indonesia's most stunning islands are a game of two halves: one is popular and incredibly well known, while its sleepy neighbour struggles to keep pace. Divided by a deep and rushing channel, Bali and Lombok are contrasting destinations in all things.

The Balinese call their home the 'Island of the Gods'. The heady mix of a balmy climate, unique culture, delightful people and great diving all adds up to one supremely good dive destination. The combination of a rich volcanic soil and some rushing offshore currents ensures there are healthy and impressive reefs with diverse diving. Even the islands that punctuate the deep-water Lombok Channel can be fascinating, as they attract some large species, such as mola-mola and manta rays.

On the other side of the channel is Lombok and, to the north, the three Gili islands. Small and sandy, no roads, no cars: there is no surprise that these are so popular with long-term travellers. All three are ringed by reefs so have become a hub for dive centres.

⇲2 Puri Jati, Siririt	
🌀 **Depth**	45 m
◐ **Visibility**	fair to good
≋ **Currents**	none

Bali's shallow northern bays act as nursery grounds for all sorts of creatures. Puri Jati is a marvellous example, a muck diving site that stays under 10 metres until a long way offshore. A shelf eventually drops steeply to depth, but the principal interest is in the shallows. The bay has only little patches of seagrass and some large-leaved halameda algae. There's not even much rubbish but, when there is, it harbours plenty of stuff. The list of critters seen over a few dives is outstanding: coconut and mimic octopus, seahorses, juveniles of frogfish, lionfish and filefish. Then there's the cockatoo waspfish, slipper lobsters, squid eggs, imperial shrimp on sea cucumbers, seasnails and cowrie shells – even cowries with imperial shrimp on them. Nudibranchs crawl along blades of seagrass, as do tozeuma and ghost shrimp, harlequin crabs, dart gobies, snake eels, garden eels, white-faced stonefish, even a frogfish just five millimetres long.

⇲1 Anker Wreck, Menjangan	
🌀 **Depth**	45 m
◐ **Visibility**	fair to good
≋ **Currents**	none

Anker is the name of a local beer but this wreck has nothing to do with the brew: it's said to be an old slave boat. The wooden hull sits on a gentle, sandy slope at about 40 metres. There is little left to see, as the timbers have decayed almost beyond recognition, but they are heavily encrusted with beautiful soft corals and small fans. The surrounds are thick with barrel sponges and flitting fish. On the gradual ascent back up and along the wall, more fans and whip corals grow from cracks and crevices in the reef until you reach shallow beds of hard corals with masses of swarming fish.

Undescribed *Dendronotid* nudibranch; harlequin shrimp hiding in the reef.

⑊3 The Liberty Wreck

🕐 Depth	30 m
◐ Visibility	fair to stunning
🌊 Currents	none to medium

The *Liberty* is definitely Bali's most famous dive and part of diving folklore. Lying just 30 metres from shore is the broken hull of a Second World War US supply ship that was torpedoed by a Japanese submarine. She lay beached for 20 years before Mt Agung erupted and pushed her down the sloping seabed. The hull broke into several sections with the top facing towards deep water to form one of the best artificial reefs you will ever see. Divers come from all over the island – and the world – to trek slowly up the pebble-strewn beach. Conditions are not always easy: if the winds and surf are up, getting in can be a real struggle.

Visibility varies by season yet, despite that, this dive is always magnificent. Finning towards the hull you pass a gang of resident oriental sweetlips (they've been in the same spot for nigh on 20 years), then the wreck quickly materializes from the blue.

Start at the stern, circumnavigate the structure to the deeper bow, then finish up on the hull. Every inch is covered in life, so much so that it can be hard to pick out a gun, winch or boiler among the corals, sponges and crinoids. You can't penetrate the holds but you can see ladders, parts of the engine and the anchor chain. At the bottom, a little past the bow, a gorgonian fan has pygmy seahorses, there are jacks swirling above, a lone Napoleon wrasse in amongst them and, on rare occasions, a bizarre mola-mola visits. The rest of the bay is good too, with lots of critters on the sea bed, such as nudibranchs and crabs.

⑊4 Sekolah Desar, Nusa Penida

🕐 Depth	34 m
◐ Visibility	fair to good
🌊 Currents	none to ripping

Nusa Penida lies right in the middle of the Lombok Channel, so is ideal for drift diving. The Sekolah Desar (primary school) sits in front of one of the most popular sections of this reef, which is a gently undulating slope that leads to a short wall with large barrel sponges. Hard corals form a carpet that is punctuated by sandy patches and outcrops with gorgeous soft corals. There is some damage – from the currents more than anything else – but tuna, mackerel and turtles are seen fairly often. However, the highlights are just as likely to be small: orang-utan and porcelain crabs, clownfish on anemones and mantis shrimp.

❝❞ Time after time, we return to the wreck and it's never been the same twice... mola-mola, vast schools of jacks, pygmy seahorses and clusters of nudibranchs.

⑤ Stingray

Depth	18 m
Visibility	poor to fair
Currents	slight

Across on Lombok, the Gili Island reefs are a testament to the work done by the Gili Eco Trust. This site is a wealth of embryonic artificial reefs. The site runs along the edge of Gili Trawangan's southeast tip. A sandy beach and lots of boat traffic mean that visibility can be pretty low across the slope that drops from about 5 to 12 metres. Small ridges project at right angles to the beach and, as you fin along, you encounter both patches of coral and the various Biorock projects. Several are already well established, with new corals coating the various struts and frames. A little further north, but down at about 17 metres, a larger one has been built. Formed of enormous organic shapes, it is starting to show good signs of growth. The animals taking refuge here include white clown frogfish and a few extremely friendly octopus. There are lots of fish, cuttlefish, nudibranchs and, of course, the omnipresent turtles, a feature of every dive in the Gilis.

⑥ Simon's Reef

Depth	24 m
Visibility	fair to good
Currents	slight to strong

Possibly the best dive in this area, Simon's Reef sits above the channel that divides Gili Air from Gili Meno. Descending to the bottom at 28 metres, you swim across to a maze-like structure of gullies and reef mounds. The raised sides are coated in fans and huge barrel sponges thriving in the strong currents that flow around and feed the lower sections of reef. Everything is in pristine condition. Amongst the oversize corals there are several muricella species fans. These are known homes for minute pygmy seahorses, if you can spot them – stay near your guide! There are also plenty of angelfish and morays. Passing over another sand channel the reef starts to rise to probably the highlight of the dive: a circular section of *Porites* hard corals has grown into what is almost a pinnacle. In the centre is a deep cut that you can carefully swim through. This area dances with the most amazing numbers of anthias – it's really a spectacular sight.

⑦ Hans

Depth	23 m
Visibility	fair to good
Currents	none

This fabulous muck dive is located off the northern rim of Gili Air. Entry is over a white sand and coral rubble slope with very little in the way of reef structure, just a few rocks and patches of coral. This environment is a haven for critters so you can hop from one curious animal to another every few seconds. A crinoid reveals a baby cuttlefish; next it's the spearing mantis shrimp, followed by the most tiny emperor angel, then several leaffish, blue and black ribbon eels and a huge black frogfish trucking across the sand. If you have the chance to do this dive more than once, you can head a little deeper to where a small outcrop is coated in cardinalfish. This rocky area is known to harbour flounders and flatheads, so the divemasters will search those out, while small cracks and crevices are packed full of cleaner shrimp and hingebeaks. Elsewhere there are juvenile sweetlips, a few moon cowries, pufferfish and filefish.

Above: an octopus on the Biorock project; Mirko's Reef in the Gilis. Opposite: a solar powered nudibranch; Komodo's Crystal Rock.

dive
log
Komodo

The long chain of islands that stretches east from Bali ends eventually at Timor. The most famous of these is tiny Komodo, home of the world's largest – and most offensive – lizard and now both a World Heritage Site and National Marine Park.

Other islands are sometimes forgotten in the rush to reach Komodo, yet this entire island chain encompasses some of the planet's most interesting geological features because it lies to the east of the Wallace Line and separates the Indian Ocean from the Java Sea.

Conditions around Komodo can be hard – currents are unpredictable and, at times, can toss you about like a washing machine. Cold water upwellings can be breathtaking too, although it's not like that all year. However, the harder conditions often correlate with the best animal-spotting seasons. This is some of the most challenging diving in Indonesia yet the reefs are spectacular, with large and small animals on every dive.

↘8 Mentjeng Wall, Sangeang	
Depth	45 m
Visibility	fair to good
Currents	none

Only just outside the Komodo Marine Park, Sangeang's southern point disguises a fantastic dive. The upper levels are covered in lush corals but the real excitement lies on the wall where you see such curiosities as colonial anemones. It bottoms out at 20 metres to a black sand seabed with masses of critters, including crinoids with ornate ghost pipefish and sea whips with gobies or tiny commensal shrimp. For the eagle-eyed, tiny boxer crabs hide under small rocks. However, the biggest attraction is the nudibranchs. At the last count nearly 40 different 'butterflies of the sea' species had been logged on a single dive.

↘9 Crystal Rock	
Depth	26 m
Visibility	good
Currents	none

At the top of the marine park, this fabulous dive has a large pinnacle linked to a small one by a saddle. As you descend, you are mobbed by huge schools of surgeonfish before an even huger Napoleon wrasse arrives to lead divers down the pinnacle wall. There are phenomenal numbers of fusiliers, midnight snappers, sweetlips and rainbow runners, while reef sharks patrol in the blue. Heading back up and towards the larger pinnacle, there are triggerfish swimming though a massive school of jacks. Finally, reaching the saddle again, there are even more schools of fish and a mob of giant trevallies.

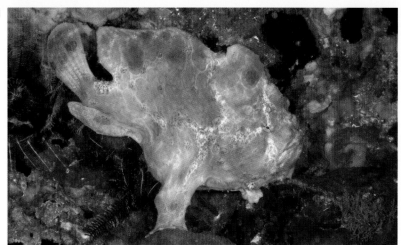

 ↘10 Cannibal Rock

🕑 **Depth**	33 m
🕐 **Visibility**	poor to good
🌊 **Currents**	none

Horseshoe Bay at Rinca Island lies to the far south of the marine park and is famous for its incredible diversity. Cannibal Rock can just about be seen from the surface. Rolling in over this submerged sea mound feels like rolling into a rainbow, as it is smothered in bright soft corals, green tubastrea corals, crinoids and iridescent sea apples. These are a sea cucumber with only a passing resemblance to red apples, especially as they poke yellow and white tentacles out to feed. Then there's the macro life: tiny shrimps in bubble corals, mushroom coral pipefish, sea snakes and orang-utan crabs. More critter life is at depth where you can see frogfish, pygmy seahorses and toxic sea urchins with their resident crustaceans. There is some pelagic life, but the visibility is variable so you may only see passing tuna.

↘11 Manta Alley

🕑 **Depth**	32 m
🕐 **Visibility**	fair to great
🌊 **Currents**	mild to strong

One of the newer sites in the area, Tora Langkoi Bay lies along the far south coast of Komodo Island. Offshore, a chain of rocky islets can just be seen from the surface, while beneath, a deep gulley cuts between the rocks. It is the movement of the tides through it that brings in plankton – and this attracts the resident manta rays. As you approach the site, you might be teased by a wing tip or two flapping in the surge zone, so you already know the mantas are in residence. There may be both Pacific and reef mantas and perhaps a dozen at the cleaning stations on the north side of the rocks or hovering effortlessly in the current swept gulley.

Giant frogfish and Bath's blenny on Cannibal Rock; a reef manta at Manta Alley.

tatawa
besar

↘12

🔽 **Depth**	24 m
◑ **Visibility**	fair to good
〰 **Currents**	slight to strong

Options, options... Tatawa can be a crazy adrenaline-rush current dive or an easy drift; at times it can even be both. It all depends on which direction you go, but whatever the currents are doing, this is an incredibly beautiful site due to the copious number and varieties of pristine corals. Starting at the north western tip, the water will often take divers to the west, almost as if it is making a point of showing off the most impressive marine life. A long stretch of reef parallels the white sand beach above; it drops from ten to about 30 metres, and everywhere you look the surfaces are shimmering with the orange tones of feeding soft corals. Punctuating the rich colours are small outcrops of hard corals where several different types of sweetlips hover and wait patiently to be cleaned by smaller fish. Further along, there are batfish in various stages, from juvenile to adult, giant trevally, a barracuda or two and several green turtles.

At different times during the day, it's also possible to dive from the northern point along the opposing side of the island. This is an equally lovely stretch of reef and, with a lighter current, you will have time to stop and look for some smaller reef creatures. Octopus are seen regularly as they wander about, and at the bottom of the slope, some whip corals protrude from the seabed so you can see their resident gobies, shrimp and, occasionally, the bizarre whip coral spider crab, *Xenocarcinus tuberculatus*.

❝❞ As one of our 'bucket list' destinations, Komodo didn't disappoint us: one day we'd be hanging out watching a parade of manta rays being cleaned, and the next, muck diving with seahorses, mantis shrimp and frogfish! The walls and pinnacles were a stunning display of colourful coral, and the sheer numbers and diversity of fish that we saw on each dive demonstrated how pristine these waters remain. *Mike and Carol Metz, veterinary doctor and practice manager, Raleigh, USA*

dive log
North Sulawesi: Manado

Bizarrely shaped Sulawesi is in the centre of the Indonesian archipelago but it's the tip of the northern arm reaching towards the Philippines that has captured the hearts and minds of both scientists and divers. Way up on this narrow stretch are two destinations with the most incredible diving. Their styles are diametrically opposed, yet they complement each other perfectly.

Sulawesi is ringed with coral reef systems so it may seem odd that most diving centres around the north. However, there are good reasons why Manado Bay, the offshore islands and the coast that leads around to the Lembeh Straits became diving hotspots. For a long time scientists believed that this small area contained the greatest marine biodiversity in the world and was at the heart of the Coral Triangle. Although research wasn't conclusive, exceptionally high levels of certain species were noted. The underlying causes are, as always, location and sea currents. This area is swept by strong northeasterly currents originating in the Pacific Ocean. In addition, many smaller counter-currents bring in rich nutrients that feed the coral reefs, which in turn sustain all the fish and marine life.

Among the most famous destinations is the Bunaken Marine Park, just off Manado. Established in 1991, there are coral gardens and steep walls with good year-round visibility and warm water. These conditions extend to the islands near Bangka just outside the park to the north. The other dive region of particular note is, of course, the Lembeh Straits.

☸ M13	Molas Wreck	
🌀	**Depth**	39 m
◑	**Visibility**	fair to good
🌊	**Currents**	ripping

Named the Molas Wreck after the nearest village, this ship is thought to be a Dutch cargo vessel that sunk in 1942. Regarded as an advanced dive due to the depth, what can actually make this a hard dive at times are the often extreme currents. You can go down the mooring line in perfectly still water only to find a complete change of pace within moments. It is worth it though, as the wreck is now a lovely artificial reef. The bow is at 24 metres, but it is best to head straight down to the propellers at 42 metres as they are heavily encrusted in coral and small sponges. Coming back up, the sides of the hull display good soft coral growth, as does what remains of the cabin. This is full of young fan corals so it can be difficult to swim through, although it is occupied by lots of young batfish. Many more are being cleaned at the bow where they can shelter from currents.

☸ M14	Lekuan I, II& III	
🌀	**Depth**	25 m
◑	**Visibility**	fair to good
🌊	**Currents**	mild to strong

The Lekuan dive sites sit along the inner curve of Bunaken's south coast at the heart of the marine park. Lekuan means 'curves' and refers to the winding nature of the wall. No matter where you descend, the topography is similar, consisting of a vertical drop coated in plenty of bright fans, sponges and soft corals. As you drop, there are small caverns where turtles take a break. They often have huge remoras sitting on their shells. Others swim up and down the wall, rising to the surface for a breath before descending. These guys are in great condition, with pristine, healthy shells. Eagle rays pass by and there are huge schools of midnight snappers. Napoleon wrasse are always about, along with blacktip and whitetip sharks, tuna and pufferfish. When it comes to smaller fish, it's the usual suspects like anthias, damselfish and butterflies.

☸ M15	Siladen	
🌀	**Depth**	17 m
◑	**Visibility**	fair to stunning
🌊	**Currents**	none to mild

The smallest island inside the marine park, Siladen is a consistently excellent dive. The sloping wall is thick with hard and soft corals and decorated by enormous clouds of ever-present pyramid butterflyfish. The currents are rarely strong, so there is plenty of time to pause and look for smaller creatures. Inside the blue vase sponges are tiny white crabs that are almost impossible to spot, so stick with your divemaster who will point these out. Scorpionfish hide in sponges too, their skin textures mimicking the surfaces around them. There are a variety of nudibranchs crawling over the wall and munching on the tunicates. Out in the blue you might spot a passing eagle ray or a small turtle. In the shallows huge swathes of leather corals compete with brain and staghorn corals, untold numbers of anemones with clownfish and even more anthias and chromis.

Bignose unicornfish (left); on the Molas Wreck; Rhinopias frondosa.

⬂16 Mandolin

🜨	**Depth**	33 m
◑	**Visibility**	good to excellent
🌊	**Currents**	slight to strong

⬂17 Sahaong, Bangka

🜨	**Depth**	33 m
◑	**Visibility**	good to excellent
🌊	**Currents**	mild to strong

Situated in the passage between Bunaken Island and Manado Tua, this has to be one of the area's more impressive dives. A sharp drop-off leads to a wall completely coated in soft corals and tunicates. It is a riot of colour that almost makes you forget you are underwater. In the depths, there are big fans and barrel sponges. Narrow shelves display long whip corals growing out in parallel rows to the light. Rumour has it that someone once thought these looked like mandolin strings. It's hard to know which direction to look: there are turtles and Napoleon wrasse swimming lazily past in the blue, while on the wall you find masses of small animals, such as balls of catfish and nudibranchs. Back on the top of the reef, if you spend some time around the bommies, there are white leaffish, orang-utan crabs and several robust ghost pipefish. Peering into the crinoids reveals squat lobsters and clingfish.

At the top of Sulawesi, but only a short trip from Bunaken, the Bangka Island dive sites are well worth a day trip. An underwater pinnacle dramatically breaks the surface; the surge and currents can be challenging but the landscape makes it unmissable. Dropping down, you pass a phenomenal number of fish. The current is doing a bit of a dance and attracts a big school of midnight snappers in from the blue until a whitetip shark buzzes them and they take off. After time at the base of the pinnacle, it's up to a plateau covered in huge step-like boulders with everything carpeted in the most stunning soft corals. The whole thing glows in bright tones of red, orange and yellow. A little further around the bend, you encounter a cluster of whip corals, thick with waving razorfish, then a tiny fan, which has an even tinier pygmy seahorse on it. The smaller creatures add a bit of scale to all the big things around.

Squat lobster living in a crinoid; whitemouth moray, and (top) frogfish nestled in a Bangka sponge.

dive log

North Sulawesi: Lembeh Straits

While many places like to claim they are best for this or that, world famous, world class, there is no doubt that this small stretch of water is actually the best at what it is: a muck diving paradise. The Lembeh Straits deliver what they promise. This is the destination for seeing weird, unusual and normally unseen marine critters.

The narrow and dark Lembeh Straits have become a 'must' for marine biology enthusiasts. With Sulawesi to the west and Lembeh Island on the east, the narrow channel between is riddled with dive sites fed by rich, volcanic nutrients. This is by no means pretty diving and visibility is always low, but it is one of the few places where you can be guaranteed sightings of some of the world's most unusual animals. You really can say 'seahorse' to a divemaster and they will ask "what type?" Although muck diving made the area's reputation, there is also some nice wall diving and a couple of Second World War wrecks.

↘18 Angel's Window	
🜨 **Depth**	24 m
◑ **Visibility**	fair to good
≋ **Currents**	slight to strong

Although the majority of Lembeh dives are critter-orientated, a few have pretty corals. Based around a pinnacle with two peaks and linked by a sand slope, the visibility here can be as much as 15 metres – not bad for the Straits. At times the currents are strong, especially across the sandy area, but there are plenty of places to get away from it. The plan is always the same: descend over the wall, down to the cave – the Angel's Window – then through that to the base of the pinnacle. There are fans on either side of the exit: one has the barbiganti pygmy seahorse on it and the miniature Denise pygmy is on the other. Ascending again, you can spend some time on the slope. There are small patches of coral and some rocks, so look around these for orang-utan crabs, imperial shrimp, leaffish and whip corals with their resident gobies. There are even squid eggs on the sand. Around the bend of the reef there is a small wall which leads to a rocky area covered in a purple hue. This is made by sergeant major eggs, and there are phenomenal numbers of sergeant majors trying to defend them against the onslaught of butterflyfish. (Curiously, this has happened on every dive we have done here across a period of 15 years.)

Soft corals in the Lembeh Straits.

jahir
pantai
parigi
hairball

⬊19 ⬊20 ⬊21

	Depth	16–25 m
	Visibility	poor to fair
	Currents	none to strong

❝❞ Anyone who has dived Lembeh knows that it's almost impossible to pick any one dive as the best or better than another. So we haven't. But here are three that hold special memories for us.

Lembeh dives are a fabulous hop from one 'pet critter' to the next; so much so that a dive log looks like a fish ID list. On **Jahir**, there are cockatoo waspfish, tiny stonefish, thorny seahorses, mating crabs, hairy crabs, decorator crabs... There are flying gurnards, frogfish in many hues, *Inimicus* (or devilfish), ghost pipefish and the Pegasus seamoth. At night the nocturnal creatures emerge: free-swimming snake eels, moon snails and tiny shells truck across the sand. This is a nursery site for flamboyant cuttlefish, with newly laid eggs often found in discarded coconut shells. Jahir is also a good spot for the mimic octopus; that's one below.

Pantai Parigi (Well Water Beach) stands out a little from the others as the sand is actually a pale beige rather than volcanic grey. Every feature on the seabed houses something of interest: a squat lobster sits on the fronds of a lonely crinoid; seapens are smothered in crabs and shrimp; a tube worm shelters five dwarf lionfish. A brown frogfish sits on the seabed, then you spot a tiny black one sitting alone in the middle of nowhere. This is also the site where divemasters perform their party trick of enticing Wonderpus out of his hole in the sand. What a gorgeous little octopus this is – all long gangly legs and beautiful stripes that he uses to appear invisible, without even faintly succeeding.

Hairball is all about the ways animals try to remain hidden. The seabed is level with black sand in every direction. There is a lot of fine silt (watch your fins!) and almost no landmarks, but it is the place to go to find hairy critters that grow skin filaments so they can hide in small patches of algae. Others use each other as camouflage: fire urchins reveal zebra crabs and other crabs carry urchins on their backs. A snake eel has a shrimp living on his nose and a coconut crab will be wrapped in three clam shells. Then there are the hairy critters: Ambon scorpionfish who are even harder to spot than hairy ghost pipefish, and all the hairy frogfish who are fishing constantly.

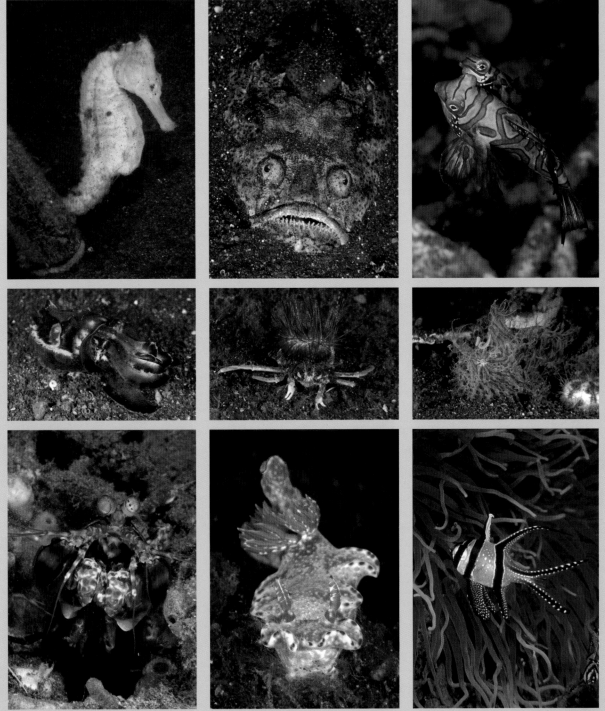

Critters in the Lembeh Straits. Top: estuary seahorse; the inimicus or devilfish; mating mandarinfish. Middle: flamboyant cuttlefish; the Urchin carry crab, and yes, that's it's name; Striped frogfish, hairy variation. Bottom: thumbcracker mantis shrimp; Many-lobed ceratosoma nudibranch; Banggai cardinalfish.

dive log
West Papua: Raja Ampat

One of the newer Indonesian regions to come under diving scrutiny is the western end of New Guinea. Officially known as West Papua but often called Irian Jaya, these waters are as remote as anywhere can be, yet are surprisingly easy to reach.

The eastern tip of West Papua is the Bird's Head Peninsula and lying offshore are a group of islands known as Raja Ampat, or the Four Kings. This lovely archipelago consists of over 1,500 small islands, cays and shoals. When the reefs around them were surveyed a few years back by a group of Australian scientists, their research registered the world's highest counts of corals, molluscs and crustaceans.

Not long after their reports hit the press a whole new dive industry developed. However, the momentum didn't stop with that one survey. Raja Ampat's reefs have been monitored frequently since and the numbers appear to rise with every new report.

❝❞Misool was a layered canvas of pastel fans that went on forever. Hundreds of fish of all different varieties. Sweetlips getting cleaned all over the place, pygmy seahorses, orang-utan crabs, beautiful shallows full of life, a living aquarium. When that feeling of euphoria does not leave, when you never want to come up, then you know that this is why we come all this way and what keeps us coming back for more.
Cindi LaRaia, president, Dive Discovery, San Francisco

↘22 Manta Reef, Jerien Island
Depth	8 m
Visibility	good to stunning
Currents	medium to strong

As the boat approaches this reef the crew watch for wing flaps and the race is on to see if there are mantas. As you drop into the water the smaller ones are flying right beneath the dive tender. The current rips across the plateau, pulling divers away from the entry point but in the same direction as the mantas. There is little coral so the strategy is to find some dead rock and use a reef hook to stay still. Waiting for just a few minutes is usually enough for them to return. Larger ones sit still, feeding in the current (no hooks required by them). You can creep closer but need to be cautious as these animals are still wary of visitors.

↘23 Melissa's Garden
Depth	25 m
Visibility	fair
Currents	can be strong

Melissa's is a flat, oval-shaped reef topped by three small rock islands. The entire area is coated in hard coral outcrops with small soft corals, masses of crinoids and fish – although fish in the singular is something of an understatement when it comes to describing the substantial numbers here. Sandy-bottomed edges are smothered in garden eels and rocky areas are home to octopus. Peek under a hard coral head to find a juvenile batfish still displaying his orange rims. Further along are snapper and sweetlips, whitetip sharks, a turtle and one huge barracuda being tailed by a school of small ones. There are smaller animals too, including imperial shrimp, mushroom coral pipefish and a juvenile rock mover wrasse. This is also a good site for spotting wobbegong sharks, while banded sea snakes appear around every outcrop.

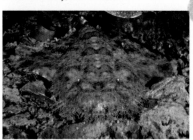  

A wobbegong shark on Melissa's; manta ray near Jerien Island; the blue water mangroves at Nampele.

⚓24 Kawe Castle and the Keep

🕐	**Depth**	31 m
◐	**Visibility**	fair to good
🌊	**Currents**	none

Kawe Island sits on the Equator and much is made of the fact that you can moor in the southern hemisphere and dive in the north. The area is noted for its dramatic underwater pinnacles. Approaching this circular, straight-sided seamount, you are met by forbidding walls that rise a castle topped with battlements. A gouge cutting through the outcrop is filled with a school of midnight snappers. At its mouth, a pink fan coral houses a whole family of pygmy seahorses. After descending to the base, a complete circuit reveals a small cave. This dungeon has a tiny exit higher up the wall. Batfish patrol outside like sentries while masses of small fish cower in black coral bushes. The sheer walls are tempered by corals and crinoids, marbled dragonets, nudis and flatworms. Another sharp gash in the wall is packed full of soldierfish and a lone barramundi cod.

⚓25 Nampele Mangroves, Misool

🕐	**Depth**	7 m
◐	**Visibility**	good
🌊	**Currents**	mild

This dive is a little notorious as saltwater crocodiles have been seen here in the past – and – yes, there were a couple of unpleasant incidents. However, these seem to be rare. The channels between the mangroves are swept by open ocean currents so the visibility is extremely good. The mangroves sit at the top of a slope edged by white sand and coral patches. What makes them so unusual, and worth seeing, are the small hard and soft corals and tiny fans that have started to grow on the tree roots. It's a pretty and curious environment. There are archerfish, and lots of small fish flitting about along with blue-spotted rays resting on the sand.

dive log

West Papua: Triton Bay

When it comes to breaking records, Raja Ampat may have started the trend, but nowhere continues the theme in quite such a spectacular fashion as Triton Bay. This relatively unexplored coastal inlet is now revealing more, and often endemic, species.

The authorities declared it a Marine Protected Area in 2008 but made sure that the needs of the local fishing communities were considered. Consequently, the reefs that run along the coast from Fak Fak to Kaimana and centre on Triton Bay are pristine. What you see – and the phenomenal numbers – are incredible. Sometimes the schools of fish are so thick you can't see past them. There is a downside, of course. The visibility can be low due to the incredibly nutrient rich water, but that is what feeds the corals and attracts the fish.

↘26 Black Forest (aka David Rock)	
🧭 Depth	20 m
🕐 Visibility	fair
〰 Currents	none

Black, white, but who's arguing? The sloping reef on this site is completely awash with black corals that are totally white. Shafts of sunlight cut through the murky visibility to reveal a snowy landscape. The vista is a bit bizarre, but hunting around these bushes reveals minute pastel cowrie shells, small pale-hued fish and young, silvery batfish. On the sand below there are nudibranchs that you have never seen before. A pink fan coral has pink pygmy seahorses and a nearby yellow fan has lemon ones. To the side of the slope there are a couple of pinnacles where Spanish mackerel and tuna are chasing the baitfish. Look in the cracks around their base for wobbegong sharks and, with a bit of luck, the recently discovered walking or epaulette shark.

↘27 Little Komodo

🌀	**Depth**	18 m
💧	**Visibility**	fair to good
🌊	**Currents**	none to ripping

This is the site where many of the species records were broken. The dive starts along a slope covered in crusting corals, sponges and tunicates. Waves of fusiliers chase tiny bait fish and pelagic fish swim after them. A cluster of protruding rocky pinnacles provide a backdrop for Similans angelfish, two or three types of sweetlips, gangs of curious batfish and groupers. It seems that every surface you look at and every crevice you stare into reveals yet another creature, so much so that you simply lose count and just enjoy the overall vista.

Swimming past the pinnacles takes you through some stiff current and then to the other side of the site. Beyond a raised ridge another set of pinnacles are completely plastered with soft corals and black corals. There are masses more fish that seem to direct you through a sun-filled cavern.

↘28 Larry's Heaven

🌀	**Depth**	22 m
💧	**Visibility**	good
🌊	**Currents**	none to medium

Triton Bay was the last discovery made by Indonesian diving pioneer, Larry Smith. The circular reef has sloping walls that lead to rubbly plateaus broken in places by some bommies. Descending to these takes you through the typical multitudes of fusiliers, rainbow runners and snappers. There are passing gangs of bumphead parrotfish before you finally reach a shelf, which is decorated by tubastrea corals, anemones and clownfish. There are dragonets on the sand and sangian crabs in sponges. If the current is running, wait on the plateau as a manta ray might come in. They do regularly.

LARRY SMITH
CMAS/YMCA/PADI M-6906

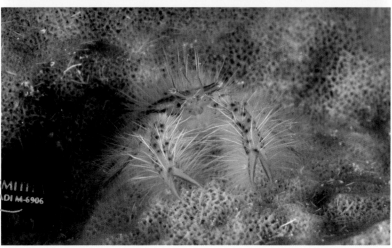

Indonesia Dive log West Papua: Triton Bay

dive log

Spice Islands: Ambon

Several hundred years ago the Spice Islands were the most important on the planet, the lone source of a commodity that, per ounce, was worth more than gold: nutmeg.

The fabled Spice Islands were so vital to 16th and 17th century trade, that they sparked many a battle between the great European seafaring powers. Now, they are visited for their mountainous rainforest interiors and incredibly diverse coastal waters. Ambon is an oddly shaped land mass almost divided into two halves; the water between is known as Amboyna Bay and it was this harbour that first attracted divers. Dive operators are now exploring further afield, around neighbouring Ceram and then southwards to the tiny Banda islands. These are dominated by the towering presence of active Gunung Api and are opening up to dive tourism.

In season, the seas tend to be calm and currents are fairly mild. Really strong currents are rare but, when they do occur, dives are often delayed until things settle down.

↘29 Tanjung Lain, Pulau Tiga

🕐 **Depth**	30 m
🔅 **Visibility**	stunning
🌀 **Currents**	ripping

Found off the west coast of Ambon, these little islands have very beautiful reefs but, at times, are subject to current patterns that mimic a washing machine spin cycle. All the same, this is an impressive area of reefs. Tanjung Lain is most notable for masses of Indian Ocean triggerfish. As you enter, the water appears almost black with them as they flit about obliterating the sun, making it hard to see the steep wall below, which is coated in feeding soft corals. At about 28 metres there is a rocky point where the currents are ferocious, but you can shelter in a bowl-shaped depression along with a blacktip shark, a bumphead parrotfish and a Napoleon wrasse. It is reassuring to see that these guys are struggling a little too.

↘30 Laha I, II & III, Ambon

🕐 **Depth**	up to 42 m
🔅 **Visibility**	stunning
🌀 **Currents**	none to strong

Also known as the Twilight Zone, these are the sites that first made Ambon hit the diver radar. Many suggest that the critters here rival the more famous Lembeh Straits. Laha I lies beneath a jetty and a load of fishing boats, then stretches away to the north. The entire area is very murky but with masses going on. There are bommies that house frogfish, patches of detritus that hide eels, crabs, saron shrimp or seahorses. In a rubble bed mandarinfish skitter about even in the daylight. At sunset they start mating, as do the dwarf cuttlefish. There are rhinopias that lurk at around 40 metres and you are likely to see fire urchins with their resident zebra crabs and Coleman shrimp. Other easy spots are pipehorses, the inimicus, stonefish and ghost pipefish.

Pulau Tiga; longnose shrimp; Flabellina nudibranch

amet
nusa laut

☸ **Depth**	25 m
◉ **Visibility**	excellent
≋ **Currents**	slight

Due east of Ambon, Nusa Laut is a small, pretty island with a landscape that gives little indication of what lies below the waterline. After mooring at the village of Amet, a ritual greeting with all the village elders takes place. They come on board to check out the tourists, which may seem a little unconventional until you learn that they have been diligently protecting their offshore reefs for many years. And that means they are absolutely pristine and full to bursting with fish. Once divers enter the water, they discover it really was worth the wait. An underwater promontory drops to a sandy slope coated with whip corals. This is edged on either side by a flat sand bar. A gang of bumphead parrotfish hang near the edge of the sand bar and just beyond them are two gigantic schools of jacks – the numbers are phenomenal. They seem unafraid of divers, continuing to move together and apart; huge waves in perfect synchronicity, a spectacular marine ballet.

Returning to the shallows takes you back over the sandy area. There are blue-spotted rays, beds of garden eels, dancing razorfish and a curious spearchucker mantis shrimp who is peering out of his burrow. The reef slopes are coated in hard corals, and if you pause above these, you see a few turtles and, possibly, a spotted eagle ray passing by. The shallows are marked by outcrops and gulleys, which harbour smaller creatures, such as tomato clownfish and shrimp in an anemone, a juvenile pinate batfish and starfish in many colours. Under another small pinnacle a cut-through is crammed full of feeding soft corals in myriad colours.

dive log Spice Islands: Banda

Famous for just one thing, the early spice trade, the Banda Islands are as lush and naturally rich today as they ever were. Back then, of course, it was all about nutmeg and the value of the coral reefs had not been recognized.

The five main islands, and a few small ones, are dominated by the towering presence of active Gunung Api. This mighty volcano influences the environment by supplying nutrients to the surrounding seas. It is an incredibly rich area: species from virtually every group can be seen on the nigh-on perfect reefs. The 'king' or raja of Banda is well known for protecting his reefs from any marauding fishermen and has done so for quite some time. The result is fantastic diving in a healthy marine ecosystem with mostly easy conditions. The seas tend to be calm and currents are fairly mild when they do occur.

↘32 Karang Hatta

🕐 **Depth**	28 m
◐ **Visibility**	stunning
🌀 **Currents**	none to slight

At Banda's eastern limits this exciting dive is over a peninsula where whitetip sharks swoop through schools of rainbow runners, triggerfish and snappers. A few barracuda appear, dashing into the throng, which then scatter rapidly making it an all-action moment – but only a moment. Along the wall the scenery is one of huge sponges mobbed by an overwhelming number of small colourful fish. There are mackerel, fusiliers and bumphead parrotfish passing by and, in the shallows, tiny juvenile, bi-coloured parrotfish that can't have been more than five millimetres long.

↘33 Mandarin City

🕐 **Depth**	18 m
◐ **Visibility**	poor to fair
🌀 **Currents**	none to slight

The most famous dive in the Banda islands starts under the jetty in Banda Harbour and extends down to around 25 metres. It is a stunning muck dive that can be brilliant at any time of day, although dusk is the best time to see the mandarinfish. Described as 'mandarins on steroids', these beauties are larger than any you will see in other places, even neighbouring Ambon. Entry is over dark sand with low visibility: this is due to currents running between Gunung Api and Banda Neira. They are not strong but fast enough to stir up the seabed. At depth you can search for, and will find, Colman's shrimp and squat lobsters hitch-hiking on toxic fire urchins. Back up the slope a little, and hiding in anything they can find, are banded pipefish, snowflake morays, coral banded shrimp, razorfish, filefish and octopus. There is much, much more as this site is prolific. It is likely you will dive it several times, which will still not seem to be enough, as you never run out of critters to spot.

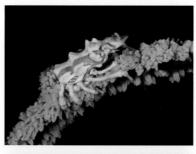

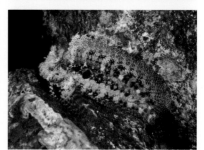

Soft corals around Banda; whip coral crab; imperial shrimp; snowflake moray; jewelled blenny.

drying out

The Indonesian archipelago has 17,000 or more islands and, sometimes it seems, almost as many dive resorts, hotels and liveaboards. Here are just a few.

Bali

This very modern island has everything you could ever want: any style, at any budget from simple to serious luxury. Some hotels have on-site dive operations but you are not obligated to use them; independent operators will arrange day dive trips as well.

Diving

AquaMarine Diving, aquamarinediving.com. In Seminyak, British-owned and managed with first-class service and top dive guides.
Blue Season Bali, baliocean.com. Located in Sanur for easy access to Nusa Penida. Customized safaris around the island.

Sleeping

Mimpi Resorts, mimpi.com. Well-located resorts in both Tulamben and Menjangan. On site dive centres and restaurants.
Taman Sari Bali, balitamansari.com. Near Menjangan in Pemuteran Bay. Bali Diving Academy is on site.
Tamukami, tamukamibali.com. Small hotel in Sanur; large rooms set in tropical gardens.
The Watergarden, watergardenhotel.com. The most charming hotel in Candidasa; each room has a private 'jungle' garden.

Lombok

There are dive centres and hotels on both Lombok and the tiny Gilis. The latter tend to cater for trainees so experienced divers should ask to do the more advanced dives.
Diving and sleeping
Manta Dive, manta-dive.com. Excellent operation on both Gili Trawangan and Air.

Villa Ombak Diving Academy, on Gili Trawangan, hotelombak.com.
The Oberoi, oberoilombok.com. On the Lombok coast opposite the Gilis.

For a different view of diving this region try Seketong on Lombok's southwest coast or head a little further east to Moyo Island, off neighbouring Sumbawa.
Dive Zone, divezone-lombok.com
Odyssea Divers, odysseadivers.com
Moyo Dive Resort, moyodiveresort.com

Bali

Although much developed in the south, Bali has a beautiful landscape, distinctive culture and is world-famous for its crafts, art, dance and music. The Balinese are Agama Hindus, an ancient religion that, to travellers, seems ever-present as it is interwoven through all aspects of daily life. It is said that there is a Balinese festival every day of the year as they are the essence of Balinese life. If you hear of one, go: etiquette requires you to stand politely back, but tourists are not resented.
Ubud This is the island's cultural heartland and full of galleries, music and retail therapy to die for. Make sure you catch a traditional dance, which will represent the everlasting struggle between good and evil.
Kintamani A cool mountain region of scenic volcanoes and crater lakes is surrounded by deep green rice paddies.
Bali Barat National Park Woodlands and coastal areas in the west house some of Bali's resident wildlife including rare birds, monkeys and iguanas.
Bedegul Mystical Pura Ulun Danau was built in 1633. On the shore of Lake Bratan, this is one of Bali's most beautiful temples.
Karangasem Dating from the 1300's, the first Balinese royal kingdom started here and left ancient palaces and temples.

Tanah Lot Bali's most important temple is built on a rocky outcrop overlooking the sea. It is worth seeing – but very busy – at sunset.
Bali Aga village, Tenganen The Aga, the island inhabitants before the arrival of Hindu Javanese, follow ancient customs and only have minimal contact with outsiders.

Lombok

Lombok is a derivative of the Indonesian word for chilli – and you will see plenty if you explore this rural island – but its size and the often poor roads mean you may not manage to do all that much.
Mataram The capital is busy and noisy but you can stop at the museum, which explains island history as part of the Balinese Kingdom.
Mayura Water Palace and **Pura Meru Temple** Built in the early 1700s by Balinese royalty, the palace has open-sided pavilions sitting on an artificial lake, while opposite, Pura Mera is dedicated to the Hindu trinity.
Mt Rinjani This active volcano last erupted in 1995. Climb through the National Park until you reach the rim and caldera lake, but the round trip takes three days.
Tanjung Not far from the Gilis, this small village has a fascinating daily farmers market.

Pura Ulan Danau in the mountains; Gili Trawangan beach; The Balinese in traditional festival dress.

Komodo

Liveaboards are the best option in Komodo as land-based dive facilities have limited access to some parts of the national park. Plus, being on a boat in Indonesia has other advantages, in particular, that the crew can monitor changing conditions. As some areas can be affected by extremely strong currents, the boat can move about as and when necessary.

Liveaboards

Dive Damai, dive-damai.com. Two luxury, custom-built phinisi schooners run by a well-respected team that have worked in Indonesia for many years.

Adelaar, adelaar-cruises.com

Arenui, thearenui.com

Dewi Nusantara, dewi-nusantara.com

MSY Seahorse, indocruises.com

Seven Seas, thesevenseas.net

Siren Fleet, sirenfleet.com

North Sulawesi

This region has many top dive resorts from budget to first class. Most have dive operators – and all other – facilities on site.

Manado

Dive resorts

Cocotinos Resort, cocotinos.com. In a picturesque bay opposite the marine park, and only a short ride to the dive sites.

Thalassa Resort, thalassamanado.com. On the coast opposite Bunaken, a professional Dutch-run operation with friendly guides.

Minahasa Lagoon, eco-divers.com

Murex Dive Resorts, murexdive.com

Two Fish Divers, TwoFishDivers.com

Lembeh Straits

Diving and sleeping

Black Sand Dive Retreat, small resort with the personal touch. Bungalows are dotted around lush tropical gardens.

Kungkungan Bay, kungkungan.com. The resort that 'discovered' diving here. Now larger and busier but still charming.

Lembeh Resort, lembehresort.com. On Lembeh Island, and built onto the hillside. Diving is run by Murex.

TwoFishDivers, TwoFishDivers.com. Well-located resort with a casual atmosphere.

For a different view of Sulawesi diving, try Gorontalo, 40 mins flight south of Manado. **Miguel's Diving**, miguelsdiving.com

West Papua and the Spice Islands

Facilities are limited in these far-flung areas, but the good news is that what is there – both dive resorts and liveaboards – is of a very good calibre. There are no resorts on Banda. For liveaboards, see Komodo, left.

Diving and sleeping

Kri Eco Resort and Sorido Bay Resort, papua-diving.com. Ground-breaking resorts on Kri Island near Sorong.

Misool Eco Resort, misoolecoresort.com. On Misool Island in south Raja Ampat.

Maluku Divers, divingmaluku.com. The only land-based dive resort in Ambon.

Temperatures rising

Indonesia is a huge country and, when it comes to diving, it's getting bigger all the time. As those who are pioneers continue to push a little further to find somewhere a little different, so the number of dive destinations within the country grows. And it seems that whenever that happens there is always a unique feature or new creature to be seen.

Take Gorontalo in Northern Sulawesi. This small city sits on picturesque Tomini Bay, where deep blue waters drop to over 4,000 metres. Coastal landscapes are of towering limestone cliffs rising vertically from the sea. Highly eroded, the walls lead beneath the waterline to complex underwater rock formations full of holes and crevasses, buttresses and deep chutes. One of the most unusual features of the bay is the diverse variety of sponges, including what has become known as a Salvadór Dalí sponge, *Petrosia lignosa*, for its surreal carved surface. Endemic species include the Blue-belly blenny, *Escenius caeruliventris*, and the Orange-back fairy wrasse, *Cirrhilabrus aurantidorsalis*.

In recent years, we have seen quite a few of the newer and less visited diving regions: we stayed on Maratua, one of the Derawan Islands off Borneo, and sailed through Buyat Bay to the south of Lembeh. We took an exploratory liveaboard trip to the other Spice Island, Halmahera, and dipped into the water around tiny Moyo, a hidden gem to the east of Bali and Lombok. It really doesn't matter how many times you go to Indonesia, there is always somewhere new to dive – and often something new to see.

Days out

Exploration on land near these diving areas tends to be focused on the natural world. Apart from an occasional trip to the closest town, if you want to add some history or culture to your dive trip, you may want to stop in Bali. That's no problem as many trips route through this island anyway.

Komodo

Everyone goes to the National Park to see the Komodo dragons. The world's largest monitor lizard grows to over three metres and weighs up to 165 kg. With huge jaws, muscular legs and sharp claws, it preys on live deer, goats and wild pigs. Youngsters spend their time in trees but adults cannot climb so hunt from the long grass. These enormous, ugly beasties are not to be trifled with: rangers escort you to the park feeding station. Solo treks are not encouraged.

North Sulawesi

Although it's not as culturally rich as Bali, there is plenty to explore in this area but you will need a whole day out to do it justice.
Minahasa Highlands Covered in spice trees and rice fields, local villages specialize in pottery or traditional house building. There is an ancient cemetery at Airmadidi full of Waruga – tombs dating back to the ninth

century. Lake Tondano lies 2,000 ft above sea level in the Lambean Mountains. The area is lush with paddy fields while nearby Lake Linow changes colour from red to green and sometimes blue. There are hot springs and many birds in the surrounding park.
Tangkoko Rainforest The most visited area in this region, the forest abuts the Lembeh Straits and is home to rare species of birds, monkeys, butterflies and the tarsius – the smallest primate in the world.

Spice Islands

Ambon The city is not a pretty place but it has lively market areas near the harbour; there are cemeteries dedicated to those who fought in the Second World War and there is a memorial for freedom fighter Martha Christina Tiahahu looming over the town. Victoria Fort was built in 1575 by the Portuguese; the huge walls facing the bay are still preserved while parts of the interior now lie in ruins. The Siwalima Museum is a charming but old-fashioned museum which aims to preserve all aspects of local heritage.
Banda Nutmeg plantations are still the main source of wealth for this island chain because nutmeg trees grow here naturally. Tours with a master horticulturist are quite something, as he picks the nuts off the trees and peels them apart, explaining the riches inside.

Banda Neira Town is an absolute must-see. In front of the Maulana Hotel is a collection of swivel guns and memorabilia. The town streets are lined with wooden Dutch colonial houses and some are being renovated – the small town museum is in one. The now deserted governor's palace can be seen but the most overwhelming sight is Fort Belgica, which hovers ominously over the town. This pentagonal structure has far-reaching views.

West Papua

Tourism really hasn't hit this area, not even for the natural world. Chances are you will be on a liveaboard that will take you for a walk on a deserted beach, perhaps to visit a fishing village or swim in a waterfall. Raja Ampat straddles the Equator, which will be announced as you pass over it with a stop made close by. The scenery around here is truly breathtakingly beautiful.

Travelling southwards, the small islands and coastal regions are breathtaking, with lush, deep green rainforest landscapes tumbling to winding turquoise waterways. There is a rare display of rock art on a cliff wall opposite Namatote Island, thought to have been drawn by wandering Aborigines.

Komodo dragon; Spice Island kids; Bunaken Marine park at sunset; the tarsius; deserted Raja Ampat beach; just picked nutmegs.

Malaysia

167 ↘ **Essentials**

168 ↘ **Dive brief**

170 ↘ **Dive sites**

172 ↘ **Dive log**

Sabah
172 Sipadan
174 Kapalai
175 Mabul
176 Layang Layang
178 Lankayan

Peninsular Malaysia
179 Tioman Island

180 ↘ **Drying out**
180 Sabah
181 Peninsular Malaysia

Creating babies: a mandarinfish pair, *Synchiropus splendidus,* doing what comes naturally when the sun goes down.
Mandarin Valley, Kapalai

destination
Malaysia

🌐 Layang Layang ⏭ p176

🌐 Lankayan ⏭ p̊

🌐 Sipadan, Kapalai, Mabul ⏭ p

🌐 Tioman Island ⏭ p179

PHILIPPINES

Sulu Sea

Kota Kinabalu

Sabah

BRUNEI

Miri

South China Sea

Sarawak

Celebes S

MALAYSIA

INDONESIA

SINGAPORE

Balikpapan

Kalimantan

Sulawe

Bali

Malaysia's diving is something of a double-edged sword. Divided by the South China Sea, part of the country borders the western edge of the Coral Triangle so is a rich and lush destination with extremely high biodiversity rankings. The other part sits in the Gulf of Thailand, an area that remains an outsider when it comes to attracting divers.

While both regions lie in Southeast Asian waters, it is the island of Borneo that is the most revered, its ocean-rimmed shores ensuring it is a magical, mystical diving realm. Descend into the waters around the northern state of Sabah to find a theatrical mix of pelagic predators living in tandem with rare and unusual creatures that are rarely bigger than your hand.

Westwards and across the sea, the smaller islands and reefs that lie off the mainland coast are totally different but still charming destinations in their own right. Pretty as a postcard, they can be a chance to escape from reality and are well worth exploring in the right season.

Drying out days are another voyage of discovery, as Malaysia once again demonstrates its split personality. This is the most multicultural of any Asian country, with Malay, Chinese and Indian influences combining to create a unique experience.

Essentials

Finding your way to Malaysia is far from difficult, although the island of Borneo, where the best diving is found, involves an extra flight from either Kuala Lumpur or Singapore and then another short hop to your final destination. Internal flights are frequent, with good connections, so you can usually get to where you need to go fairly quickly. Should you be aiming for one of the islands off Peninsular Malaysia, take advice from your resort on the best way to get there. The mainland has lovely seasonal diving but transfers are not straightforward.

Local laws and customs

Malaysia is Asia's melting pot. About half the country consists of indigenous Malay people, a third are Chinese, and the rest are of Indian descent. This curious melange of backgrounds creates an interesting and occasionally odd mix. On the mainland, some areas are strongly Muslim, so be sure to dress conservatively. The Borneo states are far more Chinese influenced, attracting substantial numbers of Chinese tourists but with quite a large population of Filipinos working in dive-related areas. Across the country people are generally friendly and helpful.

Health and safety

Apart from the usual hot sun and stinging bug warnings, there are few health issues for visitors, but be careful with drinking water. Offshore islands often rely on watermakers or importing water by tanker. Should anything out of the ordinary occur, both doctors and chemists are well trained, many in the UK.

    Generally, crimes against tourists are rare, but it makes sense to leave valuables like cash and passports in your hotel safe. Over the years, sporadic terrorist activities have affected parts of Borneo. Although the military presence is high on the islands, there are occasional incidences, which lead to government advisories recommending caution. Also be aware that Malaysia has strict laws on possession of drugs, with a mandatory death sentence.

Costs

When it comes to costs, standards and value, there is little to worry about in Malaysia. The island resorts tend to be charming but simple, with just enough creature comforts to keep most happy. The only downside is that there is little choice. The only island with more than one option is Mabul. Meals and diving will be included in a package rate, so your only extras will be souvenirs and drinks, which are not too heavily marked up. Should you choose to stop over in Kuala Lumpur or Kota Kinabalu, there are plenty of hotels in all categories. Tipping is not expected – bigger hotels and restaurants include a service charge on their bills. On the islands, most resorts have a staff fund box in reception or will leave an envelope with your final bill. What you leave is entirely up to you and should reflect the level of service you were given.

Fact file

Location	2°30'N, 112°30'E
Capital	Kuala Lumpur
Flights	AirAsia, Delta, Malaysian Airlines, Qatar, Qantas, Singapore Airlines
Internal flights	Malaysian Airlines
Land transport	Buses, ferries and taxis
Departure tax	Usually included in ticket
Entry	Visas not required for EU, USA and Commonwealth citizens
Money	Ringgit (MYR)
Language	English
Electricity	240v, plug type B (page 15)
Time zone	GMT +8
Religion	Muslim, Buddhist, Hindu, Christian
Communications	Country code +60; IDD code 00; Police 999 Internet access is patchy on the islands
Tourist information	tourism.gov.my; sabahtourism.com
Travel advisories	gov.uk/foreign-travel-advice; state.gov/travel

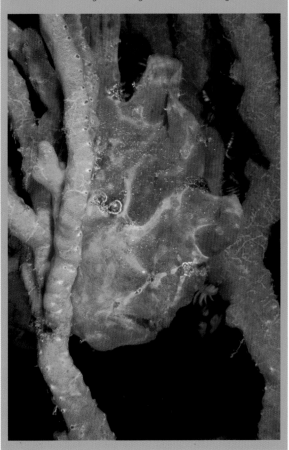

dive brief

Diving

Malaysia is a geographically widespread country with 11 'mainland' states that sit between Thailand and Singapore plus another two states and a federal territory on the island of Borneo.

When it comes to diving, Borneo – and specifically the state of Sabah – is the place to head. The name translates as the 'Land below the Wind'. Located at the top of the island, Sabah has 75% of the country's reefs and is washed by the South China, Sulu and Celebes Seas. The open ocean currents make for a diverse set of marine environments. The diving can be superb and your only problem will be choosing between resort islands.

Also on Borneo, Sarawak state and the Territory of Labuan, surprisingly, have little or no organized diving. Although Labuan has some interesting wreck dives, the unreliable conditions mean the territory is mostly bypassed.

Peninsular Malaysia, which lies to the west, between the South China Sea and the Straits of Malacca, has plenty of diving but can't compete with spectacular Sabah. The west coast is not regarded as much of a dive destination to those in the know. A history of heavy shipping, trade and industry has taken its toll on the marine environment. However, over on the east coast, a string of picturesque islands that nestle in the Gulf of Thailand are favoured by Asian divers who live close by. The diving here can be surprisingly good, but difficult transport connections mean it is regarded more as a weekend destination for training locals, especially as it is subject to seasonal weather conditions – diving is usually only possible from May to October.

Snorkelling

Location, location, location – it's all down to where you are. The diverse environments mean you can snorkel in some places and not in others. It all depends on the season, weather and sea conditions.

Marine life

The eastern coast of Borneo marks the western edge of the Coral Triangle, so the reefs there play host to an incredible range of marine creatures. Whether you see big stuff is all down to seasons: if you hope to encounter the hammerheads at Layang Layang for example, make sure you pick the right time to visit. Across all areas though, there will always be a fabulous and unusual small critter about.

> Malaysia is an interesting place no matter what part you are in, but for the very best diving, there is only one option and that's Borneo. The mainland has some real surprises, but every single resort island off the state of Sabah can promise big stuff, little stuff, more little stuff and lovely locations with friendly people. But perhaps the one thing that links them all is that the marine life is concentrated in a small space so you get to spend time in the water rather then travelling about.

The *Rhinopias frondosa* or weedy scorpionfish at Lankayan.

Making the big decision

If you are travelling a long way to dive in Malaysia it's a good idea to see more than one area. However, it's important to check seasons first, as the weather in each area can restrict diving at certain times of year. The islands off the peninsular's east coast are lovely, but experienced divers may find them a bit lacking especially as seasonal changes are most obvious here.

Sabah, however, has so many top options to choose from that it could almost be confusing. Each island resort has its own unique features, so choosing where to go should be based on what you want to see. Do you want to swim with pelagics on open water reefs or spend your time with your nose down a hole hunting for weird and wacky critters? Do you want a variety of diving or to be able to chill out on a beach? Travelling between the resorts isn't difficult, so it's possible to do a multi-centre trip. The only other thing to think about is taking a little time to see the incredible natural resources in Borneo: they are really far too good to miss.

Animal encounters

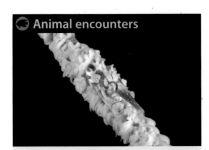

Sabah: for the big stuff, it's Layang Layang (turtles and schooling hammerhead sharks) or Sipadan (turtles, schools of barracuda and reef sharks). Kapalai and Mabul are all about the small and wacky critters, like seahorses, frogfish and the tiny *Xenocarcinus conicus* crab (above). Lankayan has its fair share of critters too, including the *Rhinopias frondosa*.
Peninsular Malaysia: colourful soft corals are a backdrop for almost every small, brightly coloured tropical fish.

dive sites

Sipadan, Kapalai, Mabul ➤➤ p172

From tiny, jungle-clad tropical islands to isolated deepwater atolls, it can safely be said that Malaysian diving pretty well has it all, especially around Sabah on Borneo.

Sipadan island is the one that kick-started the country's dive reputation and is now a legend amongst legends. Located in the Celebes Sea and away from coastal reefs, its perimeter walls drop to unimaginable depths, attracting many larger animals. Just a short distance away, Mabul and Kapalai sit on the edge of the gentle Litigan Reefs and provide a contrasting style with some of the best muck diving you will find anywhere in Asia.

Around the top of Borneo and moving into Sulu Sea, Lankayan island is a nature lover's retreat, with nesting turtles on land and a series of flat plateaux that gradually slope down to hard coral-clad shelves and a few small wrecks.

Big animal lovers are also attracted to remote Layang Layang atoll way off in the South China Sea. Nicknamed the 'Jewel of the Borneo Banks', this isolated destination has deep, open-water diving, outstanding visibility and – in season – hordes of pelagic species including hammerheads.

There is diving across on the mainland and the best is around the small, pretty islands in the Gulf of Thailand. Despite it being a strictly seasonal area, there are interesting options around Tioman island with shallow waters that are well suited to novices and trainees, plus challenging diving a little way offshore.

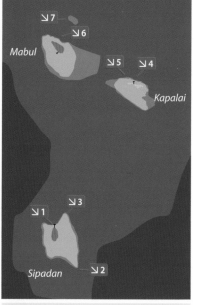

Conditions

Seasons	Borneo is mostly good all year round. However, winds patterns between October and April can restrict diving elsewhere.	
Visibility	From 5 m inshore to 40 m in open water	
Currents	Can be strong	
Temperatures	Air 22-32°C; water 26-31°C	
Wet suit	3 mm full body suit	
Training	Courses are not common – ask in advance	
Nitrox	On Layang Layang and some resorts on Mabul	
Deco chambers	Kuantan, Labuan, Singapore	

Diversity

	reef area 3,600 km²
HARD CORALS	568
FISH SPECIES	1,390
ENDEMIC FISH SPECIES	50
FISH UNDER THREAT	75

All diversity figures are approximate

Log Book

- **⬊1 Sipadan Drop-off**
- **⬊2 South Point**
- **⬊3 Barracuda Point**
- → **Mid Reef:** giant fans and black corals decorate a current fed wall
- → **Turtle Patch:** true to its name, with turtles resting on a shallow sand patch
- **⬊4 Kapalai Jetty & House Reef**
- **⬊5 Mid Reef**
- → **Recep 1:** tiny critter followed by tiny critter, followed by... you know the drill
- → **Mantis Ground:** another high-voltage dive with ground-hugging critters
- **⬊6 Paradise 1**
- **⬊7 The Oil Rig**
- → **Coral Reef Garden:** cuttlefish laying eggs on logs and stonefish in the sand
- → **Paradise 2:** clownfish and batfish by day, mandarinfish at dusk

Layang Layang ▶▶ p176

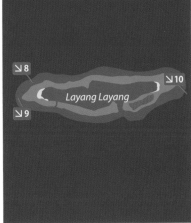

↘8
Layang Layang
↘9
↘10

Lankayan ▶▶ p178

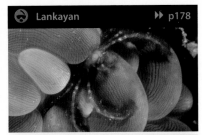

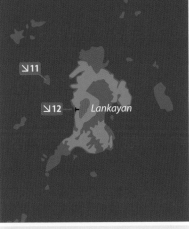

↘11
↘12 ► Lankayan

Tioman Island ▶▶ p179

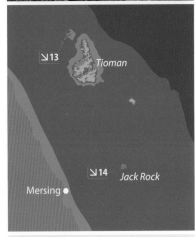

↘13 Tioman

↘14 Jack Rock

Mersing ●

Log Book

↘8 **Wrasse Strip**
↘9 **The Valley**
↘10 **Dogtooth Lair**

→ **Sharks Cave:** not so many sharks but an amazing vertical wall

→ **The Lagoon:** often overlooked but a fascinating and shallow fish nursery

→ **D-wall:** sometimes tricky but worth it in season if the hammerheads are about

Log Book

↘11 **Froggie Fort**
↘12 **House Reef & Jetty Wreck**

→ **Jawfish Lair:** resident giant jawfish and a friendly nurse shark or two

→ **Lankayan Wreck:** the remains of an illegal wooden fishing trawler

→ **Twin City:** two sea mounds separated by a gully, both rich in macro critters

Log Book

↘13 **Tiger Reef**
↘14 **Jack Rock**

→ **Pulau Chebeh:** gigantic boulders and swim-throughs painted in soft corals

→ **Pulau Jahat:** translating as Naughty Island, there's nothing naughty about it

→ **Bahara Rocks:** beneath the lighthouse, a pinnacle with soft and hard corals

Endangered oceans

Every six months, for over 15 years, a dedicated team of conservationists have been monitoring species of fish and invertebrates at sites in the Tun Sakaran Marine Park off Semporna, providing an overview of the health of the reefs. Although this is a protected area, sadly fish bombing does still occur here, as in many parts of Southeast Asia.

Yet there is hope! The Semporna Islands Project is working to stamp out this destructive activity in the Tun Sakaran Marine Park, with the cooperation of the local people, who depend on the reefs for their livelihoods.

For me, conservation is about people living in harmony with their surroundings. I became involved in this project to play an active role in the protection of the reefs and islands whilst empowering local people and enabling them to participate in the preservation of their park. A Community Ranger Scheme has been set up and, through education and awareness campaigns, we hope that the reefs will recover and the exceptionally high biodiversity can be safeguarded for the benefit of both visitors and local people.

Although it broke my heart to see the effects of destructive fishing practices, every dive gave me renewed hope. In between counting sea urchins and recording rubble instead of coral, many rare and remarkable creatures can be found. The nudibranchs, mantis shrimps, moray eels and lobsters, mean it is always worth looking closely at what seems at first to be a barren reef.

Helen Brunt, Sabah Coordinator, Semporna Islands Project

dive log Sabah: Sipadan

Sipadan is a dive legend the world over, one of those destinations that everyone knows about and wants to see. So much so that, in 2004, a move was made to turn the island into a World Heritage Site.

This deep green, circular island is rimmed by bleached white sand and encapsulated by a perfect blue sea. Sipadan is also tiny with only about a dozen dive sites. After concerns were voiced that the increasing numbers of divers were damaging the fragile ecosystem, resort operators were asked to leave, and a rehabilitation programme commenced. You can still dive Sipadan from nearby Mabul and Kapalai but numbers are restricted. Time will tell how much this policy helps to regenerate the environment and reef system.

Regardless, if you are looking to see big stuff, then Sipadan has it. Turtles are so prolific and inquisitive, they follow you around. There are phenomenal numbers of schooling barracudas, and reef sharks are easy to spot. There are small animals to hunt for in the shallows, when conditions allow, but the majority of dives are done as drifts; although they are not always that strong, the currents can quickly turn fierce, resulting in an about-face halfway through a dive.

➘1 Sipadan Drop-Off	
Depth	35 m
Visibility	fair to good
Currents	slight to strong

What made Sipadan so popular was the jetty drop-off. You could simply wander off the beach and onto the amazing wall. It was known as the best house reef in the world for many a year. Within a 10 metre or so fin, you can slip over the lip of the reef and find schools of batfish or jacks right there to greet you. You descend past small crevices and overhangs all painted with brightly coloured coral and every tropical fish imaginable. It is likely that you will see at least a shark or two, and a dozen or so turtles. At night, the shallows are alive with crabs and shrimp, the sandy beach area has shells and gobies, and beneath the jetty are many urchins, starfish and schools of catfish. To the east of the jetty, at around 18 metres, is the entrance to Turtle Cave, a series of interconnecting caverns. It is fairly dangerous inside, and full of the remains of drowned turtles: it is thought they go in at night and get lost as there is no light to guide them back out. Beware – the same could happen to divers who enter without both a torch and a divemaster.

➘2 South Point	
Depth	25 m
Visibility	fair to stunning
Currents	mild to strong

The furthest site from the island's jetty, South Point is not at all dissimilar to the neighbouring dives. In fact, nearly all the sites here have a similar profile. The island is rimmed by a steep wall that is said to eventually drop to over 700 metres. It is topped by a sloping plateau where the corals can be colourful, depending on whether the currents have encouraged them out to feed. However, where this site stands out is that it seems to be a haven for all the island's turtles. Although some people report diving here and not seeing a single one, usually there are so many that you can hardly move past them. They are incredibly inquisitive and not at all afraid of divers. One can be feeding on a coral outcrop (attracting masked and imperial angelfish or butterflyfish who scavenge for its scraps), until it sees some divers and decides they are far more interesting. Then it will desert its meal and swim over to join them. The corals on the top of the reef are a little scrappy, but you may spot a few whitetip sharks or small school of bumphead parrotfish.

Leopard shark
www.whitemanta.com

KAPALAI

Longnose hawkfish in a fan coral.

↘3 barracuda point

🧭 **Depth**	28 m
◐ **Visibility**	good to stunning
〰 **Currents**	mild to ripping

Perhaps Sipadan's most famous dive, this submerged point sits to the east of the boat jetty. The wall is sheer, and crusting corals and sponges make it incredibly colourful. As you descend, you see the full quota of schooling small fish – angels, butterflies, tangs and surgeons – but most outstanding are the number and size of the black coral bushes. Almost every one has a longnose hawkfish in it, or is swarmed by lionfish, and interspersed with gigantic fans corals.

The ever-present groups of turtles swim along with divers to keep them company; sometimes one or two will have a batfish hovering beneath his belly.

At the top of the reef the corals are less impressive, but gangs of whitetip sharks rest peacefully on the sand. Grey reef sharks approach from behind, heading for the school of jacks that are just around the bend. More turtles visit cleaning stations, while Napoleon wrasse and giant tuna pass by in the blue.

Although the dive starts along the wall and drifts towards them, the infamous barracuda school is usually spotted from the surface. There are hundreds in the ball, maybe thousands, sitting right on the top of the reef. They move slowly in perfect synchronicity, sliding apart for just a few moments only to reconfigure swiftly into a perfect spiral – simply breathtaking.

dive log

Sabah: Kapalai

Once overshadowed by its more famous neighbour, Kapalai has become known as one of Southeast Asia's best macro dive destinations.

Although charted on older maps, there is only a sand bar remaining from what was once a small island. This flat topography is similar underwater, yet the visibility here is reasonable as reef mounds are washed daily by the tides. Corals tend to be low lying to the contours of the landscape, but they're all pretty healthy and a haven for masses of weird and wacky critters.

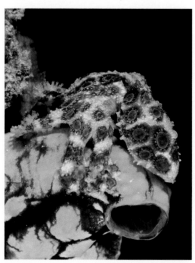

↘4 Kapalai Jetty & House Reef	
Depth	25 m
Visibility	fair to good
Currents	slight

Extending over a small drop-off, this is a dive with almost too many options: stay under the jetty in the lagoon; drop down and turn left, or right; or head down to the wreck at the bottom of the reef. Day or night, there will always be an amazing critter to see. On the fishing boat wreck are frogfish decorated with hairy splotches, morays neatly lined up in a row and, as you head back up the to the shallow reef wall, you see the spearing mantis shrimp in the sand. Sponges and hydroids camouflage families of ornate ghost pipefish, and squat lobsters sit in crinoids. There are decorator crabs, slipper lobsters and tiny shrimp.

The more exotic creatures regularly seen here include flamboyant cuttlefish and the incredible blue-ringed octopus. At dusk, visit Mandarin Valley, a patch of the reef that is just a metre or so square but where a colony of minute, glamorous mandarinfish emerge to feed and mate. As it gets dark, swim beneath the jetty to see crocodilefish and peacock flounders, sleeping parrots in their mucous bubbles and even baby nurse sharks on a fly by.

↘5 Mid Reef	
Depth	21 m
Visibility	fair to good
Currents	slight to medium

Mid Reef and the neighbouring dive site, Mantis Ground are often done together. However, if you stop to look for all the animals, you won't have time. There may be a matching pair of extravagant solar powered nudibranchs crawling on the sand, and the whip corals that reach up from it are rich with tiny animals like the well camouflaged *Xenocarcinus conicus* crab and even tinier 'bumble bee' shrimp, all jostling for prime position on the narrow surface. There are small gobies and jawfish on the seafloor, plus this site has some bigger animals, including a gang of turtles. Some healthy fan corals house spider crabs, longnose and pixie hawkfish. On our first dive at this site, one patch of finger sponges had the tiniest of pink frogfish. A year later we returned, and he was still in exactly the same place. The divemasters monitored him for the whole year and watched him grow into an adult.

Kapalai critters: an angry blue-ringed octopus and the colours of a flamboyant cuttlefish.

dive log

Sabah: Mabul

Mabul is the largest island in this area. For a long time, it was home only to the sea gypsies of the Bajau tribe but, like Kapalai, it is now a macro destination to die for.

Conditions are easy enough although, there are occasional currents that may divert a chosen dive to another day. Dives tend to be from shore and focus on sites close to the resorts, as each has a stunning house reef. If you are staying at Kapalai, the most visited sites are those under the Oil Rig and a couple of the shallow ones near to it.

⑥ Paradise 1	
🕙 **Depth**	21 m
🔆 **Visibility**	fair to good
🌊 **Currents**	none to strong

This is a cracking tour where you hop from one weird animal to the next with hardly a moment to admire each: flying gurnards, fingered dragonets, dwarf lionfish, snake eels, inimicus (or devilfish) and filefish. Even weirder fish include hairy decorated filefish, a wacky long-legged crab and longsnout pipefish. Mantis shrimp peek out of their burrows, small octopus hide in coconut shells and smaller blue-ringed octopus sneak into old beer bottles. Palm fronds get caught on buoy lines and are used by squid to lay their eggs.

⑦ The Oil Rig	
🕙 **Depth**	18 m
🔆 **Visibility**	poor to good
🌊 **Currents**	slight to medium

The massive, ugly oil derrick parked just off Mabul's shores is an exercise in nature's power over man. Humanity does its best to mess up the landscape, but nature has its cunning ways of turning that around. The pylons supporting the rig are eerie, reminiscent of a wreck dive, and swarmed by jacks and snappers. Below, the seabed is studded with detritus, yet the marine creatures have started their own recycling programmes: ropes have been colonized by iridescent sponges that shelter tiny gobies; building materials have stonefish squatters, and a giant moray called Elvis lives under an old cage. There are flying gurnards and crocodilefish carpeting the sand, ornate ghost pipefish in fans while lime green frogfish hang out in old car tyres. A pile of metal sheets and pipes has more frogfish in varying colours; morays and scorpionfish are everywhere, as are mantis shrimp and jawfish, cardinals and nesting sergeant majors. The list could go on. This is a superlative dive.

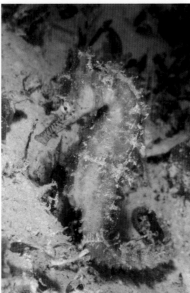
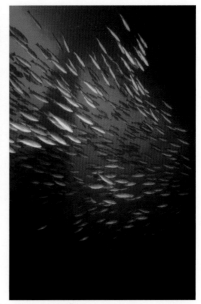

Beneath the oil rig, a frogfish pretending to be a sponge; seahorse on Paradise 1; the oil rig pylons mobbed by schools of fish.

dive log Sabah:
Layang Layang

The Spratly Islands are an hour northwest of Kota Kinabalu and, at their southern end, is Layang Layang, one of many tiny land masses whose ownership has long been fought over.

For decades, several Asian nations have laid claim to those nearest their territorial waters. As Layang Layang sits closest to Borneo, a Malaysian Navy outpost was built there to ensure Malay interest was not lost in the mêlée. And, as it was surrounded by incredible coral reefs, creating a dive resort as well seemed an obvious choice.

Layang Layang, or Swallow's Reef, is a submerged oval with just one tiny, barren island that sits on the edge of a turquoise lagoon. Steep walls, constructed of hard corals, drop away from the outer edge of the lagoon and attract masses of pelagic life. While the corals and reef life alone justify a visit, most curious is the seasonal hammerhead phenomenon. Around Easter, large schools swarm into Layang then head off again a few weeks later. At other times, turtles, reef sharks and schooling pelagic fish are common.

Conditions are variable as the atoll is so exposed: winds can whip the sea into a frenzy, and dive boats struggle to exit the channel to the outer reef. Currents can be strong and surface conditions rough. Late in the year, when the winds really pick up, the resort closes for a few months. Yet, in season, when conditions are good, they are very good and visibility seems limitless.

Picasso triggerfish in Layang Layang lagoon.

↘8 Wrasse Strip

🌀	**Depth**	35 m
◐	**Visibility**	fair to stunning
🌊	**Currents**	medium to strong

On the northern side of the atoll but at its westernmost end, Layang's dive sites tend to be sloping reefs, which makes excellent multi-level diving. Most of the time there is a current here, but it's a manageable one so you will have time to admire the reef. The gentle slope is covered in a variety of hard corals and sponges surrounded by soldierfish, triggerfish and wrasse. Many of the larger fish cluster under table corals where you can also spot boxfish, angels and butterflies. Just past 20 metres the reef drops into a sloping wall where there is a bed of waving gorgonians, whip corals and some lush soft coral growth. To the south of this dive is The Valley – if currents are strong you may see both at once.

↘9 The Valley

🌀	**Depth**	35 m
◐	**Visibility**	stunning
🌊	**Currents**	medium to strong

At first glance, this site looks like nothing much, just a flat slope with small crusting corals, sponges and a few fish. However, descend to 30 metres and the action starts: lots of small whitetip sharks and handfuls of large grey reefs appear out in the blue; there are dogtooth tuna and several giant trevally. These swoop to and fro as the currents push against the western tip of the atoll. A cluster of blackfin barracuda joins the throng, then, as you ascend, another huge ball of barracuda appears overhead. Up in shallower waters is a 'valley' scooped out of the reef where you can find large turtles resting, many juvenile whitetips under some bommies and a gigantic ball of schooling jacks.

↘10 Dogtooth Lair

🌀	**Depth**	25 m
◐	**Visibility**	fair to good
🌊	**Currents**	mild to strong

Lying to the east, this gets mixed currents. From the surface you can admire a racing pod of dolphins playing in the waves, while below, your profile becomes a zigzag pattern along the wall and slope. The dive site is named after the pack of enormous tuna that often lurks here, but it is equally likely to have schools of jacks and turtles – although every dive on Layang has turtles; you would have to be asleep to miss them. Rumour has it that this is a prime site for schools of hammerheads that appear in huge gangs around Easter, when the resort is at its busiest. At other times, whitetip sharks park at the cleaner stations for a spruce up. In the shallows, there are nudibranchs and ghost pipefish.

❝ ❞ Dive, eat, sleep in hammock under trees. Dive, eat, chat, dive, eat, sleep. Layang Layang is a relaxed and friendly place; the diving is superb, and although it was the end of the season, there was still the odd hammerhead cruising about. It was unusual NOT to see turtles on each dive, and I was starting to feel a little blasé about seeing whitetips, if that's possible...
Estelle Zauner-Maughan, chiropractor and dive instructor, Newcastle, UK

Whip and fan corals at The Valley; juvenile Clarke's anemonefish – this is the orange variation.

dive log

Sabah: Lankayan

A short distance north of Borneo into the Sulu Sea, Lankayan became a Marine Conservation Area after a survey in 2000 confirmed high biodiversity and nesting sites for green and hawksbill turtles.

Conditions are easy, strong currents only occurring every now and then. However, visibility is often quite poor due to shallow reef structures, proximity to the mainland and high levels of plankton. Diving is all about looking for the animals that thrive in these nutrient-rich conditions, although there are also several wrecks to explore.

Whitetip and nurse sharks are seen, and a very special treat is walking with blacktip sharks: the shallows are a nursery for them. You can stand in ankle-deep water and have 50-centimetre long babies swim around your toes! The resort announces the passing migration of whale sharks every year, but you can never guarantee them being there for any long-term planning.

↘11 Froggie Fort	
🕐 **Depth**	22 m
◐ **Visibility**	poor to good
🌊 **Currents**	mild to strong

Something of a surprise, the base of this sloping oval-shaped reef is ringed by rows of short, pastel gorgonians. And, beneath these is where you often find the star of the dive – a rare *Rhinopias frondosa* or weedy scorpionfish. Highly decorated and outrageously patterned, this fish is about the size of a hand. It is flat like its relative the leaf scorpionfish but has beautiful markings and fronds on its skin. Up at the top of the mound, a bed of staghorn coral reveals white leaffish among the branches, with adults sitting beside their young.

↘12 House Reef & Jetty Wreck	
🕐 **Depth**	16 m
◐ **Visibility**	fair
🌊 **Currents**	slight to medium

This is the site that gets dived most, partly because it can be done whenever you like, day or night, and partly because there are several sections to the dive. Entry is under the pier, where a rope leads to the wreck of a small fishing boat. There is lots of activity along the way: clusters of catfish, trunkfish and cardinalfish shelter inside a group of tyres, their treads coated in hingebeak and cleaner shrimps. When you reach the wreck there are puffers and lionfish, while decorator crabs and spider crabs shroud the slowly rotting timbers and a school of jacks hovers over the mast. On the way back, another rope leads past two timber pyramids. These artificial reefs attract nudibranchs and batfish. On the sand are cowries and blue-spotted rays. Finally, you could spend quite some time around the pylons and struts that form the jetty itself, as each surface is coated by small corals and sponges forming miniature reefs.

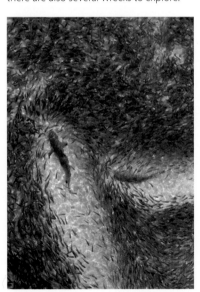

Lankayan is a nursery for juvenile blacktip sharks that hunt in ankle-deep water; one of Lankayan's wrecks; giant cuttlefish.

Malaysia's mainland is a hot destination for Asian residents. Both qualified and trainee divers head to the islands off the east coast to relax, do a little diving or continue with courses they have started at home.

The bays off Tioman Island are renowned for calm and easy diving, but far more exciting and challenging dives can be found a little way offshore. Visibility is never crystal clear, but the underwater landscape is reminiscent of the Similan Islands, with huge boulders tumbling together, creating interesting swim-throughs that attract a wealth of marine creatures. This is seasonal diving though, limiting a visit to between May and October.

dive log
Peninsular Malaysia: Tioman Island

⏱ J13 Tiger Reef	
🕐 **Depth**	22 m
◑ **Visibility**	fair
〰 **Currents**	none to strong

Off the north of Tioman, Tiger Reef consists of a series of pinnacle-shaped boulders. Entry is over the one with a mooring buoy at about five metres. You then drop to 12, swim through a crevice and make your way around all the pinnacles to see what is about. There is a lot of fish life with snappers, needlenose barracuda, Similans sweetlips and blue-spotted rays. Near the base of the dive site, in a sandy bowl, you might encounter a family of bumphead parrotfish and suddenly, all the stunning but tiny nudibranchs pale in comparison.

⏱ J14 Jack Rock	
🕐 **Depth**	20 m
◑ **Visibility**	poor to fair
〰 **Currents**	none to ripping

Named after a certain Mr Cousteau, this lone pinnacle is in the middle of nowhere, partway back to Singapore. It drops from two metres above the surface to 22 metres at the seafloor. The visibility is renowned for being awful, and currents are strong. The first part of the dive is on the side of the rock that tends to be clearer and takes you down to the base, which is covered in hard, soft and whip corals. A couple of crevices are known baby shark haunts – you can just see their tails. There are unusual nudibranchs and large starry

puffers. A bit of the dive is then spent on the murky side and then, as you come back up to about five metres on the clear side, you come into the current and one of the most amazing moments in diving – there are swarms of small silvery fish, but the excitement isn't due to their presence but rather because of the speed they are moving, both around the pinnacle and the divers. It's impossible to describe.

Turtle feeding in Tioman waters; clownfish; corals at Tiger Reef.

drying out
Sabah, Borneo

For trips to Borneo, chances are you will need a night in Kota Kinabalu. There are many hotels and even dive operations if you fancy that. However, each of the islands, with the exception of Mabul, has just one dedicated dive resort.

Kapalai and Mabul
Fly to Tawau then transfers to the islands take 1.5 hours by road and boat.
Sipadan Kapalai, dive-malaysia.com. This pretty water village hovers over a lagoon.
Sipadan-Mabul Resort and Mabul Water Bungalows, sipadan-mabul.com.my
Scuba Junkie, scuba-junkie.com

Layang Layang
Layang Layang Resort, layanglayang.com
Private island with simple but comfortable rooms built in 'longhouse' style.

Lankayan
Lankayan Island, lankayan-island.com
Transfers from Sandakan take 1.5 hours by boat. Bungalows sit nestled in the jungle.
Sandakan
Sepilok Nature Resort, sepilok.com.

Liveaboard
MV Celebes Explorer, borneo.org. The only liveaboard, this very straightforward option acts as a simple, floating hotel.

Kota Kinabalu
Sleeping
Sutera Harbour Resort, suteraharbour.com
Diving
Borneo Dream, borneodream.com
Down Below, downbelow.com

Kota Kinabalu

Take a day to see this pleasant, small city and her surrounds. The KK Heritage Walk is a guided two-hour walk around the city's landmarks and costs about RM100 per person. Those with the inclination to climb mountains will be sorely tempted to take a slightly longer break and scale Mount Kinabalu. Trips take two days so if time is short, visit Malaysia's first World Heritage Site, Kinabalu Park, and see just a little of the incredible range of plant, animal, insect and bird life. Poring Hot Springs are nearby and day trips often cover both. A slightly more relaxed day can be had by taking the North Borneo Railway journey to the agricultural region of Papar. The restored 100-year-old train chugs past mangrove swamps, villages and markets.

Sabah's rainforests

This Malaysian state is regarded as having some of the planet's most important flora and fauna species. Over half of the state has been set aside to create rainforest reserves and wildlife parks to ensure the protection of the interior and the many

unique plants and animals, although you may find this hard to believe as you pass coastal palm oil plantation after palm oil plantation. To see the real Sabah, you will need to head far inland: there are over 200 mammals living in these forests but you'll be lucky to see them as they retreat at the faintest hint of disturbance. Join an escorted walking tour to a reserve and you can stay overnight. The best time to visit is during the fruiting and flowering season from March until October. Options include the Danum Valley Conservation Area, home to Asian elephants, and the rare, endangered Sumatran rhinoceros, sun bears and clouded leopards. The Tabin Wildlife Reserve has the Borneo Pygmy Elephant, Sumateran Rhinoceros and Tembadau (a species of Asian wild cattle), while the wildlife in the Kinabatangan Wildlife Sanctuary includes proboscis and leaf monkeys and crab-eating macaques.

Sandakan

This small city on the north coast is a 45 minute flight from KK. It's pleasant enough but most people come to see the Sepilok Orang-utan Sanctuary, founded in 1964 to rehabilitate orphan orang-utans. The sanctuary consists of 43 sq km of protected land at the edge of Kabili Sepilok Forest Reserve. Up to 80 orang-utans live in the reserve, the aim being to help them readjust to life in the wild. Public access is strictly managed. At feeding times, the animals come down to platforms so are easy to see and older, permanent residents will approach visitors. There is a boardwalk trail through the forest where you can also see snakes and local plants. From Sandakan, you can catch the boat to Lankayan and also the Turtle Island Marine Park. This cluster of three small islands is where turtles come to nest. There are no established diving facilities and accommodation is limited, but it's a good day out for non-divers.

Jessica at Sepilok Orang-utan Sanctuary.

drying out
Peninsular Malaysia

Travel to the islands off the mainland east coast is best described as challenging and this, along with the seasonal nature of the diving, makes them less than popular for many diverss. If you want to stay on one, get local, up-to-date advice on how to get there. An easier option is a liveaboard that sails from Singapore.

Liveaboard

White Manta Diving, whitemanta.com Singapore-based vessel with seasonal trips to Tioman and islands on route. These are short trips but a lot of fun with all the best dives covered.

Tioman

Minang Cove Resort, minangcove.com.my
Japamala Resort, japamalaresorts.com

Tioman

Most people go to Tioman to relax, swim and dive. There isn't much else to do and chances are you won't move that far from where you are staying. The main day out is to walk across the island from Tekek to Juara on the east coast. It's a long haul uphill and takes about four hours through the jungle. Take plenty of water and catch a ferry back.

Peninsular Malaysia

Malaysia is built on its cross-cultural differences and nowhere is this reflected more than in the capital, Kuala Lumpur. If you're up for a few days of city lifestyle, KL is as lively as any, and for many, too lively. Admire the architecture that ranges from aging colonial mansions to shopping malls that could be anywhere to the state-of-the-art Petronas Twin Towers.

The historic city and port of Melaka could be worth a diversion as it's only 2½ hours away. A prosperous trading post in the 16th century, the Portuguese, Dutch and British all colonized here. For cool air, the Cameron Highlands are 1,500 m above sea level and famous for their pleasant weather, tea plantations and cool temperatures. The peninsular's East Coast is punctuated with several small cities and large towns. There is little to hold diver tourists for more than a day although places like Mersing will give you a feel for a rustic Malay sea port and Kota Bharu is an introduction to more traditional Malay culture.

Golden buddha; shopping on the East Coast

Lankayan Island; Kapalai; Layang Layang.

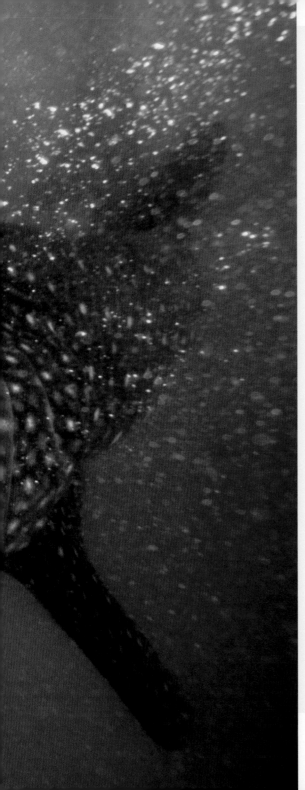

Maldives

185
↘ **Essentials**

186
↘ **Dive brief**

188
↘ **Dive sites**

190
↘ **Dive log**

190   North Malé Atoll
192   South Malé Atoll
194   Nilandhoo Atoll
195   Ari Atoll
196   Baa Atoll

198
↘ **Drying out**

Gentle giant: head-turning encounters with a feeding whale shark,
the largest fish in the sea.
Hanifaru Lagoon, Baa Atoll

destination
Maldives

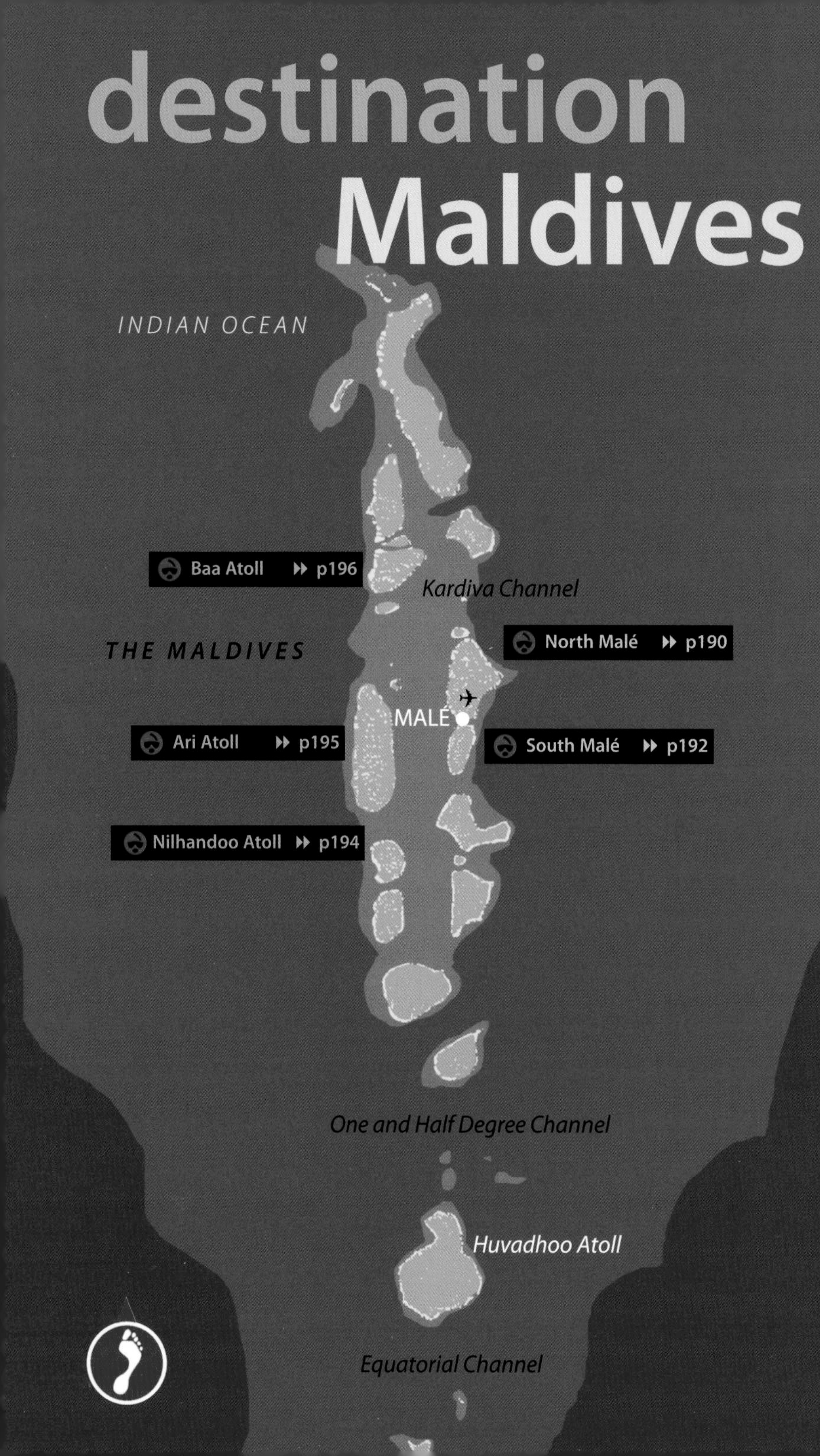

INDIAN OCEAN

THE MALDIVES

Kardiva Channel

🐾 Baa Atoll ▸▸ p196

🐾 North Malé ▸▸ p190

🐾 Ari Atoll ▸▸ p195

🐾 South Malé ▸▸ p192

🐾 Nilhandoo Atoll ▸▸ p194

MALÉ ✈

One and Half Degree Channel

Huvadhoo Atoll

Equatorial Channel

All those dreams of playing Robinson Crusoe – being cast away on your own private island and getting back to nature – can all come true in the Maldives. What's more, you can have the fantasy complete with hot and cold running water, someone to wait on you hand and foot and go diving at the same time.

Your first glimpse of the atolls will be the spectacular aerial view of her diminutive islands when you fly in to the capital, Malé. As you try to work out which is yours, rest assured that they are all equally beautiful and all have fabulous diving.

This tiny, waterborne country was bypassed for centuries due to the hazardous fringing reefs that are also its salvation. Their untarnished natural beauty, both above and below the waterline, is now its prime appeal. There are fish, fish and yet more fish, all attracted to these isolated Indian Ocean atolls, which are actually the tips of an ancient volcanic mountain range. There's other marine life too, but there is nowhere else quite like this for swimming amongst pretty fish.

Drying out time, however, isn't exactly a succession of cultural diversions. In the Maldives you make your own entertainment. Here, watching the stars in the sky can be far more rewarding than watching them on a screen.

Essentials

Getting to and around the Maldives is a fairly straightforward proposition. Flights from across the globe land at the modern international airport on Hulhule Island in North Malé Atoll just a few minutes from the capital city, which is also on an island. In fact, everywhere in the Maldives is an island but getting between them is a well-organized affair. No matter where you are staying, your resort or liveaboard operator will arrange your transfers. Depending on which atoll you are aiming for, this could be by local boat, speed boat or a thrilling ride in a sea plane.

Local laws and customs

The Maldives is a fairly strict Muslim nation, but the resorts are tolerant of other cultures. Guests are asked to respect the private staff compounds and the small mosque on every island. Women are asked not to sunbathe topless, and it is regrettable that some ignore this. Dress conservatively on non-tourist islands or in Malé and note that alcohol is only available on resort islands.

Health and safety

You're on holiday somewhere that looks like paradise so it's hard to imagine that anything could ever go wrong. Personal safety has always been an almost insignificant concern as you are mostly limited to staying on your self-contained resort island. However, it's always worth checking a travel advisory site: things do go wrong as the 2004 tsunami demonstrated. This freak disaster indicates that the biggest risk you run in the Maldives will be due to nature taking revenge: put your hands or feet down on the coral and you will get cut or stung.

There are medical facilities in Malé plus many resorts have a nurse or doctor on call. Food standards are generally high, but you should drink bottled or purified water. Mosquitos are prolific and the sun can be fearsome, so protect yourself from both.

Costs

As everything is imported into the Maldives, costs can be high. By 'everything' we mean everything – from staff to drinking water, lettuce to T-shirts. There is virtually no agriculture, no food or drink industry, no manufacturing. Hotel rates run from reasonable to astronomical plus the trend to rebuild original hotels as upper-class resorts continues. Meals are also expensive, but almost all resorts include breakfast plus many offer room rates that include lunch and dinner. The best way to keep your costs down to a reasonable level is to book an all-inclusive resort or a liveaboard as there will be fewer hidden extras. The initial outlay saves in the long run. Otherwise, everything is signed for and charges are tallied up at the end of a stay. It's easy to run up larger than expected bills so keep an eye on these to ensure you only pay what you have signed for. Tipping is expected.

Fact file

Location	3°15′N, 73°00′E
Capital	Malé
Flights	Emirates, Qatar, Singapore Airlines, Sri Lankan
Internal flights	Maldives Air Taxis and Sun Express
Land transport	Water taxis
Departure tax	Mostly included in ticket or US$12
Entry	Visa for 30 days issued on arrival
Money	The Maldivian currency is rufiyaa but US dollars are accepted everywhere
Language	The native language is Dhivehi but all European languages are widely spoken
Electricity	230v, plug type A (see page 15)
Time zone	GMT +5
Religion	Muslim
Communications	Country code +960; IDD code 00; Police 119 Internet access available in most resorts
Tourist information	Visitmaldives.com; maldivestourism.net
Travel advisories	gov.uk/foreign-travel-advice; state.gov/travel

dive brief

Diving

Fish, fish and yet more fish. There's no doubt about it, this is the place to go for them. Like no other tropical destination, the atolls here host the most amazing quantities of colourful fish due to their isolated nature. The fringing reefs provide the only habitat for many miles in any direction, so dives can feel like being immersed in a big aquarium.

On the other hand, this is not the place for prolific corals, as the shallow reefs are affected by global climate-based events like El Niño and the tsunami of 2004. However, even before these events, coral was never the main attraction. If you don't expect to see lush, colour-ridden reefs, you won't be disappointed. Despite that, there are areas with rich soft corals while hard corals live and regenerate in deeper, cooler waters.

Currents are the other defining feature of Maldivian diving and these vary with the seasons. Before you choose a resort, check what direction the prevailing winds will be coming from. Current patterns run in line with the winds and bring in clearer waters from the open ocean. May to November is the southwest monsoon. Winds transport clearer water from that direction so you will get better visibility if you go to the west of an atoll. December to April is the northeast monsoon, so at that time it's better on the east of an atoll.

Snorkelling

There are those who like to claim that you can see as much while snorkelling as you can diving and this is one place where that might just about be true. The small fringing or house reefs that encircle nearly every island are full of life. During the day, you can spend long hours floating over a shallow reef watching all sorts of pretty creatures like the ubiquitous powderblue surgeonfish. At night you can sit dangling your feet off the jetty and watch baby sharks congregate, attracted by the lights.

Marine life

Fish, fish, fish... snappers by the million, parrotfish and butterflies by the hundreds. There's never just one of something. While schools of pelagic fish such as jacks, are less common, some bigger animals are seen frequently. There are feeding stations for manta rays, reefs that whale sharks are known to haunt and a good supply of sharks, especially in the areas that are known for stronger currents.

Our first ever dives, way back when, were off tiny Bandos. On Christmas Day, we came face-to-face with a whitetip shark and were utterly, completely hooked. The Maldives have since become pretty busy, which is not to say that the islands have lost the Robinson Crusoe atmosphere that made them so famous. It's just that, these days, you need to head a lot further afield to live the castaway dream.

Lobster in soft corals.

Making the big decision

The Maldives tend to be where European divers graduate to once they have done the Red Sea. It is just a little bit further but a lot more exotic. The islands are romantic and standards are generally high. Although the greatest draw is still the marine life, these atolls now also attract those who want to sail, windsurf, be pampered in a spa or bake in the sun.

There are over 100 designated resort islands and the castaway style is cultivated and exploited at them all. Choosing the perfect one can be confusing, but most are ideal for couples while others cater for families. Some are managed by a specific nationality and that tends to attract guests of the same nationality.

Serious divers should opt for an island with a good house reef. Families may want to look for islands with bigger beaches and more facilities. Location is another consideration – the closer to the airport, the shorter the transfer time, but remote islands will be less busy. Alternatively, if you can abandon the dream of luxuriating under a palm tree, hop on a liveaboard and dive more than one atoll.

Animal encounters

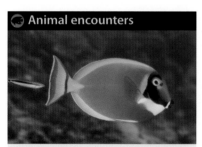

Countrywide: the variety and number of marine species vary only slightly from atoll to atoll. Small and unusual critters are less common in these waters, but keep an eye out for honeycomb morays, powder blue surgeonfish (above) and the Maldivian clownfish as well as the two endemic goby species. Mantas and whale sharks are hard to miss – as long as you are looking up.

dive sites

No matter which of the Maldivian atolls you visit, there are few differences between either the island landscapes or what you see in the underwater realm. Everywhere will have substantial fish life, well-known big animal haunts and a scattering of wreck dives.

The capital, Malé and the international airport sit on the channel that divides North and South Malé atolls. These have the most resorts and copious numbers of liveaboards making them the most dived. Slightly further afield Ari Atoll covers almost as much geographic space as its eastern counterpart. However, things are a little more spread out across open spaces.

A little to the south, Nilhandoo Atoll also has north and south segments but it's the northern area that is most explored. And with just one large resort, the diving is unhurried and relatively uncrowded.

Baa Atoll in the north has been host to tourism for some time, but has recently become far more popular. There are just a handful of resorts and a reputation for big animals, due largely to the famed – and now famously protected – schools of aggregating manta rays that congregate in this region.

North and South Malé ▶▶ p190

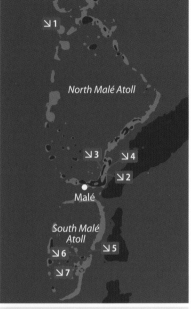

North Malé Atoll

↘1

↘3 ↘4
↘2

● Malé

South Malé Atoll

↘6 ↘5
↘7

Conditions

Seasons	The southwest monsoon is May to November so go to the west of an atoll; the northeast monsoon is December to April so go to the east of an atoll.
Visibility	Varies with location and season, from 10 to 30 m
Currents	From mild to ripping, rarely none at all.
Temperatures	Air 25-30°C; water 25-29°C
Wet suit	3 mm full body suit
Training	Courses on all islands; pre-booking is essential
Nitrox	Becoming more common; check in advance
Deco chambers	Bandos and Malé

Diversity

reef area 8,920 km²	
HARD CORALS	212
FISH SPECIES	1,131
ENDEMIC FISH SPECIES	2
FISH UNDER THREAT	26

All diversity figures are approximate

🔵 Log Book

- ↘1 **Finger Point, Eriyadu**
- ↘2 **Lankanfinolhu**
- ↘3 **Occabali Thila**
- ↘4 **Kani Corner**
- → **The Victory:** a 110-metre steel cargo ship near Malé Airport
- → **Nassimo Reef:** circular thila where oriental sweetlips jam swim-throughs
- → **Occabali Thila:** finger-shaped reef with big currents and bigger animals
- ↘5 **Cocoa Thila**
- ↘6 **Kandooma Corner**
- ↘7 **Kuda Giri**
- → **Guraidhoo Kandu:** whitetips, mackerel, and barracuda over a flat plateau
- → **Dhigufinolhu:** manta ray cleaning station in season
- → **Vili Varu Gili:** the perfect night dive, with all sorts of nocturnal critters

Nilhandoo ▶▶ p194

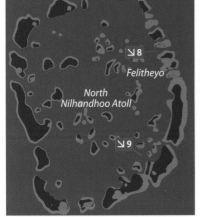

North Nilhandhoo Atoll

Felitheyo

↘8

↘9

🛈 Log Book

↘8 **Seven Stingrays**
↘9 **M'n'M**

→ **Little South Channel:** caves full to bursting with soft corals and lobster
→ **Lighthouse Channel:** hunt in open water for passing pelagic fish
→ **Filitheyo Outside:** underwater promontory with masses of fish

Ari Atoll ▶▶ p195

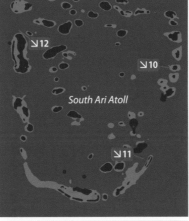

South Ari Atoll

↘12

↘10

↘11

🛈 Log Book

↘10 **Vilamendhoo House Reef**
↘11 **Maaya Thila**
↘12 **Bodhufinolhu Thila**

→ **Kalahandi Huraa:** steep sloping wall, swim-throughs and leopard sharks
→ **Angaga Thila:** silver waves of tiny bait fish avoiding tuna and whitetips
→ **Kudarah Thila:** moon-shaped reef with pinnacles, arches and fan corals

Baa Atoll ▶▶ p196

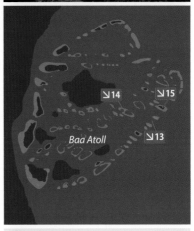

Baa Atoll

↘14

↘15

↘13

🛈 Log Book

↘13 **Kakani**
↘14 **Dhonfanhu Thila**
↘15 **Hanifaru Lagoon**

→ **Dharavandhoo:** caves and overhangs on a submerged promontory
→ **Trixie's Caves:** soft coral clad caves that punctuate a steep wall
→ **Dhigali Haa:** soft and hard corals with the Maldivian clownfish

❸ Endangered oceans

It was only a few years back that Hanifaru Lagoon was 'discovered'. Of course, the locals always knew it was there, but once the word leaked out that the lagoon could attract hundreds of manta rays at a time, its reputation hit the roof. Visitors numbers exploded and the authorities realised it needed protection. The Maldivian Government tagged the lagoon as a marine protected zone and adopted UNESCO protocols for a World Biosphere Reserve.

A code of conduct is now in place but, sadly, this means it is no longer possible to dive there. The authorities only allow snorkellers into the protected zone. Times are restricted and an entry fee is charged. Opinion is divided as to whether this was the right decision, as fewer snorkellers understand the need to protect these endangered species. There is also a visitor centre on a neighbouring island with facilities that aim to educate the masses of 'day-trippers' that arrive from local resorts. While this is not good news for divers, snorkelling in the lagoon is still exciting and will make a great diversion from all the wonderful scuba sites in Baa.

dive log
North Malé Atoll

More correctly known as Kaafu Atoll, this is home to both the capital, Malé, which you are unlikely to see before getting whisked off to a waiting transfer, and the international airport. Because of that, the resorts on islands nearby were the first to be developed and tend to be smaller but more sophisticated than ones further afield. This is because, as time has passed, the original ones have been rebuilt to higher standards.

Even though the dive sites in North Malé were the first to be explored, the diving remains some of the best in the country, with a mix of well-charted channel and thila (small submerged reef) sites. The geography creates exciting conditions for prolific marine life and there is the bonus of a few easily dived wrecks.

At certain times of year the visibility will be flawless; at others it can drop right down but then the plankton attracts the bigger animals to feeding stations. There can be substantial currents, which can be off-putting for some, but in terms of conserving the reefs it's not such a bad thing as fewer people are there to damage them. Yet, with so many resorts and the increasing number of liveaboards, many regard these atolls as a little overcrowded.

N1 Finger Point, Eriyadu	
Depth	15 m
Visibility	fair to good
Currents	slight to strong

A well-known adrenaline-rush dive: entry is over a small thila that is attached to the main reef by a sandy saddle. The current on this site can be extremely strong, but it is the reason why big animals are regularly seen here. Napoleon wrasse hover over the sand as do whitetip sharks, and then, as you descend to the point of the thila, you can spot eagle rays on a fly past. Whitetips circle just off the reef edge and even grey sharks are standing off in the blue. The thermoclines can be severe too, but it's an exciting dive. Back on the main reef where the coral is mostly rubble (natural effects taking their toll), you are likely to see octopus, a lot of small schooling fish and juvenile turtles.

Whitetip reef sharks circling over Finger Point.

⑤2 Lankanfinolhu

🕐 **Depth**	15 m
◑ **Visibility**	fair to good
🌊 **Currents**	slight to strong

At this well-known manta cleaning station, dives start with a drift along the channel, passing an occasional shark and a few fish cruising the reef until you find a depression occupied by a huge number of cleaner wrasse. Diver groups sit here and wait for the mantas to head in and get spruced up. Sometimes it's juveniles circling closer and closer, swooping between all the divers' bubbles; at other times, adult mantas arrive but hurry past the waiting divers and head straight back out into the blue. Some days they don't appear at all, or you might glimpse dozens of them further along the channel. The coral at the cleaning station has sadly been turned to rubble by all the activity.

⑤3 Occabali Thila

🕐 **Depth**	32 m
◑ **Visibility**	fair to good
🌊 **Currents**	slight to strong

Occabali sums up the best of being in a real-world aquarium. Just an hour or so north of Malé, the site consists of a circular main reef, a small narrow thila and a large coral rock creating a canyon between the thila and the main reef. The canyon is a real magnet for fish attracted by the currents that pass through. There are resident Napoleon wrasse, several tuna and schools of jacks all whizzing about. At depth there are groups of bluelined snapper and oriental sweetlips. Fish life is prolific with parrotfish, surgeons, banners, butterflies and so many others you can't absorb it all. An overhang is thick with glassfish and, as you approach them, they part in silent waves to reveal a giant grey moray behind.

⑤4 Kani Corner

🕐 **Depth**	15 m
◑ **Visibility**	fair to good
🌊 **Currents**	mild to ripping

Situated in the channel that separates Lohifushi and Kanifinolhu islands, this site can be rough in certain seasons. As you descend you see a very rubbly reef and think the time will be far from noteworthy, but then it turns into an amazing dive. There are incredible numbers of schooling fish (snappers, rainbow runners, two-spot snappers, midnight snappers, black and white bannerfish and Indian Ocean triggers), then along the reef a manta flaps overhead. Next, a scraggy old turtle swims up from the reef and leads across to a leopard shark on the bottom. Another turtle appears as you continue along, then another manta ray and right at the end, two mobula rays appear.

❝❞ My first ever trip to dive the Maldives was in 1987 when there were no direct flights and only a few tourist islands. My first trip wasn't to dive, however, I was persuaded to complete a three-day resort course after loving the snorkelling and then I was hooked! So much so, I went back again the following year to qualify, and every time there is a trip to the Maldives, I'm there! I have been 12 times in total and am never disappointed as I always see mantas and sharks.

Carole Bellars, finance director, London, UK

Octopus parading in the shallows; meeting a manta ray in Lankinfinolhu.

dive log
South Malé Atoll

With the upper rim of South Malé Atoll just about touching the bottom of the north, you could almost consider these two regions to be one and the same.

The two atolls are divided by the Vadhoo channel, with the south protected by its bigger neighbour from the more severe wind and sea conditions. Diving is mostly on the east side in the six narrow channels that carve through the rim of the fringing reef. The tides sweep in and out at a great rate and the currents can really rip! The visibility will be flawless, but at times it can drop right down, which attracts the bigger animals to feeding stations.

↘5 Cocoa Thila	
🕐 **Depth**	20 m
◑ **Visibility**	fair to good
〰 **Currents**	medium to strong

This large, flat-topped, oval-shaped reef is surrounded by a sloping wall that runs most of the way around its sides. At one end, the slope becomes quite steep and is interspersed with small overhangs covered in pastel-hued soft corals – pink, lemon and mauve. On the reef top, if the current is running, you encounter huge schools of collared butterflyfish hovering beside equally large groups of oriental sweetlips. The site is also known for green turtles and there are several in residence. You need to approach them very carefully as they take off if spooked. The adults can grow to be enormous, at least two metres from head to tail. They are sometimes seen sleeping under the ledges or moving about the plateau feeding, but mostly you see them as they take off to the surface for a gulp of air.

↘6 Kandooma Corner	
🕐 **Depth**	23m
◑ **Visibility**	good
〰 **Currents**	strong

The long, thin reef at Kandooma extends out to a point or corner where there are often fierce currents that will attract big pelagic action. More often than not, though, it won't be possible to dive here as the currents are simply too strong. Fortunately, the other, calmer side can be equally as interesting. From the flat reef top there is a small ridge and overhang that slopes down to 30 metres or so. There are lots of tubastrea corals and quite a bit of dendronephthya soft coral surrounded by masses of fish. In the overhangs you can often find small green turtles munching on some lunch, or a resting whitetip shark. On the top of the reef there are huge schools of parrotfish, black surgeonfish and rainbow runners. These appear in massive waves to feed on algae-covered rocks.

Honeycomb moray being spruced up by two cleaner wrasse; leopard shark swimming past.

kuda
giri

🕐 **Depth**	18 m	
◑ **Visibility**	fair to good	
〰 **Currents**	mild	

What makes this such a special dive is that it's really two rolled into one, with both the intact wreck of a cargo boat and a small reef pinnacle to explore. However, the real reef tends to take second place to the artificial one to its side.

The wreck lies with its hull pointing towards the reef, her bow at 18 metres and the stern dropping past 30. The hull is about 30 metres long with one cargo hold at the back, which you can enter, although it's a bit too dark and confined to penetrate very far without a torch. The outside is in perfect condition, and you can see small cup corals, sponges, tunicates and algaes colonizing the sides as you drop to the propeller at 27 metres. Ascending back to the midships section, swim past some black coral bushes to find the rear deck is enclosed by raised scaffolding. This open structure may once have had a canopy but now attracts plenty of small fish. An old, rusting cage on the deck has a resident grey frogfish inside it.

After diving the wreck it's time to head over to the pinnacle to gas off. There are some small caverns and overhangs full of fish and, up at the 10 metre mark, a bed of staghorn corals is home to even more: you can spot leaffish, filefish and even the Maldivian clownfish. Another great feature of this site is that strong currents are rare, although the visibility can drop at times.

❝❞ We descended through calm, open water to the sandy seabed a short distance from Dhigufinolhu. After finning a few metres, directly in front of us lay the remains of a small cargo boat, now known simply as the Kuda Giri wreck. No one seemed to know the boat's real name, but we were told that it sank somewhere else before being moved to create this prolific and dramatic artificial reef.

dive log
Nilandhoo Atoll

Due south of Ari, Nilandhoo(aka Faafu) Atoll is still a comparatively isolated area.

Inside the atoll, thilas are protected from strong tidal currents, making them easy sites. On the outer rim, there are plenty of channel dives and steep walls. Dive sites are never crowded but, strangely, the marine life seems more wary of divers – there are plenty of pelagics but they soon scatter at the sound of bubbles.

⬊8 Seven Stingrays	
🜁 **Depth**	28 m
◑ **Visibility**	good
🌊 **Currents**	generally strong

Highly indicative of the atoll's dive sites, Seven Stingrays is a long, flat reef with seven distinct mounds rising from its contours. These are all quite small except the last, which is far wider and only in about eight metres of water so it's a good last stop. Entry to the site starts from the north and drops you right into the current, so you drift out into the blue to search out large animals. These seem to be mostly tuna, although that all depends on the day. Back over the reef, you can count the 'stingray' mounds passing below as the current grows stronger. By the time you have reached the sixth, it can be pretty stiff and you are unlikely to stay still. There are substantial schools of yellow snapper and rainbow runners and. on the seventh mound, there are broad swathes of carpet anemones with clownfish, porcelain crabs and white-eyed morays hiding beneath.

⬊9 M'n'M	
🜁 **Depth**	19 m
◑ **Visibility**	good
🌊 **Currents**	mild

This almost circular thila is inside the reef lagoon so is quite an easy dive. It also has a distinctive structure: on the north side a perfectly straight wall drops from just below the surface to 35 metres. There are quite a few little caverns and a couple of very nice caves to swim through. These have a healthy covering of small white fan corals which are extremely delicate. There is a lot of colour here too, with the wall covered in multi-hued soft corals, sponges and tunicates. Nudibranchs crawl amongst them and mantis shrimp can be spotted on the cavern floors. The very unusual comet fish can be found here. This fish's skin is black with tiny white spots: it mimics the white spotted moray, especially if threatened. They are resident on the wall near the entry and exit point. The south of the thila has more gentle terrain and, being less dramatic, is dived less often.

Sabretooth blenny smiling from his tunicates; the wall at M'n'M; a pair of indigenous Maldivian clownfish.

dive log
Ari Atoll

The largest atoll in the country, Ari – or Alifu – atoll has resorts right around its rim along with a few on islands in the central lagoon which have access to dive sites in all directions.

The underwater terrain is consistent with elsewhere, but there's one thing that gives Ari an edge at certain times of year – the southeastern corner is regarded as a whale shark highway and you might be lucky enough to see several in a day. Visibility can be low, however, as they come here to feed when the plankton blooms.

⊠10 Vilamendhoo House Reef

Depth	28 m
Visibility	good
Currents	usually mild

This diver-friendly island has shore dives with exit numbers along the beach. Exit 10 on the northern side leads to an almost vertical wall, dropping to 28 metres before sloping to the seabed. There are scrappy coral and rocks interspersed with tubastrea corals, where you can find tiny snowflake morays and unusual nudibranchs. A cave bursting with glassy sweepers at 15 metres is the highlight, though. At its entry there are many pretty pipefish, flatworms, lots of different types of shrimp and a large grey moray waits just inside.

⊠11 Maaya Thila

Depth	20 m
Visibility	low to fair
Currents	medium to strong

One of Ari's best-known dive sites, Maaya Thila is a protected zone. You can easily swim around the thila in a single dive. Some soft coral-clad outcrops lie off one end and it is worth swimming across to them, especially if there is current, as grey sharks patrol the sandy channel. Likewise, back on the main reef, if you hit oncoming currents, you can see impressive schools of bluestripe snappers plus the resident batfish, oriental sweetlips, clown and titan triggers, octopus, morays and the ever-present powderblue surgeonfish.

⊠12 Bodhufinolhu Thila

Depth	32 m
Visibility	poor to good
Currents	medium

En route to this site, divemasters watch for tell-tale shadows and often spy a whale shark in the depths before coming across one shallow enough to snorkel with. Then it's a mad leap into the water before the magnificent beast drops down and heads away. They can be extremely nosy and will come up to the boat, providing no one is in the water splashing about, even lifting their heads up to see what's there. On the dive, visibility is low – the whale sharks come to feed on plankton – but squads of mobula rays often pass by.

Bluestripe snappers in Ari Atoll and the cave on Vilamendhoo House Reef.

dive
Baa log
Atoll

North of Ari Atoll and northwest of the Malé Atolls, Baa has been open to divers for some time, yet due to its distance from the airport, has just a handful of lovely resorts of varying standards.

The diving in this area is as exciting as the best of the other atolls, with steep-sided thilas and coral clad walls. Fish are prolific as are pelagic species. However, this area became really popular when news of the seasonal arrival of aggregating manta rays and whale sharks went viral.

↘13 Kakani

🕐	**Depth**	32
◐	**Visibility**	fair to good
🌊	**Currents**	Medium to strong

It's unusual to focus on smaller critters in the Maldives, yet this long reef, which is dotted with caverns and overhangs, has plenty. Off in the blue, there are the ever-present schools of pelagic fish, such as rainbow runners, blue-lined snappers, trevally and fusiliers. Further along the reef, the current brings in Spanish mackerel to hunt or a small nurse shark will pass by looking for a cavern to settle in. Peering into these caverns also reveals smaller creatures – morays, a few nudibranchs and plenty of gobies – but perhaps the most exciting are the two giant frogfish that are known residents. One is a pale peach colour and the other a pale blue-grey. They tend to move between the caverns and matching sponges on the top of the reef above it.

↘14 Dhonfanu Thila

🕐	**Depth**	18 m
◐	**Visibility**	good
🌊	**Currents**	mild

A classic example of a Maldivian thila dive, this almost circular reef is broken by a small tunnel that creates a swim-through, It is coated in pretty soft corals and quite a bit of black coral then, as you emerge into the crevice above, chances are you will see a grey reef shark or a small Napoleon wrasse. Along the side of the thila, there are a lot of shelves with a fair number of small creatures occupying them – morays, flatworms, crinoids and juvenile lionfish. Up on the top, is a pretty anemone with a porcelain crab, but mantas also appear here. You can try to follow them but the current is pretty strong as it sweeps across the thila top. Going back towards the crevice and tunnel and hanging right in the depression, there may be a small school of chevron barracuda.

Longnose hawkfish in black coral; soft corals coating the swim-throughs; yawning frogfish on Baa's Kakani reef.

N15	**Hanifaru Lagoon**	
Depth	0-5 m	
Visibility	good	
Currents	mild to strong	

No one quite knows why, but at certain times of the year, hundreds of manta rays converge on tiny Hanifaru Lagoon. This event seems to relate to coinciding tides, moon phases and currents. The water will suddenly turn dark with a prodigious amount of microscopic critters and even darker with the mantas who arrive to feast on the plankton. If you are there at precisely the right time, it's nothing to see 50, 100, 200 manta rays at a time – who knows how many, it's impossible to count them. There are adults in deeper water and juveniles near the surface or around the edges of the lagoon. What makes this even more astounding is that the mantas are often joined by whale sharks who arrive to feast on their fair share of the nutrient-rich water. You will feel like a mad thing from a horror movie as your head spins in every direction trying to see them all.

It was possible to dive in the lagoon until quite recently. Dive boats would moor near the edge, and watch for tell-tale signs of manta activity. There would be a rush to kit up before sinking to the bottom of the lagoon where the mantas paused over a small outcrop to be cleaned. The lagoon is currently closed to scuba divers on conservation grounds. However, snorkeling here is still an amazing experience if you are in the area at the right time.

66 99 Suddenly we saw a large shape out across the sand. We slowly made our way towards it and, as we got closer, we made out a group of three mantas slowly circling on the far side of the channel. We stayed very low and continued to swim across the channel until we were kneeling on the sand, watching the mantas above our heads. The longer we stayed the more mantas appeared and we became mesmerized by the spectacle.
Anne-Marie Kitchen-Wheeler and Matt Kitchen, cruise directors, Maldives

drying out

In the Maldives, specific islands become designated exclusively as resorts so have no local community on them. They vary in size from those that require only a 10-minute walk to circumnavigate, to the ones that take as much as an hour.

Resort layouts, facilities and atmosphere tend to be similar, so what makes each one individual is standard and hence the price, which can range from simple and three-star to a whole galaxy of sparkles.

There are far more designated resort islands than are listed here. The majority have websites, but most people book a prearranged flight and hotel package that includes meals, diving and transfers. There is a pattern of resorts periodically closing only to reopen a short while later as a far more upmarket version. Budget hotels are harder to come by, but mid-range and all-inclusive options can be good value.

North Malé Atoll
Bandos Island Resort, bandos.com. 30-mins by boat from the airport; Dive Bandos on site.
Eriyadu, eriyadumaldives.com. 1-hr by speedboat to the top of North Malé.
Kurumba, kurumba.com. 10-mins by boat from the airport; Euro-divers.com on site.

South Malé Atoll
Olhuveli Beach, olhuvelimaldives.com. Seaplane in 45-mins; Sundivingschool.com
Rihiveli, rihiveli-maldives.com. Seaplane transfer in 45-mins; Euro-divers.com on site.

North Nilandhoo Atoll
Filitheyo: aaaresorts.com.mv. 90-mins by seaplane. wernerlau.com.

Ari Atoll
Lily Beach, lilybeachmaldives.com. About 45-mins by seaplane. Ocean Pro on site.
Vilamendhoo, vilamendhooisland.com, Seaplane transfer, 45-mins; Euro-divers.com.

Baa Atoll
Coco Palm Dhuni Kolhu, cocopalm.com. 30-mins by seaplane. Dive Ocean on site.
Reethi Beach, Reethibeach.com. 30-mins seaplane transfer. Sea Explorer dive centre.
Royal Resort, royal-island.com. Transfers 30-mins by seaplane. Delphis Dive Centre.

Liveaboards
If you are having trouble choosing a resort, hop on what is endearingly called a 'safari boat' in the Maldives.

From the airport, a 10-minute transfer will drop you onto a comfy floating hotel. In much the same way as the resorts, the development of the liveaboard business in the Maldives has been fast, with an explosion in the number of boats now cruising the atolls. There are traditional wooden dhonis and smart steel-hulled motor yachts with routes that cover many of the atolls.

Carpe Vita, explorerventures.com. Large and modern boat with capacity for bigger dive groups.
Sea Queen and Sea Spirit, scubascuba.com. UK-based Maldives Scuba Tours were pioneers in the region. Two traditional, small vessels.
Maldives Siren, sirenfleet.com. An Indonesian built phinisi schooner that is somewhat unique in these waters.

Guesthouses
A fairly recent development is the option to stay on a non-resort island in a small hotel or guesthouse. These are of a good standard and will allow visitors to see a little of traditional Maldivian life. Some have a dive centre attached; at others divers are collected by a dive centre for the day's diving, returning in the late afternoon. However, you must be aware of cultural differences and respect local customs. Contact a specialist dive travel agent for up-to-date information.

Days out

When people ask what there is to do in the Maldives when you're not under the water, the answer is pretty much to get in the water. Apart from diving, you can swim, snorkel, sail or windsurf. Some resorts run night fishing trips and some run trips to other islands.

Away from the water, entertainment is centred inside the resorts. Newer resorts have fancy spas and gyms. Some have tennis courts and others will organize guest versus staff volleyball or soccer matches. Sometimes a band visits for a weekly disco but, beyond that, you can read a book under a palm tree, watch the sun setting or sit on the jetty at night and try to name star constellations.

Malé If you are staying near the capital, you could hop over for a visit. At just six square kilometres in total, it only takes about 30 minutes to walk from one end to the other. In a couple of hours you could see the new Presidential Palace, the two mosques (part of the Old Friday mosque dates from 1658) and drop into the small National Museum; it is located in the Sultan's Palace and the minimal displays include coins, jewellery, thrones and some artefacts from the pre-Islamic era. The Esjehi Art Gallery displays work by local artists but isn't open every day, or you can wander along the seafront and go to the market or a souvenir shop.

Local islands If you are near a designated locals' island you can often go across for an hour or two, talk to the kids, buy a soft drink and a T-shirt and head back.

Spas If you are looking for some post-dive body pampering, choose a resort with a spa. These are increasingly more sophisticated, with both Indian and Balinese massage programmes, yoga, reflexology and all sorts of therapies.

⊗ Undercurrents

As time goes by and development continues at speed, the Maldivian Government opens ever more atolls for tourism. There are now over 100 resorts across more than 12 atolls: Baa and Raa in the far north, once regarded as the frontier, now have six resorts between them; in the south, Meemu, Laamu and Thaa have several more, and newly opened Huvedhoo Atoll, which lies almost on the equator, has two small airports ready to service some of the most upmarket hotels in the country.

For many years there were rumours of a second major airport being built near Gan, the 1940s British naval station, but that has yet to materialize. The islands manage to retain that castaway feel but, 'undeveloped' is no longer a word most would use to describe them.

When the devastating tsunami of Boxing Day 2004 hit the region, many islands were flooded. Fortunately, these low-lying atolls escaped the more aggressive tidal effects, as the water simply rose over them and then receded. Many of the resorts used this as another reason to renovate and increase costs. Likewise, liveaboards that were once purely the domain of the adventurous are becoming classier and more luxurious.

Mexico

203
↘ **Essentials**

204
↘ **Dive brief**

206
↘ **Dive sites**

208
↘ **Dive log**

   Yucatán Peninsula
   208   Playa del Carmen
   210   The Cenotes
   212   Cozumel

   Baja California
   214   Isla Guadalupe

   Islas Revillagigedo
   216   San Benedicto
   218   Socorro
   220   Roca Partida

222
↘ **Drying out**
   222   Yucatán Peninsula
   218   Baja California

Watching me, watching you: the Great White shark, *Carcharodon carcharias,* is free to assess his caged visitors.
Isla Guadalupe, Mexico

Map labels

San Diego
Tijuana
Ensenada

UNITED STATES OF AMERICA

MEXICO

Houston
New Orleans

Gulf of Mexico

 Isla Guadalupe ▶▶ p214

Baja California
Sea of Cortez

Cabo San Lucas

Guadalajara

Cancún
Cozu

 Islas Revillagigedos ▶▶ p216

MEXICO CITY

 Yucatán Peninsula ▶▶ p

Acapulco

BELIZE

GUATEMALA HONDUR

PACIFIC OCEAN

destination
Mexico

A land of contradictions, Mexico is both a burgeoning commercial nation rife with busy industrial cities and a natural paradise of crisp white-sand beaches that act as a foil to the cartoon landscapes of cactus bushes over raw deserts.

The country's rich and ancient past is often neglected in the rush to compete with (or serve) her mighty neighbour. Yet the inhabitants of this vast land were once a superpower in their own right. Back then, it was a world where men were sacrificed in gruesome rituals or left to drown in sinkholes with no hope of escape. These cenotes are now modern-day dive sites, a unique and captivating underwater experience.

However, because Mexico has two oceanic borders, the cenotes must compete with an impressive array and variety of diving styles.

The Yucatán's coastal waters edge the Caribbean Sea and reveal both unexpected marine life and curious underwater geography with gentle reefs and also some of the fastest drift dives you will ever participate in. Meanwhile across in the Pacific Ocean, the deeper waters of the Ring of Fire teem with large animals. Most divers only dream about encounters with pelagics like those that are seen here on a regular basis.

Essentials

Wherever you live, getting to this vast nation is easy, although you will probably end up transiting through the US. There are two major airports on the Caribbean Yucatán Peninsula: Cancún and Cozumel. Either one will give access to the various dive areas nearby. Dive sites on the Pacific side are not so close to each other. The spectacular offshore islands can only be reached by boats, with Socorro departures from Cabo San Lucas on the southern tip of the Baja peninsula and Guadalupe trips from Ensenada in the north. These often start from San Diego with a drive over the border by bus.

Once you have arrived, getting around is easy enough although few hotels or dive operators will collect you, so make arrangements in advance.

Local laws and customs

Mexico is a land full of rich history and vibrant customs. Her influences range from ancient Aztec and Maya through Spanish colonialization and right up to the present day trade agreements with the US. All the coastal regions have become incredibly Americanized in recent years, so it's unlikely that you will upset anyone if you follow the usual rules of courtesy and politeness.

Health and safety

Medical facilities in the Yucatán are best described as being in a state of flux. As the area has expanded, they have struggled to keep up. Across in Baja, it's all very Americanized – this state is a geographic extension of California, and the lifestyles and services seem similar. What is interesting though, is that you can buy almost any prescription drug your heart desires... even the infamous little blue pill.

In terms of personal safety, think of Mexico in much the same way as any major western country. Some towns are raucous and lively; others are casual and laid back but, like anywhere, walking about at night showing off expensive jewellery or with a wallet in your back pocket is an invitation for trouble.

Costs

Mexico is not the cheap destination it once was. As the economy becomes more and more closely aligned with the US, so prices rise. The Yucatán was once principally rural, but development has spread right along the coast in the form of many large resorts. The Baja region is similar, and once charming villages are now brimming with top-class hotels and timeshare complexes.

This development is reflected in food and drink costs, whether you go trendy or traditional. In high season, prices often double and it's always worth checking your bill for so-called errors. On the other hand, as the US dollar is interchangeable with pesos, restaurants often give a better exchange rate than a bank.

Fact file

Location	23°00'N 102°00'W
Capital	Mexico City
Flights	BA, Continental, Mexicana, TACA, Virgin,
Internal flights	Aeromexico and subsidiaries
Land transport	Countrywide buses, ferries, taxis, car hire
Departure tax	Included in your ticket, or US$46
Entry	Visas not required for most nationals for stays of up to 180 days
Money	Mexican pesos (MXN)
Language	Spanish but English is common
Electricity	110v, plug type A (see page 15)
Time zone	GMT -5
Religion	Catholic
Communications	Country code +52; IDD code 00; Police 066 Internet access is widespread
Tourist information	visitmexico.com, discoverbajacalifornia.com and mayayucatan.com.mx
Travel advisories	gov.uk/foreign-travel-advice; state.gov/travel

dive brief

Diving

With two different coastlines, one edging the Pacific, the other on the Caribbean Sea, Mexico has two distinctive dive styles. The Caribbean side grabs the most attention as the Yucatán Peninsula sits on the world's second largest barrier reef. Referred to as the Mesoamerican Barrier Reef (rather than that other more famous barrier reef), this marine system is regarded as unique due to its length and variety of habitats.

Conditions vary enormously along its stretch: the northern Mexican end is defined by the Caribbean Current, which moves across the top of South America then travels counter-clockwise towards the Yucatán. It gets forced through the narrow channel that divides Mexico from Cuba, eddies around the Gulf of Mexico before heading to Florida. This is what gives the Yucatán its diving character: the fierce currents restrict reef creatures to those that are capable of living in this environment. Some larger pelagics are common but there is a dearth of lush corals and small creatures. However, the underwater terrain is fabulous, with plenty to explore both in the sea and inland in the underground freshwater caverns and rivers.

Across on the Pacific coast the marine world is tailored by a very different but equally dynamic set of conditions. Sitting along the Pacific Rim of Fire, this coastline and nearby offshore landmasses were formed by aeons of volcanic activity that continues to this day. Diving focuses on islands where, beneath the water, rugged geology and harsh landscapes reflect the desert terrain of Baja California. Current patterns play a strong part here too, in much the same way as they do in the Galápagos. In fact, these isolated islands look much the same and have such similar marine life they are often referred to as the mini-Galápagos. This marine realm is a magnet for really big animals.

Marine life

On the Yucatán side, reefs are typically Caribbean with pastel-toned corals and plenty of fish to admire. Small creatures like arrow crabs and shells are common but there are enough turtles and tarpon to keep everyone happy. Across in Pacific waters the balance alters. Bigger animals take first place. There are encounters with mantas and sharks, while smaller animals recede into the background.

66 99

We have spent a lot of time in Mexico – the diving is consistent and lots of fun. But what makes it really worth the trip are the differing dive styles, from the up-close encounters with marine giants to wild drift dives and the bizarre world of the cenotes. Mix it all up and you get something really special. And, remember, the ultra-modern coastal resorts are absolutely no reflection of the country as a whole, which is so much more varied, complex and fascinating.

Whitetip reef shark on patrol around Roca Partida.

Snorkelling

Cozumel's marine reputation was based on its shallow-water reserves, but many of these are now family-orientated theme parks. The mainland coastal reefs are a good option, but they are exposed to the surf which stirs up the sand at times. You can travel north to Holbox island to see the migrating whale sharks in season or snorkel in the cenotes. The Pacific areas are subject to strong currents and surge, so check conditions before leaping in.

Making the big decision

The Yucatán is defined more by what type of holiday you want rather than the type of diving. Its entire being is devoted to the pleasures of a sojourn in the sun with endless activities, theme parks and great nightlife as well as a dash of history. It is great for families – especially those with teenagers – though in high season, it may all be a bit too hyperactive. Underwater there's some unusual diving, the different styles adding a certain novelty to the experience. The Pacific, however, is really a destination for dedicated divers – once you head offshore, there is nothing but sea and the promise of a pelagic encounter.

🔵 Animal encounters

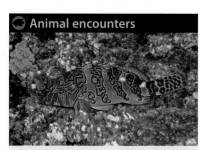

Caribbean coast: hawksbill turtles and giant barracuda are a given, so noses down to find tiny fossils and tinier shells.

Pacific islands: no need to keep fingers crossed hoping to see some of the ocean's largest animals. You may not see them all, but you will see mantas, turtles, dolphins and sharks plus the Giant hawkfish, *Cirrhitus rivulatus*, a mere 60 centimetres, above.

dive sites

Although these two regions belong to the same country, as far as the destination style, dive types and marine life go, there are really no similarities. None at all.

The Yucatán is Mexico's top tourist area and a major dollar earner, no doubt due to the two international airports, an efficient infrastructure and the massive number of coastal hotels – and because that coast fringes the warm waters of Caribbean Sea. Dive sites vary from the gentle reefs along the coast to eerie ones in underground rivers and limestone caves that contrast with the lightning-speed drift dives over tortuous topography in Cozumel.

Cozumel is perhaps best known. It was once a sleepy island until Jacques Cousteau visited in the 1960s. Diving soon became a huge part of the island's life and there are now 180 – or more – dive centres. You will rarely be on a reef on your own. On the coast opposite, Playa del Carmen has also become a major player for divers. The local reefs are not as exciting but you are much closer to the cenotes, which makes the town worth considering for such an unusual experience. The diving conditions here are easier, too.

It's a long way across the continent to Baja California, a spectacular peninsula that fades into insignificance beside the indigo Pacific Ocean surrounding it. The most amazing diving is found even further offshore, where there is nothing but open ocean and masses of massive pelagic fish. Guadalupe island has the world's most watched population of Great White sharks and while this is not quite proper diving, it is an utterly unique experience.

Baja's best diving is found around the Islas Revillagigedos, a lonely archipelago consisting of four specks of land: Socorro, San Benedicto, Roca Partida and Clarion. The tips of ancient volcanos, the area is regarded as one of nature's most unusual environments. Clarion is rarely dived, but the other islands are nicknamed the mini-Galápagos as the marine life is similar with sharks and mantas, dolphins, whales and whale sharks. However, what makes this stand out is that it is all about interaction. The mantas are so friendly they swoop in to see the divers. The dolphins come to play, the sharks approach to see what is happening. Wishful thinking? Perhaps. Guaranteed? As much as it can be.

🌐 Endangered oceans

There are few places with diving encounters that match Baja California. We came face-to-face with Great White sharks, danced with giant mantas and played with dolphins. Rather, the dolphins played with us. We met five different shark species on a single dive. And all these creatures are endangered.

At the end of each trip, there were talks about the animals we'd seen; sad talks that almost brought the adrenaline rush crashing down around our ears. We heard how the divemasters once lifted hundreds of metres of fishing nets from one site and how they came across an illegal fishing vessel. A Navy patrol boat was summoned to chase them off, but it was too late. At least the authorities did – and do – act. To help them, the Socorro and Guadalupe Conservation Funds were set up. Their main goal is to deter illegal fishermen from these protected Biosphere Reserves. More information is at guadalupefund.org and socorroislandconservation.org.

Conditions

Seasons		Isla Guadalupe: from August to October only Islas Revillagigedo: best from November to May The Yucatán: all year but the best visibility is between April and October
Visibility		10 m inshore to 40 m+ in open water, occasionally 60 m in Cozumel
Currents		Often very strong in Islas Revillagigedos and stronger in Cozumel
Temperatures		Air 20-34°C; water 19-30°C
Wet suit		3 mm; 5 mm+ for the cenotes and Pacific
Training		Available in the Yucatán and mainland Baja
Nitrox		Available but pre-booking advised
Deco chambers		Cabo San Lucas, Cozumel, Playa del Carmen

Diversity

	reef area 1,220 km²
HARD CORAL	74
FISH SPECIES	2,094
ENDEMIC FISH SPECIES	227
FISH UNDER THREAT	151

All diversity figures are approximate

Yucatán Peninsula ▶▶ p208

- ↘1 Tortugas
- ↘2 Moc-che
- ↘3 Barracuda Caves
- Playa del Carmen ●
- ↘4
- ↘3
- ● Cozumel
- ↘5
- ↘7
- ↘6
- ↘8
- Tulum ●
- ↘9

Log Book

- ↘1 **Tortugas**
- ↘2 **Moc-che**
- ↘3 **Barracuda Caves**

→ **Chun-zumbel:** masses of angelfish of every type and size
→ **X-Caret:** fast drift dive over a plateau with a nurse shark
→ **Shangri-La:** crustacean overload around this shallow plateau

- ↘4 **Dos Ojos and Bat Cave**
- ↘5 **Chac Mool**
- ↘6 **Taj Mahal**
- ↘7 **Punta Tunich/Yacab/Tormentos**
- ↘8 **Palancar Caves**
- ↘9 **The Devil's Throat**

→ **La Ceiba Reef:** shallow beach dive with the wreck of a small aircraft
→ **Santa Rosa:** drift dive along the wall before taking refuge in tunnels
→ **Paradise Reef:** nooks and crannies that shelter small crustaceans and fish

Isla Guadalupe ▶▶ p214

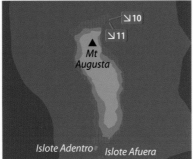

- ↘10
- ↘11
- ▲ Mt Augusta
- Islote Adentro
- Islote Afuera

Log Book

- ↘10 **The cage**
- ↘11 **The submersible**

San Benedicto ▶▶ p216

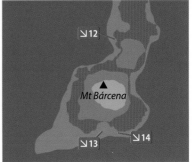

- ↘12
- ▲ Mt Bárcena
- ↘13
- ↘14

Log Book

- ↘12 **The Boiler**
- ↘13 **The Canyon**
- ↘14 **Lava Flow**

Socorro ▶▶ p218

- ▲ Mt Everman
- Punta Tosca
- Cabo Pearce
- ↘16
- ↘15
- Naval Base

Log Book

- ↘15 **Punta Tosca**
- ↘16 **Cabo Pearce**

Roca Partida ▶▶ p220

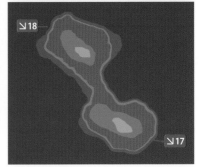

- ↘18
- ↘17

Log Book

- ↘17 **Roca Partida – South**
- ↘18 **Roca Partida – North**

dive log

Yucatán Peninsula: Playa del Carmen

The Yucatán is an incredibly diverse area, marked by centuries-old colonial Spanish cities, ancient Maya ruins, fabulous natural resources and miles of perfect white-sand beaches stretching along the coast.

The Mesoamerican Barrier Reef has almost petered out by the time it reaches this point, which is a little ironic as it's also where tourist development is at its most overwhelming.

Playa del Carmen, an hour south of super-lively Cancún, still retains a little old world charm and, just a short boat ride from the blindingly white coastal beaches, are flat reef-top plateaux swept by strong currents. Despite that, these are still fairly easy dives, far easier than those around Cozumel opposite. The currents attract a fair number of pelagic species, and visibility is better than sites closer to shore. The shallower, inshore reefs are fairly protected, but the surf stirs up the sand and visibility drops. This area is hit by hurricanes every other year or so yet always appears to recover quickly.

▶1 Tortugas	
🌀 **Depth**	19 m
◑ **Visibility**	good
🌊 **Currents**	medium to strong

At first glance this incredibly flat plateau appears to have very little life on it. The current is fairly strong and whips divers across the reef even as they descend. The corals grow to just a few centimetres and even seaplumes are only 30 centimetres high. There's little time to do more than focus on the blue vase and other small sponges that pepper the surface until you start to notice the numbers of turtles (tortugas) feeding on them. Many appear to be old and are studded with barnacles. There are quite a few more as you drift across the plateau then, near the end of it, you run into the big surprise: the resident school of tarpon. These are BIG fish, nearly two metres long, with shiny, metallic silver scales and a very grumpy expression. There seem to be dozens of them hovering effortlessly over the reef top. If you look through the gaps and beneath them, you might spot a small nurse shark.

Discovering a turtle on Tortugas; flutemouth on the reef.

↘2 Moc-che

🕐	**Depth**	14 m
◑	**Visibility**	fair
≋	**Currents**	mild to strong

Descending at Moc-che, you find a flat mound just a metre or two high that is covered in typical Caribbean corals. Small fans and seaplumes decorate the surface, all in shades of brown and beige with pale purple ones interspersed between them. Although at first glance the reef may seem uninteresting, the fish life is varied. There are lots of schooling snappers, grunts and porkfish hanging about in mixed groups. Nestling inside tiny overhangs you find soapfish and lobster, huge green morays, small, black and white blotched morays, masses of arrow crabs and periclimenes shrimp living inside corkscrew anemones. Conch shells are scattered over the sand around the mound where small stingrays and electric rays bury themselves.

↘3 Barracuda Caves

🕐	**Depth**	14 m
◑	**Visibility**	fair
≋	**Currents**	mild to strong

To the south of Playa del Carmen, this comparatively shallow reef is surrounded by low walls broken by overhangs and mini caves. The upper surface of the reef is covered in a gentle garden of soft corals and a variety of sponges. Around the edge of the reef there are a few small caverns and one is particularly good for spotting lobster. There are lots of little critters, such as arrow crabs and coral banded shrimp on the walls. Another cave, a little further along, has a resident green moray who is quite accustomed to having visitors. The great barracuda is also a resident, hence the site's name. Normally solitary, they are sometimes seen in groups of three or four around the reef, although not actually in the caves, despite the name.

The spotted cyphoma; French angelfish; an arrow crab in a sponge.

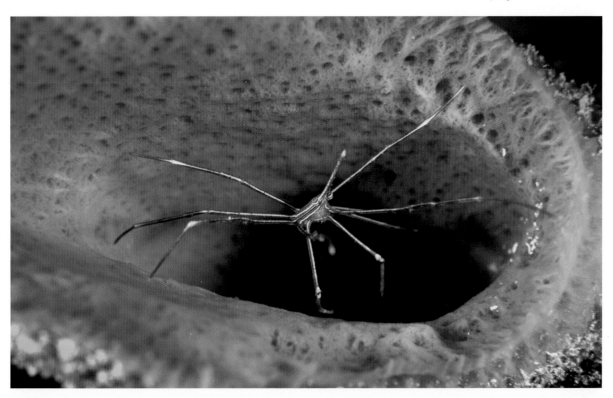

dive log

Yucatán Peninsula: The Cenotes

The Yucatán Peninsula is a limestone platform several million years old shaped by aeons of changing weather patterns. Over the centuries, the bedrock literally dissolved, leaving a vast network of subterranean rivers, underground caverns and sinkholes (cenotes). After the last Ice Age, ocean levels rose and flooded the caverns closest to the coast with seawater, while those further inland filled with rainwater.

For the ancient Maya, the cenotes were an inherent part of daily life, mythology and religion. They supplied the people with a source of fresh water, yet they believed the underworld gods lived in their depths, and people were sacrificed to appease them.

Now, these geological peculiarities form a series of unique dives. They are shallow and mostly easy. Some have guide ropes to lead the way through, but you will always be accompanied by a divemaster as there are so many unexplored passages. Even in the more complex cenotes, conditions are not difficult and you will be well briefed about being especially careful with buoyancy and to use a special finning technique.

Light floods in from fissures in the earth above or from small, secondary cenotes along the river. One of the most fascinating aspects is when you pass through a halocline – this is a phenomenon created by the meeting of seawater and fresh. The fresh water sits over the salt and forms a bizarre, mirror-like layer. Although the dives are shallow, the cenotes usually involve a lot of multilevel movement, so be careful with your ears and bear in mind that the water is pretty chilly compared to the sea.

◼4	Dos Ojos and Bat Cave	
🌀	**Depth**	11 m
🌀	**Visibility**	crystal clear, but dark
🌀	**Currents**	none

Dos Ojos, meaning two eyes, refers to two circular cenotes that sit beside each other. Entry is via a wooden platform built under the overhang of a small cave between the two eyes. The water feels icy as you jump in, especially as the surrounding jungle is so humid. And it is mosquito heaven! The first descent into an enormous yawning cave is breathtaking, then you are quickly led into a dark and gloomy passage past fragile rock formations. The route leads off towards the first 'eye' and feels quite open, with shafts of daylight shining through; you even see snorkellers swimming above. The experience becomes far more surreal as you enter tunnels that are completely black, lit only by your torch beam. Around every corner is a weird and wonderful formation: cathedral-like chambers and rocky towers glittering with minerals.

The second 'eye' is away from the busier areas, with beautiful limestone arches and doorways that lead to cavernous rooms. Stalactites hang from every available space, often converging to form thick columns. The depth is shallow all the way but there is very little daylight. At the furthest point from the entry, you finally reach Bat Cave where you can surface into air. Above the waterline the limestone cavern reveals colours and minerals that sparkle like jewels, and many tiny bats hanging from crevices. As you get closer back to the cave entrance, the dive guides like to instruct you to turn off your torch. Wait for your eyes to adjust – it's an eerie experience!

A cenote inside the forest; inside Dos Ojos; an ancient fossil buried in stone.

5 Chac-Mool

Depth	13 m	
Visibility	good	
Currents	none	

Hidden further into the jungle, this cenote feels less touristy than popular Dos Ojos – providing you arrive early enough to avoid the bus loads of day divers from Cancún. Entry is through the natural rock pool of Little Brother cenote, where you descend through a school of black catfish into a large cavern. There are several haloclines so, as you descend, the visibility decreases and the water seems to be like jelly. Below the halocline, it's a few degrees warmer. Again, there are two directions you can go – one leads to an air dome where you ascend to see the dome edges covered in stalactites that extend down into the water.

6 Taj Mahal

Depth	14 m	
Visibility	good	
Currents	none	

This far less busy site is one of the most interesting, with a variety of features. The river system runs in a straight line away from the entry, and the opening cavern drops down to jelly-like layers in 'Halocline Tunnel,' past the impressive limestone formations of 'Close Encounter' then on to 'Cenote Sugarbowl'. Rays of light illuminate massive tumbled boulders (the sugar cubes) and an old tree stump dripping in detritus from the jungle above. Further on you make a U-turn and head back to 'Bill's Hole', another tiny cenote where you can ascend into the daylight. There's a lot of decaying plant matter so good buoyancy

is imperative here. The route back parallels the start but leads past even more fanciful limestone formations with names such as 'The Candlestick', and 'Points of Light', a tiny fissure in the ceiling which shines a sharp beam onto a pile of rocks.

❝ ❞ Diving the cenotes was surreal but totally amazing. The first thing that hit me was the unreal clarity of the water; you could almost forget you were underwater and think you'd discovered the power of light. After that the urge to explore grabs you as the shapes, shadows, mystery and intrigue draw you in further and deeper. It's an awesome 'must do' diving experience.
Andrew Perkins, retail manager, Telford, UK

dive log
Yucatán
Peninsula:
Cozumel

Mexico's largest island, Cozumel is 12 miles off the Yucatán Peninsula and separated from the mainland coast by an extremely deep oceanic trench. This, along with the island's location, creates a funnel for the strong currents that flow up from the south and are then squeezed out into the Gulf of Mexico.

Cozumel's west coast is bordered by a double row of parallel reefs and, unless you are in a protected cove, the waters are never still. Move just a short way into the ocean and you will meet currents that often hit five knots – even as much as eight at times! You can descend on one dive site and ascend on a completely different one. It may sound a bit scary, but it can be a highly exhilarating experience.

This aggressive water movement has sculpted the long reefs by eating away at softer core materials, leaving a varied and complicated terrain. The area is riddled with so many tunnels, channels and grooves that, at times, the reefs feel like a giant maze.

⇘7 **Punta Tunich/Yacab/Tormentos**	
🕐 **Depth**	28 m
◐ **Visibility**	good to excellent
≋ **Currents**	unbelievable

While each of these dives is individually quite satisfying, what defines this stretch of reef – and Cozumel diving generally – is what happens when the currents pick up. And they often do, creating a triple-value dive. Dropping in at Punta Tunich, it's not unusual to hit the water and find the current is moving faster than three knots. At that level you can drift along, stopping every now and then to admire something you have spotted on the reef. However, when it's over five knots, there is no option but to move away from the wall and enjoy the passing show as you are swept along over Tunich, past Yucab Reef and onto the next section, Tormentos. You're not likely to see anything much in detail, but riding the stream is quite a rush. It also demonstrates why corals here are minimal – their delicate structures simply don't cope with the conditions. As you fly along, the ever-present schools of grunts will accompany you. There are sometimes a few creole wrasse, and you can spot angelfish or lobster on the wall or a grey ray below, who is taking it all in his stride.

A baby french angelfish using a sponge for protection; a spotted drum in changing phase.

⊠8 Palancar Caves

⊗	**Depth**	31 m
◐	**Visibility**	can be breathtaking
≋	**Currents**	slight to ripping

This popular dive starts with a quick drop down to 30 metres. From there, and rising up to about 18 metres, the wall becomes a tortuous maze of tunnels. There are architectural spires and buttresses, gullies and canyons winding to and fro between the outer wall and the inner reef. There are also countless caves and caverns but not as much marine life as you might expect. Schooling grunts and snapper appear, along with lots of small fish, several types of morays and crustaceans in the tunnels. However, you are likely to be far too busy having fun swimming through the marine labyrinth to really notice them.

⊠9 The Devil's Throat, Punta Sur

⊗	**Depth**	38 m
◐	**Visibility**	can be breathtaking
≋	**Currents**	strong to ripping

This site can only be done when conditions are just right and is restricted to advanced divers (but the definition of 'advanced' is often loose). Punta Sur is at the southern tip of Cozumel and is washed by currents, surge and some surf. The first stage of the dive involves finning into a cave system at 26 metres, which turns into a descending tunnel. Lobster and morays lurk along the passages in the dark. You continue through the tunnel until you emerge on the reef wall, before quickly re-entering another cave that leads to a second complex of tunnels. About four metres in, the tunnel narrows significantly and you enter the 'Devil's Throat'. There are several passages, including one that exits on a sheer section of wall at 37 metres. Another leads to the 'Cathedral', a vast cavern lit by beams of sun filtering through fissures in the reef. There aren't that many fish as the point is so exposed, but you still see angels and butterflyfish along the reef edge.

dive log

Baja California
Isla Guadalupe

Southwest of the city of Ensenada and 240 kilometers off the western coast of the Baja California peninsula is isolated Guadalupe island. Scarred by ancient volcanic activity, devastated in modern times by imported animals, this rare ecosytem is still one of vital importance.

It may seem surprising when you see the harsh, volcanic landscape from sea level, but Guadalupe's ecology once reflected the woodlands of American California. Now though, only sporadic trees remain and the many indigenous birds have long since become extinct due to goats being imported for food by 19th-century whalers. You are unlikely to set foot on land as there are no facilities apart from research stations.

Diving here is rare as well – a pity as the marine realm is reminiscent of California's Channel Islands. And while the land based flora and fauna has suffered terribly, the sea creatures thrived. Guadalupe is a refuge for Northern Elephant Seals and Guadalupe Fur Seals, and is now a sanctuary for all the seal species that rest on its rocky shores.

It's because of the seal populations that this has become one of the best places in the world to see the Great White Sharks. Face-to-face, up close and personal.

Cage diving

This is a highly regulated affair, with an official on all boats to ensure it's done the right way. Chumming is not allowed, but chunks of tuna are placed inside hessian 'teabags' and floated just below the surface. The smell attracts the sharks, but they can't access the goodies inside. The crew do throw tuna tails out on ropes but haul them back in if the sharks try to snatch them.

Divers can enter the cages at will, and stay as long as they like, as the depth is just three metres and air is supplied via a constant 'hookah' surface system. The only restrictions are not being a hog if others are waiting for their turn, and the water temperature, which is a chilly 19ºC. Visibility is usually good. You are also briefed not to lean out of the cages as "it's not the shark you're watching that will get you but the one behind you." So guess how many people follow that rule?

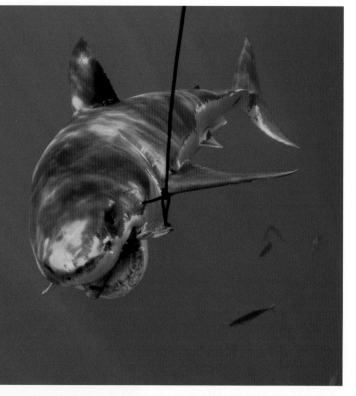

" " My last boat ride took two hours – toured Manhattan. Fun. I don't fear boats... I DO fear water. Drowning mostly. I get disoriented in my pool. I'm not sure why I chose to cage-dive with Great White Sharks. Oh, I remember... I'm *obsessed* with sharks. Seeing a Great White has consumed me my whole life.

A friend steered me towards Isla Guadalupe. Five day trip, three days in the water. Did I mention I'm afraid of water? And not SCUBA certified? I board and think about sharks for the 20 hours it takes to get to the island.

The next day, I wake up (ok bolt up), run to the back deck to see MY FIRST GREAT WHITE! I thought it was two sharks then realized it was the dorsal and tail of *one*. Time for my first dive. Down I go. Within a minute I'm seeing a 15-foot shark – three feet from me! I jump back. Everything slows down... It doesn't seem real. I relax and get some amazing pictures. "This is awesome. That's a Great White! I have to pee. Diver up!"

My adrenaline is pumping. I fling my mask into the ocean. Whatever! It's not every day I see a Great White within touching distance. And get into the water with one.

Rich Rubin, DJ, KROQ-FM, Los Angeles, USA

↘10 The cage	
🕐 **Depth**	3 m
◐ **Visibility**	good
🌊 **Currents**	none

↘11 The submersible	
🕐 **Depth**	15 m
◐ **Visibility**	good
🌊 **Currents**	none

At dawn the most curious divers are up and waiting on the back deck. The cages have been floating at surface level since the previous night and the teabags of tuna are dropped into the sea as the first cups of coffee are poured. Anticipation is rife and, before the sun breaks over the horizon, a black fin breaks the surface. You will never see so many divers move so fast to be the first in. No more vaguely cynical comments about this not being proper diving; the crew smirk (they've seen it all before), cage lids are raised, hookahs grabbed and divers drop. And there, right in front of your face is a Great White. A five metre long beastie swims right past, the nose here, the tail way back there. As time goes on there are more. Some are full-grown adults, some smaller. A few are tagged and you start to recognise individuals. They swim around and below the cage, vanish beneath the boat and circle back. When they disappear from view, it's time to get out, drink something hot, visit the bathroom, then get back in.

For qualified divers only, the next trip into the water is in a submersible cage. This one only takes two divers and a divemaster with extra safety equipment. It is winched down into the blue from a boom arm, stopping at around 15 metres. The water temperature is a bit cooler and the view surprisingly different. At depth you are in shark territory; down here they swim faster and far more freely, swooping to and fro. You watch them pause as they approach the cages above, monitoring the activity curiously before swimming off then fading away in the distance. Next thing you know they are barrelling towards you again at speed, spinning past with a friendly grin (or menacing grimace depending on your personal state of mind) then heading away again. You ascend to the deck – another part of the experience that should not be ignored as it is the best position to appreciate just how enormous this apex predator is – before you re-enter the shallow cages where it all happens again.

The cage diver's day: the crew dropping the cages into the sea; throwing out a tuna tail at dawn; Rich and Sheri finally leave the cages to warm up; diver down again; hanging out of the cage to get closer!

dive log Islas Revillagigedo: San Benedicto

Sail for 24 hours across the open ocean southwest from Cabo San Lucas on the Baja Peninsula to reach the isolated Revillagigedo islands. Sitting firmly on the Pacific Ring of Fire, these islands are the location of a unique and fascinating marine ecosystem.

There are strong similarities between the three islands and, surprisingly, few named dive sites. However, each one is explored at least twice on different levels or in opposite directions.

San Benedicto is usually the first stop on any liveaboard trip. Sunrise over still active Bárcena volcano reveals a rugged landscape. The island was deeply scarred by the last eruption in 1952 and, beneath the surface, the scenery of strong rocky walls and volcanic boulders reflects what you can see above.

Nautilus Explorer
From Alaska to Mexico and beyond…
www.nautilusexplorer.com

⓷12 The Boiler

🜚 **Depth**	32 m	
◑ **Visibility**	good	
🌊 **Currents**	moderate but variable	

The most anticipated dive here, The Boiler is known as 'the' manta site. A short surface swim takes you to a circular pinnacle. The top sits at about six metres, with several other pinnacles to the sides. Fin past sheer walls made up of millions of thin layers, almost like stacks of paper, to get a first glimpse of the indigenous Clarion angel then finespotted, green and zebra morays. Around the bend, and up over a plateau, you are likely to come face-to-face with a giant Pacific manta ray: flapping to and fro, this graceful creature is more than interested in being interactive with the divers as they arrive. Accustomed to the attention, she works the group, sliding from one diver to the next, seeming to say hello to each in turn. It's hard to ascend (watch your air!) but a second dive here just gets better as more mantas arrive each one with distinct differences in body patterns.

⓷13 The Canyon

🜚 **Depth**	26 m	
◑ **Visibility**	good	
🌊 **Currents**	moderate but variable	

On the south of San Benedicto, this dive is meant to be the hammerhead site. It's also meant to have some strong currents but, typically, it's current one dive and not the next. Sometimes even current one minute and not the next. Descending beneath the boat, you swim to the anchor chain then head east until you hit a barrier reef of tumbled rocks. It's a long way from pretty but there are lots of fish: Clarion angelfish, redtail triggerfish in big groups, juvenile king angels, guinea fowl and porcupine puffers plus the giant electric ray. There is a special spot where divers are told to wait for the hammerheads to appear but, as is the way, they may not be there. And that's because they might be sitting just over your shoulder watching. Turn too quickly and you will scare them off. Unlike the mantas, these sharks tend to be skittish: always there but never close.

N14 Lava Flow	
Depth	32 m
Visibility	good
Currents	moderate but variable

Daily weather conditions dictate where and when you can dive, but this site, directly under the huge lava flow, is well protected. The topography is naturally rockier, with lots of swim-throughs in the shallows. As you drop in you meet a green turtle, but within milliseconds a manta appears. She is completely black, unlike the Boiler's chevron mantas (which have the arrow-shaped white collars across their wings) and look like sleek stealth bombers. More appear, smaller juveniles who are a little less curious and stay behind the adult female. Redtail triggerfish arrive in clusters, there are spotted boxfish and some of the biggest scorpionfish ever seen: the stone scorpion is 18 inches long and quite flat. Clarion angelfish dance around the area's other indigenous fish, the Clarion damsel, then, at the end of the dive, a very friendly octopus moves across the rocks.

The indigenous Clarion angelfish and Clarion damselfish (bottom); chevron manta ray.

66 99 We came around the corner of the pinnacle to see Sten, our divemaster. He flapped his arms at us and we responded with the universal 'where?' signal of both hands up. 'Manta, what manta?' we both thought... then with impossibly perfect timing a giant rose from behind him to fill our field of vision. This genuinely enormous female came towards us, turned and looked into our eyes. We must have passed muster as she slid sideways, oh-so-slowly, to hover in our bubbles. She wriggled and giggled, swooping in and out to play, wrapping her wings down and around us each in turn, glancing below to ask for more.

dive log Islas Revillagigedo: Socorro

Another overnight sail and you wake up at Socorro, the largest island in the group. Arriving at dawn, you watch the sun rise over sloping Mount Evermann, which last erupted in 1993, although this eruption was a submarine one and not far from the Punta Tosca dive site.

Diving starts after checking in at the naval station on the southern coast. This is the only community on the island, with just 250 or so people. After formalities are completed, the boat will set sail to either west or east, depending on the weather.

⬇15 Punta Tosca	
🔆 **Depth**	30 m
🔵 **Visibility**	good
🌊 **Currents**	moderate but variable

Lying on the western coast of Socorro, this site is a submerged tongue-shaped promontory that extends out from the coast at depth. The topography is very interesting, with several diverse sections to explore. Surface currents can be strong, but they drop away as you reach the reef top and are easy to avoid by moving to

the opposing side of the ridge. One side is an almost vertical wall made of huge rock slabs stacked on top of each other like some ancient Aztec fortress. The wall is covered in small green sponges and tiny feathery corals. Legions of lobsters – the hugest you think you will ever see – crawl across the surfaces, disturbing the well-camouflaged giant hawkfish. At 30 metres, the ridge is broken by sand and, beyond that, there are several more rocky outcrops. This area attracts reef sharks, and you can hear whale song reverberating through the sea.

🐟 Silky smooth

An activity that will certainly not be to everyone's taste is the opportunity to go snorkelling at night with silky sharks. Once the sun goes down, the lights from the boat attract flying fish to hunt across the surface of the water. Their arrival then attracts the silkies, but these sleek creatures soon get diverted to swim around and beneath the boat, curious to watch the activities on board. On our trip, there were only three, but the crew say that sometimes there are as many as ten in attendance.

After watching the sharks from deck for a short while, it's time to slip into the water – no splashing allowed – to see them at close range. Silky sharks grow to 3.3 metres and are renowned for their 'silky' smooth skin, which is a light beige-grey on top and white on the tummy. It can be hard to see them, as all your excited buddies get in the way and the torches attract a lot of planktonic matter.

A mother and baby dolphin came to join the party; then one of the divemasters noticed a tiny seahorse floating in front of his mask. What this poor little creature was doing so far up the water column, no one knew, so he was gently scooped into a plastic bucket and taken away from all the activity for fear he would become a snack for the sharks. This was the first seahorse seen in the Socorro area by the crew.

↘16 Cabo Pearce

Depth	34 m
Visibility	good
Currents	moderate but variable

Descending the line that leads down from the surface buoy, you arrive on the top of a narrow tongue-shaped promontory. There's a choice to be made – to go either left or right – but both routes will lead down to a deep area at its tip where sharks are often seen. Naturally, if you expect to see them, there won't be a single one but instead, there are often pairs of mantas, some with the hugest remoras hitchhiking on them. The rest of the dive will be lost to admiring these majestic and very friendly beauties.

A second dive is planned to explore the rocky surfaces of the promontory, where there are lobster, slipper lobsters and an octopus. Unfortunately for the smaller critters, it won't be long before the sunlight fades again, forcing you to look up. Yet another manta is hovering overhead and demanding all your attention, even while you are being mobbed by massive, mixed schools of Clarion angels and triggerfish.

By late afternoon, the currents often pick up so the final dive of the day is done beneath the sheer, vertical island walls. Towering overhead, these are carved with patterns more sculptural than any work of modern art. Beneath the waterline lies a bed of huge, rounded boulders, all coated with a furry carpet of algae. Poking around them, you can find octopus in the throes of a romantic moment. Giving them some privacy, you soon find several others who are more interested in reacting to their visitors than each other.

Opposite, a black jack on patrol. Right, Clarion angels and triggerfish; an octopus on display; green turtle with his barnacle.

dive log

Islas Revillagigedo: Roca Partida

The craggy, guano-coated twin pinnacles of remote Roca Partida, thrust aggressively up from a dark and choppy ocean. Just 100 metres long and much less wide, the island falls equally dramatically down to the depths of the Pacific.

As you approach in the dive tender you will instantly see that the conditions can be a little tougher here, with surf hitting the base of the walls. However, entry into the water is actually away from the cliff walls, so you rarely end up inside the surge zone. There is always some current, which hits the two ends of the island, north and south. Luckily, this is never so strong that you can't swim through it, and it's the current that makes Roca Partida the dive spectacle that it is.

⌄17 Roca Partida – South	
Depth	39 m
Visibility	good
Currents	moderate but variable

If you really wanted to, you could fin right around this dramatic rock in a single dive but, if you did, you would miss a lot of marine life: there is something on every surface or out in the blue, just waiting to be seen. Dropping in by the rock's curved south point means divers might have to swim down through current to find calmer waters – and just might encounter mantas doing the same. They whizz effortlessly around the point, see the divers and greet them with a belly roll before taking off again. After laughing at the precocious show-off, you can admire the steep walls where every crack and crevice is home to an animal. There are minute rainbow

scorpionfish, twice-spotted soapfish, the Panamic fang blenny and sally lightfoot crabs. The frustrating thing about these dives is that, just as you start to discover more unusual small creatures, yet another gorgeous manta ray appears. These sadly endangered animals are so playful, you just have to desert whatever else you were looking at. After they flap away you can return to the walls where wide shelves are stacked with whitetip sharks. Smaller caves have two or three juvenile sharks nestling with a giant green moray who appears to be acting as a surrogate mother, keeping the young sharks cosy by wrapping its sinuous body around them.

Clockwise opposite, Roca Partida residents: the guinea fowl pufferfish; leather bass (the juvenile uses the spiny urchin to its side as camouflage); a trio of silvertips; rainbow scorpionfish; giant damselfish; Galápagos shark.

roca
↘18 **partida**
north

⊘ **Depth**	45 m
◑ **Visibility**	good
≋ **Currents**	moderate but variable

Crossing from the main ship to dive Roca's northern point you just might be met by a pod of bottlenose dolphins – a tantalizing taste of things to come. As you roll in, you find you have dropped right into the centre of the pod! One youngster approaches: he hangs perfectly vertically, just waiting until everyone is in the water. Then he flips his tail and takes off rapidly to collect the gang, bringing them back to play. The dolphins do what you always hoped they would – they spend time with you, darting to and fro, returning to your side. The encounter takes you way too deep, but there is no way you can resist swimming with them.

Moving back up to a sensible depth near the northwestern tip, you run straight into a heaving mass of jacks and giant trevally. There is a shelf at 33 metres which is a good place to look for sharks. You don't have to move far, as they keep passing by at this level – a lone hammerhead hovers at the edge of vision; a group of silvertips spin in quite closely, then away and a Galápagos shark just about kisses your fins. This corner is very active and, as you ascend, you see more hammerheads (sadly still too far away) and another silky shark. Moving up to about 15 metres to start gassing off, you can visit two small caves that are always loaded with whitetip sharks. Ten or 12 at a time sit piled on top of each other: adults on top of babies on top of adults. A few flashes from the camera and they take off, circle for a moment then descend and settle again, prepared for another photo session.

❝❞ The smallest dolphin paused by my side, moved away a little, then paused again. It was an invitation to play. so I joined in, until I realized the cheeky creature had taken me down past 40 metres!

drying out
Yucatán Peninsula

Choosing where to stay in the Yucatán should be based on what type of diving you want to do. Whether you are on the coast near Playa del Carmen or over on Cozumel island, there is a big variety of accommodation options with almost as many dive centres and more restaurants than you could ever try in a short holiday.

Playa del Carmen

Transfers from Cancún airport take up to 90 minutes.

Diving

SeaLife Divers, sealifedivers.com. On Mamitas Beach, value dive packs include local reefs, Cozumel and cenote diving.

Dive Cenotes, divecenotes.com

Sleeping

Acanto Hotel, acantohotels.com. Central location and just back from the beach.

Condo Ali, luxury 2-bed villa with good access to both the beach and all nightlife. Book through seamonkeybusiness.com.

Cozumel

Transfers from Cozumel airport take less than 60 minutes.

Diving

Deep Blue, deepbluecozumel.com. Custom packages for experienced divers.

Del Mar Aquatics, across the road the Casa del Mar hotel, see below.

Sleeping

Casa del Mar, casadelmarcozumel.com. Resort-style hotel on a quieter section of the coast north of town.

Casa Mexicana, casamexicanacozumel.com. In the very centre of town and opposite the waterfront.

Chichén Itzá on the Yucatán Peninsula; dive centre on the beach; Mexican child selling balloons.

Days out

Cozumel, Playa del Carmen and Cancún No matter where you stay, these are easily accessible from each other. Holiday activities include skydiving, kayaking, golf and jungle treks. Cancún is a purpose-built tourist city and highly commercialized, which may not suit everyone, while the others are a little more relaxed and retain a Mexican feel.

Chankanaab National Park, Cozumel The original marine park in this area is a shallow lagoon that's a great place to get your toes wet if you're not a diver, but you can dive here as well. There are snorkelling facilities, and the botanical garden has hundreds of tropical plant species and many iguanas.

Tulum An hour's drive south from Playa del Carmen, this ancient site was both a Maya seaport and an astronomical centre. It sits in the most breathtaking location facing the rising sun and looking over the sea.

Xel-há North of Tulum, this once natural complex of waterways and mangroves is now a themed park with lagoons, cenotes, ancient caves and jungle walks. A good day out for those with kids and non-divers.

Xcaret Just south of Playa this is touted as an eco-archaeological park. There are some marine-based activities plus a Museum of Culture and Archaeology and a replica Maya Village. Special evening events include dance extravaganzas and ancient ball games.

Sian Ka'an Biosphere Reserve This UNESCO World Heritage Site covers an area of rare coastal wetlands with 20 or so archaeological sites, over 100 mammal species and 300 bird species. It is also a nesting site for two species of endangered sea turtles.

Holbox On the very northeastern tip of the Yucatán, tiny Holbox island sits just off the coast. The seas close by are a known whale shark highway. Between late June and August, it is said you can snorkel with more than you can count on all your digits.

Chichén Itzá West of Cancún, this sacred Maya city is the best known in the area. Its pyramid is something of an icon with 91 steep steps to the top – if you climb it, your calves will be sorry. There are many other buildings, including an observatory and a ball court. An ancient Olmec ball game was played here and gave a whole new meaning to the term 'sudden death'. The winners (or losers, no one really knows which) were decapitated after the game.

Baja California

Baja's principal diving destinations can only be reached by liveaboard. A small cluster of large, steel-hulled vessels cruise the Mexican Pacific. They are stable and comfortable, which is important for the long crossings to these islands.

Isla Guadalupe itineraries depart from San Diego. Transfers are by bus to Ensenada in Baja California Norte and take two to three hours. Islas Revillagigedos liveaboards leave from Cabo San Lucas on the tip of Baja California Sud. Flights are to San Jose del Cabo with transfers of up to 90 minutes.

Liveaboards

Nautilus Explorer, nautilusexplorer.com. This stable and substantial vessel can accommodate 26 divers. A fabulous crew and some lovely touches like hot drinks and on-tap fresh cookies between dives.

Rocio del Mar, rociodelmarliveaboard.com
Sea Escape, seaescapeliveaboard.com
Solmar V, solmarv.com
Baja California

Sleeping

El Encanto Inn, elencantoinn.com. In the heart of the historic San José del Cabo and right in the artists' quarter; this town is a charming stopover destination.

Sleeping

Wyndham Hotel, wyndham.com. Directly opposite the Cabo San Lucas marina where liveaboards (and cruise ships) dock, this is a convenient but very lively and busy area.

Days out

San José del Cabo Anyone who has ever travelled through the heart of Mexico will be delighted to see that the centre of this small town still retains a traditional air. Prior to colonization it was a provisioning stop for Spanish galleons and famous pirates like Sir Francis Drake. Historical sites include The Mission, a Jesuit fort and mission that was built in 1733 on what would become the main town square. The imposing exterior has an ornate ceramic mural of native Indians on the front and contrasts strongly with the simplistic interior. The Plaza, lying in front of the Mission, is a lovely cobbled square edged by many Spanish colonial buildings, including the city hall. At night the plaza attracts buskers and acrobats, musicians on a bandstand or dancers on the stage. The enormous fountain is ringed by sculptures of famed local dignitaries. The quiet streets that lie behind the plaza are the Artists' Quarter, attracting both artists in residence and many galleries showing the works of well-known Mexican artists. It's well worth touring and well worth leaving your credit card behind.

Cabo San Lucas On the southernmost tip of Baja, is this highly developed and highly touristy town. This once idyllic small fishing harbour has become a busy marina that is swarmed upon almost daily by the occupants of visiting cruise ships. There are touts for game-fishing trips, beach trips, snorkelling, paragliding and so on, and anyone walking around the marina is fair game. Beyond the pier, and at night, it calms down somewhat and you can sit at a marina-side restaurant to enjoy the view. Shops, restaurants and nightlife are all on tap for anyone who likes a busy stopover.

San Diego

An added bonus of going to Guadalupe is a stopover in one of America's nicest small cities. Central San Diego is compact and easy to get around with a very good public transport system. Before the transfer to Mexico departs, take a walk around the 1860s Gaslamp Quarter and Balboa Park, which is promoted as America's largest urban cultural park. Both are must-see's. If you have kids, there's SeaWorld, and for those interested in naval life, you can tour the supercarrier *USS Nimitz*.

San Jose del Cabo – restaurant or art? Roca Partida; Cabo San Lucas marina; San Diego harbour.

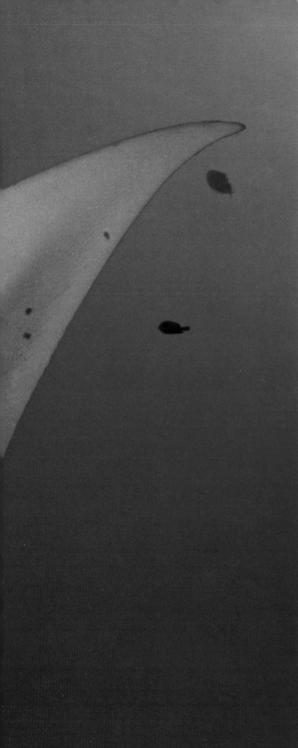

227
↘ **Essentials**

228
↘ **Dive brief**

230
↘ **Dive sites**

232
↘ **Dive log**

232 Chuuk
235 Republic of Palau
240 Yap

242
↘ **Drying out**

242 Republic of Palau
243 Yap and Chuuk

Micronesia

Bath time: the manta ray, *Manta alfredi,* glides in for a spruce up from cleaner wrasse and butterflyfish.
German Channel, Palau

destination
Micronesia

Guam

Philippine Sea

PACIFIC OCEAN

🦶 Yap ▶▶ p240

● Kolonia

🦶 Palau ▶▶ p235

● Koror

🦶 Chuuk ▶▶ p232

Weno ●

Flying in to Micronesia is quite an experience. The aerial views are of awe-inspiring beauty: handfuls of green islands sprinkled over the deep blue Pacific Ocean.

There is no development here, no high rise, no motorways, just never-ending seas that promise – and deliver – some remarkable diving experiences. The island groups of Palau, Yap and Chuuk are like a set of triplets: all charming but, for divers, each with its own distinct personality.

Palau is precocious, leaping to the fore to show off her many marine talents; she has a bit of everything and something for every diver. Yap is shy, modest about her attractions, yet quietly proud of her year-round manta ray populations. Further east lurks Chuuk, moody, mysterious but much admired for her Second World War wrecks. Although each has its own specific features, they are all set against the backdrop of a prolific marine realm born of the deep ocean trenches of the Western Pacific.

Micronesia sits quietly apart from the 'real' world. These islands have developed at differing paces: one rushing headlong towards a western future; one shying away from any outside influences; and one that's not sure which way to jump. The challenge is in being open-minded – you think you know what to expect, then you realize you didn't have a clue.

Jayapura ●

INDONESIA

Essentials

There's hard to get to, there's expensive to get to, and then there's Micronesia. But don't give up, as there are huge rewards for those who make the effort to visit these miniscule Pacific islands. Neither the Federated States of Micronesia (Yap and Chuuk) nor the Republic of Palau have a national carrier, and airline routes from nearby come and go. There are regular departures from Manila, Tokyo, Seoul and Guam, a US Territory. You will need to go through American immigration there but, if you are doing a multi-centre trip, it's often the best option.

Local laws and customs

These islands, often loosely grouped together as Micronesia, were originally inhabited by seafarers from Indonesia and the Philippines. Their ancient cultures were sophisticated, with highly structured social groups but, as each island developed in isolation from each other, so their cultures differ. There are many variable nuances when it comes to social etiquette, so be very respectful of the elderly, the role of the family in traditional village life and the positions of both sexes. It's best to ask a local, as times are changing rapidly. Play it safe and dress modestly everywhere.

Health and safety

With no specific inoculations or warnings and good medical facilities on all these islands, health worries are minimal. However, there can be a little trouble in paradise: each of these islands is rushing headlong into joining the modern world and the effects of this need management from within. The islands may seem calm on the surface and local issues are unlikely to affect tourists, but be aware that road, alcohol and drug offences are treated with a strong hand. Any display of affection (even holding hands) can be frowned on, as is homosexuality. If you were to notice any unrest it would be in Chuuk (Truk), where unemployment and hence social problems are the most pronounced.

Costs

These islands could be described as expensive when compared to neighbouring Asian destinations, but costs aren't so high as to be prohibitive. Drinks and meals are a little bit more than what you might expect to pay in the US, an easy comparison as all the islands use US dollars. There is very little in the way of agriculture, so nearly everything has to be imported. With no specific 'cuisine', meals tend to be international style. Hotel choices are limited, and standards are a little lower than you would hope for the rate paid. Palau has the best options; Yap has just a handful, and the lower-end places are not really worth investigating. Chuuk has only two land options and these are similarly priced. Tipping is expected everywhere.

Fact file

Palau
Location	7°30'N, 134°30'E
Capital	Melekeok

Micronesia
Location	6°55'N, 158°15'E
Capital	Palikir

Flights	Major carriers to Guam, Manila, Seoul, Tokyo with onward connections
Land transport	Taxis or use private options
Departure tax	Manila: US$20; Palau: US$20; Chuuk: US$15
Entry	Visas not required but check US regulations for transiting through Guam
Money	US dollar
Language	English is widely spoken
Electricity	110v, plug type A (see page 15)
Time zone	Palau and Yap: GMT +9. Chuuk: GMT +10
Religion	Various Christian denominations with many fringe and evangelical forms
Communications	Palau country code +680; FSM country code +691; IDD code 011; Police 911 Internet access is patchy but improving
Tourist information	visit-palau.com; visit-micronesia.com for both Chuuk and Yap; visityap.com
Travel advisories	gov.uk/foreign-travel-advice; state.gov/travel

dive brief

❝❞ **Our first trip to Micronesia was on an extended trip to see all three of these islands at once. A week in Palau gave us great diving but not enough time to explore the cosmopolitan island lifestyle. Five dive days in Yap gave us manta after manta encounter but no time to see the charming southern reefs, and six days on Chuuk – on land – was enough. But, oh to have been floating over that amazing lagoon on a boat. The question is, would we go back? Yes, to Palau – and we have – and another yes to Yap in a heartbeat; but to Chuuk? Maybe one day, but only if we could get on a liveaboard.**

Diving

It can be a little misleading but the word Micronesia is often used to describe all the islands in the Western Pacific as well as being the formal name of the Federated States of Micronesia. In reality, the only reason these islands are grouped together is that, after the Second World War, the UN and US formed federations of certain Pacific island groups. Some of these lasted and some didn't. Each island has its own history, influenced by wars, colonialism, missionary infiltration and geopolitical interests right up until today.

Each has its own marine features too. The three most visited destinations are the Republic of Palau and, in the Federated States of Micronesia, Yap and Truk Lagoon – more properly known as Chuuk. As you fly in to Palau you get your first view of just how breathtaking the landscape is. (Sell your grandmother for a window seat or you'll find yourself sitting on a stranger's lap.) Once you hit the water you won't be disappointed, as the diving can be equally breathtaking, especially when you come face-to-face with more sharks than you thought still existed in the ocean.

Yap is famous for another marine giant: her resident manta populations, although there is much more, and Chuuk is equally famous for a single reason – her renowned lagoon, which is littered with wrecks. If you are into wrecks and war history, this is an unrivalled diving destination.

Snorkelling

This is another of those location, location, location moments. The majority of wrecks in Chuuk are beyond 20 metres deep, so snorkelling will be limited, but there are some wonderful aeroplane wrecks in shallow water near Eten Island.

Over in Yap, the mangrove-rimmed channels and coastal reefs can be murky with some strong currents during tidal changes, so you will need to be advised by your dive team. In Palau, there are lots of beautiful white-sand beaches with offshore reefs where a snorkel can be rewarding, but these sites are not likely to be where the dives are. Parts of the Rock Islands are closed to protect nesting species, such as turtles, but of course, Palau does have one of the planet's ultimate snorkelling destinations: the Jellyfish Lake.

Diving on Siaes Wall in Palau; The Jake, a slow-flying reconnaissance seaplane.

Marine life

Divers come to these islands for the large and famous animal populations: the sharks in Palau and the mantas in Yap. However, diversity is high and the macro life in these seas can be good, as long as you take time to look for it.

Making the big decision

As this is likely to be the least convenient dive trip you will ever make, there is no question that you should do at least two islands together, three if you can swing the time. However, that will mean taking the best part of three weeks, four if you really want to do it properly. Flight links between the islands are sadly not as good as they once were, so you may lose up to two days getting there and another two each time you transit between islands. If you have less time, then Palau and Yap can work well together. It would be hard to see Palau in less than a week. Yap needs four or five days; any less in low season and you risk missing the mantas. Chuuk? Well, a week if you are on a liveaboard, four or five dive days from land, though you may still not see as much as you should.

Animal encounters

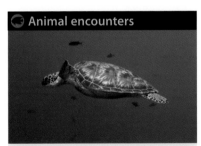

Palau: Napoleon wrasse, whitetip reef sharks, manta rays, grey reef sharks, turtles, blacktip sharks and a few thousand jellyfish. Did we mention the leopard sharks?

Yap: almost as many mantas here as sharks in Palau, plus a few sharks, batfish, cuttlefish and gorgeous mandarinfish.

Chuuk: the amazing, almost intact vessels are classic examples of ocean reclamation, so hunt in the colourful soft corals for pretty fish and small critters.

dive sites

Each of these tiny Pacific Islands has a huge reputation for a unique marine feature or two. Conditions vary too, due to individual influences from the local geography.

Palau has the most impressive range of dive styles, with steep walls, wrecks and submerged limestone caves, but by far the most popular attraction has to be the sharks. It's the reason to go and go again. This one small country has proven that turning your territorial waters into a shark sanctuary and then policing it really does work. Conditions can be challenging, with strong currents on many dives, but these are unavoidable if you want to see the big animals. On the other hand, you can also snorkel in a mill-pond calm lake with a gazillion velvet-smooth jellyfish.

Biodiversity is also highest in Palau and decreases the further east you go. A short distance away, Yap's topography, both above and below, is flatter. Actually four islands sandwiched together and divided by murky channels that wash nutrients into the sea. This area is subject to wind patterns – when the breezes are up on the windward side, dives are done on the other. It's these conditions that keep the manta rays close by. They are as guaranteed as any event in the marine world can be.

Micronesian Chuuk, also known as Truk Lagoon, is the legendary location where a whole fleet of Japanese planes, cargo carriers and warships sit on the seabed. There is little else, as the reefs outside the lagoon have been battered both by man and nature. Truk is another mirror-smooth destination, but the dives tend to be deep, with most well beyond 20 metres and some at 50 metres plus. Dives need to be planned carefully but currents are rare with just occasional surface movement, and visibility is good year-round.

Chuuk – Truk Lagoon ▶▶ p232

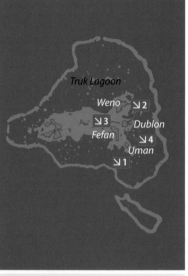

Truk Lagoon

Weno ↘2

↘3 Dublon

Fefan ↘4

Uman

↘1

Log Book

↘1 **Sankisan Maru**
↘2 **Nippo Maru**
↘3 **Kenshu Maru**
↘4 **Fujikawa Maru**

→ **The Emily:** wreck of a flying boat lying in shallow water; a Zero fighter is near by

→ **Rio de Janeiro:** a submarine support vessel now resting on her port side

→ **Yamagiri Maru:** used to transport goods from the Solomons until torpedoed

→ **Heian Maru:** lying on her port side revealing her name welded on the hull

Conditions

Seasons	Year-round diving but with the most rain between July and October.
Visibility	10 m inshore to 40+ further offshore
Currents	Can be strong in Palau and Yap, none in Truk
Temperatures	Air 26-32°C; water 28-30°C
Wet suit	3 mm shorty or full body suit
Training	Courses in Palau or Yap
Nitrox	Check with your resort or liveaboard
Deco chambers	Palau, Yap, Chuuk and Guam

Diversity
combined reef area
5,490 km²

	Micronesia	Palau
HARD CORALS	330	350
FISH SPECIES	1,228	1,469
ENDEMIC FISH SPECIES	6	1
FISH UNDER THREAT	23	26

All diversity figures are approximate

Palau ▶▶ p235

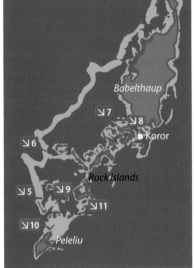

🕓 Log Book

📍5	Blue Corner
📍6	Ulong Corner and Channel
📍7	Teshio Maru
📍8	Chandelier Cave
📍9	German Channel
📍10	Ngedbus Coral Garden
📍11	Jellyfish Lake

→ **Blue Holes:** four holes in the reef top that lead down into a huge cavern

→ **Siaes Tunnel:** a deep tunnel through the reef always occupied by circling jacks

→ **New Drop Off:** steep wall decorated with clouds of pyramid butterflyfish

→ **The Jake:** an almost intact Navy floatplane nestling on a shallow reef

→ **Peleliu Wall:** on the southern tip where currents create a ripping drift dive

Yap ▶▶ p240

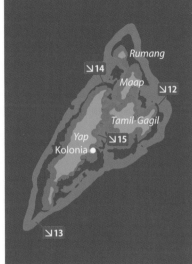

🕓 Log Book

📍12	Valley of the Rays
📍13	Lionfish Wall and Yap Caverns
📍14	M'il Channel and Manta Ridge
📍15	Mandarinfish Dive

→ **Goofnuw Mini Wall:** immense schools of batfish hovering over hard corals

→ **Gilmaan Wall:** vertical wall that hides leaffish and moray eels

→ **Peelaek Corner:** sandy plateau a few passing turtles and a few more mantas

→ **Gapow Reef:** vertical wall meets terrace meets a second wall

🕓 Endangered oceans

There is a new trend in a few countries, including Palau, that you may or may not approve of – the nautilus dive. It involves putting a couple of dead chickens into a fishing cage then dropping it down to great depths. Goodness knows who ever worked it out but it seems this rarely seen nocturnal cephalopod likes chicken meat. Once the cage is down at dusk, the scent attracts the nautilus and, overnight, a few wiggle into the cage and have a very good dinner, thank you very much! They then get stuck and are hauled up to 15 metres to amuse the tourists.

A lot of divers are not happy with this practice, and it has to be said that no one knows what affect bringing these beautiful creatures up to the reef in daylight will have on them. However, the females do ascend to shallow waters to lay their eggs, which take between eight and 12 months to develop and hatch.

On questioning the crew, we were told it was traditional to capture the nautilus in this way to sell the shells. By paying the local fishermen for the capture and release service instead, the nautilus live to tell the tale. Sales of their shells on this island at least have been substantially reduced.

dive log
Micronesia: Chuuk

Standing on a flawless beach, beneath a rustling palm, looking at a perfectly calm sea, it's hard to imagine the devastation caused during two short days in 1944. It's not until you get below the water that Chuuk's wartime history really hits you.

The Japanese Imperial Fleet valued Chuuk's completely enclosed lagoon, thinking that the few entry and exit channels would make it easy to defend against a naval attack – but it also made it a trap. On 17 February, Operation Hailstone blitzed this so-called impenetrable fortress and an estimated 100 American planes annihilated the entire Japanese fleet stationed in Truk Lagoon.

There are 40 or so shipwrecks lying on the lagoon floor, and each and every one is a rich artificial reef, an incredible tour through a moment in history and a testimonial to her purpose: you will find the remains of tanks and jeeps, anti-aircraft guns, torpedo tubes and far more ammunition than you care to think about. There are broken aircraft and abandoned submarines, but you won't find any human remains: as many as could be recovered were returned home, an action regarded as vital to Japan's religious beliefs.

You also won't see as many artefacts as you may have thought. Sadly, many small items have been systematically plundered – by tourists desperate for a souvenir, by locals trying to profit from selling artefacts and by local fishermen who have salvaged explosives for their own use.

↘1 Sankisan Maru	
🔻 **Depth**	48 m
◑ **Visibility**	fair to brilliant
≈ **Currents**	no

Regarded as Chuuk's prettiest wreck, the *Sankisan's* history is unknown. She may have been Japanese, launched in 1942, or American, launched as the *Red Hook* and later captured by the Japanese. Whatever the truth, the ship was around 4,700 tons, 112-115 metres long and nearly 16 metres wide. Sitting off Uman Island, her demise was caused by strafing from American aircraft but there are no accurate records confirming this. As a dive, the *Sankisan's* reputation is for coral gardens – a strange introduction to the wrecks in the lagoon. As you descend over the hull, the view is one of rainbow-hued reefs rather than disintegrating metal. Divers visit the first hold, which is carpeted in bullets and shells, then swim back up to deck level, past the remains of a few vehicles, before descending down into the next hold. This has a truck and a flat-bed lorry, plus boxes full of medicine bottles, their contents an ominous, chalky white. The divemasters then swim through a warren of corridors to a third hold, where there are spare parts for engines. On the deck, the midships section is quite broken up but covered in corals. Metal joists and beams drip with colour and you meet fish you normally see on a coral reef: longnose hawkfish, moorish idols and mimic filefish. On the way back up, you can investigate the incredible growth on the foremast. Plan another dive to see the ruined stern and the remains of the propeller and rudder which are down at 48 metres.

Inside and outside the *Sankisan Maru*.

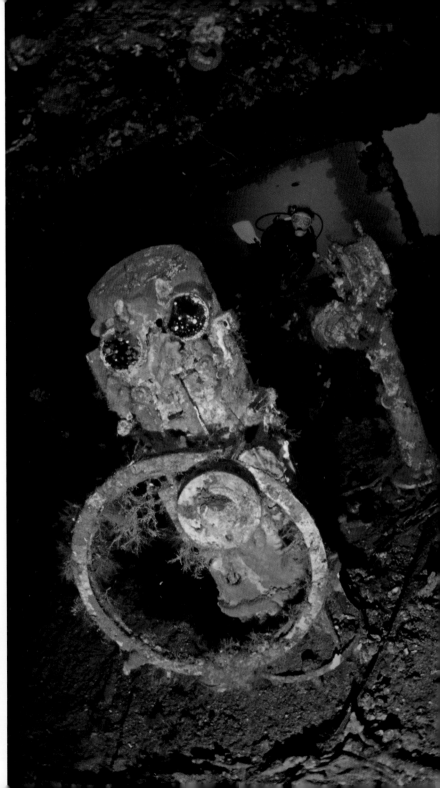

🔱 Nippo Maru	
🧭 **Depth**	38 m
◐ **Visibility**	fair to excellent
🌊 **Currents**	no

The *Nippo* was built in 1936 in Kobe as a cargo-passenger vessel, then requisitioned in 1941 and refitted to carry water tanks, ordnance and munitions. She arrived in Chuuk in a convoy transporting troops a week before being hit three times in the midships area by 500-pound bombs. The *Nippo* was discovered in 1969 by the Cousteau expedition near Eten Island, although her location was 'lost' until the late 1980s when the ship's bell was discovered, engraved with both English and Japanese characters. At 107 metres long, the remains of the *Nippo* could easily take three dives to investigate fully and, as she is sitting at over 50 metres, dives should be carefully planned. The stern is most impressive. As the light fades and the hull takes on that ghostly quality, a series of three howitzers emerge. To their side are a series of gun mounts and a barrel gun platform. Inside the deepest hold is more artillery, while the next one heading upwards has medical supplies, bowls, wheels and tyres. Another has water tanks, shells and beer bottles.

To the port side of the deck is a preserved armoured tank, although its turret gun is missing. A final entry is made into the shallowest hold – and perhaps the most harrowing – where you are reminded what went on here. Surrounded by a swathe of bullets are several gas masks.

Medicines and the bridge on the *Nippo Maru*.

◺3 Kenshu Maru

❂ Depth	17 m
◐ Visibility	fair to good
≋ Currents	no

Originally a passenger and cargo ship, the *Kenshu Maru* had been transformed into a transporter by the time it was targeted by US forces, although it took three attacks for them to take her down. She was first hit by a bomb and set afire in December 1943 so was run aground to keep from sinking. On 17 February, 1944 she was hit on the stern by a bomb dropped by US aircraft then, a day later, she was attacked again – a torpedo hit amidships, and she promptly sank. Despite all that, much of the wreck is in perfect condition: the bow gun is intact as is the engine room. One hold is full of bottles and plates, and the wheel house still has its signalling devices inside. Soft corals are now growing around parts of the hull.

The *Kenshu Maru* (below) and Fujikawa (above).

◺4 Fujikawa Maru

❂ Depth	34 m
◐ Visibility	fair to excellent
≋ Currents	no

Perhaps the most dived wreck, the *Fujikawa* was a passenger ship until, in 1940, it was requisitioned by the Imperial Navy to be used as an armed transport ship for the delivery of aircraft and spares. She was damaged at anchor in Kwajalein and then towed to Chuuk for repairs, arriving on 31 January 1943. The *Fujikawa* is an easily accessible dive but is showing obvious signs of wear, probably as she is upright and one of the shallower dives. There is plenty of interest on the deck at around 17 metres. Descent is straight down to the impressive, coral-encrusted bow gun, which rests at about 12 metres, bathing in the sun's rays. Her coating of crusting hard and soft corals is incredibly lush, although you can hardly see them for the number of fish that swarm around. Just below the

gun mount on the deck are two memorial plaques: one for the ship itself and another for well-respected local explorer and diver Kimiuo Aisek. The two front holds are full of aircraft paraphernalia: propellors, wings, engines and the fuselages of four aircraft said to be Zero fighters. Heading out of the second hold you can swim through the engine room, a maze of walkways and engines still lit by sunshine filtering from above. One cabin still has a bathroom area where you can see wash basins and urinals. All the holds heading to the stern can be investigated, but the most curious is the last, full of sake bottles, china and mess kits.

dive log

Republic of Palau

The legend goes that these islands were formed after the birth of a boy named Chuab. He grew into a giant, consumed all the village's food and even some of the other children. The villagers were so worried they decided the only solution was to kill him. They built a bonfire and tricked him into standing in the middle of it by saying it was for a special feast. The fire engulfed him and he fell into the sea. The parts of his body that protruded from the sea became the many islands of Palau.

Geographically, these islands are either limestone or volcanic (not human, obviously) and nearly all are ringed by reefs that drop to extreme walls perforated by caves and tunnels. Koror, the capital, and Malakal, the harbour, are linked by road bridges, and the lagoon nearby has enough wrecks to give Chuuk a run for its money. A little south are the picturesque Rock Islands, where you will find the stunning Jellyfish Lake, an unmissable experience. At the bottom of the chain is Pelilu Island, which was the scene of a terrible land battle in the Second World War. The islands sit between the North Pacific and the Philippine Sea so their marine realm is influenced by both.

⑤⑤ **Blue Corner**	
🕐 **Depth**	33 m
🜂 **Visibility**	good
≋ **Currents**	medium to ripping

Palau's most famous dive site is justifiably renowned – a spectacle of truly epic proportions. Entry is over the edge of a wall that curves outwards to a promontory. Divers often drop straight into a massive school of chevron barracuda, or sometimes it's an equally large one of jacks. Next, it's a swim along the perfectly vertical wall to a deep crevice lined with fan corals. The wall is pretty enough but mostly ignored, as just beyond this point is where divers ascend to the plateau above and hook on to a rock to wait for the show.

Looking down, there are a few grey reef sharks in the deep and then, on the other side of the plateau, a jumbo school of jacks appears. It's when the current lifts to rip-your-mask-off levels that the real action starts. More sharks – greys, blacktips and whitetips – appear and swoop across the vista. They are surrounded by schooling fish, such as fusiliers and redtooth triggers. Napoleon wrasse swim in and out and you notice a few turtles sitting on the plateau behind, calmly chomping on the sponges. The sharks circle closer and closer, while masses of fish seem to hang off their tails. The greys and whitetips continue patrolling along the front of the wall, sometimes followed by blue trevally; at other times, there is yet another school of barracuda. Eventually, you have to lift off; the current will take you either along the reef rim, over beds of hard coral with the whitetips still cruising below, or back over the plateau to spot morays and turtles.

ulong
↘6 **corner**
and channel

⚙ **Depth**	31 m
◐ **Visibility**	stunning
≋ **Currents**	medium to strong

Ulong Island is a very pretty one but, far more significantly, it sits by an exceptional, if somewhat exposed, diving area. Ulong Corner and Channel are swept by currents that constantly attract sharks – and divers. Entry is over the channels outer corners, where a wall edges a natural amphitheatre. Divers hook on at the top of the wall and wait for the show to commence. There are always small whitetip sharks waiting in the wings, but they tend to move away as the larger and more inquisitive grey reef sharks approach those waiting in the front rows. The greys swoop in so close you almost feel the need to pull back, but they are very accustomed to their daily visitors and only ever curious.

After a while, it's time to move the show down the channel and, unhooking from your rock, you are swept away, followed by juvenile whitetips, schools of snappers and trevally. The current can be frisky so it's off for a rollercoaster ride between the gorgeous, soft-coral-clad walls with schools of big-eyes and snappers. About half way along the channel, you reach an extensive patch of lettuce leaf corals that smother the sloping wall. There are unbelievable numbers of fish tucked between them – butterflyfish, red soldierfish and two-spot snapper all fighting for space. A few sharks and a turtle keep you company towards the end of the ride, but they disappear as soon as the current spits you out over a patch of bright white sand.

☑7 Teshio Maru	
🕐 **Depth**	24 m
🕑 **Visibility**	good
〰 **Currents**	none

☑8 Chandelier Cave	
🕐 **Depth**	10 m
🕑 **Visibility**	excellent at the top
〰 **Currents**	none

Palau's war-era wrecks are nowhere near as famous as those in Chuuk, but they are still great dives. The *Teshio* is one of the few that lies outside the Palau lagoon where the visibility is the best. This was a Japanese cargo ship that was sunk in 1944 by a US fighter plane. It was trying to escape at the time and now lies on its starboard side. Apart from a hole in the hull caused by a torpedo, the vessel is almost intact. There are coral clad anchors and a small gun mounted at the bow. It is safe to explore inside the two forward holds if you have a torch, although few people take the time out to do that as there is so much more to see around the outside of the hull and down on the seabed. Few artifacts are found within the superstructure, and much of the engine room is damaged from salvaging. The propeller has been salvaged too, but the rudder and shaft are easily seen. Large sea whips and sponges drip off the hull.

In a lovely cove just across from the port at Malakal is this incredible hidden cave system. Entry is just before a buoyed-off area, which stops boats mooring too close. The cave mouth is four metres down and perhaps five metres wide but as soon as you go inside, it opens to a gaping space. At one time – and we are going back millennia here – these caves were open to the air. Rainwater would trickle down through the porous limestone to create hanging stalactites, the drips hitting the surfaces below forming stalagmites. After the ice age, seawater levels slowly rose, flooded the caves and concealed the entrance. As you enter the first and largest cave, the stalactites are quite rounded, perhaps reshaped by the movement of seawater. Swimming past these you get to enter each of the next three chambers in turn and can ascend inside them to surface in the spaces where an air gap still allows fresh water to percolate through

from the land above, creating spectacular sculptures. The formations are breathtaking, glittering with absorbed minerals and appearing as pleats of fabric or pencil-thin icicles. It's incredibly pretty, but some find it claustrophobic. Ensure you stay well above the bottom to avoid stirring up the silt and take a good torch (or two).

Descending over the *Teshio Maru*; investigating Chandelier Cave.

⇘9 German Channel	
Depth	33 m
Visibility	good
Currents	medium to ripping

Another of Palau's best known and most popular dives is found in this man-made channel. During the German occupation in the early 20th century, phosphates were mined on Angaur. A hole was blasted through the reef to allow transport boats access to town. The channel now connects the inner lagoon with the open ocean and brings in nutrients and plankton.

Swimming down the channel towards the mouth of the lagoon, there are some coral outcrops with a few small schools of fish, but the marine topography is mostly perfectly flat with a bright-white sand seafloor. However, as you approach the channel mouth, you also approach the manta cleaning stations. Divers kneel in semicircles a little way back and hope the mantas arrive. Even if they don't, it is likely there will be a few grey reef sharks and whitetips or even a passing leopard shark. If the currents are right, the mantas can be seen either feeding on plankton at the mouth of the channel or as they get a spruce up from the waiting butterflyfish or cleaner wrasse. Their visits are not as constant as at some cleaning stations, but when the mantas are there, they stay for quite some time. Unfortunately, this can mean that there are a lot of divers as well, and the visibility drops as all that lovely white sand gets badly stirred up.

⇘10 Ngedbus Coral Garden	
Depth	18 m
Visibility	good
Currents	medium to ripping

The most southerly island in the chain is Peleliu, location of a horrendous battle during World War II. More recently, the island was hit by Typhoon Bopha and some of the more impressive outer reefs were damaged. All the same, the ones near the top of the island are in good condition and the reefs make a contrast to the big animal dives elsewhere. They consist of a backdrop of hard corals that slope away gently from the coast. The dive at Ngedbus is a healthy coral garden that starts in less than a metre of water and drops to about 22. The reef is broken by crevices that lead back towards the shore and these harbour and protect a range of smaller creatures. Juvenile whitetip sharks can be seen sheltering in caves, while the corals camouflage leaffish. Cuttlefish are seen regularly too, as are blue ribbon eels if you go to the bottom of the reef and watch for them in the rubble.

Leaffish (above) and cuttlefish are seen around Peleliu island.

S11 Jellyfish Lake	
Depth	33 m
Visibility	good
Currents	none

The marine lake known as Jellyfish Lake, but locally as Ongeim'l Tketau, is found on Mecherchar Island. Although it's the one everyone sees, there are actually 70 or so found in Palau. Their depths are salt water and fed by hidden channels that lead in from the sea, while the top layer of water is fresh, diluted by rain. The animals that live inside these lakes have adapted to exploit this unusual environment.

Reaching this particular lake requires a trek through the jungle, up a steep and very slippery track. It can be quite hard going, but it only takes 10 minutes before you descend to a pontoon overlooked by emerald hills and surrounded by thick mangroves and forest.

The water in the lake is murky around the edges, which are well shaded, with just an occasional polka-dot cardinalfish hovering around. However, as you snorkel across the lake you see one, then another, until suddenly there are hundreds of pale apricot, mastigias jellies, plus an occasional moon jelly. The mastigias lost their capacity to sting, as their only predator is a small anemone that lives beneath the mangroves. They spend their days circumnavigating the lake, following the movement of the sun's rays. As you snorkel, be aware of what you are doing with your fins – a hefty kick will destroy any jelly you make contact with.

❝ ❞ They feel like floating jello... no, no, more like cold oatmeal... no no, more like a soggy sponge after you've done the dishes... millions of jellyfish pushing, pulsating and slithering to get in the sunlight as they glide across your neck, arms and legs. Another reason why this was one of my best ever dive trips.
Phil Tobin, diamond broker, Portland, USA

dive log
Micronesia: Yap

From the air Yap appears to be a single triangular island. However, on closer inspection, you realize her gently rolling landscape is divided by three channels into four tightly-knit land masses: Yap, Tomil-Gagil, Maap and Rumung.

These shallow channels are lined by dense mangrove swamps and edged by seagrass. The water is nothing if not murky, but head seawards, over the surrounding lagoon, and it's all change. Where the surf breaks against the reef, the visibility clears to reveal coral-clad hills and valleys. Fifteen miles to the east is the Yap Trench, one of the deep water trenches that form part of the Pacific Ring of Fire and one reason why large pelagic species are attracted to the islands.

Yap's resident manta populations may be world famous, but sharks congregate here as well. The area is also becoming known for its macro life. There is a good selection of small and often wacky reef-building animals to look for if you can just drag yourself away from the mantas.

⚓ Valley of the Rays	
🕐 **Depth**	16 m
◈ **Visibility**	medium to great
≋ **Currents**	mild to strong

At this site on the east coast, plankton-rich waters flow through the shallow channel and into the deeper valley. There are three cleaning stations that attract the mantas – Merry-go-round, Carwash and Manta Rock. The dive involves swimming from one to another until you find them. At first this seems hopeless, until you suddenly notice a grey wing flap. Effortlessly, a manta glides in leading a gang. They are so close you could touch them; you know that, as you sit captivated on the sand just a few feet away, they are watching you too, no doubt with barely disguised amusement. More arrive in small groups, taking turns at the cleaning station, then move off again. At the same time, those waiting in line pull into the channel behind, so you need to have eyes in the back of your head.

❝❞ The mantas appeared like a squadron of bombers, approaching the shallows in formation, gently finning their wing-tips to stay stationary. We lay underneath them in awe, closer and for longer than we could have hoped; in the end it was our air supply that ended the dive, not the departure of the mantas.
Sue Laing, managing director, Sydney, Australia

↘13 Lionfish Wall and Yap Caverns

🌀 **Depth**	26 m
◐ **Visibility**	good to great
〰 **Currents**	mild to strong

There are dives all the way to the south of Yap where the reef veers away from land. The water can be a bit rough, as the surf pushes in from different directions, but the walls become much steeper than those on the east and much prettier. The vertical surface of Lionfish Wall drops to about 45 metres and is covered in pastel tree-fern corals. There are moray noses sticking out and even a lionfish or two. More prominent though, are the incredible number of big-eyes, coral trout and groupers. Looking into small cracks and crevices, you can spot leaffish, carpet anemones with 'popcorn shrimp' crawling on them and nudibranchs. The terrain becomes rockier as you move along the wall to the Yap Caverns. These cuts and tunnels in the reef wall are just big enough to swim in and out of. You are likely to meet a young whitetip en route, and one cavern harbours a substantial school of copper sweepers. Above the caverns for a safety stop are carpets of cup corals, dragonets and lots of anthias.

↘14 M'Il Channel and Manta Ridge

🌀 **Depth**	27 m
◐ **Visibility**	medium to great
〰 **Currents**	mild

The ride through the channel that divides Yap from Tomil-Gagil is a mysterious tour through mangroves and past villages with their traditional buildings and meeting houses. At the mouth of the channel the boat moors over one of Yap's most famous sites. In the middle of M'Il Channel is a manta station. Divers wait on the rubbly bottom, but if the rays haven't arrived within about 10 minutes the divemasters head off down to Manta Ridge. Along the channel are outcrops of coral, anemones and clownfish, but you'll be keeping your eyes on the blue to catch a glimpse of what's out there. It could be a manta ray speeding past, a flock of eagle rays or a small shark. At the ridge is another cleaning station, and here the mantas arrive silently to sit over everyone's heads, waiting to be cleaned by the small fish that are on duty for the day. This is the area where, between December and April, the mantas come to mate, doing belly rolls and acrobatics to impress each other.

↘15 The Mandarinfish Dive

🌀 **Depth**	9 m
◐ **Visibility**	poor
〰 **Currents**	none

A few minutes from Manta Ray Bay but inside the channel are a cluster of small, uninhabited islands. The divemasters know several residential areas for mandarinfish: in less than 10 metres of murky water are some stands of coral surrounded by rubble. Descending seconds before dark, you spot the male mandarins skittering about, but they are still wary in the fading sunlight. As it gets darker, they become more active, chasing the ladies around the reef until, eventually, they begin mating. Rising up into the water column, they are disturbed, inevitably just before spawning, by the equally numerous but very aggressive – and hungry – pyjama cardinals.

Lionfish on his namesake wall; male mandarinfish displaying.

drying out

Palau

Traditional village meeting house; the Rock Islands from the air; remains from the battle in Peleliu.

Palau has a reasonable choice of hotels at varying standards. The best ones for divers tend to be on or near Malakal with easy access to the harbour. Cheaper ones are in less pretty locations but are still good quality and ideal for a short stop pre- or post-liveaboards.

Most dive related businesses are under 45-mins or so from the airport and tend to multi-task, so dive centres have restaurants or are in a hotel or have a liveaboard – or a mixture of all these.

Dive centres

Fish 'n' Fins, fishnfins.com. At diverse dive operation with daily programmes, dive courses, photo facilities, the Ba-ra-cu-da restaurant and two luxury liveaboards.
Sam's Tours, samstours.com. With day trip diving, courses, shop, bar and restaurant. They also run land-based tours. Affiliated to Palau Siren, based at Sam's dock.

Liveaboards

Ocean Hunter I & III, oceanhunter.com. Part of Fish 'n Fins see above.
Palau Siren, sirenfleet.com. Delightful phinisi schooner with great on-board facilities, and a top crew. At Sam's Tours.
Solitude One, solitude-liveaboards.com. This new steel-hulled vessel is the largest in Palau at 52-metre long.

Sleeping

Comfort Suite, peci-palau.com. Simple but comfortable option near Sam's Tours.
Sea Passion, palauseapassion.com. Good location on the bay, nice bar and dive centre on site.
The Carolines Resort, carolinesresort.com. Small boutique hotel away from the town and coast. Traditional Palauan bungalows.
West Plaza Malakal, wphpalau.com. One of a series of locally owned hotels with huge rooms. The Palm Bay Bistro and Brewery is opposite.

Palau

Palau's history reaches back centuries to a once highly family-orientated, matrilineal society: during the Stone Age women were in charge of the finances and the men had to ask permission to spend! More recently, periods of European colonialism led to the Japanese occupation during the Second World War, which was followed by a period of American rule. Independence was finally granted in 1994. The result here, unlike Yap and Chuuk, is actually a fairly cosmopolitan atmosphere created by the curious melting pot of cultures. At the moment, the biggest influence is probably Chinese, with a fair number of residents coming from Japan, the Philippines, America and Europe.

It's easy to get a feel for the island: on Koror in the town centre is the National Museum as well as the Etpison Museum, which has some art and ancient artefacts. The International Coral Reef Centre (aka aquarium) is at M dock. However, the best day out is one that takes a tour around the largest island, Babeldaob. These are tailor-made to your personal interests but can cover traditional villages that still retain their ancient men's meeting houses (called a Bai) or old stone sarcophagii wrapped in legends. The national capital, Melekeok, is a lonely but impressive structure modelled on the White House. One real highlight is the mysterious stone monoliths at Ngarchelong in the far north. There are breathtaking views from here over the Pacific. The tours also divert to a local crafts store that displays carved storyboards, which are wooden panels that tell old tales. You are unlikely to see much else in the way of crafts, except perhaps some old money beads in a shop. One thing you might still see, though, is the use of turtle shell and corals for making knick-knacks. Don't buy these, as the trade is frowned upon and in many other countries is illegal.

If you are on a liveaboard and reach Peleliu, there are short tours that take in the Second World War sites, the museum and memorials. This is an educational and interesting tour thats points out the harsh realities of the war.

drying out
Yap and Chuuk

Places to stay and dive are minimal on both islands are minimal but access from the airports is quick and easy.

Yap
Resorts

Manta Ray Bay Hotel and Yap Divers, mantaray.com. Lovely rooms, a good restaurant (The Mnuw), and a unique PADI Speciality Manta Ray Awareness course.

O'Keefe's Waterfront Inn, okeefesyap.com. Delicious New England style inn beside Yap Divers; great bar.

Yap Pacific Dive Resort Resort, yap-pacific.com. Uphill from the coast with an on site dive centre.

Chuuk
Resorts

Blue Lagoon, bluelagoondiveresort.com The better located resort and dive centre with a good restaurant and lovely rooms.

Truk Stop, trukstop.com. A modern hotel right in the centre of town. The dive operation is well regarded.

Liveaboards

Odyssey Adventures, trukodyssey.com American-run liveaboard.

SS Thorfinn, thorfinn.net. This vessel appears to be more budget orientated.

Truk Siren, sirenfleet.com. New vessel and part of the charming Siren Fleet.

Yap

The ancient Yapese empire was a powerful one but almost unknown until European explorers came looking for riches like spices and *beche de mer*. Many foreign countries influenced life here, until the Japanese took hold during the two World Wars. Control then passed to the US. Despite this, Yap remains the most traditional of these islands. The village chief holds sway over his clan; the sexes live fairly separate lives and there is a resolve to keep traditions alive.

People are friendly but come across as shy. If you are out walking, say hello to anyone you pass, don't step across sitting people and always ask before photographing someone. Also, carry something: empty hands are said to show signs of a troublemaker!

Take a morning to see compact Kolonia, the capital. From Manta Ray Bay, walk around the coast towards the hospital, stopping at the Yap Art Gallery to admire the work of local artists. Then go back towards town and up the stone path by the defunct Ocean View Hotel – a stone money disc marks the route, which is lined with plants and flowers. At the top you come to a paved road where you can turn left and go past St Mary's Church, head right all the way up Medeqdeq Hill or go straight across and down a slippery stone path to Chamoor Bay. In the bay is the Ethnic Art Institute where you find women weaving cloth or men carving. Another walk leads from here to the village of Balabat, known as the stone money bank, as the road is lined with a large collection of *rai*, the huge stone discs that were used to display the wealth of a village.

Chuuk

Unlike Yap, contemporary history seems to have eroded much of Chuuk's past. Foreign contact arrived in a similar way and had much the same effect, until it culminated in the total occupation of these islands by the Japanese Imperial Navy during the Second World War.

Chuuk is now Micronesia's most populous state, with the highest quota of government senators, yet it appears to be struggling in the modern world. Island life was once based on a clan system, but this is no longer apparent. The elderly are still greatly respected and women bow to men, but both unemployment and alcoholism are rife.

There are few facilities for general tourism. The airport is comparatively sophisticated, so your first view of the town as you drive through may come as a shock. You could take a day to explore recent history: these cover Nefo Cave, the Japanese War Memorial and Lighthouse, from where views over the lagoon are revealing. There are few chances to see other islands except Eten; its shape changed when the Japanese excavated the hill for an airfield: now it resembles an aircraft carrier. The Officer's quarters are standing despite US bombing.

Crafts are rare, but you will see lovesticks: a slender, dagger-shaped wooden rod that was traditionally carved on Fefak. Male islanders carved their personal notches on the lovestick for a would-be sweetheart. At night, the chap would kneel beside the thatch wall opposite where his intended lay sleeping, poke the stick through the wall and entangle her long hair, hopefully awakening her but not her family.

Yap's stone money; the high street in Kolona; recovered war artefacts; the edge of Truk Lagoon.

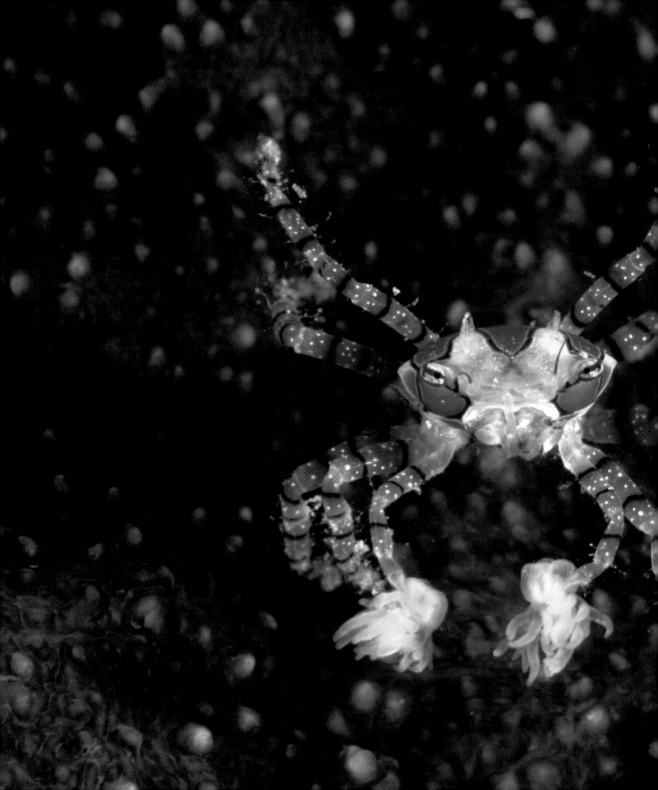

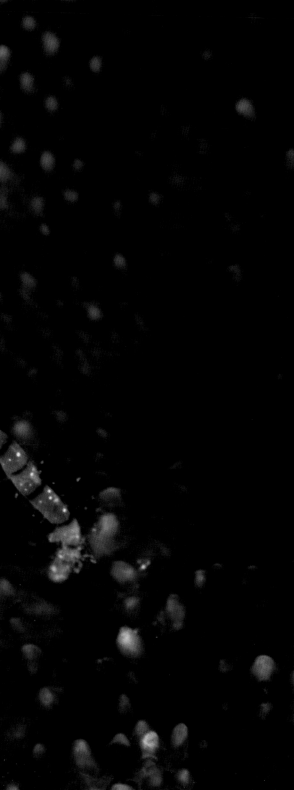

247
↘ **Essentials**

248
↘ **Dive brief**

250
↘ **Dive sites**

252
↘ **Dive log**

New Britain
252 Kimbe Bay
253 Fathers Reefs
254 Witu Islands

Papua New Guinea
256 Loloata Island
258 Tufi

260
↘ **Drying out**

Papua New Guinea

Small creature, big attitude: the one centimetre wide boxer crab, *Lybia tesselata*, carries stinging anemones for protection.
Midway Reef, New Britain

Papua New Guinea is perhaps the last frontier. Not the easiest of places to get to, it is a destination for those serious divers who want undiluted adventure. The landscape is one of high drama both above and below the water line. There are towering mountain ranges where roads simply don't exist and chilly highland forests that plummet down to lush, tropical coasts; idyllic islands face sheer-sided fjords and lead to some of the world's least explored and most impressive coral reefs.

Marine biodiversity is just about the highest on the planet with some of the richest and most pristine reefs in the world and home to almost every marine creature you could ever hope to see, from the tiniest of pipefish to pods of spinner dolphins. This is an outstanding dive experience with consistent year-round conditions.

On land, it is said there are still places where visitors have failed to tread; where indigenous tribes live traditional lives beyond the realm of western comprehension. You're unlikely to see a lot of tribal culture as it's all so remote, although small villages close to dive resorts are unfailingly friendly and welcoming.

PACIFIC OCEAN

destination
Papua New Guinea

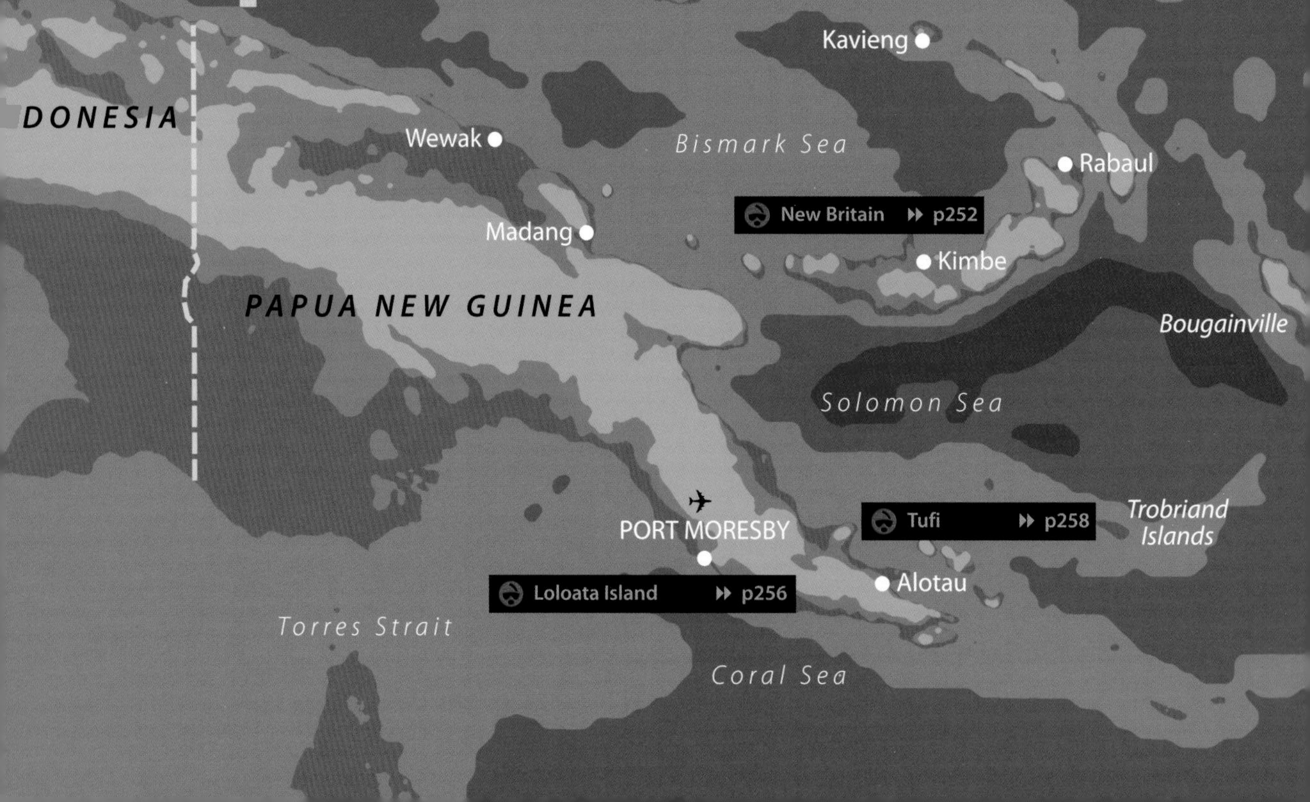

Kavieng

DONESIA

Wewak

Bismark Sea

Rabaul

New Britain ▶▶ p252

Madang

Kimbe

PAPUA NEW GUINEA

Bougainville

Solomon Sea

Tufi ▶▶ p258

Trobriand Islands

PORT MORESBY

Loloata Island ▶▶ p256

Alotau

Torres Strait

Coral Sea

Essentials

Because Papua New Guinea has so little in the way of mass tourism – such a bonus these days – getting there will cost. There is simply not enough competition to bring flight prices down. Air Niugini has inbound flights from several Asian cities, but the cheapest routes are from Australia; these are often Qantas codeshares. However, any flight from anywhere to PNG can be hard to find, so hunt around for deals, especially as you are sure to need an internal flight as well. There are plenty connecting the outer islands. Dive resorts arrange transfers; just hop off the plane and look for the person who is looking for you. There are so few tourists, it will all be terribly obvious.

Local laws and customs

With its strong colonial influences, daily life in PNG tends to feel westernised. Even if you go into a local village, you won't feel too out of place. Missionary groups have had so much impact that many people regard themselves as Christian, although traces of original cultures still shine through. Resorts are casual with few pretensions and if you visit a local village, will advise on dress codes. In Port Moresby smart casual is the way to go.

Health and safety

Standards are good in resorts and hotels, so health concerns only include the usual tropical warnings on sun, mosquitoes and so on. There is one thing to note, though – the only decompression chamber is in Port Moresby. As much of the diving here is deep, and because the water is warm enough to keep you under for long periods in a day, be aware of what your dive computer is telling you. Be safe rather than sorry. Outside Port Moresby, there are few issues, but the city has a reputation for not being the safest place in the world – don't carry valuables about and keep out of the city centre at night as it attracts a lot of unemployed people. Alcohol problems lead to petty crimes and muggings.

Costs

PNG is one of the world's more expensive diving destinations, mostly due to flight prices. Although it's just a stone's throw from Australia, the logistics of importing goods is rarely straightforward. There is little road transport across the mountainous main island so everything has to come by plane or ship, a slow and costly affair. This is amusing when chef says, "sorry no eggs, the plane is late!" It's less amusing three days in a row. The knock-on effect is higher rates in the resorts, which are mostly run by ex-pat Aussies, so at least they never run out of beer. Tourism numbers are comparatively low, so there are few choices for either general tourism or diving, but the good news is that the resorts and liveaboards do, generally, include all meals and diving in their rates. Although the initial cost may seem high, a trip here will be good value. Tipping is not expected.

Fact file

Location	6°00′S, 147°00′E
Capital	Port Moresby
Flights	Fly to Manila, Hong Kong, Singapore, Sydney or Brisbane then connect to Air Niugini
Internal flights	Air Niugini, Airlines of PNG
Land transport	Provided by all dive operations
Departure tax	30 kina airport tax
Entry	Visa issued on arrival at Jackson Airport (100 kina) or from your closest embassy
Money	Papua New Guinea kina (PGK)
Language	English and Tok Pisin
Electricity	240v, plug type E (see page 15)
Time zone	GMT +10
Religion	Christianity mixed with indigenous
Communications	Country code +675; IDD code 05; Police 000. Internet is available but may be satellite-based
Tourist information	papuanewguinea.travel and pngdive.com
Travel advisories	gov.uk/foreign-travel-advice; state.gov/travel

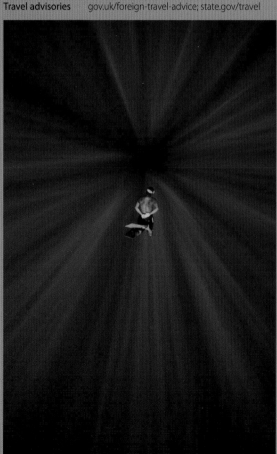

dive brief

Diving

The string of islands that make up Papua New Guinea sit inside what is known as the Coral Triangle. This refers to the islands and reefs that stretch from The Solomons, past PNG to Indonesia then north through Borneo and up to the Philippines. Sitting on the edge of the Pacific Ring of Fire, the volcanic band that encompasses the entire ocean, this region is known to be the most biodiverse on the planet.

PNG waters are home to an extremely high percentage of all tropical reef species plus the country boasts every significant marine ecosystem – from atoll systems to seagrass beds and mangrove deltas that cover over 40,000 square kilometers. No matter what your personal underwater interest might be, you are bound to find it somewhere in the country.

In such a hugely diverse environment what attracts many divers, is the smaller reef-building life, the nursery areas full of weird and wacky creatures. However, there are also substantial amounts of Second World War paraphernalia littered around, as many parts of the country were occupied by Japanese forces.

Another major bonus is that there is no particular dive season. It matters little what time of year you go, as conditions are fairly consistent. A final consideration is that PNG diving is as close to unlimited as you will ever get. Liveaboards schedule five dives a day; most resorts have three boat dives and you can dive from shore whenever you like.

Snorkelling

Many offshore reefs tend to be very deep, starting at around 15 metres but dropping off to unfathomable depths. However, as the visibility is often fabulous, floating over these would be quite a blast. There are exceptions reefs near Port Moresby, for example, have reduced visibility as they are affected by shipping and the tidal flow moving over the shallow seabeds. On the other hand, there are masses of coastal reefs further afield that are just a few metres deep and have good visibility.

Marine life

For any diver who is interested in tropical marine life, this area is almost unsurpassed. From the smallest of creatures – minute boxer crabs and ghost pipefish – to uncountable schools of barracuda and jacks, it's all here.

Like many people, it took us a long time to commit to going to Papua New Guinea to dive. Until we'd been, we just couldn't see the value in upping our travel budget enough to cover the extra costs the journey involved. Then a friend dragged us along and, of course, once we had done it, we realized there was no reason to think up excuses again. This is a superlative destination for serious divers.

Diving on Cyclone Reef near Tufi.

Making the big decision

When it comes to considering a trip to Papua New Guinea, you have to get your head around the comparative cost. Yes, it is far more expensive than neighbouring Indonesia, and no, it's not so completely, utterly different. But it is different enough and it is one of those remote frontiers that you really should see – and dive – at least once in your life.

Once you have made the mental adjustment, selecting a specific area to go to can be more difficult. To travel so far and only do one small part of the country would be a waste. To get the most out of your time and the flight costs, do more than one dive region. No one resort or boat is better than the other. All have their own style, whether it's romantic views from colonial bungalows or dive-your-brains-out liveaboards targeted at underwater photographers. The diving is consistently fabulous right across the country. Initial costs may seem high, but this is a great value-for-money destination.

🌐 Animal encounters

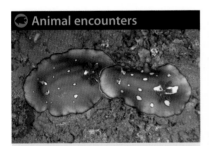

Countrywide: there are many small creatures in PNG from pygmy seahorses to boxer crabs. There are plenty of big ones too with sharks and barracuda, tuna and bumphead wrasse. Even small critters tend to be on the large size: nocturnal Ocellated platydoris nudibranchs (above) are 25 centimetres long and one of the biggest members of this species.

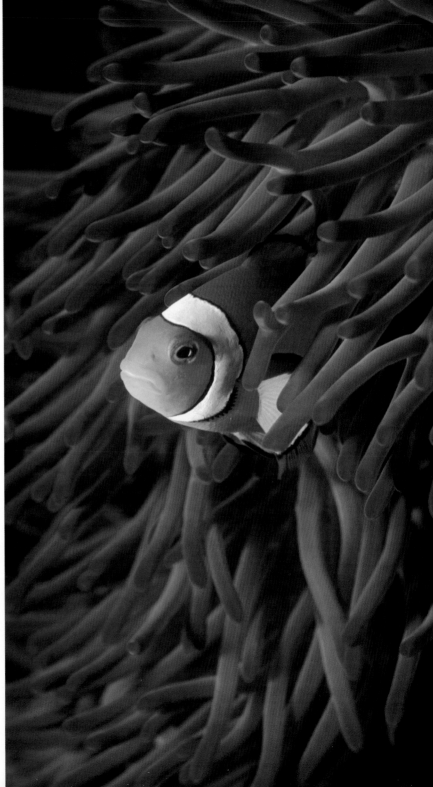

dive sites

New Britain – Kimbe Bay, Fathers Reefs, Witu Islands ▶▶ p252

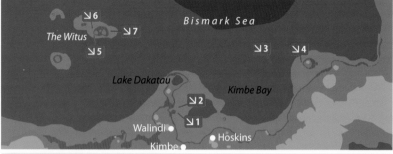

Bismark Sea

The Witus

↘6 ↘7 ↘5 ↘3 ↘4

Lake Dakatau

Kimbe Bay

↘2 ↘1

Walindi ● Hoskins

Kimbe

The main island of Papua New Guinea is a melange of geographic features. Extreme mountain ranges lead to coastal plateaus then on to diverse marine environments. Just offshore from Port Moresby, Loloata Island is a miniature version of this natural world and a haven for many unusual marine creatures – and one very rare one – plus some spectacular shipwrecks that are now rich artificial reefs. Meanwhile, across on the east coast, Tufi sits above some of PNG's most impressive terrain. Deep fjords cut sharply through the coastal cliffs that tumble down to mysterious inlets. This is where reefs get into recycling, and they win.

Second only in size, New Britain lies to the northeast in the Bismark Archipelago. It's the largest island in group and has 21 volcanoes that can be rather frisky at times but also supply nutrients to the water. Kimbe Bay is famous for iridescent colours on pristine corals, while the Fathers Reefs are – surprisingly – defined by crystal-clear waters despite the pitch black sand close by. A little further away, there is dramatic diving at the Witus around the remains of a submerged volcanic crater.

No matter where you go though, conditions are fairly consistent. Some say the best visibility is from January to April but that seems an unnecessary statement as the comparison is between excellent and really excellent. Currents can be strong, a benefit to the marine life, but, as there are so many dive sites, avoiding them is never an issue.

Log Book

↘1 **Restorf Island**
↘2 **Susan's Reef**

→ **Kimbe Island:** wall dive that attracts grey reef sharks and bumphead parrotfish
→ **English Shoal:** steep pinnacle where hammerheads, white tips and grey reefs patrol

↘3 **Jayne's Reef**
↘4 **Midway Reef**

→ **The Arches:** dramatic arch linking the reef to a pinnacle
→ **Jurassic Park:** night dive off Lolobau Island to look for *Ocellated platydoris* nudibranchs
→ **Kilibob's Knob:** sharks patrolling the channel between two pinnacles

↘5 **Wiray Bay**
↘6 **Dickie's Place**
↘7 **Lama Shoals**

→ **Swap Tinny Reef:** schooling butterflyfish, rainbow runners, midnight snappers and sweetlips
→ **Lama Reef I & II:** series of reefs with huge barrel sponges, batfish, leaffish and so much more
→ **Wiray Bay:** a whole ID book's worth of crawling critters

⊗ Endangered oceans

If you ever make it to New Britain and if you get to stay in the jungle-clad bungalows at Walindi Resort, take some time out to wander along the road to Mahonia Na Dari. Meaning 'Guardian of the Sea', this conservation body was set up with assistance from the resort to teach local people about looking after their reefs. Kimbe town is a hub for industries including palm oil and coconut plantations, cocoa and timber logging. Somehow, it just doesn't make sense for the islanders to devastate the natural resources on which they rely to make a living.

In the past, the people had limited understanding of the environment – even today, some children never learn to swim – so the aim is to educate future generations then have them manage the protected areas. At the same time, closing reefs will allow them to recover. This programme has been so successful in Kimbe that it is being integrated into Papua New Guinea's National School Teaching Curriculum.

Loloata ▶▶ p256

● Port Moresby

Loloata

↘9

↘10

↘8

🔵 Log Book

↘8 **End Bommie**
↘9 **Suzie's Bommie**
↘10 **MV Pacific Gas wreck**

→ **MV Pai:** the almost intact wreck of a small prawn trawler.
→ **Pumpkin Patch:** lots of everything ignored in favour of the lacy rhinopias.
→ **Lion Island:** the rotting hull of the *Lady Jules* is now a micro-critter haven
Quayle's Reef: sea snakes and pygmy seahorses hiding on sea fans

Tufi ▶▶ p258

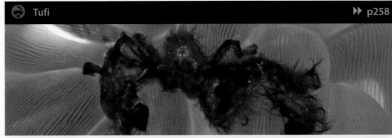

Sefoa ●

Tufi ● ↘11

↘13

↘12

Baga ●

↘14

🔵 Log Book

↘11 **Tufi Pier**
↘12 **Tufi Bay**
↘13 **Bev's Reef**
↘14 **Cyclone Reef**

→ **Minor's Reef:** named for the *Notodoris minor* nudis seen here along with big schools of fish
→ **Marian's Reef:** circular reef with a depressed crater in the top used by resting sharks
→ **Mulloway Reef:** strong currents that attract jacks, barracuda and tuna

Conditions

Seasons	Diving is year round. There are dry and wet seasons, but the changes aren't significant except in the area around Loloata.
Visibility	10 m inshore to 'infinity' in open water
Currents	Rarely strong enough to bother anyone
Temperatures	Air: coast 24-35°C; highlands 12-28°C Water: Loloata 25-30°C, elsewhere 28-30°C
Wet suit	3 mm full body suit
Training	Courses are not generally available, email in advance to make arrangements
Nitrox	Available in some resorts/liveaboards
Deco chambers	Port Moresby

Diversity

reef area 13,840 km²

HARD CORALS	517
FISH SPECIES	2,586
ENDEMIC FISH SPECIES	71
FISH UNDER THREAT	61

All diversity figures are approximate

WALINDI DIVING

MV FeBrina

dive log
New Britain: Kimbe Bay

New Britain island is just a 50-minute flight from Port Moresby and forms the nation's northern barrier with the Bismark Sea. This is one of PNG's best known and most spectacular diving regions.

Kimbe Bay on the north coast is ringed by a dramatic volcanic landscape and is the heart of this amazing destination. There is quick and easy access to some adrenaline-pumping dives, with the added bonus that you can dive from land or on a liveaboard.

Grey reef shark, and razorfish hiding amongst the whip corals in Kimbe Bay.

↘1 Rest Orf Island	
🕐 **Depth**	18 m
◐ **Visibility**	fair to good
〰 **Currents**	slight

Just 30 minutes from Walindi, this is a true picture-postcard island. The tiny, white-sand beach leads down in a semicircle to a small reef wall that extends on either side to a sandy seabed. This is dotted with patchy coral outcrops that support some brightly coloured soft corals, which in turn create homes for critters such as the hard-to-spot dendronephthya crab. Around the base of these outcrops you can also spot crabeye gobies and other tiny bottom dwellers such as flounders. Titan triggerfish nest here as well, so you need to keep an eye out for them. At depth there are some really good whips and fans and different shades of black coral that flourish in the currents. The entire reef is decorated with flitting tropical fish and clownfish in their host anemones.

↘2 Susan's Reef	
🕐 **Depth**	50 m
◐ **Visibility**	fair to good
〰 **Currents**	slight

Just a little way from Rest Orf Island, this incredibly pretty dive site consists of a submerged ridge that connects a small reef to a much larger one. The channel between the two is what makes it such an outstanding dive. The currents that are funnelled through the space encourage the growth of a fantastic number of bright red whip corals, and these seem to coat almost every surface. One stand of them is alive and dancing with silvery razorfish who reflect the sun's rays as they turn their bodies this way and that, trying to remain hidden. A variety of coloured crinoids cling on to the gorgonian fans and sponges, while masses of curious fish hang off the walls. Longnose and pixie hawkfish are common residents, as are angelfish and parrotfish.

dive log
New Britain: Fathers Reefs

Marking the outer edge of Kimbe Bay, the Fathers are a group of three volcanic cones that protrude from the horizon and hover ominously over the coast.

Underwater, these landmarks mutate into steep sloping walls surrounded by countless pelagic fish species. Dive Conditions are similar to those inside the bay although currents tend to be stronger. The visibility is amazing and looking down over the reefs tops feels like looking through air.

▨3 Jayne's Reef	
Depth	36 m
Visibility	good to stunning
Currents	can be strong

▨4 Midway Reef	
Depth	30 m
Visibility	infinity
Currents	slight

This steep-sided circular pinnacle is coated with whip corals and fans, and swarms of jacks pass by. Despite the currents, it's easy to spot minute creatures even at depth – a huge barrel sponge has sangian crabs on it, while pygmy seahorses reside on a fan known to the divemasters. The reef top is quite rubbly, due to the effects of tide and currents, but this is also a prime area for octopus. At the right time you can see them mating, one extending a tentacle to attract another. Eventually, the male will insert his specially modified arm into the female to transfer his sperm packet to her. There are small hawksbill turtles who are very friendly, swimming right up to divers. In amongst the small corals are orang-utan crabs and tiny commensal crabs living in the algae.

Midway is a circular reef with a small saddle connected to a secondary pinnacle. On the main section, the wall drops steeply to reveal Napoleon wrasse hovering over incredibly thick beds of staghorn coral with anthias, fusiliers and damsels darting in and out. Schooling snappers dash past anemones with their commensal clownfish who dart up at divers. Over at the saddle, a handful of grey sharks are on patrol, while schools of big-eye trevally and surgeonfish circle above. The macro life is impressive as long as you take time to look for it – so much is camouflaged by the dense hard and soft corals. Squat lobsters hide in the crinoids, dendronephthya crabs in the dendronephthya coral and popcorn shrimp on carpet anemones. Lucky divers might even spot a boxer crab!

Fathers Reefs: two dendronephthya crabs in their soft coral; gigantic fan coral masking a dive.

dive log

New Britain: Witu Islands

This cluster of volcanic islands rises from very deep water. Garove, the largest and busiest, is a sunken caldera, shaped like a horseshoe and opening to the south.

These waters are incredibly nutrient rich. The open water reefs a short sail from the coast attract massive schools of pelagic fish, while the many small bays around the islands have black sand seabeds that are a haven to weird and wacky small animals.

↘5 Wiray Bay	
Depth	22 m
Visibility	good
Currents	none

This bay off Wiray Island feels very primeval, as the surrounding hills are clad with thick jungle dripping with vines while birds squawk overhead. The black sand seabed has algae, the odd log and a few coconut husks, but very little coral. The divemasters hop from one seemingly barren spot to the next to show off the critters: halimeda and sangian crabs, sand divers that puff up their necks, dark panda clownfish, popcorn shrimp in cauliflower-shaped anemones and so much more. At night, there are masses of cone shells – literally hundreds. There are many tiny dwarf scorpionfish and decorator crabs that cover themselves in bright green balls of algae. The biggest surprise, though, is the huge platydoris nudibranchs, possibly the largest there is. These will pair up, linking head to tail then travel at speed across the sand.

↘6 Dickie's Place	
Depth	22 m
Visibility	fair to good
Currents	none

Named after the late and much admired Dickie Doyle, who ran the cocoa plantation fronting this small but perfectly formed bay, this macro dive site is quite shallow and divided by a ridge. On one side is a small reef but, again, the dark sand seabed is the star of the show. This is the place to see seagrass pipehorses, a tiny pipefish that wraps its tail around blades of grass. There are also minute black mantis shrimp, the saddle back clownfish and several twinspot lionfish. At night, bumblebee squid emerge from their hidey-holes, along with seahares, more decorator crabs and pleurobranchs. Down on the ridge the branches of an old decaying tree attract squid that are mating and laying their eggs. This is quite a lively spectacle, as the boys fight over the girls who trying to fend them off as they attach the eggs to the log.

Witu Bay residents include chromodoris nudibranchs, halimeda algae crabs and sangian crab.

↘7 lama shoals

🕐 **Depth**	45 m
◐ **Visibility**	stunning
〰 **Currents**	can be strong

Lama Shoals sums up the best of diving in New Britain waters. It's always non-stop action; you can dive it at any time of day, and there always seems to be something going on. But what really captivates is the water clarity, it feels like diving in air. You simply hang in the blue and watch the dramas of this prolific reef unfold.

The reef is a long oval and drops off to extreme depths. When the currents lift, this dive site is revealed in all its glory. They are fairly consistent but not so aggressive as to make this a drift dive. Yet these currents bring in both pelagic fish and the nutrients that feed the corals, fans, and sponges that plaster every available surface.

As you descend below the boat, whole forests of black coral bushes are showing off, tones of gold and silver flickering in the sun. Midnight snapper, sweetlips and longnose hawkfish nestle in the bushes. A few bigeye trevally hang around them, but these are obviously stragglers, as you see when you descend further and meet the most enormous school of them. And this is just the start of the action. Further along the wall, another shoal appears above, then a third far below. Schooling barracuda stand off in the blue, possibly wary of the large dogtooth tuna cruising along the wall, or maybe it's the arrival of some spanish mackerel, which in turn are disturbed by the passing rainbow runners.

The top of the reef is around 15 metres where plenty of smaller creatures balance out the dive. Scorpionfish and grumpy-faced false stonefish nestle amongst small

corals, while lionfish hover beside the fans. Schools of unicornfish and pyramid butterflies add to the colour. Good spotters may see several types of moray living behind swarms of tiny purple fairy basslets. The reef shallows also have a covering of coralliomorpharians. These rather attractive creatures look a little like anemones and are related to them but have a far more powerful sting. At the end, pause for the school of batfish that reside near the safety stop rope. They are good entertainment for the deco-stop you are bound to have after this dive.

" " Several years have gone by since our trip to PNG. The names of most dive sites are long forgotten but not this one and not the pure joy and awe of seeing the tallest and most amazing funnel of barracudas.
Patricia Tobin, sales manager, Portland, USA

dive log

Papua New Guinea: Loloata

A few miles south of the nation's capital, Port Moresby, lies this haven of marine splendour. Loloata Island Resort is under half an hour from the airport, 15 minutes from shore and on the edge of the Papuan Barrier Reef. The resort gets a good through-flow of diver and non-diver traffic, which adds to its charm. One night you might dine with some fellow divers, the next, an Australian politician.

The island itself is a long, oval shape with a steep central hill ringed by a flat, craggy strip. There is nothing on the island apart from the resort, which is also an unofficial wildlife reserve with many rescued native animals.

The dive reputation is one of a serious muck diving haven with critters in every shape, size and colour, including almost guaranteed sightings of the splendid lacy scorpionfish. The reefs themselves are impressive hard coral growth is substantial, soft corals pretty and colourful. The reefs host plenty of schooling fish including jacks, groupers and snapper. Then there are the wrecks. Local waters are littered with them, although they've mostly been scuttled over the years for the benefit of divers.

Unlike the rest of PNG, seasons here are notable. There are two doldrums (April to May and October to December) when the sea is calm and the visibility is better. December to April is wetter and June to October is drier. Diving is still year round.

↘8 End Bommie	
Depth	22 m
Visibility	fair to good
Currents	mild

This site is a well-known haunt for the rare *Rhinopias aphanes* or lacy scorpionfish. The main reef has a saddle that connects it to a smaller circular outcrop with lots of pristine corals along the outside wall. One section is smothered in tubastrea, purple and white soft corals, and vast numbers of anthias all darting in and out. However, it's on the flat reef top that the divemaster will point out the rhinopias – there's no chance of seeing one of these perfectly camouflaged creatures on your own. The resident one is black, with yellow and white patterns on his skin and transparent areas in his fins, making him very hard to distinguish from the surroundings.

Oriental sweetlips by the hundreds on Suzie's Bommie.

⬂9 Suzie's Bommie

🕐	**Depth**	27 m
◑	**Visibility**	fair to good
〰	**Currents**	can be strong

Suzie's cone-shaped pinnacle rises from 30 metres to about 10. Around the base are some good fans and plenty of fish but the further you ascend, the thicker the fish life becomes. Sweetlips shelter against the tubastrea along with pairs of barramundi cod. There are masses of anthias and then you encounter huge numbers of oriental sweetlips, snappers, surgeon and batfish. These all school together in a massive ball. A lone Napoleon wrasse hangs around with the other species. In the corals, there are leaffish in varying colours – olive, lime and silver – and marbled dragonets. Longnose hawkfish free swim around whip corals, and mantis shrimp run out of their burrows.

⬂10 MV Pacific Gas wreck

🕐	**Depth**	39 m
◑	**Visibility**	fair to good
〰	**Currents**	can be strong

Originally owned by Pacific Gas, this cargo vessel was scuttled in 1986 to create a dive site. Strong currents wash over her, so she has filled up with lots tubastrea and small soft corals. The propellers are sitting at 45 metres, while the main cabin at the stern rises up to over 20 metres. There is less coral cover at depth but plenty of jacks and a couple of big groupers. Back up at the bow, some gear wheels are exposed. Two leaffish sit on them and a moray has a cleaner shrimp in his mouth. Travelling up the mast for a safety stop, there are masses of anthias, sweepers and crinoids. There's even a resident dendronephthya crab hiding in some soft coral.

The Pacific Gas wreck and the bizarrely decorated *Rhinopias aphanes*, or lacy scorpionfish.

Papua New Guinea Dive log Loloata Island

dive log

Papua New Guinea: Tufi

Tufi village sits right on the top of a tropical fjord. Originally built as a Second World War base, the dive resort is only accessible by an hour's scenic flight from Port Moresby. The views are to die for and the walk down to the dive jetty involves a daily greeting ceremony with the local villagers.

Inside the bay, the dives are classic muck; consequently visibility is low. However, lying offshore are some fantastic reef systems. The water is gin-clear, corals lush and massive schools of pelagic fish seek shelter around them. A little further away, several war-era wrecks are worth a visit if weather allows. If you miss them, it hardly matters though, as Tufi Bay has its own wrecks, reminders of when US forces were stationed here.

⊠11 Tufi Pier	
🕑 **Depth**	12 m
◐ **Visibility**	fair to good
🌊 **Currents**	none

For serious muck-diving aficionados, there is nothing quite like this. You name it and you'll probably see it here. Just below the jetty are decades of detritus, but no matter what ugly old bit of rubbish you look at, it will be a thriving marine colony. Kitting up on the wooden jetty, you can admire the juvenile batfish lurking just beneath the surface, then descend to three metres to find handfuls of ornate ghost pipefish, pairs of robust ghost pipefish and a lone hairy ghost pipefish. Inspect a crate to find nudibranchs crawling over it or an old beer bottle for a blenny or two. Seahorses and frogfish live around the pylons and, hiding in amongst the algae, are scorpionfish, lionfish and cowries. If you do this dive at dusk, you may spot a pair of harlequin shrimp preparing their supper by killing a starfish then eating it limb by limb, or one of the resident mandarinfish that come out to feed under cover of darkness.

TUFI DIVE

N12 Tufi Bay

Depth	42 m
Visibility	fair to good
Currents	none

Heading downwards from the jetty past all the magnificent macro life, there is a solitary coral rock where young pinnate batfish live, their orange outline glowing like neon. Still descending, you eventually reach 40 metres. The seabed flattens out into a dark and silty place. Scattered across it is the detritus from the Second World War base. When the American forces shipped out, they dumped many of their unwanted items into the bay. You can see engines and chains and ponder their original use. There are the remains of a patrol boat that still has its engine and, inside the hull, is completely covered in cleaner shrimp and small cardinals. Nearby is a nearly intact Land Rover. Its screen is encrusted with muck and small flat corals are forming on the surface. Just a few feet away is a torpedo tube, with the torpedo still in it.

N13 Bev's Reef

Depth	32 m
Visibility	fair to good
Currents	none

A couple of hours out from Tufi towards the D'Entrecasteaux Islands are some of the best reefs in the area, with clear water and plenty of pelagic life. Bev's is one of the closer reefs to shore and does have some damage on the top. This is caused by wave and storm action, as the site is quite exposed. Circumnavigating the reef edges you see colourful soft corals with schools of mating surgeonfish hovering above them. The walls harbour critters like flabellina – and many other – nudibranchs. Eagle-eyed spotters might see a ghost pipefish, crocodilefish or the blacksaddle coral grouper, which is white with yellow and black markings. As you ascend back to the flat plateau, you are surrounded by a huge number of fish: schools of spanish mackerel, chevron barracuda, jacks, yellow tailed snappers, damsels and angels.

N14 Cyclone Reef

Depth	50 m
Visibility	good to stunning
Currents	slight

In 1975 a cyclone swept across this reef. It rearranged the submerged terrain and even created a small island that is now used by birds. There are two dives here: one is a pinnacle connected to the main reef via a 26-metre-deep saddle. There are a lot of black coral bushes full of fish that sit on the branches like nesting birds, plus schools of yellow tailed snappers, rainbow runners and tangs, grey reef sharks. The other dive is on the wall which drops to 60 metres. A large depression on the reef top attracts masses of schooling fish, a real soup of species: snapper, spanish mackerel, tuna and juvenile whitetip sharks. Down below, grey reef sharks patrol the wall, which is coated in more colourful corals. This is also a good location for spotting the king of nudibranchs, *notodoris minor*, and even a manta ray or turtle in the blue.

Dinner time for a pair of harlequin shrimp (left); a loaded torpedo tube rusting on the sea floor; a harlequin ghost pipefish; diving Cyclone Reef.

drying out

Tourism is a very small industry in PNG. Across the country, the number of resort choices is minimal although standards are good. Nearly all coastal resorts are diver-friendly.

With the exception of Loloata Resort just south of Port Moresby, all dive regions need to be reached via an internal flight. Sometimes there will be a land transfer to the resort as well. However, due to the isolated nature of these destinations, all rates tend to be packages that include transfers, diving and meals.

Papua New Guinea
Port Moresby
Airways Hotel, airways.com.pg. Located at the airport so ideal for overnight stops.
Loloata Island
Sleeping and diving
Loloata Island Resort, Loloata.com. Just 30-mins from the airport, this charming dive resort is also an option for short stays.

Tufi
Sleeping and diving
Tufi Dive Resort, tufidive.com. On the top of a fjord and under an hour by small plane to the airstrip, aka, the football field.

New Britain
Kimbe Bay and the Bismark Sea
Sleeping and diving
Walindi Plantation Resort, walindi.com.Nestled in a coastal jungle with marvellous views, Walindi is also the home port for MV Febrina.
Liveaboard
MV Febrina, febrina.com. Febrina is a legend amongst liveaboards with a reputation that speaks for itself.

Other options
Lissenung Resort, lissenung.com
Tawali Resort, tawali.com
MV Golden Dawn, mvgoldendawn.com
MV Chertan, chertan.com

Wild tales from wild places

I have some very wild tales about travelling through Papua New Guinea to see her primitive and mesmerising cultures. I've been up the highlands to see the Huli Wigmen and the Mudmen of the Waghi Valley. But my favourite trip was by canoe to visit remote villages on the Sepik River in northern PNG.

After 12 days of diving, this was an unreal contrast. The only person who dared to come with me was my brave friend Sandy. We slept in rural villages on the river. It was hotter than hell and humid to match, mozzies and no breeze. Our guide was from one of the villages and all the people knew him – but they hadn't seen white people for ages. It was fun to see how they reacted to us

My aim was to search out some old and unusual handicrafts, not the copies that you can buy down in Port Moresby, beautiful though they are. Our guide got the gist of what I was after and well after we went to sleep, people would appear from all over to show him their old pieces. Some I would not take as they were very important and ancient, regarded as spirits from their ancestors.

I was amazed by my meetings with these very special people and I am so grateful that they wanted to share their past with me. I have a story from each villager about the items I bought from them so they will all be catalogued and maintain their ancestral story. Papua New Guinea is just an incredible place.

Days out

Nature has taken an interesting turn in Papua New Guinea: it has the world's third largest rainforest, and the jungles host as many bird and plant species as nearby Australia, with endemic species like tiny tree kangaroos, the enormous Queen Alexandra Birdwing butterfly and the world's largest pigeon. Perhaps most importantly, the islands are home to 38 of the world's 43 birds of paradise. While access to very remote areas can be difficult, there are organized tours that will give a taste of the real country.

Port Moresby

While the centre of Port Moresby may be best avoided, there are a few attractions worth seeing. Take a trip to the National Museum & Art Gallery on Independence Hill. The building is based on traditional architecture and the displays will give you a feel for some local arts and culture. The National Capital Botanical Gardens are worthy of a couple of hours as they have an extraordinary collection of tropical plants including native trees and palms, heliconias, cordyline and pandanus. Most impressive though is a display of orchids unique to Papua New Guinea. There is also a section of enclosures that contain native birds, including a few birds of paradise (but not the really flamboyant ones) and the world's largest pigeon.

The highlands

As most of PNG is smothered in steep mountains, almost half her population lives in the highlands. The incredibly lush vegetation and lack of roads over steep terrain has ensured that much of this region has remained well protected from prying eyes. Conditions are simple, with some tribes virtually unknown to white people who are regarded with curiosity or suspicion. The villagers conduct their lives far removed from first-world concerns. Some areas are considered unsafe due to tribal warfare though this is mostly a cultural event and rarely affects tourism. Parts of the Southern Highlands are easily accessible and are home to the Huli Wigmen, the most photographed people in the country.

Sepik River

The mighty Sepik River is 1100 km long and up to 1.5 km wide. Flanked by flat lowlands and mangrove swamps, it is a natural highway for the Sepik people. This is a unique ecosystem for plant, bird and animal life. Yet what attracts tourists is the intensely spiritual nature of the Sepik people. The Haus Tambaran (spirit house) is integral to daily life: men gather to discuss village business and hide sacred objects from women. The Sepik's unique handicrafts (crocodile totems and legends carved on cooking tools) are a huge draw for those who sail – or canoe – up the river to visit the tribes.

Trekking

If you are into trekking you could walk the 96 km Kokoda Trail from Port Moresby to Kokoda, then on to Tufi. This Second World War supply route was used by Australian Forces (ably helped by the Papuans) in 1942 to stop the Japanese advance on Port Moresby, a key target as an air assault could be launched from here to northern Australia. Somewhat easier would be one of the half-day walks organized from Tufi leading up the eastern ridge towards Mount Trafalgar and stopping at villages on the way to talk with the women and children before you reach the end of the fjord. On the way are hornbills, parrots and cockatoos and spectacular scenery. Baga village is 2 hours' walk along the fjord's western ridge. There are other villages near Tufi – Kupari Point Village often invites guests to traditional events. Similar day trips are arranged from Walindi including the nearby Nature Centre, which is home to the Mahonia na Dari (Guardian of the Sea) Project and focuses on conservation and marine education.

MV Febrina collecting divers; Kupari Village.

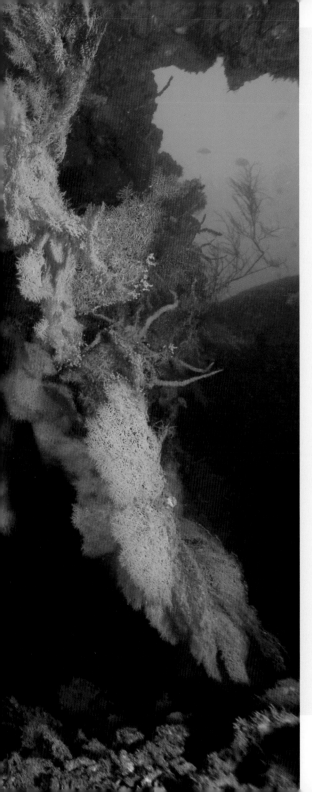

Philippines

265
↘ **Essentials**

266
↘ **Dive brief**

268
↘ **Dive sites**

270
↘ **Dive log**

Luzon
270   Anilao

Mindoro
272   Puerto Galera

Palawan
274   Tubbataha
276   Coron

The Visayas
278   Panglao and Balicasag
280   Cabilao
281   Negros Oriental
284   Moalboal

286
↘ **Drying out**

A wreck by any name: golden fan corals shine through the gloom
on the *Taiei Maru*, aka The Okikawa.
Coron Bay, Palawan

destination
Philippines

The islands of the Philippines are surrounded by the second largest expanse of water inside the Coral Triangle, and form its northern apex. The country is just a short hop from more popular routes for well-heeled divers, so it should come as no surprise that the diversity of marine species ranks as high as anywhere in the region, even competing with neighbouring Indonesia.

Sandwiched between the Pacific Ocean and the South China Seas, the reefs are tantalizing, thick with tropical fish and colourful gardens of coral. In some areas there is a wealth of unusual small marine animals, while in others there are swarms of pelagics or the chance to explore a fleet of Second World War wrecks.

Considered something of an enigma, the outlying islands retain a charming sense of the past. Idyllic sea views are interrupted only by rows of bancas – brightly painted timber and bamboo outriggers – lined up awaiting the next day's quota of divers. It would be hard to beat the romance of sitting at night under a coconut palm on a snow-white Philippine beach, cool sand between your toes, wondering what the next day will bring.

Babuyan Islands

Philippines Sea

Luzon

MANILA ●

Anilao ▶▶ p270

South China Sea

Puerto Galera ▶▶ p272

Mindoro

Busuanga

Samar

Coron ▶▶ p276

Panay

Leyte

Palawan

PHILIPPINES

Cebu ●

● Puerto Princessa

Negros

Visayas ▶▶ p278

Bohol Sea

Tubbataha ▶▶ p274

Mindanao

● Dava

▲ *Mount Apo*

Sulu Sea

MALAYSIA

Celebes Sea

Essentials

There are many airlines that will deposit travellers in Manila including, these days, Philippine Airlines whose network has now expanded to cover Europe. However, many of the best diving regions are more easily accessed from Cebu in the Visayas, where there is a second international airport. From these major hubs, you are likely to need to make a small hop to another island, with internal connections usually made by either a ferry or fast catamarans. Because of this, hotels and operators rarely include transfers from the airport in their rates – it's one of the peculiarities of Filipino dive trips. However, you will be given full instructions and advice.

Local laws and customs
Filipinos are deeply religious, though it's easy to forget that as you stand beneath a city skyline obliterated by posters depicting American movies, pop stars and mobile phone companies. Move your eyes just a little to see that the rest of the horizon is lined with churches. This was a Spanish colony for 350 years and 85% of the country is Catholic. The country was sold to America in 1898 and remained a US possession for 50 years. American influence may seem dominant but, deep down, the Filipino nature is devout.

Health and safety
Manila has many healthcare facilities but the islands have fewer and standards vary. Health risks are low but AIDs is spreading, as is the sex trade, so be wary. Insect-borne diseases are almost unheard of in coastal areas, but malaria is a problem in Palawan.

When it comes to safety, geography is all important; most government advisories warn against travel to Mindanao and the Sulu Archipelago as these are bases for the extremist Muslim Abu Sayyaf group. The good news is that dive regions are nowhere near these and are mostly unaffected. Manila and Cebu are typical busy cities but, once you are on the islands, life is relaxed with no specific dress codes or courtesies to be observed. It is unlikely that you will find anything to trouble you, but be aware that the penalties for any form of drug use are severe.

Costs
The Philippines are very good value. Resort styles vary by both cost and quality, with most in the two- to three-star range. These can be simple and basic but, in more popular areas, dive-specific resort standards are higher. Whatever you book, the quality will be reflected in the room rates so compare carefully. Likewise, food and drink costs can be aligned to location, with beachside bars and restaurants cheap and always charming.

When it comes to tipping, dive resorts and smaller hotels will simply leave a tips box on the reception desk. High-end resorts add service and taxes, but elsewhere, rounding up the bill seems to be the done thing.

Fact file

Location	3°00'N, 122°00'E
Capital	Manila
Flights	Air Asia, Cebu Pacific, Philippine Airlines, Qatar, Qantas, Singapore Airlines, Silk Air, United Airlines
Internal flights	Asian Spirit, Cebu Pacific, South East Asian Air
Land transport	Jeepney buses, ferries and taxis
Departure tax	US$30, if not included in your ticket
Entry	No visas required for stays up to 30 days
Money	Philippine pesos (PHP)
Language	English and Tagalog plus regional dialects
Electricity	220v, plus types A/C (see page 15)
Time zone	GMT +8
Religion	Roman Catholic
Communications	Country code +63; IDD code 00; Police 166 Internet access is patchy but improving
Tourist information	experiencephilippines.org morefunphilippines.co.uk morefuninthephilippines.com.au
Travel advisories	gov.uk/foreign-travel-advice; state.gov/travel

dive brief

Diving

Can you imagine a country with 7107 (or so) individual islands all ringed with coral reefs? That must be something like 70,000 dive sites to choose from. What a concept.

The Philippines are located within the Pacific's Ring of Fire and, just as significantly, make up a segment of the Coral Triangle. This imaginary boundary is bordered by nearby Indonesia, the Solomon Islands, Malaysian Borneo and the Philippines. Within this small space there are more marine species than anywhere else on the planet – more varieties of coral, more fish and more critters.

The Philippine islands have their fair share of this wealth and, in fact, research indicates that the levels of diversity may be far higher than was previously thought. There are luxurious coral reefs, awesome walls, mysterious wrecks, critters by the bucket load and countless marine reserves. This dive destination once suffered from a reputation for serious fish bombing and environmental damage to the reefs, so you may be surprised at the number of small exclusion bays that are patrolled by local villagers. Local people have learnt

the value of creating protected nursery grounds, if only to be able to fish beyond the no-go zones. There are also two UNESCO Biosphere Reserves and two World Heritage Sites.

Underwater, the conditions are fairly easy-going. The islands are naturally tidal and currents can be strong at times, but dive centres sensibly divert to protected sites when necessary. Visibility is usually good, murkier in the shallows and crystal clear in oceanic open waters.

Snorkelling

For the non-diver who likes to join in the fun, the Philippines is a feast. Small reefs run right up to the beach, shallow drop-offs are protected and currents are fairly predictable. The water is warm and usually clear enough for surface-huggers to still get a good peak below the water line.

Marine life

With so much diversity, you can safely assume that you will see a high variety of tropical species, both pelagic animals and reef-based fish and critters. However, a few dive regions in the Philippines are

There are certain things about diving in the Philippines that boost it up a level to compete with some of the best we have ever done. The country almost ranks as an addiction – we have returned time and time again, and while each trip is good, sometimes a curve ball presents itself as a totally new experience that threatens to become one of the best ever. And Pescador's Sardine Run is that dive.

Giant frogfish nestled into an elephant ear sponge.

particularly seasonal with diving restricted to a few short months each year. Go out of season and you are likely to lose your diving. If you want to see something specific, check before you book.

Making the big decision

No matter where you go, the Philippines is a friendly, welcoming country with plenty to offer the travelling diver – not least a well established dive industry across a wide range of destinations. There are only a few liveaboards so, if you are not a boat person, to get a broader view of the country it's best to choose two slightly different destinations and build a two-centre holiday: a week of wrecks and one of macro, say. For the more isolated atolls, a liveaboard is the only way to go, but you could add some time at a more lively island resort afterwards. There are a variety of dive types in each area so, if you simply want to kick back and relax in just one place, that will work too.

Animal encounters

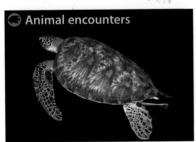

Countrywide: the Philippine Islands have always been regarded as a superlative macro destination as there are masses of amazing teensy-tiny, reef-building critters. However, if you choose your destination carefully, there will also be encounters with the ocean's giants. Around Tubbataha, turtles and reef sharks are prolific and in the Visayas there is a good chance you will see a whale shark, even if it's only a fleeting glimpse.

dive sites

There are, loosely speaking, two directions to go for Philippine diving. If you start in Manila, you can drive south to the Verde Island Passage, an oceanic highway that is regarded as the country's most biodiverse. Anilao, which sits above it, and Puerto Galera, below, are much loved by locals.

From here, a few liveaboards travel to Palawan (or you can get flights from Manila) on the western edge of the country. This is the access point for two unique diving regions: Coron, where many Second World War era shipwrecks sit on the seabed, and the Tubbataha World Heritage Site, which is way out in the middle of the Sulu Sea and the best area for (almost) guaranteed big animal encounters.

Heading in the other direction, Cebu airport ensures that reaching the diving areas in the Visayas is also easy. This region has more delicious white-sand-edged, coral-ringed islands than you can possibly imagine. There is a huge variety of dive sites with reefs, walls, steep drop-offs, shallow bays and caverns surrounding the islands of Panglao, Balicasag, Cabilao and several others. A short way south, the coast off Negros Oriental does its best to rival some of the world's best critter havens but with open-ocean Apo Island close enough to vary the pace. And last, but not least, the channel between Cebu Island and Negros, is the place to head for the Philippines very own Sardine Run.

Conditions

Seasons	Weather patterns are highly variable and hard to predict. In general, from June to October is rainy and November to February is cool and dry. There is a risk of typhoons in May.
Visibility	10-40 metres
Currents	Variable by area; only occasionally strong
Temperatures	Air 23°-32°C; water 25°-30°C
Wet suit	3 mm shorty or full body suit
Training	Courses in most resorts, standards vary
Nitrox	Not easily available
Deco chambers	Manila, Batangas and Cebu

Diversity

reef area 25,060 km²

HARD CORAL	577
FISH SPECIES	3,172
ENDEMIC FISH SPECIES	121
FISH UNDER THREAT	100

All diversity figures are approximate

Anilao ▶▶ p270

Anilao •   • Mabini

• Bagalangit

↘1   ↘3   ↘2

Log Book

↘1 **Dead Palm**
↘2 **Mainit Point**
↘3 **Secret Bay, east and west**
→ **Twin Rocks:** a slope with what remains of a capsized barge and lots of batfish.
→ **Basura:** night dive or muck dive, this is a renowned critter hunt
Sombrero: a swathe of boulders coated in small corals and loads of nudibranchs

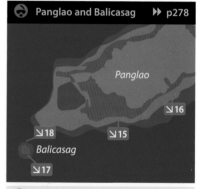

Panglao and Balicasag ▶▶ p278

Panglao

↘16

↘18   ↘15

Balicasag

↘17

Log Book

↘15 **Alona Beach Sanctuary**
↘16 **Arco Point**
→ **Snake Island:** a submerged plateau with strong currents that attract sea snakes
→ **Pamilican Island:** sloping reef, small caves and (maybe, perhaps) a manta ray
↘17 **Black Forest**
↘18 **Divers Dream**
→ **Cathedral Wall:** schools of butterflyfish and moorish idols off Balicasag Island
→ **Balicasag Sanctuary:** nursery ground for juveniles on a protected coastal stretch

Puerto Galera ▶▶ p272

🔖 Log Book

- ↘4 **Alma Jane Wreck**
- ↘5 **Boulders**
- ↘6 **Nudi Wall**
- → **Giant Clams:** this dive is all about the seahorses, but there are some clams
- → **Sabang Bay:** a patch of seagrass with pegasus sea moths and flying gurnards
  Shark Cave: one of the deepest dives here, but it lives up to its name

Tubbataha ▶▶ p274

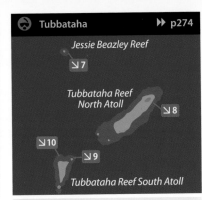

🔖 Log Book

- ↘7 **Jessie Beazley**
- ↘8 **Shark Airport**
- ↘9 **Black Rock**
- ↘10 **Eiger Wall**
- → **Malayan Wreck:** sitting exposed on the reef, the dive below is a mass of turtles
- → **South Rock:** a sharp wall and a fun drift dive with the whitetip sharks

Coron ▶▶ p276

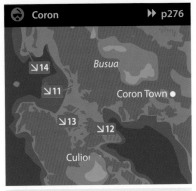

🔖 Log Book

- ↘11 **Wreck of the Taiei Maru**
- ↘12 **Wreck of the Kogyu Maru**
- ↘13 **Wreck of the Akitsushima**
- ↘14 **Dibutonai Reef**
- → **Dynamite Point:** no evidence of that, but masses of enormous corals and sponges
- → **Siete Pecados:** the 'seven sins' reveal rare tunicates and strapweed filefish

Cabilao ▶▶ p280

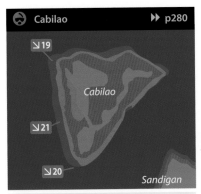

🔖 Log Book

- ↘19 **The Lighthouse**
- ↘20 **Gorgonia Wall**
- ↘21 **South Point**
- → **Talisay Tree:** the pretty gets forgotten in favour of giant and painted frogfish
- → **Cambaquiz:** a sandy channel between two small walls with all sorts of fish
- → **Paradise:** vertical wall with blennies and gobies, spider and orang-utan crabs

Negros Oriental ▶▶ p282

🔖 Log Book

- ↘22 **Coconut Point**
- ↘23 **Sanctuary**
- → **Rock Point, Apo:** enormous barrel sponges across a sandy shelf
- ↘24 **Atmosphere Reef**
- ↘25 **Masa Plod Sanctuary**
- ↘26 **Dauin**
- → **El Dorado Reef:** a circular bed of hard corals hides frogfish and cuttlefish
- → **Bahuru:** a dusk dive that is known for mandarinfish and octopus

Moalboal ▶▶ p284

🔖 Log Book

- ↘27 **Dolphin House**
- ↘28 **Kasai Wall**
- ↘29 **Pescador Island**
- → **Tongo Point:** a microcosm of reef life with almost everything you can think of
- → **Club Serena:** sloping bay dotted with symbiotic clownfish and anemones
- → **Pescador Cathedral:** swim through the cave for a stunning view to the surface

dive log

Luzon: Anilao

About 10 kilometres long and jutting into the waters of the Verde Island Passage, the Calumpan Peninsula's steep hills and craggy shores continue below the surface to a series of stepped terraces. These harbour a surprising amount of macro life. Directly opposite Anilao are Maricaban island and the Sombrero, a flat-topped pinnacle ringed by surf, which makes it look like a classic Mexican hat.

The diving here is quite special, although for some years the reefs had a reputation for being wrecked by poor fishing practices. Education by environmental and conservation groups has ensured that the area has now rejuvenated and dives close to shore are rife with soft corals; open water dives are alive with pelagic fish, while the tip of the peninsula has amazing muck dives that cluster around hot water sea vents.

◤1 Dead Palm	
Depth	25 m
Visibility	poor to good
Currents	slight to medium

One of the many dive sites that parallels the rocky shoreline, this series of slopes and terraces drops down to 35 metres or so. The divemasters stop at 25 metres as a golden fan has a family of the *Barbiganti* pygmy seahorses on it – including some pregnant males. Moving north along the reef, the seascape is one of small outcrops and huge barrel sponges punctuated by a few large pink fans. Octopus nudibranchs, morays and blue-spotted rays prowl around these and every surface seems to be decorated with multi-coloured crinoids.

◤2 Mainit Point	
Depth	27 m
Visibility	fair to good
Currents	slight to strong

Cazador Point is the most southern on the peninsula and, just offshore, some volcanic boulders break the surface and mark this dive. To the east there is a little damage but the closer to the boulders, the better it gets. There the reef is outstanding, coated in black coral bushes and hard corals with masses of crinoids adding colour. At the western end there are anthias, fusiliers and butterflies, anemones and clowns, a small school of needlenose barracuda and a gang of batfish. And then there are all the blue ribbon eels, morays and rays.

❝ ❞ Anilao offered the best of muck diving, especially as darkness fell. Seahorses and appeared frequently, complemented by rhinopias, the two-ringed and coconut octopus and the dazzling flamboyant cuttlefish...
R. Duncan Kirkby, professor, Grenada

▼3 Secret Bay, east and west

✦ **Depth**	28 m
◑ **Visibility**	fair to good
≋ **Currents**	slight

The dark sand bay beside Mainit Point was deserted until a large hotel complex was built and its secret status was no more! The sandy beach leads to a bed of rounded pebbles, then to a long, slowly descending slope. It's hard to describe this as a muck dive as there is very little muck. The seabed is quite barren but the critter life is truly superlative. On the western side of the bay a flat scrappy bed of sponges and algaes provides camouflage for the smallest, whitest frogfish you are ever likely to see. At under an inch long, even as adults, they are virtually invisible. Common seahorses have only been seen once or twice, but there are fire urchins, squat lobsters, jawfish, mantis shrimp and many juvenile fish that are hard to identify.

Diving towards the eastern side of the bay you pass many of the creatures met on earlier dives, like the aggressive panda clownfish and peacock flounders in the shallows. However, on this side, down at about 25 metres, the seafloor flattens out into an enormous jacuzzi. Streams of bubbles percolate from hot water vents in the seafloor revealing the volcanic activity in this region. There is less animal life just here – too warm perhaps – but heading back up the slope there are dwarf lionfish, scorpionfish and many incredibly beautiful, unusual nudibranchs. Other species include dragonets, lots of commensal shrimp and goby partnerships, sea snakes, tiny octopus, cowries, squid and masses of mantis shrimps.

The residents of Secret Bay on the Calumpan Peninsula include, clockwise: *Cuthona kanga*, a nudibranch from the Aeolid sub order (named for Aeolus, Greek god of the wind); seahorse; hingebeak shrimp; squid; mantis shrimp; white frogfish (this one is an adult and the size of a thumbnail); Orange and Black Dragonet (that is its proper name); crinoid shrimp.

Philippines Dive log Luzon: Anilao

dive log

Mindoro: Puerto Galera

The top of Mindoro island creates the bottom edge of the Verde Island Passage. Some say this narrow body of water is the most biodiverse on the planet. Competition for that accolade is strong, but you could be forgiven for blindly agreeing as you cross it accompanied by a pod of pilot whales and frolicking dolphins.

These waters were first declared a marine reserve way back in the mid-1930s; in 1973 they became a UNESCO Man and Biosphere Reserve. However, this is also one of the busiest shipping lanes in the country and extremes of weather can conspire to cause damage to some of the shallow reefs. From a diver's point of view, this may not seem particularly obvious; drop onto any dive site around the Puerto Galera promontory and it's soon clear that marine diversity here is high regardless.

↘4 Alma Jane Wreck

🕓 Depth	31 m
🔵 Visibility	fair to good
🌊 Currents	slight

On the edge of Sabang Bay, and just a few minutes from shore, are a range of small shipwrecks. They are all good dives, but perhaps the best of them is the *MV Alma Jane Express,* an old cargo boat that was scuttled in March 2003 to make an artificial reef. She was a 60-ton, 35-metre-long steel-hulled cargo ship built in 1966 and is now sitting upright at 30 metres. Little remains to indicate her past working life. but the boat has become a special dive as it attracts a huge number of pelagic fish. Dropping to the rudder you meet the first school of curious batfish then, when you ascend, there is a larger group hovering around the metal framework at deck level. There are schools of fusiliers, snappers, golden rabbitfish, lionfish and a solitary flutemouth that follows divers around.

↘5 Boulders

🕓 Depth	26 m
🔵 Visibility	fair to good
🌊 Currents	slight

Sitting on the boat beneath an almost vertical cliff wall, you are faced with a series of large boulders that break the surface. Rolling back into the water between them, you find some of the most dramatic terrain around this coast. The boulders seem to have tumbled down from the cliff, forming swim-throughs that create a winding path down to the level base of the site. Although you might want to stop to explore the caves and tunnels, the divemasters signal to head down to the flat base of the reef. A rubbly area is coated in sponges, hydroids and a swathe of algae and this is the spot to start searching for the resident thorny seahorses – and it's no problem to find them. They are always there, along with peacock razorfish, the usual range of clownfish in anemones, nudibranchs, blue-ribbon eels and young cuttlefish. More of a surprise as you move back up to the boulders is when the divemaster you are with goes absolutely crazy. You know he has found something but he's too excited to tell that you he's just seen a stunning, and rather unimpressed, blue-ringed octopus. This sort of thing doesn't happen all that often, but when it does...

Blue-ringed octopus displaying the full extent of its fury.

nudi
wall

🌀 **Depth**	21 m	
◐ **Visibility**	fair to good	
〰 **Currents**	slight	

A short boat trip from Sabang Beach, and more correctly known as Sinandigan, this site represents what diving here is all about. The topography is a bit unusual: despite being part of a wall, the dive focuses on a slope between two almost vertical sections of reef. This patch is renowned for being full to bursting with nudibranchs. And not just a few species, but countless different ones, including some that you are unlikely to have seen before. The dive starts at the smallest of fan corals with half a dozen pygmy seahorses on it. You can spend a huge amount of time admiring these tiny creatures so you need to force yourself across to the slope. Once there, you hardly fin a metre before spotting a nudi, then another and another. There are also wildly patterned flatworms, orang-utan crabs, snowflake morays and masses of small fish.

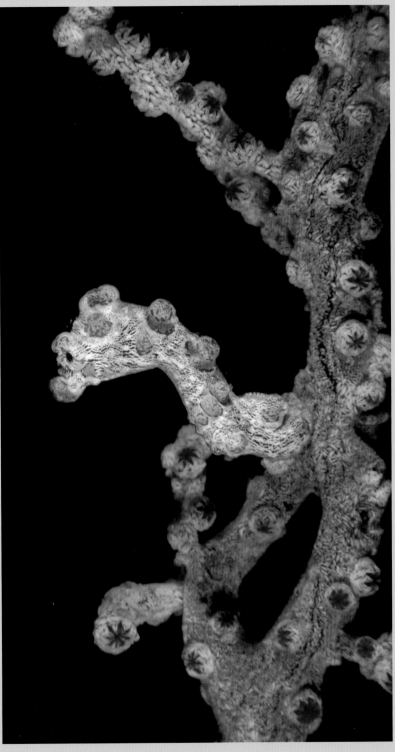

dive log
Palawan: Tubbataha

The island province of Palawan is just about as far west as you can go and still remain inside Philippine waters. It is an area famed for its outstanding natural landscapes as much as for its incredible underwater realm.

Palawan is also frequently targeted by divers, as liveaboards heading for the unique Tubbataha National Marine Park sail from its port. It's a long sail out but, when you finally arrive, it's to steep-sided walls that rim oval reefs with visibility to die for. In the open water, reef sharks, barracuda and tuna all cruise by at a lazy pace. Rays flit by and turtles ponder over reef tops.

This huge open space is in the middle of the Sulu Sea and highly exposed, so it can only be dived in the late spring. At other times potentially rough seas make the crossing nigh on impossible. Currents are variable and most dives are drifts. While this is not the prettiest of reef systems – reef tops have been damaged by past illegal fishing and coral growth is inhibited by natural weather conditions – this is definitely the place for big guys.

⬛ Jessie Beazley	
🕐 **Depth**	32 m
◐ **Visibility**	good to great
≋ **Currents**	slight to strong

Jessie Beazley Reef is the first stop boats make. The dives along the walls follow the tides and currents. The reef to the north is in good condition with a shallow top level rising to five metres and the deepest wall dropping to a sandy seabed at about 60 metres. The walls are covered in fans and branching corals with plenty of hawkfish.

However, the main action is off in the blue where there are masses of pelagic species including barracuda and tuna, several shark species (but only whitetips come in close) and quite a lot of schooling fish. Heading southwards, the reef has the added bonus of a slightly prettier upper level. There are big stands of *porites* hard corals that house lots of small colourful fish, pufferfish and lobsters. This section is also a great night dive; in the shallower areas there are saron shrimp peeking out from the coral, decorator crabs, tiny squat lobsters and seahares.

Manta ray at Black Rock; whitetip resting at Shark Airport.

ꙥ8 Shark Airport

Depth	35 m
Visibility	stunning
Currents	can be strong

One of the north atoll's gentler dives: a long slope drops away from the reef rim before turning into a wall. Dotted with caves and crevices, this drop has visibility so amazing you can see for miles – or so it seems. The wall is decorated with sea fans and soft corals. Jacks, rainbow runners and the ever-present whitetips hover on the tails of snappers. Heading back up, the slope pans out into a long strip of sand – the 'airport' – surrounded by coral heads. This ledge is almost always covered in whitetip sharks which rest here in neat squadrons.

ꙥ9 Black Rock, South Atoll

Depth	38 m
Visibility	stunning
Currents	slight to strong

The geography of the south atoll is a little gentler than the sharp walls of the north, and this sloping reef is a good example of the dives here. It eventually drops well beyond where you should be – you really have to watch your gauges for depth when the visibility is so clear. The wall is covered by a substantial number of fan corals interspersed with enormous barrel sponges that are swarmed by schools of bright reef fish. Thick schools of rainbow runners are broken by an occasional tuna or barracuda while, on the wall, there are squirrel and soldierfish, lionfish and moray eels. Eagle rays have been seen here but most exciting, on the right day, are the mantas. They are not a regular attraction but, when they do arrive, there are often several of them. It is most likely that you will get to snorkel with them rather than dive, as they hang around near the surface for hours at a time, lazily flapping about.

ꙥ10 Eiger Wall

Depth	38 m
Visibility	stunning
Currents	mild to strong

Sitting between the north and south atolls, this site is subject to some fairly strong currents. Entry is over a flat reef top, then a very steep vertical wall drops sharply to over 50 metres. Swimming downwards you pass some humungous gorgonians and, as you reach the 30 metre mark, you can see a lot of soft corals below. A cavern at 38 metres reveals its upper surface is just dripping in small white soft corals, like an upside-down snowstorm. Ascending back up the wall you pass a few more sharks, including some blacktips, before arriving on the top plateau to be greeted by a school of jacks silhouetted against the sun.

Corals on Eiger Wall; turtles are seen on every dive.

dive log
Palawan: Coron

The second of Palawan's dive attractions is Coron, which became famous due to the shipwrecks that litter the seabed. The remains of the Japanese Fleet are seen as second only to those in Truk Lagoon.

To the east of Coron Bay is the Sulu Sea, to the west the South China Sea, so you could expect this location to be subject to strong currents as the sea moves around the islands. Instead, the channels and bays are mirror calm and currents are minimal. These conditions attracted the Japanese in the Second World War; they moored a number of support ships here that were later bombed by US forces.

To date around a dozen wrecks have been located and their historical value is boundless. For divers, they are particularly attractive as they are so much easier to dive than Truk: this lagoon is shallow and calm. To an extent, that is also to its detriment as the visibility is never very clear. However, Coron isn't just wrecks: small reefs here are in good condition too.

N11 Wreck of the Taiei Maru

Depth	28 m
Visibility	fair
Currents	none

The *Taiei Maru* was an oil tanker which, at 180 metres long, is one of the larger wrecks in Coron. She sits upright on the seabed with a slight list to the port side. The buoy is hooked on at 10 metres and the deck is at 15-ish so there is plenty of time to look around. After descending, it's a good idea to head straight down to the rudder. Swarming around this are masses of pelagic fish: schools of batfish, yellow snappers and some sweetlips. The seafloor reveals animals, including some unusual nudibranchs. The divemasters then take an unusual turn and swim through the narrow propeller shaft behind the rudder, emerging 30 metres later in the engine room. This is a very tight passage so once you are inside you must go forward. Most people will find it easier and just as much fun to head back up to near the deck, from where you can penetrate some of the well lit holds and the engine room.

N12 Wreck of the Kogyu Maru

Depth	37 m
Visibility	fair
Currents	none

This Japanese freighter is 158 metres long and was carrying construction materials, supposedly for building an airfield. She is now lying on her side with some of those still inside the holds. After dropping down the mooring line, which is tied to the central bridge, it's best to fin downwards past the mast before entering the nearest open hold. Inside are rolls of fencing or some other diamond-shaped, webbed material. (They are heavily coated in silt so it's hard to see precisely what the material is.) The next hold along has some bags of cement and an almost intact bulldozer inside. It's a little easier to pick out shapes here. Next, you can swim through parts of the engine room before heading back up to the mast area where the black corals are very lush and there are lots of fish. The top level is actually the side of the hull (now facing up) and is covered in a huge amount of lettuce leaf and leather corals.

The deck of the *Taiei Maru* and inside its engine room; descending on the *Kogyu Maru*.

S13 Wreck of the Akitsushima

Depth	38 m
Visibility	fair
Currents	none

The only warship sunk inside Coron Bay, this seaplane tender was 118 metres long and 16 wide. The visibility can be murky and seems to get worse the further down you go. The hull lies on its side with a lot of gold and silver black corals coating the two masts that jut horizontally out over the seabed. Beneath these you can find a school of young, teenager stage, batfish. Finning inside the wreck you could explore the holds, which originally covered three levels, but time will be against you. On the deck are two circular gun placements and a crane, which was used to lower the seaplanes down into the water; it is now lying a short distance away on the seabed.

S14 Dibutonai Reef

Depth	15 m
Visibility	fair to good
Currents	none

There are many delightful bays sitting off even more delightful islands around the edges of Busuanga and Coron. Dibutonai is one. It is ringed by a classic, shallow fringing reef where you would never get much deeper than 15 metres without a shovel. The sandy bottom has seagrass beds – with large balls of stripy catfish – and there are anemone and clownfish combinations dotted about. The water in these shallows is very warm, possibly stopping the corals from becoming really prolific. However, many small animals such as nudibranchs and flatworms hide in what is there. Juvenile pinnate batfish seem common and seahorses are rare but seen.

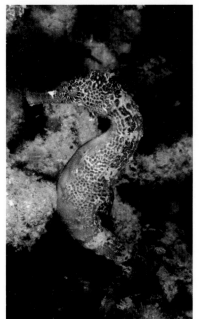

Philippines Dive log Palawan: Coron

66 99 The water in Coron Bay may be murky but it is the constant flow of plankton and nutrients that has turned each of these wrecks into a sumptuous artificial reef

dive log

Visayas: Panglao and Balicasag

It's just a quick hop from Cebu to Bohol, a large island renown for its natural attractions and interesting history, but it is the nearby smaller islands that attract divers as they are ringed by glorious coral reefs.

Panglao is the most popular as it is connected to Bohol by a causeway. Alona Beach was the first to be developed and is now a lively place with many beach-front hotels, yet it still manages to retain that 'no news-no shoes' feel. There are great dive facilities and many stunning dive sites all within minutes of shore. A short sail away is the satellite island of Balicasag, which is completely ringed by sloping reefs. There is a marine sanctuary so the environment is well protected and shelters the marine life.

Cabilao is a little further to the north and can be reached on a day-long dive trip, or you can stay there – the island is as lovely as any in the area. Like Panglao, these reefs have shallow, flat tops that drop away to walls, but one of Cabilao's features are extensive areas of good hard corals. Another is that from December to April there is the chance to see migrating hammerhead sharks, although sightings are rarely reported these days.

◲15 Alona Beach Sanctuary	
🕐 **Depth**	12 m
◑ **Visibility**	good to great
〰 **Currents**	slight to medium

◲16 Arco Point, Panglao	
🕐 **Depth**	28 m
◑ **Visibility**	good to great
〰 **Currents**	slight to medium

Pristine Alona Beach is very shallow, so much so that at low tide boats struggle to cross it. To protect the reef from damage, a section is buoyed off and the area below is now a sanctuary. At high tide the reef is at 10 metres and, at its edge, the drop-off descends to about 20 metres. The wall is cut with vertical crevices and there is a broad array of corals and fans, tunicates and small sponges. It's colourful both day and night, but the reef top is definitely the best night dive in the area. Inspection of the many small outcrops reveals endless weird critters. There are tiny cardinalfish, flatworms, shells, nudibranchs, frogfish, cuttlefish, cuttlefish nabbing cardinalfish and lionfish preying on whatever they can.

East of Alona, a blue hole about two metres wide leads from the reef top, through a submerged point and then emerges on the wall at about 20 metres. The tunnel is lined with soft corals and whips, lots of small morays and fish. After exiting the cave you swim to the base of a completely vertical wall where there is one of the largest purple fan corals you will ever see. A patch of tubastrea coral is a known haunt for giant frogfish. The wall winds in and out, lined with plenty of corals, then it's back up to the sandy flat reef for a safety stop. You can go critter hunting over the sand, where there are motionless pipefish, ribbon eels, pufferfish and many sand dwellers like the *inimicus* or devilfish.

The cave at Arco Point; smiling snake eel; juvenile stumpy-spined cuttlefish in the Alona Sanctuary.

⬛17 Black Forest, Balicasag

🌀 **Depth**	33 m
🔵 **Visibility**	good to stunning
🌊 **Currents**	slight to strong

Balicasag's principal dive site, Black Forest, is a swathe of incredibly prolific black corals that shimmer in tones of gold and silver whenever the current is running enough for them to extend their tentacles to feed. Black corals tend to be found in deeper waters, but the ones here grow right up to 30 metres. It is thought that they have adapted to the shallower depth as they are living in the shadow of the island. Cool water upwellings supply deep-water nutrients so the corals are fooled into thinking they are deeper than they are. There are many animals hiding around the branches – giant frogfish and flutemouths are regular finds. Meanwhile, out in the blue are massive balls of jacks and even larger schools of barracuda. Batfish and moorish idols join the throng; then, as you ascend, ledges and patches of sloping sand house many nudibranchs, pipefish and some tiny scorpionfish.

⬛18 Divers Dream, Balicasag

🌀 **Depth**	28 m
🔵 **Visibility**	good to stunning
🌊 **Currents**	slight to strong

Also known as Divers Heaven, this section of Balicasag starts on a slope covered in an array of hard corals before dropping swiftly to around 35 metres. This part of the wall is sharper than elsewhere on the island and is interspersed with cracks and caverns to investigate. There are some fan corals and more black corals, but the focus tends to be out in the blue where there are more schools of jacks and barracuda. The turtles are huge and very curious of divers to the point that they desert their meal of jellyfish to approach. Meanwhile, the jelly gets instantly smothered in both cardinalfish and a scrawled filefish who rush in to pick at it as well.

dive log

Visayas: Cabilao

⇘19 The Lighthouse

Depth	30 m	
Visibility	good to stunning	
Currents	slight to strong	

This dive is noted for exceptional visibility, but this can come along with some fierce currents. It's these that were said to bring the hammerheads to this site. The top of the reef slopes quickly down to a wall that is interspersed with cracks and crevices, which are full of corals, sponges and tunicates. In the shallows a seagrass bed has creatures such as catfish, tiny caverns full of banded pipefish, stone, scorpion and leaffish. If you were staying here, obviously, it would be a great night dive.

⇘20 Gorgonia Wall

Depth	34 m	
Visibility	fair to good	
Currents	slight to strong	

A classic multi-level dive, this reef runs along the shoreline and beach in front of La Estrella resort. The dive attracts some current at certain times of day: you can stay at five metres or so to stay out of it, or drop all the way to the base of the wall which is actually at 60 metres. Stopping at a more sensible depth, around 30, you can see a shelf a fair way below that is completely coated in black coral bushes and huge fans. It all appears to be in extremely good condition, then as you ascend back to a lesser depth you swim past small caverns full of fish. As you come up to around 10 metres, the scenery changes again to patchy coral outcrops. These act as home to banded pipefish and balls of catfish, then, finally, at the top are some seagrass beds where frogfish and seahorses are sometimes seen. The variety of marine life here is staggering.

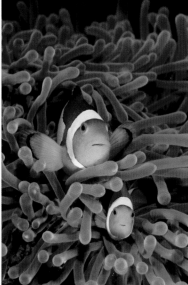

⇘21 South Point

Depth	22 m	
Visibility	fair to good	
Currents	slight to strong	

Heading to Cabilao's southern tip, the landscape changes to a sharp and craggy coast. Beneath this is probably the most spectacular hard coral growth you will encounter in the Visayas, as good as almost any part of the region. The wall drops for some way but the best corals are actually growing between about five and twelve metres. They are all in pristine condition and in the afternoon, when this dive is usually done, they are bathed in rays of sunlight. At the top, the table corals have spread to extreme widths, which allows them to catch more light. Dancing in and out of the branches are countless anthias, chromis and damsels. They drop out of sight as you approach, reappearing as you pass by. Off in the blue you may spy some jacks as they chase the endless schools of minute baitfish that are chasing even smaller plankton.

Reef lizardfish getting a gill clean from a cleaner wrasse; false clown anemonefish; Great phyllodesmium nudibranch.

dive log
Visayas: Negros Oriental

Running parallel to Cebu island, Negros is a draw for divers who target the contrasting dive regions near Dumaguete on the coast and Apo Island a short way offshore.

Apo is a pretty island three kilometres across and topped by a lighthouse. The shoreline swaps between dark rock boulders and bright white beaches that lead down to the now protected reefs. The island's highly successful marine sanctuary is run by villagers with great enthusiasm, and as time goes on, it is becoming more and more of a model for well-planned ecotourism. Dive wise, this is big blue territory with all sorts of pelagic species.

⬇22 Coconut Point	
🕐 **Depth**	28 m
💧 **Visibility**	stunning
〰 **Currents**	slight to ripping

This is Apo's big-thrill experience, a point that catches some very strong currents, and as ever it's the currents that attract the fish. The dive starts over a flat reef with good hard corals. It then slopes to a tongue with steep walls, where jacks, snapper and rainbow runners patrol. A sandy cut gives shelter if the current is really ripping and from here you can watch turtles, groupers, Napoleon wrasse and whitetip sharks. Schools of big eye trevallies compete with Spanish mackerel, barracuda and midnight snappers. The sloping section of this site is a very good place to look for turtles – one friendly resident is very old and his shell is encrusted with barnacles – and sea snakes are always on the prowl.

⬇23 Sanctuary	
🕐 **Depth**	20 m
💧 **Visibility**	good to excellent
〰 **Currents**	slight

It is interesting to see how a sustainable marine project can work to the benefit of both the local people, whose lifestyle has improved, and the surrounding environment. Diving inside the sanctuary is limited to a small number each day but, if you manage to do this, it's well worth it to see the swathes of hard coral and the small fish that are attracted to this safe haven. There are always clouds of fusiliers, butterflies, angels, sweetlips and different species of surgeonfish. The two most interesting patches are the clam beds, where the sanctuary monitors growth and spread, and the area of clownfish and anemones. You could spend most of the dive playing with the nemos!

dive log
Visayas: Negros Oriental

The coastal reefs off the eastern side of Negros were once regarded as being overfished. But, after a small marine sanctuary was established and local fishing communities learned about the value of the dive dollar, the area became riddled with sustainable fishing projects.

The reefs below Dumaguete city are some of the best macro dive locations you will ever find. This is not a pretty-pretty marine realm: the sand is dark, there is plenty of detritus to be seen and a fair number of artificial reefs. For aficionados of muck diving, this is the perfect description of a day underwater: simply think of a critter, mention it to the divemaster and off you go to see it.

⬊24 Atmosphere Reef

🕐 **Depth**	24 m
🔆 **Visibility**	fair to good
🌊 **Currents**	slight to strong
🌊 **Dive type**	shore

Located in front of Atmosphere Resort, and consequently regarded as their house reef, this part of the coast is a protected zone and an amazing beach dive. Entry from shore is over a patchy sloping reef but a sandy channel leads downwards, past some small bommies, until you reach the base of the slope. This flattened area is so full of small critters you have to be careful not to run out of time. There are crinoids housing shrimp, nudibranchs, jawfish and mantis shrimp in the sand. Descending over a field of low-lying hard corals, you might spot an enormous black banded sea snake. These differ from the more usual sea kraits as their bands are thicker and less defined. At the top of the reef, but to the north, a seagrass bed is a good area to offgas and hunt for ornate ghost pipefish and juvenile cuttlefish.

⬊25 Masa Plod Sanctuary

🕐 **Depth**	22 m
🔆 **Visibility**	fair to good
🌊 **Currents**	none
🌊 **Dive type**	day boat

One of the first sanctuaries in the area, this one is roped off so that no fishing can take place, not even with a hook and line. This means that the fish life within these boundaries is prolific. The reef falls gently down to about 25 metres and is covered in patches of hard coral. It's one of those dives where the closer you get to the sand, the more you will see, as so many of the creatures take refuge under the corals. There are huge groupers and even larger, juvenile whitetip sharks, plenty of triggerfish species and some sweetlips. On the sandy edges near the corals, and under little crevices, are mantis shrimp, pipefish and balls of catfish. Young batfish hide here too; they are still quite skittish, as are the young blue-spotted stingrays. Looking out to sea from the reef, you may even spot some passing tuna.

Juvenile whitetip at Masa Plod; slender crinoid shrimp in disguise.

◹26 **Dauin**	
❤ **Depth**	30 m
◐ **Visibility**	fair to good
≋ **Currents**	slight
◡ **Dive type**	day boat

For those interested in small cryptic marine dwellers, this is simply heaven. For those who would give their right arm (or more likely their camera) for a glimpse of a ghost pipefish, cuttlefish or even a mimic octopus, this ranks right up there with the best. There are several sites within Dauin Bay, with different nicknames depending on who you are diving with – Cars, Secret Corner, North or South and the Rubbish Pile are just a few.

Wherever you start, you will head across the crest of a dark sandy slope then down to the flat seabed. On the way there are logs surrounded by balling catfish, old car tyres with dwarf lionfish and flying gurnards. A little further along snake eel noses poke from the sand, then it's down to a hollow where a crinoid houses tiny ornate ghosties. At the base of the slope, a rubbish pile is the homepatch of several seahorses, morays, flamboyant cuttlefish and stonefish encounters. A little north of here, the wrecks of some old cars are smothered in life – lionfish, scorpions and batfish. There is even a rare, juvenile zebra batfish on occasion. Or you could turn south and fin back uphill to spin along the edge of the coral sanctuary with its baby sharks and butterflyfish, then back along the crest until – if you are really lucky – you spot the mimic octopus. Finally, there is a patch of seagrass in shallow water that makes a perfect, extended safety stop. In fact, you can spend a very long time here hunting for critters in amongst the green blades. There are more frogfish, seahorses, juvenile razorfish, fingered dragonets, devilfish, and a spectacular find for patient spotters is the Pegasus seamoth.

Dauin residents: ornate ghost pipefish mating pair; juvenile zebra batfish; seahorse; adult rockmover wrasse; pufferfish in hiding; black banded sea snake; flamboyant cuttlefish; clown frogfish.

dive log

Visayas: Moalboal

◢27 Dolphin House	
🕐 **Depth**	22 m
◑ **Visibility**	good
〰 **Currents**	mild

◢26 Kasai Wall	
🕐 **Depth**	15 m
◑ **Visibility**	good
〰 **Currents**	slight to medium

Because this dive leads downwards from a bay, it starts over a hard coral-clad slope that descends slowly to around 20 metres before suddenly dropping off to a wall that stops at beyond 40 metres. However, the most interesting section is just over the rim of the wall where there are a lot of small caves to be investigated. Dolphins are rarely, if ever, seen but there are nearly always turtles nestling in these caves or following the divers along the reef wall. Deeper than this, there are some big fan corals where the divemasters have been known to spot pygmy seahorses but, as time is limited at that depth, it's better to stay near the caves and look for residents. At night, the slope of the bay is good for hunting out bottom dwellers such as small flounders, decorator and hermit crabs, shells and octopus.

If divers had gills, you would start at one end of this coastal stretch and drift all the way to the very far end. The topography of the sites tends to be fairly similar, so it's a good idea to do each one at specific depths to see the various levels. Kasai is perfect for the shallower depths where all the surfaces of the vertical wall are coated in pastel-hued soft corals and fans with lots of smaller fish resting inside them. There are also substantial numbers of golden black coral bushes, each with a school of razorfish clustered around them. Although you could head down to the base of the reef wall, the shallows are better for spotting small groups of striped snappers and sweetlips hovering over the hard corals. Moray eels and sea snakes live amongst these; there are nudibranchs and small fish like gobies on the sand.

Tucked behind Cebu's west coast is a channel of water that divides it from Negros Island. The Tañon Strait was declared to be a protected zone back in the 1990s as the channel is a migratory path used by whales and dolphins. A decade later, areas inside the strait became official marine parks and sustainable fishing is now practised.

The heart of the dive industry here centres on the town of Moalboal, although there are dive sites and resorts up and down the Cebu coast. The scenic coastline winds gently along the island with small bays providing havens for shore dives. However, each of these drops to sharp dramatic walls. The conditions are mostly easy, the visibility is good and the marine life is plentiful. But, and this is the big but, the main reason for coming to this area is to experience the Sardine Run at Pescador Island in the channel.

Razor fish clusters and black corals along Moalboal's walls.

pescador
island

❖ **Depth**	21 m	
◐ **Visibility**	fair to good	
〰 **Currents**	slight	

A few years ago, this was regarded simply as a beautiful dive but not so unusual or unique. Then a humungous ball of sardines appeared. They stayed for a while, long enough to attract all the relevant predators and capture the attention of dive centres. Naturally, comparisons were made to the more famous South African Sardine Run. Then, as suddenly as they had appeared, the sardines disappeared. It was quite an event, if only a short-lived one. However, a couple of years later, the sardines returned and – so far – have stayed. Chances are that this is a seasonal pattern.

The ball can usually be seen from the surface, but entry is made a short distance away, as the brief is to hover in the shadow of the reef wall and wait for the mass of fish to move towards the island. Hundreds and thousands, no, millions of tiny flashes of silver are clustered just off into the blue and, as you watch in awe, the immense sardine ball starts its approach. The sun is obliterated by masses of, shimmering ribbons of silver until, suddenly, the solid edges start to disintegrate and a gigantic tuna comes barreling in at great speed, launching himself into the body of the sardine school and splitting it into myriad smaller groups, nabbing and taking prey, then disappearing off into the distance.

As quickly as they disperse, the sardines regroup into a tighter ball, only to be blown apart a second time as a gang of jacks intent on eating a big breakfast force the school asunder once more.

❝❞ **The rest of the diving was fine, typical of the tropics, but none of it even faintly compared to Pescador. The Sardine Run was eerie, moody... and almost overwhelming.** *Sean Keen, construction manager, Bexhill-on-Sea, UK*

drying out

Across such a large country, there is bound to be a huge selection of resorts that have excellent dive facilities. Once you have decided on a region, remember to balance standards with budgets. You really do get what you pay for, and this is especially true with liveaboards.

Liveaboards
Most liveaboards in the Philippines run countrywide schedules, moving vessels around to match the best seasons.

Philippine Siren, sirenfleet.com. Delightful phinisi schooner with great on-board facilities, service and a top crew. Wide range of routes across the country.

Atlantis Azores, atlantishotel.com/azores
Discovery Fleet, discoveryfleet.com
Expedition Fleet, expeditionfleet.com
M/Y Vasco, dive-vasco.com

Luzon
Anilao
Transfers to resorts in this region are by road and take 2½ hours from Manila.
Crystal Blue, charming small resort with on site dive centre, great food and views. crystalblueanilaodivingresort.com
Halo Dive Resort, halodiveresort.com
Dive Solana, divesolana.com

Mindoro
Puerto Galera
There is no airport so transfer by road to Batangas (2½ hrs) then 45-mins by boat.
Atlantis Dive Resorts, atlantishotel.com. Full-service, diver-focused resort with excellent facilities in lively Sabang Bay.
El Galleon Diving Resort, asiadivers.com
Marco Vincent, marcovincent.com

Palawan
Both Coron and Tubbataha are best dived by liveaboard and in fact, you can only get to Tubbataha that way, see left.
Coron
Discovery Divers, Decanituan, ddivers.com
Dive Link, Uson, divelink.com.ph
Sangat Island Reserve, sangat.com.ph

Visayas
Bohol
The islands and resorts around Bohol are about 3 hrs from Cebu airport.
The Ananyana, ananyana.com. Top-class resort on Panglao with on-site dive centre, spa and restaurant.
La Estrella, laestrella.ph. On Cabilao
Oasis Bohol, Panglao, oasisresortbohol.com

Dumaguete, Negros Oriental
There is an airport but road and sea transfers take 4-5hrs from Cebu airport.
Atlantis Dive Resorts, atlantishotel.com. Sister resort to Atlantis in Puerto Galera.
Atmosphere, atmosphereresorts.com
Bahura Resort and Spa, bahura.com
El Dorado, eldoradobeachresort.com

Moalboal, Cebu
Club Serena, clubserenaresort.com
Magic Island, magicisland.nl
Turtle Bay, turtlebaydiveresort.com

City stopovers
If your flights to Manila or Cebu airport require a stopover night, these hotels are comfortable and convenient.
Heritage Hotel, millenniumhotels.com. International-style hotel, 8-mins from Manila airport; transfers included.
Plantation Bay Resort, plantationbay.com Just 20-mins from Cebu airport on Mactan Island. Colonial style rooms in a fun resort.

Retail therapy on Apo Island; Philippine Siren in the Visayas.

Days out

Anilao There isn't much in the way of land attractions here although villages are pretty and worth exploring. Inland from the coast are mountain plains and ridges, which appeal to trekkers, and the smallest volcano in the world, Mt. Taal, is located at the centre of the Taal Lake.

Puerto Galera The main town, Poblacion, was once a fishing village and has banks, restaurants, shops and a public market. Beside the Catholic Church, the Excavation Museum displays ancient Chinese pottery and artefacts found in the area. If you need a change from seawater to fresh, there are waterfalls at Tamaraw, near the village of Villaflor (14 km from Puerto Galera). These have a natural swimming pool at the base. Mangyan Village is home to Mindoro's once coastal nomads. These tribes have tried to avoid any outside influences in order to protect their own culture. Nearby, Small Tabinay River has gold-digging sites.

Coron Arrive in Coron Bay by boat and you will never forget the breathtaking vistas of towering, sharp volcanic walls dotted with small green trees clinging on for dear life. Inside the channel the walls give way to soft and gentle hills, then it all drops into the deep blue sea. Busuanga is the largest island in the group and attracts those who like to get out into the great outdoors. There are river, mountain and jungle walks, hot springs and horse-riding. This is also the location of Coron Town, which is quite small and easy to explore on foot. You could stick to the market, souvenir or pottery shops or trek the 720 steps up Mount Tapyas for a 360º scenic view. Calauit Island, lying off the northwest tip of Busuanga, is an animal sanctuary with both endemic and African animals: zebra, giraffes and gazelles live alongside the local Calamian deer and Palawan peacocks. Culion Island is the best known in this area, famous for once being a leper colony. Established in 1906, the community grew when families

followed their afflicted relatives there. It was said to be the safest place in the country during the Second World War as the Japanese would not set foot on the island for fear of getting ill.

Bohol Spend a lazy day walking around Tagbilaran, the island capital and location of an old Spanish settlement. There are a few 17th- and 18th-century churches and some attractive tree-lined plazas, colonial homes and a small museum. However, the most famous Bohol attraction is the Chocolate Hills, a weird landscape of more than 1,200 grassy mounds that look like someone tipped up bags of sugar in rows. In the summer, the 30-50m high domes turn brown as the grassy vegetation dries out, transforming the area into rows of 'chocolate' mounds. The province is also home to the world's smallest primate, the tarsier. This truly diminutive creature is endangered. Visit the Tarsier Research and Development Centre at Corella. There is a netted enclosure where the tarsiers are fed, bred and monitored. Alternatively, take the tarsier trail through the forest and watch out for one.

Negros The busy city of Dumaguete is home to Silliman University. The shops and markets are fun to visit and there is some colonial architecture including an 18th-century bell tower. The botanical gardens, zoo and aviary are worth a visit. Casaroro Waterfall is an hour by car in the Valencia Mountains. The small nature reserve nestles in the river valley. Hiking for an hour takes you to the waterfall, which drops into a stunning natural swimming pool. Another day out is to Twin Lakes. Located in the mountainous area above San Jose, and inland from Dumaguete, Balinsasayao and Danao Twin Lakes are a haven of pristine flora and fauna. Kayakers can rent a small *banca* and cross to the deserted side of the lake under a dark forest canopy.

Diving bangka at Alona Beach; fish market; the diminutive Tarsier; local jeepney bus.

291
↘ **Essentials**

292
↘ **Dive brief**

294
↘ **Dive sites**

296
↘ **Dive log**

Egypt
296 Sinai Peninsula
298 South coast
300 Brothers Islands
301 Far south

Jordan
304 Aqaba

307
↘ **Drying out**
307 Egypt
309 Jordan

Red Sea

A lonely sentinel on the sand: an American M42 Duster with
self-propelled anti-aircraft canon finally laid to rest.
Aqaba, Jordan

destination
Red Sea

The lands surrounding the Red Sea are steeped in legend and ancient history. According to the story from Exodus, it was here that the waters parted to save the Israelites from the Egyptian army. Across the centuries, great races populated the lush river valleys, intensely dry deserts and hidden rocky gorges, all the time building unrivalled monuments and developing technologies we still rely on thousands of years later.

The name of this body of water is something of an enigma. The most popular explanation is, that every now and then, a seasonal bloom of red algae turns the sea a pink hue. Even so this sea is far from red: intense blue waters mask the rich coral reefs of the world's most northern tropical sea.

Seven nations border this narrow ribbon of water, with Egypt grabbing the lion's share of diver attention. Yet the land of the Pharaohs may not be what you expected: coastal resorts are highly developed and ancient monuments are a long way away. And, while a million or so divers descend on Egypt year after year, a small and intrepid band choose to avoid the crowds and venture instead into easy-going Jordan, where the dive sites are calm and peaceful and history is just a stone's throw away.

ISRAEL

CAIRO

Petra

JORDAN

Eilat

Aqaba ▶▶ p304

Sinai Peninsula

SAUDI ARAB

Sinai ▶▶ p296

EGYPT

Sharm el Sheik

El Gouna

Hurghada

South Coast ▶▶ p298

Nile

Red Sea

Safaga

Brothers Islands ▶▶ p30

El Quesir

Marsa Alam

Far South ▶▶ p3C

Aswan

Hamata

Essentials

If you live anywhere in Europe, you will know that getting to the Egyptian Red Sea is easiest and cheapest by charter flight. Flying scheduled is far more comfortable but it's also more complex, and in the end, it's only a few hours on the plane. If you are coming from further afield you will probably need to fly to Cairo, routing through the home base of whatever airline you choose, and then swapping to an Egypt Air internal flight. Jordan is pretty much limited to scheduled flights to Amman with a short connection to Aqaba on the coast.

Local laws and customs

Both countries are principally Muslim but the Red Sea towns are highly tourist-savvy and fairly easy-going. However, what you can get away with on the coast may be frowned upon in Cairo or Amman so dress modestly. Jordan is better known for its levels of tolerance, but women should play it safe and cover bare skin while in towns or at religious sites. People everywhere are highly hospitable; always eat with your right hand if you are with a local, and never expect to finish a meal in Jordan. If you clear your plate, they will think you are still hungry and will bring more food.

Health and safety

Tutankhamen's Two-step, Pharaoh's Revenge... you guessed it, euphemisms for a classic case of Egyptian stomach upset. While standards are high in Jordan, you will be lucky to get to Egypt and back without at least a minor dose, especially in places that target tourist tastebuds. Local cooking is often fresher and worth trying. Keep up your fluid levels to help combat tummy troubles and avoid dehydration. These countries get very hot – summer temperatures can reach over 50°C, so get a high factor sunscreen.

Before booking your flights, it's worth checking an official travel advisory site. It doesn't matter what country you are visiting, things can go wrong. The political unrest seen in Cairo in recent times is a prime example. However, the Red Sea resorts are a different kettle of fish, and tourists are always treated as welcome guests.

Costs

Package trips that include flights, room and diving are exceptional value but it is harder to judge costs if you travel independently. Eating out is easy to budget for as there are many restaurants in many styles. Where you are limited to a resort, meals and drinks can be pricey. However, many towns have supermarkets, so use those for incidentals like mineral water to keep costs down.

Tipping – *baksheesh* – is a way of life in both countries. Salaries are low in the service industries, so 'donate' an Egyptian pound or two to everyone, from cab drivers to the chap who watches your shoes when you a visit a mosque. In restaurants, consider adding 10%. Jordanian workers are a little better paid and less expectant of a tip, but 5% or so will always be appreciated.

Fact file

Egypt	
Location	27°00'N, 30°00'E
Capital	Cairo
Jordan	
Location	31 00 N, 36 00 E
Capital	Amman
Flights	Alitalia, British Airways, Egypt Air, Emirates, KLM and Royal Jordanian
Internal flights	Egypt Air; Royal Jordanian
Land transport	Countrywide buses, trains, taxis, mini-buses
Departure tax	US$20 when leaving Jordan
Entry	Visas are required and will be issued on entry. The Egyptian fee varies according to nationality from US$30-60. In Jordan, the fee is fixed at $30.
Money	Egyptian pounds (EGP); Jordanian dinar (JOD)
Language	Arabic but English is common
Electricity	220v, plug C in Egypt; type G in Jordan (p. 15)
Time zone	GMT +2
Religion	Muslim, with small Christian minority groups
Communications	Egypt country code +20; IDD code 00; Police 0 Jordan country code +962; IDD code 00; Police 191. Internet access varies but is available at a cost
Tourist information	egypt.travel; visitjordan.com
Travel advisories	gov.uk/foreign-travel-advice; state.gov/travel

dive brief

❝ ❞ When we learnt to dive so long ago, the swimming pool in central London made our training dives in Cyprus look exotic. In turn, those dives meant our first trip to the Red Sea took on the status of a pilgrimage. Our first foray was to Jordan; on the next we went from Aqaba to Sharm by ferry. But after several trips to the area we got a hankering to go further and spent the '90s traversing one continent after another. We've been back to both countries since and have been reminded that this is one of the world's better coral reef systems. At the right time of year. in the right part of the sea, with the right operation, you will find some great diving.

Diving

At 2,240 kilometres long, 380 kilometres wide and up to 2,150 metres deep, the Red Sea is a vital lifeline for the countries that border her shores. The northern end is enclosed – or was until the building of the Suez Canal – while the southern opening that leads to the Indian Ocean is extremely shallow, preventing the deep ocean currents from entering the gulf.

The surrounding deserts and extreme temperatures create the highest salinity in any open sea yet, despite this, it sustains one of the world's more prolific marine systems. Being isolated from both the Indian Ocean and the Mediterranean Sea (originally) means this most northern tropical sea has an unrivalled biological set-up. Almost 10% of her species are endemic: they might look like something you've seen somewhere else but chances are they're a unique form. Crustaceans, cephalopods, molluscs – they're all there, along with substantial schools of reef fish and plenty of pelagic fish.

Whether you've headed for the far south of Egypt or the tiny strip of coastline owned by Jordan in the far north, the appearance of the dives will be fairly similar, with a typical backdrop of extensive hard coral formations. Seasonal variations can be marked, though. The summer months are exceptionally hot and, when it's windy, you will know all about it.

Winters can be surprisingly cold and surface conditions can be very choppy, so getting beneath the surface can be far more comfortable than sitting above it. The marine life seen from one season to another can differ substantially too, with bigger pelagics seen more often in the winter. Plankton blooms are linked to temperature changes and can occur at any time, as can a change in the currents.

Snorkelling

Even if you don't dive, it's worth heading out on a boat with the divers, as many offshore reefs can be snorkelled. There are also many easy beach-side reefs. However, before leaping into the water, ask a dive centre or hotel for advice. Sadly, a couple of years back, there were a few high-profile incidences of shark attacks, but these are very rare. The only other issue will be the weather. Be very aware of how harsh the sun can be – as the water here is cool, you may not realize that you are burning.

Schooling chevron barracuda at Elphinstone Reef.

Marine life

The majority of divers who dive the Red Sea do so regularly and tend to see much the same things: anthias, butterfly, clown and angelfish are common, while blue-spotted rays, turtles and morays are an every-dive occurrence. But you can also be surprised by anything from a tiger shark or manta ray to tiny seagrass ghost pipefish and frogfish.

Making the big decision

The Red Sea is only a stone's throw from Europe and, although you can dive much of it, the Egyptian coast is by far the easiest section to reach. The infrastructure is highly diver-focused and it is reasonably priced, especially for Europeans. Choosing a specific destination inside the country is only difficult in that there is little difference between the resort areas: a little bigger or smaller, a lot busier or a little quieter. As long as you accept that wherever you go there will be many others with you, this will be one of the most reliable places you will ever dive. Jordan appeals more to independent travellers and divers or simply those who like to float about in a world of their own. It's a small area, so the variety of sites will never compete with its neighbour yet the marine life is the same and the reefs remain uncrowded.

Animal encounters

Across the Red Sea: keep an eye out for occasional visits from Oceanic whitetips and dugongs, but you are far more likely to see the full range of butterflyfish like the masked pair above, and friendly cuttlefish. A more unusual encounter is the delightful Spanish Dancer that is frequently seen at night, very often up and dancing in the water. And of course, there are the wrecks. OK, these are not animals but there is sunken ship after sunken ship, and each one has become an incredible and rich artificial reef.

dive sites

From top to bottom, the Red Sea relishes its role as a diving heartland. In the far north, Jordan has the smallest section of coastline in the Red Sea and is a reminder of how diving here used to be. Dive sites are quiet and peaceful yet still display many of the same features as the more popular waters to the south.

Sharm el Sheikh on the tip of the Sinai Peninsula was the birthplace of Egypt's dive industry. Once sleepy fishing villages have grown almost beyond recognition, with ever-more resorts spreading both north and south along the coast. Much-loved dive sites, such as Ras Mohammed, and famous wrecks like the *Thistlegorm* are as popular and busy as ever.

Moving south and across the Straits of Gubal, several small ports and coastal towns are now marketed as the 'Red Sea Riviera'. Hurghada and Safaga are very popular as their less prolific inshore reefs still maintain the potential to surprise. However, sail out a little way from the coast and the offshore reefs turn up the intensity. Around six hours' sail from the coast, the distant Brothers Islands have potentially breathtaking diving in a pristine environment although access is limited.

Egypt's final dive frontier is reached via Marsa Alam in the far south and continues until you are almost on the Sudanese border. Pristine hard corals, unusual sites and some unexpected pelagic species are making this an increasingly dived region.

Sinai Peninsula ▶▶ p296

Sinai Peninsula · Straits of Tiran · Na'ama Bay · Sharm el Sheik · ↘1 · Tiran · ↘3 · Ras Mohammed · ↘2

🔵 Log Book

↘1 **The Tower**
↘2 **Ras Mohammed**
↘3 **The Thistlegorm**

→ **Ras Nasrani:** steep wall at 'Christian Headland' leads to lush reefs and caves
→ **Woodhouse Reef:** a long, current-swept reef with jacks, tuna and turtles
→ **The Dunraven:** the remains of a sail and steam hybrid vessel built in 1873
→ **Gordon Reef:** blue-spotted rays beneath and dolphins up above

South coast ▶▶ p298

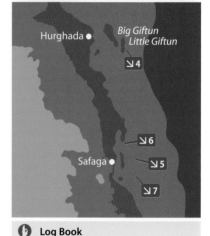

Hurghada · Big Giftun · Little Giftun · ↘4 · ↘6 · Safaga · ↘5 · ↘7

🔵 Log Book

↘4 **Little Giftun**
↘5 **Tobia Arba**
↘6 **Panorama**
↘7 **The Salem Express**

→ **Shabroah Umm Gamar:** remains of a patrol boat scattered over the reef
→ **Abu Kefan Wall:** lovely coral-clad wall with tuna and barracuda in the blue
→ **Sha'ab Saiman:** a pretty coral garden with sharks and eagle rays

Conditions

Seasons	In Egypt, July and August are extremely hot. December and January can be cool and windy. Aqaba is marginally hotter in the summer and cooler in the winter but a little less windy.
Visibility	10-40 m
Currents	everything from none to raging
Temperatures	Air 20-30°C; water 20-29°C
Wet suit	Summer: 3 mm full body suit; winter: 5 mm+
Training	Courses available everywhere, standards vary
Nitrox	Available everywhere
Deco chamber	Sharm el Sheikh, Hurghada, El Gouna, Marsa Alam in Egypt; Aqaba in Jordan

Brothers Islands ▶▶ p300

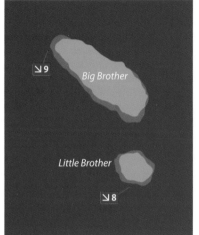

↘9   Big Brother

Little Brother

↘8

Log Book

| ↘8 | **Northern Point, Little Brother** |
| ↘9 | **The Aida, Big Brother** |

→   **The Numidia:** remains of a British cargo ship off the tip of Big Brother

→   **The Pier:** multiple Napoleon wrasse and enormous balls of silver baitfish

→   **Little Brother, south wall:** amazing soft coral wall and a gorgonian forest

Far south ▶▶ p301

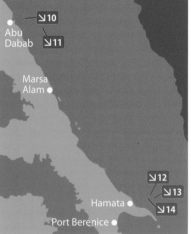

↘10
Abu Dabab   ↘11

Marsa Alam ●

↘12
↘13
Hamata ●   ↘14

Port Berenice ●

Log Book

↘10	**Abu Dabab Bay**
↘11	**Elphinstone Reef**
↘12	**Sha'ab Claudio**
↘13	**Sha'ab Malahi**
↘14	**Abu Galawa Soraya**

→   **Sha'ab Sattaya:** renowned for being home to a pod of spinner dolphins

→   **Sha'ab Ini:** clusters of tightly packed coral pinnacles with dancing fish

→   **Sha'ab Bohar Soraya:** free swimming moray eels patrol corals in the sand
Zabargad Resort Reef: leap off the jetty to meet barracuda and batfish

Aqaba ▶▶ p304

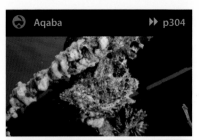

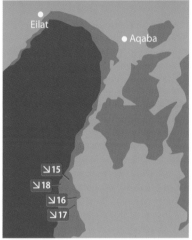

Eilat ●

● Aqaba

↘15
↘18
↘16
↘17

Log Book

↘15	**Cable Canyons**
↘16	**Japanese Gardens**
↘17	**Gorgon 1**
↘18	**Cedar Pride and M42 tank**

→   **Cazar Reef:** shallow fringing reef, home to all the usual Red Sea residents

→   **Eel Gardens:** swathes of garden eels in the sand and a towering pinnacle

→   **First Bay:** frogfish and hard corals, hard corals and more frogfish

→   **Yellowstone Reef:** a small wall with black corals and moray eels

→   **King Abdullah Reef:** narrow crack in the fringing reef leads to turtle encounters

Diversity
combined reef area 3,850 km²

		Jordan	Egypt
	HARD CORAL	120	143
	FISH SPECIES	552	826
	ENDEMIC FISH SPECIES	1	3
	FISH UNDER THREAT	25	43

All diversity figures are approximate

dive log

Egypt: Sinai Peninsula

Diving around the Sinai Peninsula is legendary. This area is definitely one of those 'must do' places: home to Sharm el Sheik, Ras Mohammed (Egypt's first marine park), the Straits of Tiran and the Straits of Gubal where many a wreck is found. And despite the large numbers of dive boats, operators and divers, this is an area of distinctive beauty.

Egyptian dive tourism was born in a tiny fishing village which developed out of all recognition to become the upscale resort now known as Sharm el Sheikh. There are hotels and dive centres, restaurants and more hotels. At its heart is Na'ama Bay, a crescent-shaped cove that just manages to retain a little of the town's early charm. It's a lively place, with lots to do: golf and camel riding, trips into the desert with a Bedouin guide or tours to a medieval site. Yet the focus remains pretty much dive, dive, dive – and party. Bars and restaurants abound. On either side of Na'ama, the resorts in Shark Bay and Sharm El Maya are good for those who like things a little less frenetic. For a more relaxed scene (but nowhere here is all that peaceful) you can go north to one of the smaller centres along the coast towards Israel. Dahab, in particular is popular with those who like a quieter life with fewer visitors, both on land and in the water, yet the diving is still impressive. St Catherine's Monastery and Mount Sinai, where Moses received the Ten Commandments, are nearby.

If you are a novice and want to gain experience, there are plenty of dives to practise on: shallow wrecks, pretty reefs, drifts and caves – it's all there. For more experienced divers, there's all of that plus some deeper wrecks and more exposed conditions. The downside, though, is the numbers. You will never be the only boat moored at any site. Sometimes there are so many you need both hands, and a toe or two, to count them.

⚓ The Tower	
🕐 **Depth**	20 m
◑ **Visibility**	good
〰 **Currents**	slight to medium

This shore dive is incredibly popular both day and night, as the topography is a lot fun. The entry over the reef can be a little tricky at low tide, so divers can take a spectacular short-cut through a small cave. The mouth is part way across the reef top and, as you swim downwards, it opens into a much wider passage that then exits onto the reef wall. You could drop as deep as 40 metres, where you may encounter a whitetip or two, but the most interesting parts of the dive are under 20 metres. The marine life is a microcosm of all things Red Sea: masses of anthias flitting in and out of soft corals, moray eels, butterflies, lionfish and plenty of crustaceans. At night every surface is alive with shrimp and decorator crabs, which are attracted by the moonlight shining through the opening.

Octopus are Sinai regulars.

◹2 Ras Mohammed	
Depth	20 m
Visibility	good
Currents	can be very strong

◹3 The Thistlegorm	
Depth	25 m
Visibility	fair
Currents	can be strong

Off the southern tip of Ras Mohammed are several dives loosely known as 'Ras'. The actual sites mostly referred to are the twin peaks of Shark Reef and Jolanda. Their joint status derives from dives starting on one and finishing on the other. A submerged sea mound is separated from the mainland by a shallow channel: rising from it are the two peaks linked by a saddle. The dive starts off as a drift at Shark Reef where a wall drops dramatically into the blue. You float past swarming orange anthias and over colourful corals. Reef sharks (black and whitetips) are often seen; less common are hammerheads. Next you pass over the saddle then it's on to the coral gardens at Jolanda. You may spot a few cargo remains from the freighter of the same name, but the wreck itself dropped into the deep during a storm in the '80s. The dive finally ends in the shallows.

The Straits of Gubal, the narrow stretch of water that leads to the Suez Canal, are a shipping graveyard. The most renowned dive in the strait is the *HMS Thistlegorm*, a British cargo vessel bombed during the Second World War en route to resupply troops. Now she is like a deserted shop, with holds full of motorbikes, engines and toilets that never reached their destination. Conditions are highly variable – when it's calm, it's an easy dive but, if the wind and waves pick up, it's not a place for novices. The hull sits almost upright and is pretty much intact. Descent is down a line tied to the forward section from where you swim into a few of the holds then down towards the stern. This took the brunt of the bomb blast, but you can still see the crew quarters and some anti-aircraft guns. Off to one side, if you can tear yourself away, is a locomotive engine on the sand.

Descending on the *Thistlegorm*; at Ras Mohammed.

dive log

Egypt: South coast

Once a small Bedouin encampment, Hurghada expanded into a major resort after an international airport was built there and, within a few years, all the other small towns in the area followed suit.

This is Egypt's biggest beach resort, stretching for many kilometres north and south of downtown Dahar. The coastline is connected by a single road lined with resorts, restaurants, shops and facilities for all sorts of sports from diving to golf. Dahar itself is a working town, busy, messy and typically Egyptian.

Offshore, the reefs once suffered from misuse and over-diving. However, in 1992 operators formed a conservation group and the reefs are now safeguarded under the same rules as Ras Mohammed. They are regenerating well, although those closer to shore are not as profuse as you might hope.

For a sense of seclusion not found in Hurghada, there are other resorts towns. El Gouna is a custom-built resort that turned the desert into a maze of palm tree- and hotel-studded islands surrounded by lagoons. Access to the wrecks in Gubal is easy from here. An hour in the other direction, is the shipping port of Safaga. A handful of hotels have on-site dive centres and, as it is less busy, local reefs are in fairly good condition. Surface conditions can be rough as Safaga is also a favoured destination for windsurfers.

⬇4 Little Giftun	
Depth	28 m
Visibility	fair to good
Currents	slight to medium

A short sail offshore from Hurghada are Big and Little Giftun islands. These are popular sites for novices and trainees so the corals are not at their best, especially in the shallower areas. However, the wall on Little Giftun is an exception. Entering the water opposite the lighthouse, you drop in to find a current that will carry you on a drift through a forest of pink and yellow fans. Longnose hawkfish hide in these and scrawled filefish try to do the same. There are a lot of schooling fish and giant morays that free swim along the wall.

⬇5 Tobia Arba	
Depth	19 m
Visibility	good
Currents	mild

Although it's called the Seven Pillar, there only seem to be five – well, at least that's all you have time to find on an average dive. These rocky pinnacles rise from a flat seabed and are marked by interesting hard coral shapes. Small caves are full of glassy sweepers; overhangs protect lots of butterflyfish couples, while swathes of coral cover the walls and host countless anthias. You can swim through small tunnels and find moorish idols while on the sand there are seagrass ghost pipefish and, at night, Spanish Dancers.

Hard corals forming a prolific reef; flounder in the sand; Napoleon wrasse.

66 99 The Salem finally appears peaceful, succumbing slowly to the elements as they take her back into the usual cycle of nature.

↘6 Panorama	
Depth	33 m
Visibility	good
Currents	none to mild

Regarded as one of the area's most prolific reefs, this long coral mound can be dived from several points. On all sides, gentle slopes lead down to 25 metres or so, then the sudden drop-off falls to unreachable depths. The northwest corner is lacking in soft coral growth but there are plenty of overhangs along the walls. Turtles and morays hide amongst the craggy rocks formed by the cover of hard corals. The opposite corner is more colourful, with some fans brightening the view; whitetip sharks are regular visitors, and there are a surprising number of bottom-dwellers like crocodilefish and blue spotted rays.

↘7 The Salem Express	
Depth	22 m
Visibility	good
Currents	mild to medium

A controversial addition to the dive list is the wreck of the *Salem Express*. In 1991, this passenger ferry was heavily loaded with pilgrims returning from Mecca. She was only a few hours short of Safaga when she strayed off course and hit Hyndman Reef. The impact smashed a hole in the starboard bow and forced the bow visor open. The vessel rapidly took on water and sank on her starboard side within minutes, causing a huge loss of life. Many operators will not dive here but many will, and you will be briefed on treating the site with the respect it deserves. Suffice it to say that any trophy hunting would be exceptionally bad form. The *Salem* lies on her side at 32 metres. There are many signs of the people who were on board at the time, with suitcases and life rafts rotting quietly on the sea floor. Small corals are forming across the hull; pipefish and octopus hide in crevices and puffers hover like silent sentinels.

dive log
Egypt: Brothers Islands

El-Akhawein, also known as the Brothers Islands, took their place in diver folklore after the surrounding marine park was reopened a few years ago.

Big and Little Brother are a six-hour sail from Hurghada and the crossing can be rough, but once you are there, you find a flawless reef system that surrounds the two harsh rocky islands. The corals are still pristine – get your buoyancy right – and, as they are the only reefs for miles, they attract a large number of pelagic fish. It is said that you can also see Oceanic whitetips, thresher and hammerhead sharks but these only appear when the currents are running. These can be strong, so less experienced divers may find the going tough.

Moorings are limited and tucked away on the calmer sides of these tiny islands. The authorities are supposed to restrict the number of permits given to liveaboards but appear to over-supply them. Don't be surprised if your promised four days here ends up being less than two because your captain can't find a vacant spot.

⛴8 Northern Point, Little Brother	
Depth	38 m
Visibility	infinity
Currents	mild to strong

Opinions on currents are relative to what you have done, but a truly strong current will threaten to rip the mask from your face. Fortunately, at Little Brother the pace can be fairly easy-going at times – it all depends on what season you are there. Entering at the northern point of the island, a tongue-shaped section of reef leads seawards. This section usually produces a faster, drift dive where the currents push eastwards and, hopefully, there's a chance to see thresher sharks. These graceful, long-tailed creatures are usually quite deep but you often get a quick glimpse from above. It's more likely that you will see grey reef sharks or a solitary hammerhead passing by.

⛴9 The Aida, Big Brother	
Depth	36 m
Visibility	infinity
Currents	mild to strong

Big Brother is marked by a tall lighthouse, which is manned by the military and dominates the pancake-flat vista. The *Aida II* is the best known of the wrecks here. She was a supply boat that, in 1957, was transporting personnel to relieve troops on the island. Despite heavy storms and rough seas, the captain decided to try and reach the island but struck the rocks and sank. She now lies on an extremely steep slope with her bow resting at 25 metres or so and her stern at around 60. Her propeller isn't reachable within sport diving limits so all you will manage is a quick glimpse but the entire vessel is now rich with hard and soft corals, attracting a wealth of fish.

Bannerfish on patrol; masked pufferfish at rest.

dive log
Egypt: Far south

In long distant times, the village of Marsa Alam marked the junction with the Red Sea's coastal road and a lone road that led inland to Edfu on the Nile. More recently, it became the site of a small military airport, which grew to become an international one, and the region rapidly expanded as a tourist destination.

Ancient records reveal some interesting history, although you are unlikely to see much evidence of the original trade route to the Nile or of the ancient Egyptian and Roman mines for gold, gems and marble.

The current focus on tourism is intense, with the coast road sporadically bordered by new clusters of hotels, then stretches of nothing but desert. Further south, the coastline is unique in that much of it is mangroves and seagrass areas, which are protected by law. Finally, and almost as far south as you can go whilst still remaining in Egypt is the tiny town of Hamata. Blink and you could miss it – there are only a few hotels, no shops and nowhere to go.

The diving is comparatively uncrowded and the area has some of the best hard corals in Egypt. Hamata is also the access point for the Fury Shoals. Less than eight miles from shore, Fury is regarded as the last frontier, as the reefs sit on the rim of a deep undersea shelf. Liveaboards also leave Hamata for Zabargad Island and St John's.

⛵ **Abu Dabab Bay**	
Depth	14 m
Visibility	fair
Currents	none

This horseshoe-shaped bay makes a deep indentation in the coastline. Enclosed by a lovely beach, the bay remains shallow a long way out from shore, with the seabed almost completely covered by seagrass. It is this habitat that has made Abu Dabab famous for its permanent residents. One is a male dugong: he is one of seven known to live in the area; the others evidently have havens further along the coast. The bay is also home to 10 green turtles: nine females and a male. Visiting them involves a long swim at less than two metres. The bay gradually slopes until you find a ridge at about 12 metres. The seagrass beds end and turn into silty dunes punctuated by patches of vegetation. It's near this point that you are more-or-less guaranteed to see the turtles, and you would be very unlucky to see less than half of them. They are completely unphased by the divers approaching, even to within a few inches, and keep chomping away at the grass, eating about 40 kilograms a day. Watching these giants eat, ascend to breathe and descend again is unforgettable. Sadly, the dugong is far more elusive: although he

can be seen at any time during the day, sometimes he is not seen for days on end.

The remainder of the bay can be quite interesting – it's not just about these large animals. On one side lies a small section of patchy, flat corals and some rocks that harbour blue spot rays, nudibranchs and lionfish. Jacks and snapper hover over the grassy seabed and sea snakes wind their way through it. Schools of squid seem to be another permanent feature, although they are wary of diver bubbles. The outer edges of the bay have small walls and caves, and divers can be dropped off in a RIB, swimming back to shore.

Crocodilefish camouflaged by rubble; turtle in Abu Dabab Bay.

elphinstone
reef

↘11

🌀 **Depth**	32 m
◐ **Visibility**	stunning
≋ **Currents**	can be ripping

This long, oval-shaped reef is another Red Sea legend: a dive with a well deserved reputation even though that reputation was partly built on how little you get to dive it. If the currents are wrong or too strong, you are out of luck; if the wind is up you may not even get from shore to the reef. However, if you are there when conditions are just so, you may see some of the big pelagic species that make it so famous. And if not – who cares? There is so much life in one small place that only a grand cynic would fail to be impressed.

Dives start at the northern end of the site. It's about 30 metres down to a level plateau but the reef drops a long way beyond. Divers wait on the plateau to see if there are any large animals and are usually rewarded by dancing schools of chevron barracuda and glimpses of various reef sharks. The famed oceanic whitetips are only seen regularly in winter when conditions are least cooperative.

When it's time to ascend, you can swim to either side of the reef, depending on the currents, and onto magnificent walls of soft corals and black corals. There are a lot of fish, not just the obligatory anthias, but masses of coral trout, some pipefish, jacks in the blue, butterflies and angels and tangs. You could list fish for ages, but suffice to say, it is all very, very lively. By the time you reach about 15 metres, the scenery changes to a cover of perfect hard corals where there are schools of snapper and free-swimming morays.

❝❞ Depending on your mind-set and even allowing for its near mythical status, you might think this is one of those 'all or nothing' dives but let me tell you, you would be wrong. It has a serious Plan B. Elphinstone might have the ability to provide amazing pelagic sightings but it also has limited chances to get it 'just right'. Currents and wind mean you might miss going, but we did go and sadly missed the much hoped-for Oceanic whitetips. We were more than a little disappointed as we started our ascent, but it was then that Plan B hit with a serious assault on the senses: a raging rainbow wall of lush corals enhanced by a massive variety of fish. In the end, it was an incredibly memorable dive and certainly one to add to the Log Book. Been there, seen that, got the stamp.

Andrew Perkins, retail manager, Telford, UK

🔶 Sha'ab Claudio

🕐 **Depth**	16 m
🕐 **Visibility**	good
🔷 **Currents**	mild to strong

From the surface it's hard to judge what this dive is going to be like: the brief of 'enter over the dark path and go into the cave' only really makes sense once you are in. Beneath what appears to be a solid reef top is a warren of narrow crevices that lead to a cathedral-like cave. Well lit by sun rays that pierce parts of the reef, there are tunnels between sections, openings to the outer edge and all sorts of nooks and crannies filled with snappers and copper sweepers. The floor of the main chamber is sandy with a shelf-like rock embedded in it. Beneath it lives a coral banded shrimp and a blue-spotted ray moves between the sand to the shelf, parking himself in front of the shrimp. On the outer edge there are swathes of stunning hard corals that mask the entrances and, at times, some current. But you can easily find your way back inside by following the many free-swimming morays as they go.

🔶 Sha'ab Malahi

🕐 **Depth**	16 m
🕐 **Visibility**	good
🔷 **Currents**	mild to strong

Fondly named the 'Crystal Maze' by the local divemaster, this reef is as stunning a dive as Sha'ab Claudio. There are several sections to the site, so it's potentially more than one dive, but the best bit is the 'maze' of tunnels on the southern side. Entering the water on the outer reef edge, you are faced with too many choices of which way to enter, but once inside there are a multitude of twists and turns between bommies and pinnacles. It's great fun swimming through the large tunnels spotting more copper sweepers and squirrelfish as you go. Some of the corals inside the tunnels are a little damaged but there are fabulous shapes in the rocks, and at the far northern end of the site, you can exit onto a section of the most brilliant, pristine hard corals. Returning south to the boat by going around the edge, a pinnacle stands to the side like a sentinel and is home to some clownfish in their anemone hosts.

🔶 Abu Galawa Soraya

🕐 **Depth**	18 m
🕐 **Visibility**	good
🔷 **Currents**	mild to strong

This reef splits into sections: off one end lies the wreck of an American sailing boat that went down in the '80s. Lying on her side, the 17-metre long hull is completely intact, its insides full of glassfish, coral banded shrimp and pipefish. The outside is nicely coated with corals and the metal railings are still quite shiny in places, so the overall shape is easy to see. As you swim around the outside of the reef, you encounter more fabulous hard coral outcrops and also some current. A channel leads to a lagoon-like depression in the reef top full of rich hard coral formations.

The Crystal Maze; free swimming moray at Sha'ab Claudio; the remains of a yacht.

Red Sea Dive log Egypt: Far south

dive log
Jordan: Aqaba

The Hashemite Kingdom of Jordan is tucked away at the northernmost tip of the Red Sea and sandwiched between Israel and Saudi Arabia. It owns just a miniscule stretch of coast with access to the coral-rich waters in the Red Sea – a feature that gives it a certain amount of exclusivity.

Marked by the rapidly expanding city of Aqaba, this tiny segment of the Red Sea sees far fewer scuba divers than the busy and popular resorts further south in Egypt or even neighbouring Eilat. Jordan's coast is only 27 kilometres long yet there is some first-class diving around the shallow coral gardens just moments from shore. The reef structures are generally in good condition, made up of hard corals decorated by a scattering of brightly coloured soft corals and often edged by sloping seagrass beds.

With all the usual Red Sea creatures and fairly similar reef topography, what really distinguishes Aqaba for divers is that the majority of sites are shallow and accessed from shore. The water temperatures are a little cooler here, more so in winter, but conditions are easy, allowing for long dives on quiet reefs where it is unusual to see other divers.

↘15 Cable Canyons	
🕐 **Depth**	32 m
◑ **Visibility**	good
🌊 **Currents**	mild to strong

Aqaba is home to one of the strangest and most evocative artificial reefs that you are ever likely to dive. From the entry point, you swim across a series of valleys until, at the end of the third one, you swim around a submerged headland to enter a gully at depth. Looming overhead are a series of enormous and ghostly metal pipes that bridge the valley to give it structural support. These protect the high-power electricity cables than run the length of the canyon and connect the Jordanian grid to Egypt. On either side of the canyon, long lines of metal cages and rocks that disguise the work have created a whole new set of reef structures, a haven for minute, growing corals and juvenile fish. It could have been very ugly, yet soft corals, fans and sponges have taken hold on the structures, softening the vista. Somehow the effect is a bit like a dam, with light flooding down the valley and silhouetting the pipes, creating a view reminiscent of a scene from a James Bond movie.

Aqaba - Jordan
Sea star
PADI 5* IDC (2500)
info@aqabadivingseastar.com
www.aqabadivingseastar.com

↘16 Japanese Gardens

Depth	14 m
Visibility	excellent
Currents	none

It comes as a surprise to many but several of the shallower, shoreside reefs in Jordan are full of small and unusual creatures, some of which are far more familiar in far distant Asian waters. These coral gardens are close to the famed *Cedar Pride* wreck but the dive diverts to the south across a wide swathe of seagrass. The hard corals are pristine and the first coral pinnacle is home to a couple of very grumpy devil scorpionfish. There are lionfish hovering around the pinnacle, pipefish hiding in crevices, pufferfish, reticulated morays, clownfish in their anemones, blennies, gobies... it's a never-ending list. Coming back over the seagrass bed is equally impressive with long snout pipefish, dwarf lionfish, Pegasus sea moths and a truly ugly stonefish buried in the sand.

↘17 Gorgon 1

Depth	16 m
Visibility	good
Currents	mild to strong

Defined by a natural channel cut in the fringing reef, this dive really stands out for a single but astounding coral pinnacle. Just about 10 metres high, one side is swamped with glassy sweepers and, approaching them, you see they are hiding a swarm of lionfish. Surprisingly, the lionfish are only swooping through the sweepers (which they usually eat) until they become more interested in divers and follow you around for the rest of the dive. There are lots of angelfish too, and nestled in the crevices are bright pink stonefish, pale-coloured devil scorpionfish and small turtles.

Aqaba's smaller reef residents (clockwise): common lionfish; long-tail ceratosoma nudibranch; redeye hovering goby; double ended pipefish; stonefish; geometric morays; frogfish; Pegasus sea moth.

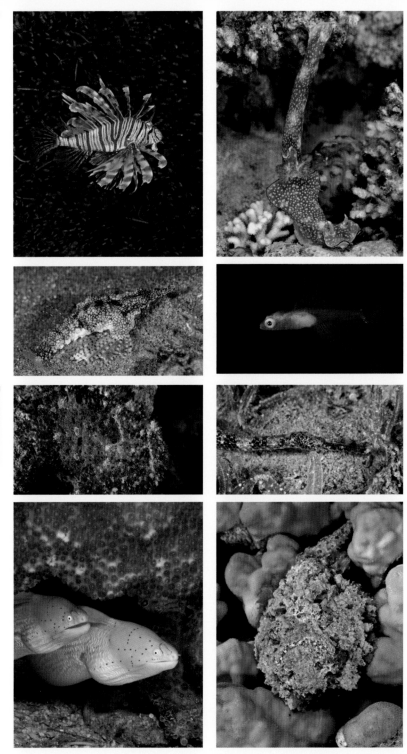

🧭 **Depth**	26 m
◐ **Visibility**	stunning
〰 **Currents**	can be ripping

Jordan's most famous dive has a well-deserved reputation. This 80-metre-long Lebanese cargo ship was scuttled by King Abdullah in November 1985 and now lies about 130 metres from shore on its port side, bridging two coral reefs. After finning down a long sandy slope and across a seagrass bed, the hull appears through the gloom. The deck is facing out to sea and can be reached by swimming under the hull and between the two reefs, before ascending again to explore the rest of the vessel. The side facing into the currents shows corals developing on the surfaces, especially around the bow. You can swim into the holds from beneath the crow's nest, although there isn't much to see inside, then down to the propellor.

When it's time to ascend, you can offgas on another great wreck, the M42 tank. This unexpected vision sits isolated and lonely on the sand in just six metres of water. Usually referred to as 'the tank' the vehicle is actually an American M42 Duster with a self-propelled anti-aircraft canon that was used by the Jordanian army in the 1960s. In 1999, it was scuttled to create an artificial reef and is now sporting soft and hard coral growth. Small fish occupy the cracks and crevices while the space beneath has become a haven for an enormous number of lionfish and a few devil scorpionfish lurk motionless on the sand.

66 99 I can visit the Cedar Pride every day and never get tired of it: there are so many nooks and crannies, doorways and windows to explore that it's nearly impossible to see it all on one dive. The mast alone is covered in beautiful soft corals, and brightly coloured sponges, surrounded by huge shoals of glass fish and hunting lionfish. All this and the occasional visiting turtles and barracuda... I am never disappointed. *Suzanne Al Qadi, PADI instructor and marine biologist*

drying out

Egypt

The Egyptian Red Sea coast has untold hotel and diving options, many of which are linked together. The majority of divers arrive on pre-booked packages to take advantage of this, but independent travellers are not obliged to dive and stay with the same company.

In fact, although some of the operations listed here were once working in tandem with each other, they may not be any more. It's worth checking websites to see who is currently working with whom. Virtually all hotels tend to be large resort complexes. Consider choosing a higher level of hotel than you might normally, as an Egyptian three-star is less impressive than a similar property in other countries.

Sharm el Sheik
Sharm area hotels are spread across the three bays that make up the town, Sharm El Maya, Na'ama Bay and Shark Bay. The majority of hotels and dive centres are usually about 20-30 minute transfer by road from the airport.
Diving
Red Sea College, redseacollege.com
Sinai Divers, sinaidivers.com
Sleeping
Hilton Hotels, hilton.com. In all three bays.
Camel Dive Club & Hotel, cameldive.com
In the centre of Na'ama Bay.

Hurghada, El Gouna and Safaga
Reaching Hurghada hotels from the airport takes around 20-mins. However, El Gouna is a 1-hr drive and Safaga, 2-hrs.
Diving
Divers Lodge Hurghada, divers-lodge.com
Emperor Divers, emperordivers.com
In El Gouna and Hurghada.

Sleeping
Hilton Hotels, hilton.com. Three hotels in Hurghada, all with dive centres.
Hotel Shams Safaga and Diving Centre, shams-dive.com.

Marsa Alam and Hamata
Marsa Alam is about 30-mins from the airport, Hamata is a 2-hr drive.
Diving
Emperor Divers, emperordivers.com
In both Marsa Alam and Hamata.
Orca Dive Clubs, orca-diveclub.com.
Sleeping
Zarbagad Dive Resort, zabargad.net

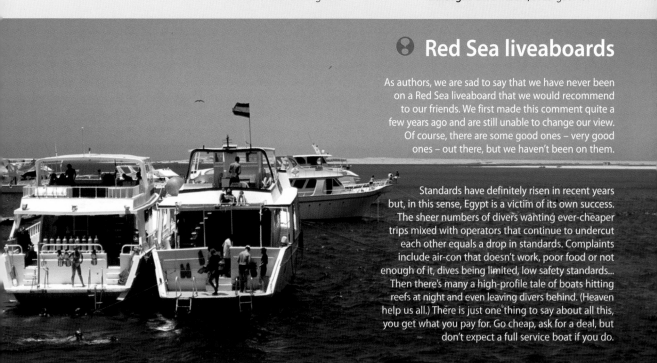

Red Sea liveaboards

As authors, we are sad to say that we have never been on a Red Sea liveaboard that we would recommend to our friends. We first made this comment quite a few years ago and are still unable to change our view. Of course, there are some good ones – very good ones – out there, but we haven't been on them.

Standards have definitely risen in recent years but, in this sense, Egypt is a victim of its own success. The sheer numbers of divers wanting ever-cheaper trips mixed with operators that continue to undercut each other equals a drop in standards. Complaints include air-con that doesn't work, poor food or not enough of it, dives being limited, low safety standards... Then there's many a high-profile tale of boats hitting reefs at night and even leaving divers behind. (Heaven help us all.) There is just one thing to say about all this, you get what you pay for. Go cheap, ask for a deal, but don't expect a full service boat if you do.

drying out

Egypt

The great pyramid of Cheops; cooking bread in Cairo; Hamata resort; camel on Safaga beach.

Days out

Ras Mohammed National Park Contrary to popular belief, at least in diver brains, Ras isn't just about diving. Landside there are some fantastic, 'other world' landscapes to admire plus rare mammals, thousands of birds and some unusual flora species.

St Catherine's Monastery Dating back to AD 300, this religious site is worth a visit for its varied history. Now owned by the Greek Orthodox Church, there is a collection of illuminated manuscripts, works of art and of course, the site of Moses' Burning Bush. The monastery is still home to several monks.

Mount Sinai This is where Moses is said to have received the Ten Commandments. To reach the top it's either 4000 steps or a 3-hour walk along a winding path, but many make the pilgrimage at sunrise when the views are stunning.

Bedouin camp Trek across the desert on the back of a camel until you reach traditional Bedouin camp and can enjoy dinner under the stars.

South coast Once you leave the Sinai, there aren't a huge amount of cultural excursions. From Hurghada, Safaga or El Gouna but you could arrange to visit a couple of ruined, ancient Roman sites: Mons Porphyrites is where a stone called Imperial Porphyry was mined and there remains of temples and fortresses. Mons Claudianus was a Roman settlement in the 1st and 2nd centuries AD and the base for mining a grey granite. The ruins include a Pantheon, Hadrian's Villa and an unfinished temple.

Likewise, cultural excursions and day trips are non-existent in the area around Marsa Alam and Hamata. There are ruins of an old emerald mine, but no emeralds; the temple of Seti I, but you can't go inside and the remains of an extensive Ottoman fort at El Quesir– but no tours. You get the picture... for the moment, come to this area and dive, although that's bound to change soon.

Cairo

Egypt's capital is a shock to the system. Hot and completely manic, it's a non-stop pulsating, gyrating, merry-go-round of people. There are close on 16 million in the capital and you will feel that they are right in your face. But to go to Egypt and not see the pyramids? A day in the city will give you a chance to sample her incredible history. Head out to Giza, admire the Sphinx, then, unless you are horribly claustrophobic, stretch your calf muscles by walking down the 45-degree ladders inside the great pyramid of Cheops. Take a camel or horse ride a short way into the Sahara, look back at the pyramids and imagine what they would have been like all those centuries ago.

Afterwards, head back into the centre and visit the Egyptian Museum. Gaze on the face of god-king Tutankhamen (if you can get close enough – the museum is always crowded) before heading to one of the city's bazaars for a little retail therapy. This is definitely best undertaken with an Egyptian guide or you will find the hassle-factor overwhelming. Finally, at sunset take a Nile dinner cruise: terribly touristy but at least you can say you've done it.

Luxor

For culture buffs, it probably makes sense to add a few days to your trip and explore Luxor otherwise, a day trip from Hurghada will be a long, hot and very dusty day. The tour will take you across the Nile valley and on to the Valley of the Kings and the Temple of Queen Hatshepsut. Later, it's back to Luxor to see the Colossi of Memnon and the outstanding Temple of Karnak, ancient Egypt's most impressive feat of engineering.

Before booking, check travel advisories. If you are taking a longer tour for either city, hotels will be included. If not, the major international chains are all there and worth researching into to get an idea of locations, prices and standards.

drying out
Jordan

Aqaba in Jordan is the polar opposite to the tourist centres on the Egyptian Red Sea coast. Hotels are mostly small and independent, as are the diving centres.

The usual plan is to stay in the town centre, which is fairly relaxed: you can choose places to eat and drink, wander the stores and shops and generally feel part of this vibrant small town. The dive centres then collect divers each morning.

Diving
Dive Aqaba, diveaqaba.com. Day boat diving from a town-centre-based operation.
SeaStar, aqabadivingseastar.com. Great beach-based dive centre about 15-mins from town with transfers included.
Sleeping
Captain's Hotel, captains-jo.com. Small but comfortable boutique hotel.
DoubleTree, doubletree3.hilton.com

Days out

Jordan has hosted many civilizations over the centuries from the Judean, Persian and Babylonian empires through Pharaonic Egypt, the Romans and the Ottomans until it spawned the native Nabatean civilization, which left the awe-inspiring remains at Petra. Then there are Crusader castles, natural wonders like Wadi Rum (best known for its connection with British officer T. E. Lawrence) and the Jordan River where Jesus was baptized by John the Baptist. The river fizzles out in the Dead Sea at 423 metres below sea level.

Amman

Evidence of many past civilizations can be seen in Amman but, even though the city was built on ancient stones, Jordan's capital is now a very modern city. A little sprawling and not ideal for wandering on foot, it has are some unmissable sites. Jabal Amman, or downtown, is where to find the souks, markets, museums and ancient monuments. Hovering above the city is Citadel Hill, topped by the Temple of Hercules. The Roman forum and the Roman theatre – with room for 6,000 spectators – was built around AD 150.

Jerash

Dating back more than 6,500 years, the city's golden age came under Roman rule and it is now generally regarded as one of the best-preserved Roman provincial towns in the world. It was hidden for centuries in sand before being excavated and restored over the past 70 years. You can wander the colonnaded streets, temples, theatres, squares and fountains.

Petra

Hidden in the desert, but easily reached from Aqaba, visiting ancient Petra is an absolute must. Wander downhill through a narrow gorge carved between soaring rock cliffs. A sharp turn reveals an ancient facade that was cut into the surrounding cliffs – The Treasury is the best known of Petra's sights as its sudden appearance from nowhere is totally overwhelming.

However, there is much more to this ancient city. Two thousand years ago, camel caravans passed through loaded with spices, textiles and merchandise from distant regions so the city flourished. The Nabataean people learned to harness precious water, allowing the population to thrive while building its monumental centre. Eventually, though, the foreign traders found new routes and the city fell into decline.

The Treasury at Petra; boats in Aqaba harbour; welcome tea; donkey caravan and (left) Jerash.

313
↘ **Essentials**

314
↘ **Dive brief**

316
↘ **Dive sites**

318
↘ **Dive log**

318 Russell Islands
321 Florida Islands
322 Marovo Lagoon

324
↘ **Drying out**

Solomons

Camouflage catastrophe: the leaf scorpionfish, *Taenianotus triacanthus*, failing to get a perfect colour match.
Twin Peaks, Mbulo Island

destination
Solomons

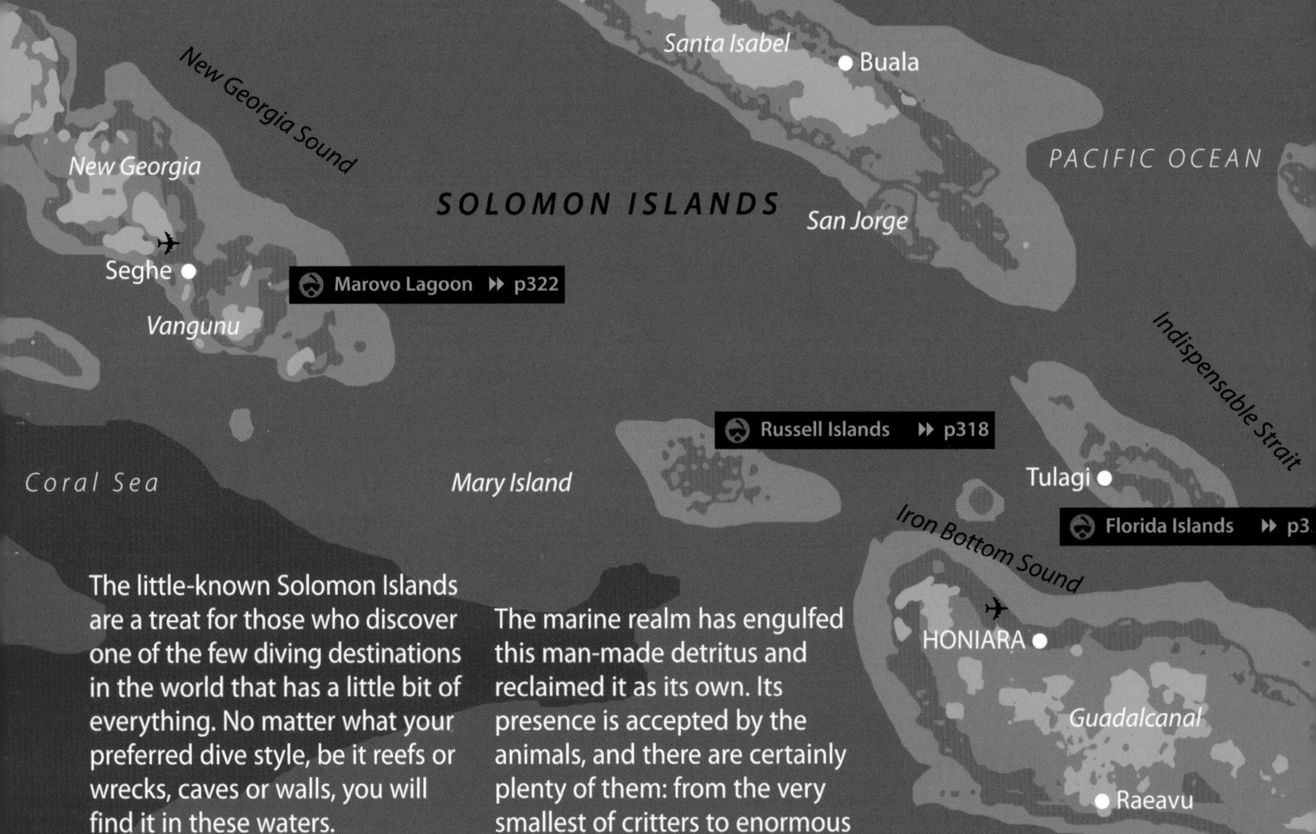

Santa Isabel
● Buala

New Georgia Sound

New Georgia

PACIFIC OCEAN

SOLOMON ISLANDS

San Jorge

✈
Seghe ●

🌀 Marovo Lagoon ▶▶ p322

Vangunu

Indispensable Strait

🌀 Russell Islands ▶▶ p318

Coral Sea

Mary Island

Tulagi ●

🌀 Florida Islands ▶▶ p3

Iron Bottom Sound

✈
HONIARA ●

Guadalcanal

● Raeavu

The little-known Solomon Islands are a treat for those who discover one of the few diving destinations in the world that has a little bit of everything. No matter what your preferred dive style, be it reefs or wrecks, caves or walls, you will find it in these waters.

This string of islands are now part of the vital Coral Triangle and, as such, have very high levels of marine diversity. No one knows quite what's there, simply because the reefs are less explored than some better known areas nearby.

The Solomons saw some of the longest battles of the Second World War, and the evidence of that is littered across the seabed.

The marine realm has engulfed this man-made detritus and reclaimed it as its own. Its presence is accepted by the animals, and there are certainly plenty of them: from the very smallest of critters to enormous schools of pelagic fish, you will find something from almost every marine species group.

Life in the Solomons today reflects little of its history. Gone are the headhunters of ancient times, the European colonists and over zealous missionaries, and despite recent political turmoil, this is a country populated by laid-back and friendly islanders.

Essentials

There is only one straightforward way to reach the Solomon Islands and that's from Brisbane in Australia, although there are flights from other, equally remote Pacific islands. Internal transport links from the capital, Honiara, are more prolific with frequent internal flights connecting all the smaller islands. There is a network of large passenger ferries and public boats, known as canoes, but standards and distances make flying a more practical option. Alternatively, to get better coverage of the country's diverse diving, it is much easier to hop on a liveaboard, with no transfers or internal land travel required.

Local laws and customs

The people of the Solomons are mostly Christian and, no matter where you are, the people are devout. Outside Honiara, the way of life is based on a system of clans or families in which the headman rules. If you do go exploring independently, it is best to contact him. Local people are open and friendly, but tabu (taboo) is an important part of daily life especially when it comes to male/female relationships. For instance, couples shouldn't touch each other in public, and a woman mustn't stand taller than a man! Female tourists should always cover their thighs and shoulders. Some other curiosities are that shaking hands is thought unnatural, as is looking directly into someone's eyes.

Health and safety

Medical facilities in the Solomons are highly variable, but the bigger issue is that there are few chemist shops, so it's important to have a good first aid kit with you. Resorts and liveaboards will be able to assist you, but it's best to be prepared. Having said that, there isn't much to guard against, with the notable exception of malarial mosquitoes. Use a repellent on land and cover up at dusk. Over the last decade, the Solomons have suffered from a couple of political coups, but the unrest seems to have settled. Like many small nations undergoing constant change, crime against travellers is rare but increasing. You are only likely to encounter petty crime in Honiara.

Costs

The Solomons' economy is not exactly buoyant. The post-colonial legacy and political instabilities mean that tourism comes at a price. It's not so much that it's expensive, but prices can seem high for the quality you get. This is one of the reasons for going on a liveaboard – everything is included except alcohol, which is charged at US rates. Accommodation and meals in Honiara are a hit-and-miss affair and, although stopping there for a night or two might be unavoidable, island-based resorts are by far the better choice if you prefer a land-based diving holiday. Tipping isn't expected and may be regarded as wrong in some places. If you want to be generous, gifts may be more appropriate than cash.

Fact file

Location	8°00'S, 159°00'E
Capital	Honiara
Flights	Solomon Airlines from Brisbane
Internal flights	Internal flights by Solomon Airlines
Land transport	Small planes and motorized 'canoes'
Departure tax	SBD$40
Entry	EU, US and Commonwealth – valid passport and return ticket required for stays of up to 30 days
Money	Solomon Islands dollars
Language	English and Pijin English
Electricity	240v, plug type E (see page 15)
Time zone	GMT +11
Religion	Various Christian denominations
Communications	Country code +677; IDD code 00; Police 911 Internet access not yet widely available
Tourist information	visitsolomons.com.sb and flysolomons.com
Travel advisories	gov.uk/foreign-travel-advice; state.gov/travel

dive brief

Diving

Presented with a nation that covers about 1.4 million square kilometres of the South Pacific and has 992 islands all ringed by coral reefs, you may feel overwhelmed by the prospect of choosing which will best suit your diving requirements. But the decision is made easy because there's not much choice. As the Solomon Islands only get something like 5,000 visitors a year, tourism-focused facilities haven't taken over the place and there are just a handful of options for divers. The islands are all delightful, but with resorts located on so few, the most expedient option is to visit several regions by hopping onto a liveaboard for a week or two.

This is a diving destination that holds the rather impressive accolade of a little bit of everything. There are walls, reefs, caves and, of course, a whole range of Second World War wrecks resting on the seabed. Pelagic species are plentiful on some sites, while macro animals are more prolific on others – but most of all, there is a selection of both on most dives.

However, what you won't get is huge numbers of each of these things. As the divemasters are first to admit, these waters have variety rather than quantity. Research that was undertaken a decade back resulted in the country being ranked in the top 10 most biologically diverse on the planet when around 500 different corals were surveyed. This promoted the Solomons into the Coral Triangle.

The Solomons also have year-round diving. Like anywhere tropical, there is a wet season, but rainfall is intermittent and the water temperature is uniformly warm.

Snorkelling

Many reefs start only a few steps from the beach and just below the water line but are often murky in the shallows due to fresh water run-off. All island resorts have easy access to shallow reefs and some are great for snorkeling. Really strong currents are rare, so you can snorkel almost everywhere, just check conditions first.

We asked our cruise directors what had kept them in the Solomons for so many years... living in a tiny cabin, working around the clock to show their demanding divers around. The answer was pretty much what we expected: a little bit of this, a bit of that. Every dive has something a little different to the one before. By the end of the cruise, we couldn't have agreed with them more.

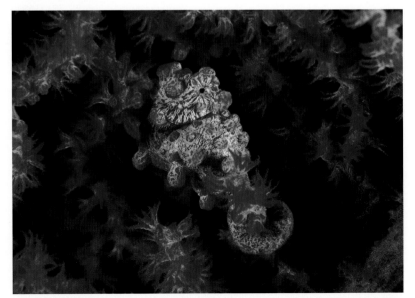

The diminutive pygmy seahorse, *Hippocampus barbiganti*.

Marine life

Whatever you might hope to see on a tropical reef, you are likely to see it here. There's big stuff (sharks, rays and turtles) and schooling stuff (barracuda and jacks). At the other end of the scale, there is some great muck diving (nudibranchs, leaffish and the inimicus), plus animals that have become famous drawcards elsewhere, such as the pygmy seahorse.

Making the big decision

Many divers are attracted to the Solomons despite knowing little about them. It's one of those places that has a certain mystique. The dive industry is small, which makes it feel rather like an exclusive club. Others may have been and passed on the word, or the reputation on of the liveaboards has filtered through. No matter what has attracted you, you won't be disappointed. Australians, who are on the doorstep, tend to go to the island resorts, but to get the most out of this distant island chain, the best way to go is definitely being escorted around on a boat. Either way, it's the variety of diving that keeps divers happy.

Animal encounters

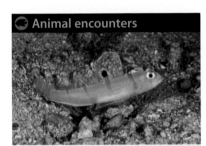

Countrywide: although each of these island groups does have its own set of unique marine features, these are mostly to do with changes in dive styles. For unusual creatures, keep an eye out for white bonnet anemone fish, schools of funny little archerfish that hover under mangrove roots and shoot insects, unusual bloodspot nudibranchs and the charming yellow striped Randall's shrimp goby (above).

dive sites

While the marine life seen in the Solomons is fairly consistent from one island group to the next, what makes each worth seeing – rather than just stopping on only one – is the variety of dive styles and how they keep changing. The Russell group consists of two main islands, Pavuvu and Mbanika, along with a cluster of smaller, volcanic land masses. Dive sites include dramatic, shallow cave systems that cut back beneath the coast and emerge into pools surrounded by coastal forest. There is a plethora of shipwrecks, some war-era and others more recent. Slightly to the west, Mary Island (more correctly known as Mborokua) is an inactive volcano and the centre for pelagic hyperactivity.

One of the world's largest lagoon systems, Marovo is a unique environment in that it has a clearly defined double barrier reef. On one side, there are several volcanic islands and, on the other, long chains of smaller, flat islands. The fringing reefs in between combine to create a rare marine terrain plus there are more World War II wrecks lurking on the seafloor.

The four main islands in the Nggela – Florida – group have tortuous coastlines edged by white-sand beaches. Their proximity to the main island of Guadalcanal and capital, Honiara, led to several US bases being built and later abandoned there. Now, it's a destination for exciting dives around prolific and diverse reefs that are just a short trip from the capital.

Russell Islands ▶▶ p318

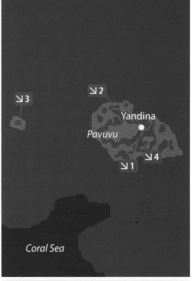

Coral Sea

Pavuvu
Yandina

Log Book

↘1 **The wreck of the Ann**
↘2 **Leru Cut**
↘3 **Barracuda Point, Mary Island**
↘4 **White Beach**

→ **Karamolun Point:** small fish taking refuge on a submerged peninsula
→ **Custom Cave:** wide cave on a sloping wall with nudibranchs and soft corals
→ **Mirror Pool:** small cave system ending at a pool mirroring the forest above.
→ **Mary Island Wall:** deep dive with whip and fan corals and cruising whitetips

Conditions

Tropical regions only

Seasons	Diving is year round although from December to April tend to be the wetter months.
Visibility	5 m inshore to 40 m in the open
Currents	Mostly mild
Temperatures	Air 30-34°C; water 27-29°C
Wet suit	3 mm shorty or full body suit
Training	Courses are available in the resorts at Uepi and Gizo; prebooking is advised
Nitrox	Available on liveaboards, but enquire in advance at resorts
Deco chambers	Honiara and Townsville, Australia

Diversity

	reef area 5,750 km²
HARD CORALS	497
FISH SPECIES	913
ENDEMIC FISH SPECIES	0
FISH UNDER THREAT	7

All diversity figures are approximate

Florida Islands ▶▶ p321

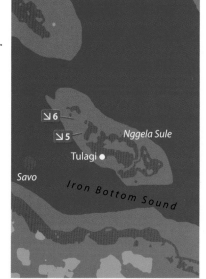

Savo

Iron Bottom Sound

Tulagi ●

Nggela Sule

↘5
↘6

Marovo Lagoon ▶▶ p322

Seghe ●

Vangunu

Marovo Lagoon

Nggatokae

↘7
↘8
↘9

🌐 Endangered oceans

Even as far back as Darwin and his contemporary Alfred Wallace, it seems there was always a perception that the countries around what we now call the Coral Triangle were important to the planet. But, as time went on, scientists would change their thinking on where the world's most prolific species hotspot was. They would agree, disagree and agree to disagree. It took until the post-war era for corals to be accepted as a vital indicator, and in the 1950s a table of worldwide coral genera was plotted. This noted Indonesian and Philippine waters as the centre of coral diversity but also included Australia's Great Barrier Reef. This changed again when global distributions were compiled at species level and clearly indicated that the Indonesian-Philippine archipelago was the real centre of diversity.

Finally, in the first decade of this millennium, it was agreed that the most biodiverse region on our planet was a triangle bordered by the Philippines, Malaysia, Indonesia and Papua New Guinea. Additional research resulted in the Solomons being included and a bit of politics added East Timor to the cluster.

The Coral Triangle at its inception recorded having 605 zooxanthellate corals – or 76% of the world's total species – making this province the world's highest conservation priority. Inside the Coral Triangle, the highest levels are said to be in the Bird's Head Peninsula off Indonesian Papua. which reveals at least 574 species.

🔵 Log Book

↘5 **Tanavula Point**
↘6 **Velvia**

→ **Devil's Highway:** a known manta ray cleaning station from October to May
→ **Mbike Ridge:** a seamount with scattered bommies to the sides
→ **Tanavula West:** turtles and blacktip sharks surfing in some frisky currents
→ **Sandfly Passage:** sandy gulley with crocodilefish and soft corals

🔵 Log Book

↘7 **Lumahlihe Passage**
↘8 **Wickham Island**
↘9 **Who Maru I & II**

→ **Kokoana Passage:** little (pygmy seahorses) and large (whitetip sharks)
→ **Lagoon Point:** multi-level reef known for octopus and commensal shrimp
→ **Twin Points, Mbulo Island:** more little (leaffish) and large (chevron barracuda)
→ **Mbili Shallows:** rubble-strewn seafloor with gobies, leaffish and nudibranchs

dive log Russell Islands

Northeast from Guadalcanal are the Russell Islands. Pavavu is said to be the largest of 'a thousand and one islands' and is covered in coconut plantations. Land is leased from customary owners and planted with palms. The islanders then collect the fallen coconuts and take them to the main town of Yandina to sell.

The rest of the time the islanders live a fairly traditional sea-bound life. Long days are spent in dugout canoes floating over the coral reefs that completely ring these small islands. If there isn't a section of reef, it's usually because there is a small cave complex. Coastal Pavuvu is riddled with underwater caves and tunnels that lead inland then emerge on land as tiny tree-lined pools. The diving is easy, with little in the way of currents. Boats can avoid strong winds simply by sheltering on another side of an island. This is also the location of the rather romantically-titled Sunlight Channel, a haven for the US forces in the Second World War and now a fantastic dive site.

⚓1	The wreck of the Ann	
🌀	**Depth**	36 m
◐	**Visibility**	fair to excellent
〰	**Currents**	mild

Deliberately sunk just over 20 years ago, this wreck of a cargo boat is completely intact and sits virtually upright on a sandy slope close to the shore. The visibility is often so good that you can see all the way from the bow to the stern. The decks are covered in huge elephant ear sponges in several different colours. The wheelhouse is full of glassy sweepers, with a few hungry lionfish prowling around them. There is just one gaping hold, which appears to be completely empty but, if you take some time, you may spot both pipefish and nudibranchs. Back up on the deck, the mechanical winches are now covered in crusting corals. When it's time to ascend for a safety stop, you can off-gas on the nearby reef. It's a bit patchy, but there are several different types of clownfish and anemones. Some have cleaner shrimp and some, porcelain crabs.

Swimming through Leru Cut; the wreck of the Ann; white bonnet anemonefish.

⇘2	Leru Cut	
Depth	20 m	
Visibility	fair	
Currents	none	

Tucked into this tree-lined coast, this dive is a little murky due to sediment and run-off but, despite that, it's quite a spectacle. A deep cut in the reef wall forms a shallow cave that narrows before leading beneath the island. When you get to the end, you can ascend into a pool surrounded by the deep green jungle. Inside the cavern are pretty rock formations and the filtered rays of light are very moody. Back out on the reef, there are schools of rainbow runners, bumphead wrasse and midnight snapper hanging about, while on the wall are ornate ghost pipefish hiding in crinoids.

⇘3	Barracuda Point, Mary Island	
Depth	40 m+	
Visibility	excellent	
Currents	mild to strong	

A short sail due west of the Russell Islands lies isolated Mary Island, a completely inactive volcano. Although the island is ringed by steep walls and coral reefs, her star attraction lies in a tongue-shaped promontory that juts out from the coast with sloping drop-offs on either side. As you enter the water you are met by a huge ball of jacks that circle ceaselessly over the top of the tongue, then, as you descend downwards towards the point, you find another smaller ball. Continuing even further, there are solitary dogtooth tuna passing by, small gangs of chevron barracuda and then countless numbers of needlenose barracuda. Amongst it all, grey reef sharks patrol to and fro across the reef and, in the evenings, they hunt amongst the balls of jacks. Down at 30 metres plus, on the tip of the tongue, there are a lot of whip corals, fans and many different coloured elephant ear sponges. A few more whitetip sharks circle in to watch the divers. Back on the top of the reef, the hard corals are pristine and swarming with smaller, colourful fish as well as several Napoleon wrasse that follow divers curiously.

66 99 The grey reef shark moved ever closer to the ball of jacks. Suddenly, he whipped his tail and zoomed right into the middle of the ball. The jacks split into a million directions, like some fantasy firework. The shark sped away with his catch and the jacks slid back into formation. Just as if it had never happened.

white
beach

⬂ 4s

🌀 **Depth**	45 m+	
🌓 **Visibility**	fair to excellent	
🌊 **Currents**	mild	

This absolutely stunning site is in Sunlight Channel by Mbanika Island. Diving centres around a munitions dump from a US supply base that was hidden behind the mangrove ringed coast. When the troops shipped out at the end of the war, they simply dropped everything from their base into the sea.

Once moored up, divers come and go as they please, a fantastic option as the site has huge potential. In the shallows there are three flat-topped barges that were originally lined up along the shore and tied to wooden pylons. These have rotted away and the barges now sit below sea level. Their surfaces are coated in small corals and critters like blennies, pipefish and nudibranchs. There's another dive under the nearby mangroves, where you can watch schools of archerfish shoot jets of water at the flies in the trees above; the other extreme is the deepest part of the dump, where you will find many larger discarded items: there's a tractor and a crane and several other vehicles. Coming back up the reef, you pass loads of mechanical litter – even steering wheels that are so encrusted with coral you almost don't recognize their shape, plus old bombs, torpedos and loads of bullets, now coated in healthy crusting corals.

❝❞ Our favourite critter dive was at White Beach. All the equipment left behind by United States Marines was pushed into the sea, creating an artificial reef inhabited by many weird animals. The site is a treasure hunt of sorts – the treasure being scads of beautiful gobies, nudibranchs and pipefish, lionfish, mantis shrimp and several species of clownfish. A bonus was finding these critters hiding among the abandoned jeeps, mortar shells and other artefacts.

Steve and Suzanne Turek work for the Department of Fish and Game in California

dive
log
Florida
Islands

The closest group to Honiara, the Florida Islands border the north of Iron Bottom Sound. During the Second World War, the main island of Nggela Sule was garrisoned by the Japanese, who hoped to build a seaplane base. The area was liberated by US forces and then became a base for their war effort.

The impact of the war meant that almost all pre-war plantations were destroyed. These had been the mainstay of the local economy and very little was done to re-establish them or introduce other forms of employment to the Floridas. These are now very quiet places with little happening other than a bit of dive tourism. The dives, however, are far from quiet, for these are some of the country's most exciting and diverse reefs.

At White Beach: bullets and blennies; archerfish in the mangroves; the remains of a pier. A spider crab on Velvia.

⛴5 Tanavula Point	
🧭 **Depth**	28 m
🔅 **Visibility**	good
🌊 **Currents**	mild to strong

This long, sloping reef is a dog-legged shape. As you descend at the start of the dive, you see a thick covering of sizeable fan corals that rise above patches of hard coral. There are some enormous pink gorgonians that are known homes for the barbiganti pygmy seahorse. These tiny creatures are hard to spot, so hang by the divemasters. It's much easier to spot adult barramundi cod and their madly fluttering juveniles. As you travel around the crook in the reef, the currents start to pick up. You may get caught in a pressure point where the currents merge, but this attracts some pelagic life – blacktip sharks are often spotted out in the blue, eagle rays fly past and there are schools of rainbow runners and jacks.

⛴6 Velvia	
🧭 **Depth**	35 m
🔅 **Visibility**	good
🌊 **Currents**	mild to strong

Named after the photographer's favourite film, this open sea mound has a flat top with isolated coral mounds but is mostly sand and coral rubble. However, the sides drop all around to walls rich with life and fans. The deeper you go, the more lush it becomes. Nestling in cracks and crevices are large green morays and lobsters. There are sharks off in the blue, but the focus is more on small creatures – nembrotha nudibranchs, octopus and mantis shrimp, plus masses of nesting fish. Damselfish are particularly active, and you can see them herding newly born babes just millimetres long right up to youngsters of an inch or so. Aggressive sergeant majors also guard their eggs, while clownfish couples can be spotted aerating the next generation.

dive log
Marovo Lagoon

This complex reef system runs for around 100 kilometres from end to end and is bordered by several substantial volcanic islands and an unusual double barrier reef.

Inside the lagoon there are mangrove islets and sand cays, raised reefs and freshwater swamps. Rivers and streams carry sediments off the volcanic slopes and into the lagoon. Much of the diving is inside the lagoon or in the channels that lead in and out. The water is shallow and highly nutrient-rich so visibility is rarely fantastic, certainly not much over 20 metres. Some of the barrier islands, such as Uepi, which are long, narrow islets, sit between the ocean-facing fringing reefs and lagoon-side fringing reefs. Only 20 or so islands are inhabited, with coconut farming and fishing being the main cash earners. The lagoon has been promoted as a potential World Heritage Site due to its incredible environmental diversity.

⛴7 Lumahlihe Passage	
Depth	36 m
Visibility	fair
Currents	mild to medium

This channel lies between two uninhabited islands that edge Marovo and has several dive options. You can travel along both sides and the outer walls on either the incoming or outgoing tides. The channel walls are steep-sided and eventually drop to 50 metres or so on the outside of the lagoon. There are plenty of fans and soft corals making the site really colourful, although the visibility can be low due to run-off from the lagoon during tide changes. Several fans have the Denise pygmy seahorse on them and there is a resident black leaffish. Travelling along the wall, small fish include longnose hawkfish and decorated dartfish. On the top of the wall is a sandy channel coated in garden eels and surrounded by small coral outcrops. Amongst them are bloodspot nudibranchs, moray eels, small bumphead parrotfish and crocodilefish.

⛴8 Wickham Island	
Depth	28 m
Visibility	poor to good
Currents	medium

Wickham is an incredibly pretty island, a classic tropical speck of white beach backed by greenery. The dive is just the opposite, a little murky and definitely 'mucky'. It starts at a small promontory that leads away from the beach and drops quite sharply to over 30 metres. The wall is covered in good fans and soft corals, crinoids and whips. It's all very colourful and pretty, but the real action starts once you rise back up to the sand slope that extends from the beach. At depths of around 12-15 metres the whole seabed turns into a fantastic muck dive. There are more varieties of shrimp than you would care to name, similarly gobies in the sand and then there are harlequin crabs, seahorse, inimicus – or devilfish – and mantis shrimps. You can even spot some curious commensal relationships such as a black cucumber with two tiny fish living on it. This is a great night dive.

Life in Marovo Lagoon: a nocturnal round crab; corals on the wall of Lumahlihe Passage; roughhead blenny.

All Japanese warships were named after a place and tagged maru, meaning return. The theory was that the boat would then return home safely, but these two cargo boats didn't, and no one knows what they were called originally. They are sitting a few hundred metres apart from each other in a section of the lagoon where the Japanese moored their supply ships. The first sits on the sand at 40 metres deep. On the bow is an anti-aircraft gun and, just below, the anchor is still in its hawser. At the stern, there is a huge gash in the side where it was torpedoed, and you can see signs of the ship's original purpose, such as cable reels and winches. The wreck is covered with a lot of black coral bushes, with longnose hawkfish and small yellow damsels flitting about. On the mast, there is a circular depression that houses a coral trout and, surprisingly, a large cluster of Debelius shrimp.

The second vessel is quite similar but it is resting in shallower water. The Japanese version of a 50 millimetre Howitzer sits on the bow. You can see the large gash where a torpedo went through one side of the hull and then bent the other side out of shape. This structure is also smothered in lots of yellow and white black coral bushes and there are plenty of fish here too.

Longnose hawkfish; on the *Who Maru* (right).

drying out

Heading across the Pacific to dive the Solomon Islands is most likely to involve hopping onto the lone liveaboard. This floating hotel is by far the most practical and thorough way to see – and dive – the Solomons, although there is always the option to stay at a land-based resort.

Either way, you shouldn't need more than an overnight stop in the capital city, Honiara. If you do have to have a stopover, which is likely due to ever-changing flight schedules, bear in mind that standards are not what you would expect of most capital cities.

Liveaboard

Bilikiki Cruises, bilikiki.com. En suite cabins, spacious dive decks, unparalleled service and food – look forward to the canapés and cocktail hour as the sun goes down. Itineraries vary slightly by season.

Other options

Tulagi Dive Centre, tulagidive.com Simple resort in the Florida Islands.
The Gizo Explorer Hotel and **Dive Gizo**, divegizo.com. On the waterfront in the centre of town.
Uepi Island Resort, uepi.com. On the edge of the Marovo Lagoon, a real get-away-from-it-all resort.

Honiara

Solomon Kitano Mendana Hotel, kitanomendana.com. On the stretch of town beach, various room styles and pool.

The Solomons' war wrecks

Honiara, sits on the little-known island of Guadalcanal – little known except to those who know their Pacific war history.

The Battles of Midway and the Coral Sea may be more famous but the battles fought here were regarded as pivotal during the Second World War. The Japanese had been advancing through Micronesia and across the north of New Guinea. Unopposed, they made for the Solomons with the intention of building an airfield. When America became aware of this threat to their vital communications link to Australia, they decided an offensive was imperative.

Guadalcanal was the first American amphibious counter-offensive of the war and highly risky as the forces were at the farthest extreme of their supply chain. It was also one of the longest battles in the Pacific, running for six months. Eventually the Japanese were driven off, with Imperial Headquarters privately admitting defeat and ordering an evacuation. They had been gone for some time before US operations realised what had happened. Naval losses off the north coast of Guadalcanal were so great that the area became known as Iron Bottom Sound.

There are a variety of ships and planes sitting at the bottom of the sound but the largest warships are beyond safe sport diving limits. Visibility is rarely good in this area. Elsewhere, the Solomons are riddled with Second World War-era wrecks, some of which are more accessible.

Days out

Honiara This capital city is small, busy, hot and dusty, with (as one of our American buddies says) few redeeming features. With apologies to the local people, who are always very friendly and welcoming, Honiara is worth little more than a night. Chances are you will have to stay a night due to flight schedules, so while you are there, drop into the tiny museum to see the miniscule displays, then wander the shops along the main road. There are a few souvenir shops with good crafts. the prices are lower than what you will see on the islands, but so is the quality.

Everything of note in town is within walking distance. If you want to go a bit further, perhaps to see some of the war history, a taxi would probably be easiest. They are unmetered, so negotiate a price for a tour.

World War II sites If you are interested in Second World War history, you can visit the US War Memorial at Skyline Ridge, with its description of the Guadalcanal Campaign, and the Japanese Peace Memorial on Mount Austin, which is surrounded by red hibiscus and white frangipani, the Japanese national colours. There are panoramic views over the capital, Iron Bottom Sound and the Florida Islands. The Gifu, a Japanese defensive position, is a short drive away and was an important forward command post in their attempt to win back Henderson Airfield. Bloody Ridge is also situated close by – this is called Edson's Ridge after the Edson Raiders who defended the ridge against the Japanese onslaught.

Island visits There's not much to do or see on the smaller, remote islands other than admire the lovely scenery. However, while cruising, liveaboards schedule stops in local villages. These take an hour or two and are perfect for a glimpse of island life. Homes are still built traditionally with local timber and thatching, and the islanders are very proud of the way their villages look: gardens have orchids much like the average English garden would have roses. You are met by children carrying flowers, and the giving of small gifts such as toothbrushes and pens is appreciated.

Wander the daily fruit and vegetable market, where the women sell the surplus from their own gardens, and then the displays of handicrafts by local craftsmen. Carved wooden bowls and masks are superlative, but the prices aren't rock-bottom. Bartering is expected or you can take things like old snorkels and dive masks to part exchange. As these people rely on fishing for their diet, snorkelling gear is a useful swap. It is also likely that you will experience one of those traditional song and dance events, as the local people are striving to keep their traditions alive by performing age-old dances for the passing tourists. It is amusing to see lengths of plumbing pipe substituted for bamboo canes to create musical instruments.

Visits from the islanders One of the joys of being on a liveaboard is the frequent visits from the islanders. No matter where you are, local people come out to visit the big ship. They paddle out in their wooden dugouts to trade vegetables and flowers, watch the divers or simply have a chat. The crew of Bilikiki take an active role in the lives of these people both personally and commercially.

Bilikiki; islanders visiting the big ship; visiting children in a local village; returning from a dive; island in Marovo Lagoon.

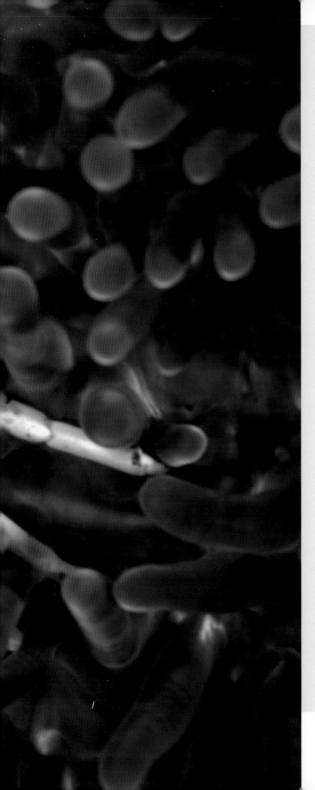

Thailand

329
↘ **Essentials**

330
↘ **Dive brief**

332
↘ **Dive sites**

334
↘ **Dive log**

Thailand
334 Gulf of Phuket
336 The Similans
340 Surin and
Richelieu Rock

Myanmar
342 Mergui Archipelago

344
↘ **Drying out**

Hey, look at me! The tiny spotted porcelain crab, *Neopetrolisthes maculatus* trying to grab some attention.
Koh Tachai, Andaman Sea

destination
Thailand

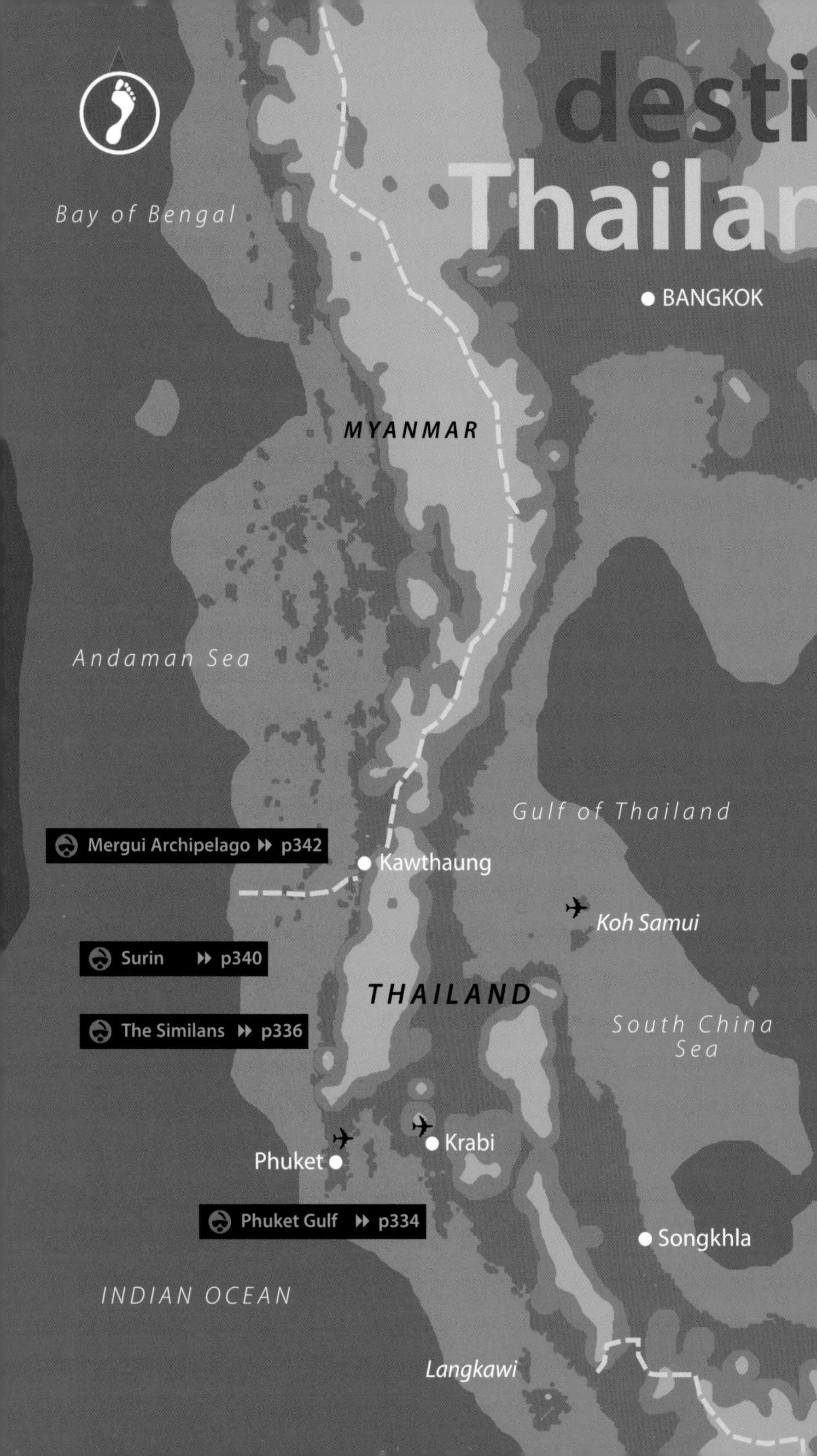

● BANGKOK

Bay of Bengal

MYANMAR

Andaman Sea

🐾 Mergui Archipelago ▶▶ p342

● Kawthaung

Gulf of Thailand

✈ *Koh Samui*

🐾 Surin ▶▶ p340

THAILAND

🐾 The Similans ▶▶ p336

South China Sea

✈ ● Krabi

Phuket ●

🐾 Phuket Gulf ▶▶ p334

● Songkhla

INDIAN OCEAN

Langkawi

Sitting right on the western edge of Southeast Asia, Thailand could be regarded as the region's dive outsider. Geographically beyond the borders of the Coral Triangle, Thailand still reflects much of the marine beauty of her neighbours, yet her principal dive sites are far more influenced by the effects of the Indian Ocean than the Pacific.

From the shallow reefs south of Phuket to the high drama of the Mergui Archipelago over the border in developing Myanmar, the diving can be impressive. These seas may not be as rich as those further east – biodiversity rankings are lower by quite a way – but with more than their fair share of pelagic animals, you can forgive them almost anything. Especially as this is one of the places where you are most likely to get to dive with that most revered of gentle giants, the whale shark.

When it's finally time to let the nitrogen leach out, days on land can be a treat. The culture is lavish – think orange-clad monks and golden Buddhas – nightlife is heady, the cuisine outstanding. And the contradictory elements of tradition, religion and cutting-edge modernity are held firmly together by the charming people.

Essentials

Thailand is one of Southeast Asia's easiest countries to travel to and in. There are international airports right around the country, a decent bus system, trains linking north to south and ferries to all the islands. As the best diving is based in the south of the country, international flights via Singapore are often the most practical option and the city is great for stopovers. For that matter, so is Bangkok... it all depends where you started from. Airport transfers are rarely included in hotel bookings though, so ask in advance for one to be arranged.

Local laws and customs

Thailand requires more than a passing nod to etiquette: never touch a Thai on the head, and never show the soles of your feet or use a foot to point, as that's considered an insult. The Thai Royal Family are much revered, so criticism is never allowed. Buddhist monks warrant equal courtesy, and women should never touch one. If you visit a temple or are away from the beach, sensible, modest clothing is preferable. On the beach, well, anything goes!

Health and safety

In tourism-focused areas, standards are high and decent medical facilities are available should you need help. Basics, like aspirin and insect repellent, are easy to get. There is little risk of malaria in the coastal regions but be very smart when it comes to extra-curricular activities – AIDS and HIV are common. Independent travel requires a dose of common sense: some border areas should be avoided (fortunately, these are not dive areas) and travellers on public transport can be targeted by petty criminals. Likewise, in resorts where nightlife can be wild and outrageous, there are incidents of theft, and drink spiking does happen. Women should be aware that they may get hassled. Note that penalties for the possession of drugs are severe and can include the death penalty.

Costs

Thailand is good value for money for divers. With substantial numbers of hotels, guesthouses, dive companies, liveaboards and restaurants, competition is strong and prices competitive. Although everyone's version of value varies, you can easily get a decent meal with a local beer or two, while sitting under a coconut palm at sunset without having to pull out a credit card.

Myanmar

After the political reforms of 2011/12, tourism is steadily growing. If you are on a liveaboard that includes Mergui, you will be away from any difficult areas and your crew will know the ropes, whether you need a chemist or want to visit a temple. The social norms are much the same as in Thailand, but somewhat more conservative. The Burmese people are delighted to have visitors – make it clear you are delighted to be there and they will welcome you.

Fact file

Location	15°00'N, 100°30'E
Capital	Bangkok
Flights	AirAsia, Bangkok Airways, Singapore Airlines/Silk Air, Thai Airways
Internal flights	Bangkok Airways, Jetstar, Thai Airways, Tiger
Land transport	Good countrywide bus connections, trains and ferries to all islands
Departure tax	Included in your ticket
Entry	EU, US and Commonwealth – valid passport required for stays of up to 30 days
Money	Thai baht (THB)
Language	Thai but English is widely spoken
Electricity	220v, plug types A/C (see page 15)
Time zone	GMT +7
Religion	Principally Buddhist
Communications	Country code +66; IDD 001; Tourist Police 1699 Internet access is widespread but often slow
Tourist information	tourismthailand.org; myanmarburma.com
Travel advisories	gov.uk/foreign-travel-advice; state.gov/travel

dive brief

Whenever we're asked why we keep returning to Thailand – or why we recommend it – we can only quote some of the special moments... floating over the crystal clear, turquoise waters of the Similans; dawn on the Burma Banks watching whales breach; the time the light went out at Richelieu Rock as a whale shark swam over us – and when we met another in the Mergui Archipelago a day later. Finding a perfect pink ghost pipefish on a perfect pink coral; exploring the inky depths of a wreck at night. And simply knowing that below lies a marine adventure that's hard to rival. We've never been disappointed diving off Thailand's west coast.

Diving

Thailand's diving is defined – or perhaps confused – by its position between two seas. The western coast faces the Andaman Sea in the Indian Ocean and is heavily affected by its deep water currents and contrasting monsoons. May to October sees driving, onshore winds pushing in from the southwest. By November, calmer conditions return to the Andaman Sea as the monsoon swaps over to the northeast and the Gulf of Thailand, where the wind patterns have the opposite seasonal effect.

There are coral reef structures along both coastlines but on the west these are far more extensive, particularly around the offshore islands. All the way from south of Phuket island, right up into the distant Myanmar waters, there is fantastic diving. Sea fans, hard and soft corals are plentiful. There are enormous granite boulders with spectacular swim-throughs and swarms of colourful fish. Sharp, rocky pinnacles rise from the depths and submerged reefs offer protection in more isolated regions.

In contrast, the Gulf of Thailand and her islands are subject to their position in a very shallow sea. At less than 60 metres deep and with twice daily tides, the reefs are susceptible to heavy sedimentation and river run-off. These harsh conditions have restricted reef diversity and coral numbers. There are some very decent dive sites around a few of the southern islands, which are extremely popular with the gap year set. It's a good destination for a few months in the year, but it pales in comparison to the opposing coast. Also, the further north you go, heading towards Bangkok, the more likely it is that visibility will disappoint.

Snorkelling

Thailand is a mixed bag: currents can be unpredictable and occasionally strong offshore plus wind conditions can change rapidly, making surface conditions rough. However, these observations apply more to specific dive sites such as the exposed pinnacles visited by liveaboards. While snorkelling around those sites may be off-putting for all but the strongest swimmers, there is decent snorkelling from all the lovely, white sand beaches in the Similans as well as the Phi Phi Islands and in nearly all coastal areas.

Rare nudibranchs, *Dermatobranchus ornatus*, which eat gorgonians.

Marine life

Despite being outside the Coral Triangle, the reefs in this section of Andaman Sea are lush with hard and soft corals that attract and support a substantial variety of species. These tend to be fairly typical of the tropics and include everything from manta rays and whale sharks down to the tiniest crustaceans.

For those expecting marine life similar to other Southeast Asian countries, you do get that, but as the Andaman Sea faces into the Indian Ocean, it is subject to more rigorous ocean current patterns. These bring in clearer waters, which in turn, create a greater interchange of species from further afield. The visibility is better and sunlight reaching down to the reefs ensures lush coral growth.

Making the big decision

Diving Thailand is one of those must-do scenarios. And, once you go, chances are you will want to go back. However, this area is highly seasonal, so first of all decide when you can go. If it's between November and May, then you've chosen the perfect season, as the entire western side of the country is open for diving. For qualified divers, there is no better way to explore the wonders of the Andaman Sea than on a liveaboard while novices and lundlubbers will love the access to the Phi Phi Islands and surrounding areas.

If you are limited to the other months, you could consider the Gulf of Thailand as the drier weather at that time will make a better holiday, although not necessarily the best diving.

Animal encounters

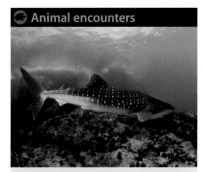

Across the Andaman Sea: there may be some of the most pristine and prettiest soft corals you will ever see, countless lovely, colourful fish, masses of pelagic fish and almost as many molluscs, crustaceans and cephalopods, but honestly, the best thing you can see in either of these countries? It has to be whale sharks.

Thailand Dive brief

Fan coral-clad reef at Koh Doc Mai.

dive sites

As Thailand's western coastline borders the edge of the Andaman Sea, its marine ecosystem is influenced by the far larger Indian Ocean, where water temperatures are warmer than in either the Pacific or Atlantic Oceans. This restricts the levels of phytoplankton and means that the levels of marine life are lower than in the neighbouring countries that make up the Coral Triangle. Fish species are the best example, with both Indonesia and the Philippines having recorded around 3,000 species, while Thailand has a mere 1,500 – although that is still far more than somewhere like Egypt, with just over 800, or 500 in the Galápagos. All the same, in the Indian Ocean, the Andaman Sea is one of the most diverse areas, with the reefs leading from around Phuket and up into Myanmar supporting many exciting and colourful creatures.

Apart from water temperatures, there are localized conditions that affect the varying dive areas. Three well-developed holiday centres – Phuket, Krabi and the Phi Islands – form an imaginary gulf that has some delightful day-trip diving. However, the seabed in this enclosed area is very shallow and visibility is rarely

brilliant. Yet, because of that, the soft corals are outstanding, as they feed on the nutrient-rich waters.

This area is often overlooked by many divers as Phuket is also the most popular departure point for the Similan Islands, the ultimate Thai marine park with its picture-postcard islands and glorious reefs. Sail out on a liveaboard to explore the differing east and west sides before going further north to Koh Bon and Koh Tachai. Technically part of the marine park zone, these open water pinnacles have different geology and far more dramatic underwater topography. They also attract a lot of big stuff, making them a prelude to legendary Richelieu Rock, the do-not-miss dive of the country and quite possibly of your life.

The most distant stop for many Thai-based liveaboards are the waters of the Andaman Sea but across the Myanmar border. Although these have been dived for many years, they remain relatively unexplored, yet they often equal those in Thailand. Distant outposts attract high numbers of sharks while the shallow reefs closer to the coast reveal plenty of smaller creatures.

⊘ Endangered oceans

When it comes to organized conservation projects, Thailand can rightly pat itself on the back. There are researchers counting cetacean numbers (it is said there are 22 species of marine mammal in Thai waters); programmes to monitor rare dugongs and Irrawaddy dolphins, and others that identify individual whale sharks, count whales or rescue turtles. There are some working on the reforestation of mangrove forests and those that monitor coral regrowth, a priority after the devastating tsunami of 2004.

Conditions

Seasons	The Andaman Sea is best from November to May. Other months are subject to monsoon patterns so diving is restricted.
Visibility	5 m inshore to 'infinity' in the Andaman Sea
Currents	Mostly mild except on exposed pinnacles
Temperatures	Air 30-34°C; water 27-30°C
Wet suit	3 mm full body suit
Training	Courses available in Phuket, Krabi or the Gulf
Nitrox	Available on land, may be limited on liveaboards
Deco chambers	Pattaya, Bangkok, Phuket and Koh Samui

Diversity

	reef area 2,130 km²
HARD CORALS	428
FISH SPECIES	1506
ENDEMIC FISH SPECIES	20
FISH UNDER THREAT	109

All diversity figures are approximate

Gulf of Phuket ▸▸ p334

Similans to Surin ▸▸ p336

Myanmar ▸▸ p342

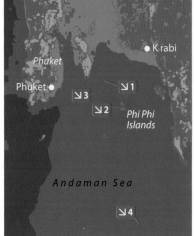

Phuket

● Krabi

Phuket ●

↘ 1

↘ 3

↘ 2

Phi Phi Islands

Andaman Sea

↘ 4

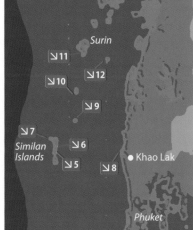

Surin

↘ 11

↘ 10   ↘ 12

↘ 9

↘ 7

↘ 6

Similan Islands

↘ 5   ↘ 8   ● Khao Lak

Phuket

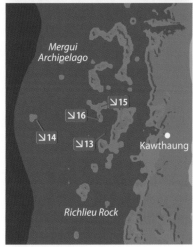

Mergui Archipelago

↘ 15

↘ 16

↘ 14   ↘ 13   Kawthaung

Richlieu Rock

🕐 Log Book

↘1 **King Cruiser**
↘2 **Maya Wall, Phi Phi Lei**
↘3 **Shark Point, Hin Musang**
↘4 **Hin Muang (Purple Rock)**

→ **Koh Racha Yai:** delightful bays that feel like diving in swimming pools
→ **Koh Racha Noi:** sister island to Racha Yai, submerged boulders and lots of critters
→ **Koh Doc Mai:** aka Flower Island, low visibility but pretty underwater garden
→ **Koh Yawa Bon:** a gentle and safe introduction to cave diving
→ **Koh Bida Nok:** hard coral after hard coral punctuated by flitting fish

🕐 Log Book

↘5 **East of Eden**
↘6 **Elephant Rock**
↘7 **Christmas Point**
↘8 **Boon Song Wreck**

→ **Breakfast Bend:** nudibranchs crawling in the shallows with titan triggers
→ **Beacon Point:** reef, beach and wreck dives all named Beacon
→ **Donald Duck Bay:** a calm bay and just perfect for a night dive

↘9 **The Pinnacle, Koh Bon**
↘10 **Koh Tachai**
↘11 **South Point, Surin**
↘12 **Richelieu Rock**

→ **West Ridge, Koh Bon:** underwater promontory with schooling fish
→ **Turtle Ledge, Koh Surin:** true to its name, turtles on a shallow reef

🕐 Log Book

↘13 **Western Rocky**
↘14 **Burma Banks**
↘15 **North Twin**
↘16 **South Twin**

→ **Three Islets:** aka Shark Cave, three small islets that break the surface
→ **High Rock:** aka One Tree island where a lone tree tops a submerged pinnacle
→ **Stewart Island:** arches and caves that cut through a long reef
→ **Fan Forest:** lots of fans competing with cephalopods for attention
→ **Taung La Bo Island:** lots of small creepy crawlies in the seagrass

dive log

Thailand: Gulf of Phuket

Embracing some of the country's most iconic scenery, the body of water ringed by Phuket and the Phi Phi Islands, along with the nearby town of Krabi, is the starting point for diving in Thailand.

All the dive sites in the Phuket Gulf are accessible from any of these points, so you can stay at any one and still dive the whole area. Phuket has it all, from the loud and raucous but very pretty Patong Beach to flat, broad Chalong Bay, which is also the departure point for most dive trips. For somewhere a bit less developed, head to Krabi: it was originally the haunt of long-term travellers but despite their increasing popularity, the local beaches and islands have managed to achieve a comfortable balance. The final option for island lovers are the famous Phi Phi Islands. These are the ones that attract serious crowds as they really are intensely beautiful, with steep limestone cliffs dropping to gorgeous sweeps of sand.

The dive sites closest to Phuket tend to have reduced visibility, due to water that flows from mainland rivers, but visit any site that's offshore by an hour or so and the difference can be surprising.

↘1	King Cruiser	
🌐	**Depth**	31 m
◐	**Visibility**	fair
🌊	**Currents**	slight to medium

The *King Cruiser* passenger ferry was en route to Phi Phi when it found itself several kilometres off course. It ran into a pinnacle and sank slowly. There were 500 people on board but fortunately no loss of life. In just a decade the hull has become a prolific artificial reef. Sitting upright on the seabed at 32 metres, the wreck is 85 metres long and 25 metres wide. There are the most amazing numbers of fish swirling between the two rudders. Small sardine-sized silver baitfish are preyed on by gangs of lionfish and, swimming between the two hulls, you see the giant barracudas that lurk here, no doubt equally well stuffed with all the smaller fish. Ascending upwards, the hull is well covered in newly developing corals, sponges, oysters and barnacles. This wreck can't be penetrated, as the cabin sections are starting to collapse, but you can peer in through the old window holes and see the passageways that would have led to the cabins.

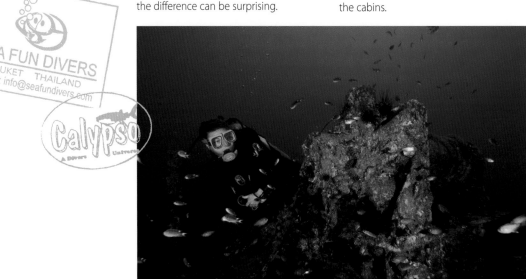

On the wreck of the *King Cruiser*.

Shark Point (Hin Musang)

Depth	16 m	
Visibility	low	
Currents	slight to strong	

The story goes that a dive company owner called this reef Shark Point to get people to go there. It really should be called Soft Coral City or something similar. The dive starts near an exposed pinnacle that has a strong surf and surge pushing across it. Below is an extensive series of pinnacles, bommies and outcrops, all plastered with enough soft corals to wow even the most hardened diver. The visibility can be as low as five to seven metres, which divemasters describe as a good day. Regardless, the reefs are very beautiful, with lots of barrel sponges ringed by ever more soft corals and fans. There are some interesting macro critters lurking on the sand: stonefish, nudibranchs, dragonets and stingrays. The coral bommies are colonized by extensive gardens of waving anemones, each with apricot-coloured skunk clownfish living inside. A nearby hard coral table has a dozen white-eyed morays nosing about.

Hin Muang (Purple Rock)

Depth	25 m	
Visibility	good to excellent	
Currents	mild	

If you ask the divemaster what you'll see, the likely response will be anemones and clownfish. And what an understatement that would be. This totally submerged reef is aptly named. Purple-hued anemones form enormous carpets; then there's the purple and pink soft corals that drip down the gully and, if you look closely, you'll see that the whole reef has purple-toned fish: scorpionfish, lionfish and even octopus display indigo hues hoping to stay hidden. There are some bigger animals hanging around too, but it's hard not to focus on all the tiny critters hidden in the folds, branches and crevices. The macro life is wonderful. Tiny caves are full of purple cleaner shrimp and, occasionally, you'll find rarer creatures hiding along with them. Ornate ghost pipefish – in shades of purple – are often seen by those who take the time to look. It's the furthest south of these sites, so the visibility is better here.

Maya Wall, Phi Phi Lei

Depth	20 m	
Visibility	fair to good	
Currents	mild to strong	

Just beyond Maya Beach, this dive is a continuation of Phi Phi's dramatic topside scenery. The wall of the island and a row of enormous granite boulders that sit a few metres away form a long enclosed channel. Swimming through this becomes an encounter with several large turtles and a lot of fish. At the end of the channel the boulders are more sporadic, creating lots of nooks and crannies to investigate. The hard corals are interspersed with brightly hued fans, and there are a huge number of impressive 'comb' corals that grow vertical branches. A shallow cave has nudibranchs, clown triggerfish and the Similans angelfish.

Soft corals at Shark Point; lionfish preying around the fan corals in the Phi Phi Islands.

dive log
Thailand: The Similans

For many people a dive trip to Thailand means just one thing – the Koh Similans National Marine Park. This chain of tiny islands is around 55 nautical miles north of the island of Phuket and ringed by perfect beaches and amazing coral reefs.

These nine small islands ('similan' means nine in Malay) were established as a marine park in the 1980s. What makes them so attractive for divers is they have two completely different sides. To the east, each island has pure white-sand beaches leading down to equally white sea floors where classically pretty coral gardens slope gently to about 30 metres. The diving is easy and the pace is calm. In contrast, the western side of the chain is far more dramatic, with currents that swirl around huge submerged granite boulders with spectacular swim-throughs. It often feels a bit like diving between skyscrapers that have been reclaimed by the sea. Visibility rarely drops below 20 metres and can reach mythical proportions.

Marking the northern limits of the national park, but beyond the Similans chain, are Koh Bon and Koh Tachai where the geological features change to steep-sided granite outcrops. Koh Bon is just an hour north of Similans No 9 and has steep, grassy cliffs. A cavernous hole perforates part of the island's steep walls so you can see right through to the other side. The main reef runs to over 45 metres deep and is almost completely coated in soft corals, while the deeper sandy parts are where you may see pelagics. A little to the side is the famous Pinnacle dive site.

Koh Tachai is another 25 kilometres further north and is a greener and lusher island. Due to consistent currents, this is a promising area for encounters with large schools of fish.

Ornate ghost pipefish; the blue-ringed angel is called a Similans angelfish in Thailand; an Emperor shrimp living on a sea cucumber.

↘5 East of Eden

🕐	**Depth**	21 m
◑	**Visibility**	good to excellent
🌊	**Currents**	slight

↘6 Elephant Rock

🕐	**Depth**	28 m
◑	**Visibility**	good to excellent
🌊	**Currents**	can be strong

Off Similan No 7, this sloping wall drops to a secondary reef encrusted by rainbows of huge soft corals and bigger fans. Masses of glassy sweepers flit and dance around them like sparkling stars. Tuna and trevally swim by in the blue, while the upper reef hides plenty of delicate small creatures like ornate ghost pipefish. You can even spot the indigenous Similans sweetlips here. At night, the site reignites with nocturnal activity. Nestling in almost every crevice are cleaner shrimp or tiny pink crabs. Hermit and arrow crabs scramble everywhere. Stay completely still, but divert a torch beam a little away from the wall and you will be rewarded with tiny, shy cuttlefish peeking out from matching crinoids. Heading back uphill to the sandy sea floor, decorator crabs are on the prowl, along with cowries and cone shells. A stealthy octopus will wait for the right moment to nip out for a quick meal.

This is one of the Similans' most famous dive sites purely because of the unusually shaped granite boulders that reach up from invisible depths, emerging on the west of the island. On land, one cluster is said to mimic the shape of an elephant's head. Beneath the water, boulders tumble over each other to form a complex of arches and tunnels and some of the most dramatic swim-throughs in the entire chain. Small fans nestle into the crevices for protection from the surge, while critters crawl on the sheer rocky surfaces. Small tubastrea trees add a hint of green, while hawkfish perch on their branches. There are many sea cucumbers on the sand, which host fantastic imperial shrimp; mantis shrimp skitter about in the rubble with blennies, while gobies bob up from the rocks. Back up around the boulders there are groups of trevally and schools of small yellow grunts under a ledge.

⛵7 Christmas Point

🕐	**Depth**	20 m
👁	**Visibility**	excellent
🌊	**Currents**	mild to strong

Wonder how this one got its name? The site marks the top end of the Similans chain and the visibility here can be very, very good, no doubt because it is swept by clear open ocean currents. These can be strong at times and surface conditions a little rough, but below there is a good reef with the classic Similans scenery of square-cut boulders interspersed with bright-hued fans. On one side of the dive, there are some large stony arches to swim through and these are mobbed by schools of fish. Trevally are quite common. Down on the rubble-strewn seabed are blue and black ribbon eels, lots of spotted jawfish and lovely, pure white egg cowries displaying their jet-black mantles. Occasionally you may find a leopard shark resting here. This is also a good site to spot the indigenous Similans sweetlips, clown triggerfish, puffers and angelfish.

⛵8 Boon Song Wreck

🕐	**Depth**	18 m
👁	**Visibility**	poor to good
🌊	**Currents**	slight to mild

The *Boon Song* is the hull of a tin dredging boat. Also known as the Bansak wreck, as it lies off Bansak beach on the coast, it sank in 1984 and appears as a solid square of metal resting on the seabed. Visibility can be poor, due to the silty surrounds, but it really doesn't matter as it is a haven for a wealth of tiny critters. Circumnavigating the hull is like a treasure hunt – there are unbelievable numbers of nudibranchs, plus estuarine stonefish, tiny flounders and unusual miniature spindle cowries on whip corals. There are honeycomb and blotched morays in crevices, lionfish and tiny peacock flounders. You can also see some of the mechanical parts from the boat's past life such as gear wheels and metal scoops. The wreck is also known for resident leopard sharks that nestle on the sand and a school of porcupine puffers that hover constantly over the top deck.

> 66 99 Our trip to Thailand was my first liveaboard. I have to say the quality of the boat, diving, fish diversity and the company of new buddies spoilt me forever more. I can instantly calm myself down after a stressful day by thinking about my very first whale shark, gliding so gracefully over my head, the cuttlefish I was watching instantly forgotten. That trip was one of many firsts. Whale sharks, ghost pipefish, octopus, cuttlefish and, of course, the beginning of my continuing fascination (bordering on obsession) with nudibranchs – plus my 100th dive with all the silky sharks on the Burma Banks. Friendships I still cherish and experiences I will never forget. The Similans and the Burma Banks opened my eyes to the world underwater.
>
> *Estelle Zauner-Maughan, chiropractor and dive instructor, Newcastle, UK*

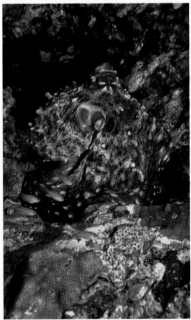

A common octopus; juvenile cardinalfish sheltering in the bell of a jellyfish; the Stricklandi nudibranch was named after the divemaster who found it.

⬛9 The Pinnacle, Koh Bon

🌀	**Depth**	35 m
◐	**Visibility**	poor to stunning
〰	**Currents**	generally strong

This sharp-sided pinnacle rises from who knows where to 20 metres, its rocky surfaces smothered in yellow soft corals and golden-toned fans, all surrounded by yellow snappers. The effect of sunny hues in the dark water is rather surreal. Leopard sharks rest on a ledge, while off in the blue are mingled schools of jacks and batfish. There could be as many as 200 – perhaps more – as the water is thick with plankton. The soup attracts masses of fish to feed: it's an incredible sight, but hovering at such depth means a safety stop on the nearby shallow reef. You may be rewarded with a glimpse of a manta as you both swim through the small channel between the pinnacle and the reef. No doubt, it was attracted by the seasonal smorgasbord.

⬛10 Koh Tachai

🌀	**Depth**	35 m
◐	**Visibility**	good to excellent
〰	**Currents**	generally strong

Southeast of Koh Tachai, the currents are nearly always swift; a mooring rope leads down to where it's possible to shelter from them. Descending, you pass bommies coated in soft corals and crinoids that add splashes of brighter colours. At the base of the reef a resident school of batfish hovers around a cleaning station, a lone sea snake passes a gang of pufferfish and a carpet anemone reveals eggshell shrimp (with white spots showing through the insides of their transparent bodies) and porcelain crabs. Near the boulders there are masses of swooping jacks; trevally and mackerel nip in and out to feed on glassy sweepers, and, to complete the collection of pelagic fish, a massive shoal of chevron barracuda swirls above the pinnacle.

dive log
Thailand: Surin

After Koh Bon and Koh Tachai, the next stop on liveaboard routes are the islands in the Surin National Park. These are the final land masses before Myanmar waters.

There are five islands and two underwater pinnacles in the park; these attract turtles and reef sharks, Spanish mackerel and barracuda. The offshore currents can be tough but the shallow coastal waters have extensive hard coral reefs. Although these are not as impressive as some of the others in this region, they are dived mostly at night while moored up. And this is all because the main target is 20 kilometres from Surin, the dive site that has it all – Richelieu Rock. An hour to the east, this isolated pinnacle rises from 40 metres and extends to the surface. As a dive, it is completely, justifiably famous. In fact, if the gods are smiling on you and your dive buddies, this could be the one do-not-miss dive of your life.

≥11	South Point	
🌀	**Depth**	20 m
🜂	**Visibility**	fair to good
≋	**Currents**	none

A short distance from the jetty on North Surin, this bay makes a great night dive and is usually done at night as a precursor to arriving at Richelieu Rock, as you cannot moor overnight there.

The seabed is a mix of sand and coral rubble, although there are some very good hard corals in patches. The staghorn corals are alive with critters. It's easy to spot large grey morays as they poke their noses out to feed, and the crustaceans are incredibly prolific. A torch beam will highlight the reflective eyes of large, bright red crabs, tiny hermit and decorator crabs on the sand, coral crabs and green-eyed dancing shrimp hiding up in the branches of the staghorn. It's worth looking in the crevices for young lobsters and saron shrimp. These hairy, highly patterned shrimp are never seen in daylight. Scorpionfish move out onto the sand to feed as well, so are far easier to see than they would be during the day, as are crawling fish like flounder.

Banded sole undulating over the sand; the Splendid red spooner crab, which measures 150 centimetres across the carapace.

richelieu
rock

⬇ **Depth**	32 m
◈ **Visibility**	stunning
≋ **Currents**	none to strong

The idea of describing the splendour that is Richelieu Rock in a paragraph or two is more than a challenge – it's nigh on impossible. This isolated, submerged hill is without doubt the dive site that has it all, from the tiniest of critters to the ultimate in grace, size and beauty: the whale shark.

Entering over the top of the rock, it's worth heading straight down to the base, where there are masses of healthy, brightly coloured soft corals and several enormous groupers. Back on the slopes there is a wealth of smaller creatures to admire: lion and trumpetfish, sea snakes, cowries, angels and butterflies, seahorses, clownfish, and mantis shrimp. There are minute harlequin shrimp pairs and masses of nudibranchs. Then there's the bigger guys: turtles, reef sharks, barracuda, potato cod and even occasional mantas. Every surface seems to house yet another fascinating resident. But at all times keep an ear out for the sounds of manic tank banging. This is the signal that a whale shark has been seen and you should make a mad dash towards the sound. When the conditions are right, you may be lucky and see several in a day. Both adults and juveniles are attracted to this isolated reef, which is one of the few places in the world where you can still dive with them. Pay these gentle giants the respect they deserve.

dive log
Myanmar: Mergui Archipelago

Sail a short distance north of Richelieu Rock and you cross the border into Myanmar. The past political situation made this a questionable trip for some but, with recent changes, the area is now regarded as open for tourism.

It always was for many divers, as this part of the Andaman Sea is well worth diving; the scenery is truly beautiful, the marine life is superlative and reefs are relatively untouched. This extension to the Thailand routes has long been a favourite of liveaboard operators, who extended their itineraries to include these remote reefs. After a quick stop at the border town, Kawthaung, the boat resumes the trip to the Mergui Archipelago.

⊠13 Western Rocky	
🕐 **Depth**	25 m
◐ **Visibility**	excellent
≋ **Currents**	slight

How do you improve on diving Richelieu Rock? Simple, sail up to Western Rocky. This area was closed for some time to let it regenerate but it now rivals its neighbour. Sheer walls plummet vertically to ring a submerged pinnacle. The sides are coated in glistening cup corals and bright crinoids. There is a soaring cathedral-like arch at the end of the south wall and, finning through it, you are surrounded by masses of stripy snappers. Further east, a series of smaller pinnacles are coated in fan and soft corals and smothered in glassy sweepers. Banded sea snakes investigate tiny caves where porcelain crabs shelter in huge carpet anemones. Schools of squid take refuge in the lee of a wall and sharks hide in the caverns. You might even be lucky enough to meet that young whale shark.

⊠14 Burma Banks	
🕐 **Depth**	25 m
◐ **Visibility**	excellent
≋ **Currents**	slight

It's a great pity that when a site gets well known as the place to see sharks, it also gets a bit too well known to fishermen. A few years ago the Burma Banks were bereft – not a shark to be seen. However, more recently, they have returned and the area is once again a great shark-spotting destination. The Banks consist of several different sea mounds, but Silvertip Bank is the most visited. The plateau is carpeted with lots of small fans and some pretty, soft corals. Peer down into the depths and you're likely to glimpse the whitetips that pass by. Other species make irregular appearances – reef sharks, nurses and even large silvertips. They swoop around divers and seem quite curious but slide away just as easily. The rest of the dive has dogtooth tuna and octopus, while much smaller fish include rockmover wrasse and sand gobies. Yet all that gets lost in the excitement when the crew sets up a bait bucket. This attracts a few wary young silvertips and the regular star of the show, Max, a resident nurse shark.

66 99 I'll never forget it... one day after I saw my first ever whale shark on Richelieu Rock, I rolled into the water at Western Rocky and dropped to five metres to wait for the others. And there, right below me... a baby whale shark. Utterly unbelievable.
Jill Keen, financial advisor, Bexhill-on-Sea, UK

↘15 **North Twin**		
🌀 **Depth**	24 m	
◐ **Visibility**	fair to good	
〰 **Currents**	mild to strong	

↘16 **South Twin**		
🌀 **Depth**	30 m	
◐ **Visibility**	fair to excellent	
〰 **Currents**	none to slight	

North and South Twin Islands sit about 20 kilometres apart. Currents can be strong and, when they're not, the visibility goes way down. At the bottom of the island a pinnacle drops from just below the surface to about 30 metres, where a series of large granite boulders create swim-throughs that are thick with seafans and purple soft corals. The marine life is a real contrast – one minute, a nurse shark appears, lazily swimming past then off into the blue, then a few seconds later you spot minute flabellina nudibranchs crawling along a hydroid, competing for the tastiest bits to chew on. Fish life includes butterfly and angelfish, parrotfish, surgeonfish and, if you pause to look at the fans, you will catch the resident hawkfish staring back at you.

A little larger than her sister at a kilometre long, South Twin dives are comparatively easy with gentle conditions around the bays to the south. Granite boulders tumble down from the side of the island and onto a sloping reef. Visibility is usually good as you swim past small soft corals and fans, discovering many critters along the way. There are blue ribbon eels, honeycomb and yellowmargin morays. Shells are prolific, with spider conchs and gorgeous cowries. The tiger cowrie is easy enough to spot, but not the *Mauritia maculifera* cowrie, which has no common name but definitely lives here. There are so many nudibranchs, it's a struggle to remember which species you have seen and, even with a picture, you can't identify some.

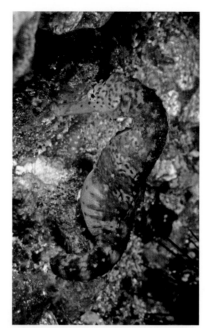

Thailand Dive log Mergui Archipelago

drying out

The western coast of southern Thailand has international airports at Phuket and Krabi. Both places have a massive number of hotels in all styles and price ranges so you will be spoilt for choice. Dive shops tend to be independent so collect divers from hotels each morning. Liveaboards are no longer as numerous as they once were but there is still a good selection. Most focus on short trips to the Similans, but some still run week or 10-day trips that go as far as the Burma Banks.

Phuket

Diving

Calypso Divers, calypsophuket.com. Local day trips and overnight trips to Phi Phi.
Sea Bees Diving, sea-bees.com. In Ao Chalong and Khao Lak, north of Phuket.
Sea Fun Divers, seafundivers.com. Local day-trip specialists with a range of courses.

Sleeping

Ao Chalong Villa and Spa, aochalongvillaandspa.com. Small, quirky resort near Chalong Jetty with a superb restaurant. 50-mins transfer. .
Kata Minta, kataminta.com. Boutique hotel just off Kata Beach. Airport transfer, 60-mins.

Phi Phi

Sleeping

Bay View Resort, phiphibayview.com. Large resort complex on Phi Phi Don. Transfers from Phuket by ferry can take up to 4-hrs.

Ao Nang, Krabi

Diving

Aqua Vision, aqua-vision.net
Scuba Addicts, scuba-addicts.com

Sleeping

L Resort, theresort.com, previously lovely Wanna's Place, now upgraded.

Liveaboards

Diving the Andaman Sea beyond Phuket is best done by liveaboard. There are many operators from budget to luxury but, of late, there have been big changes to the local scene. Longer trips may include the waters just over the Myanmar border; your operator will handle all the necessary formalities. Check out:

MV Black Manta, whitemanta.com
MV Mermaid I, mermaid-liveaboards.com
SY Diva Andaman, divamarine.com

✪ The tides of change

The popularity of diving destinations can change direction as often the tides that are so vital to our oceans. However, at times, this vital and expected movement in our oceans does something it shouldn't. Thailand, when we started diving, was incredibly aspirational and, although it took quite some years before we had saved enough to go, we made it. As one of our first big liveaboard trips, the journey from the Similans to Burma still ranks as one of the best ever.

And then there was the tsunami. On Boxing Day in 2004, the tide went out, but it did so in minutes. The sea disappeared from view, then came back as a massive wall of water. The lands surrounding the Andaman Sea, from India and Sri Lanka to Thailand and Indonesia, were all terribly affected. The tragedy was unprecedented.

It's no surprise that the Thai diving industry faded away; people stayed away out of shock, then out of respect. As time went by, there were reports that much had been lost on the reefs, so divers started going elsewhere. Some will say that the marine realm has never quite recovered, yet reefs are designed to regenerate. New corals are growing; fish are breeding and the dives are still exciting.

There have been changes in the fortunes of the Gulf of Thailand too. Ever-popular with the backpacker set, the tiny islands that surround Koh Samui have some good seasonal diving and are favoured learn-to-dive destinations. Yet, these supposedly idyllic islands have a reputation for social problems, rather than natural ones. Common sense is everything, of course, but take care.

Days out

Gulf of Phuket There is a lot to do on and around the island of Phuket if you can force yourself away from the marine realm. On the island itself, Wat Chalong Temple is one of 29 Buddhist monasteries but by far the most important. The buildings are very ornate. Thalang National Museum contains ancient artefacts and exhibits on the famous Battle of Thalang. The Phuket Aquarium on Cape Panwa is surprisingly good with a turtle hatchery, jellyfish exhibit, a walk-through tunnel and nature trails. And, of course, there is always Phuket Town, a retail therapy haven. If you're there in April, you'll catch Songkran, the Thai New Year water festival. Masses of Thais fill plastic bins with water and ice, drive the streets then ditch them over the unwary. And they do love dousing tourists! The tradition behind this lively event lies in the cleaning of hands to wash away of bad thoughts or actions. Great fun and completely harmless so join in the spirit of the day.

For longer days out, Khao Sok National Park, is a protected lowland rainforest with animal conservation projects, canoeing and elephant treks. Koh Tapu, aka James Bond Island, is incredibly pretty and equally touristy. Day trips pass Nail Island and a sea gypsy village. If you don't stay on the Phi Phi Islands you can always catch a ferry there and retread Leonardo di Caprio's steps for a day by visiting Maya Beach, where The Beach was filmed. Krabi Town has good shops, and from here you can easily reach the Tiger Cave Temple with its nature trail and many shrines set in caves. It's all of 1,237 steps to the mountain-top statue of the Buddha.

Similans to Myanmar There is little to do on any of the Similan Islands apart from a beach walk every now and then although a couple don't allow visitors. Once you reach Kawthaung, you'll be itching for a bit of culture. The town is fairly small but worth disembarking for, with some lovely small craft shops and a few good restaurants where you can sample the fabulous local cuisine. The temple on the headland is worth the walk if you have time.

Bangkok Completely manic, outrageously noisy and entertaining beyond belief, 24 hours in the capital guarantees a high-voltage stopover. A single day's itinerary will give a taste of the city's best features. Start by taking a three-wheeled tuk-tuk ride to the Grand Palace, a superlative example of traditional architecture. Inside the complex is Wat Phra Kaew, the Temple of the Emerald Buddha, Thailand's most sacred. Next, walk the short distance to the Chao Praya River. Pass by the unusual Royal Barges Museum then on to Tha Chang Pier. Hop on the Chao Phraya Express river boat to lovely Wat Arun, the Temple of the Dawn, which is opposite. Re-embark for a short cruise upriver and back, for a local's view of Thai river life. Hop off at Thra Phra Arthit jetty and walk to the place for cheap designer goods, Khao San Road. This travellers' hang-out is full of shops and good restaurants. Thai food ranks as one of the world's top cuisines with its unique blend of the four principal taste sensations – hot, sweet, sour and salt. Be bold and walk into any restaurant where you see locals eating something good. Finally, for a touch of class, take a taxi to the museum at Jim Thompson's House. Credited for creating the silk industry, his home is now full of interesting exhibits.

If you have a second day, within easy reach of Bangkok is the ancient Siamese capital of Ayutthaya, a World Heritage Site with amazing ruins of temples and palaces. Damnoen Saduak is famous for the floating markets where canals are packed with boats piled high with fruit and vegetables and there is the River Kwai if you are interested in war history.

Sleeping

The Peninsula Bangkok, bangkok.peninsula.com.
Holiday Inn, ichotelsgroup.com.

New Year festival in Phuket town; sleeping Buddha at Ao Chalong; moored in the Similans; spices and herbs typical of Thai cooking; Thai river boat in Bangkok.

Resources

348
↘ **Marine biodiversity**

350
↘ **Marine conservation**

352
↘ **Diver training**

354
↘ **Health and first aid**

356
↘ **Marine nasties**

358
↘ **Acknowledgements**

360
↘ **Directory**

365
↘ **Index**

Losing count. Is it even possible to tally coral species in the world's most prolific realm?
Penemu Wall, West Papua, Indonesia

marine biodiversity

When you consider that seven tenths of the planet is covered in water, it may seem curious that most divers' hit-lists are confined to the equatorial belt. But there is good reason. This is where the majority of accessible marine life resides.

All oceans are teeming with life, but many seas are too deep and too cold to encourage the development of all but the most specialized species. These conditions also make many areas off-limits to sport diving.

The warm waters that surround the equator are known to have remained tropical for millions of years. High light levels and sun-heated waters encourage reef growth and provide time for marine species to diversify. This simple equation ensures that tropical waters are just that much richer than temperate waters. Yet nothing is ever really that simple. The world's oceans – and diving zones – are also influenced by deep water plates, ridges, submerged volcanoes and marine currents. It has been accepted for many years that the waters in the Indo-Pacific region, from Madagascar in the west to the Galápagos in the east, are far richer than those of the Atlantic. However, Southeast Asia is the specific region that displays the highest levels of biodiversity. This is due to its position in the Pacific Ocean, in a geologically complex region known as the Pacific Ring of Fire: a deep water string of submerged volcanoes encircle the Pacific and were a key element in the formation of the Earth's crust and, many centuries later, resulted in an array of biologically unique island ecosystems and species.

The Coral Triangle

While past scientific research suggested that the area around the top of Indonesian Sulawesi was the Ring of Fire's epicentre, more recent studies have introduced the Coral Triangle. This is the area enclosed by Southern Indonesia, eastern Borneo, up to the Philippines, then across to Papua New Guinea and the Solomons. Studies conducted throughout this region have confirmed it is the global centre of marine biodiversity. Covering 5.7 million km^2 (about half of the area of the United States) this area has over 600 reef-building coral species (which is 75% of all species known to science) and more than 3,000 species of reef fish.

These figures vary by country, with species numbers reducing the further away from the centre you go. For example, Indonesia

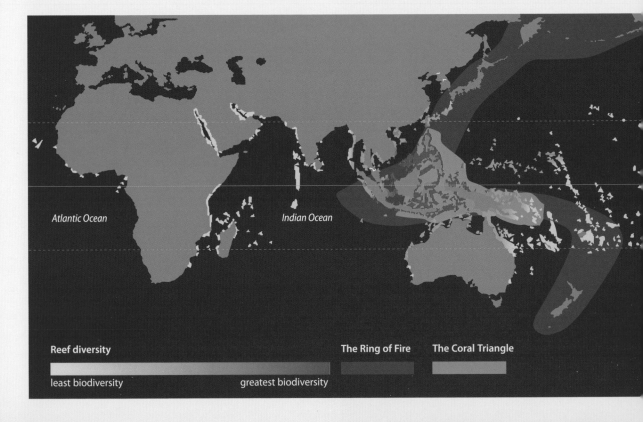

Atlantic Ocean

Indian Ocean

Reef diversity

least biodiversity   greatest biodiversity

The Ring of Fire   **The Coral Triangle**

has around 3,600 species of fish, including 138 damselfish. Papua New Guinea has 100 damsels, but by the time you reach Fiji there are just 60. Way over in the Galápagos the number drops to 18, while the Caribbean has a mere 16 across its entire sea. Australia, always the exception to the rule, has the highest numbers of damsels at 142, but that is because the continent covers tropical, temperate and cold waters.

The Indo-Pacific versus the Atlantic

Global patterns of reef and coral development started way back in the Triassic era, a mere 250 million years ago. It was during this time that the continents broke up, disconnecting certain sections of sea from others. This resulted in the Atlantic being isolated from all the other oceans so it formed reefs with distinctly different characteristics. Localized marine life was thought to be prolific in this period, but a few million years later, the Ice Age kicked in and the entire region was subjected to mass extinctions. Melting ice water flooded into the Atlantic, reducing its temperature enough to decimate the animal populations, leaving just a small refuge in the area we now know as the Caribbean. Many of the species that had been common to all coral reefs did not survive this period and left just seven genera in common with the Indo-Pacific. Although conditions settled, species diversity never did regenerate and left this one ocean lagging behind all others.

Global reef area — km²

Region	km²
PACIFIC	115,900
SOUTHEAST ASIA	91,700
INDIAN OCEAN	32,000
CARIBBEAN	20,000
RED SEA & GULF OF ADEN	17,400
ARABIAN GULF & SEA	4,200
ATLANTIC	1,600
EASTERN PACIFIC	1,600

All diversity figures are approximate

Species diversity and discovery

The other reason for higher species diversity in the Asia-Pacific basin is the way in which ocean currents transport cold waters around the planet. The Indo-Pacific area is partly protected from Arctic waters by the Russian and Alaskan land masses, and this allows marine life to flourish in the shallower, warmer waters – the zone where most coral reefs thrive.

This information is by no means a reason to ignore one sea or country for another. While diving in Asian waters is more likely to be a journey of discovery than it is elsewhere, new species are discovered across the world on a regular basis. Across the millenia, unique geological forces have created a variety of marine environments and many endemic species. You may not see a pygmy seahorse in the Caribbean, but you also won't see an indigo hamlet in Thailand.

66 99 **We feel surprise when travellers tell us of the vast dimensions of the Pyramids and other great ruins, but how utterly insignificant are the greatest of these, when compared to these mountains of stone accumulated by the agency of various minute and tender animals! This is a wonder which does not first strike the eye of the body, but, after reflection, the eye of reason.**

Charles Darwin, April 12, 1836, on his theory of atoll formation.

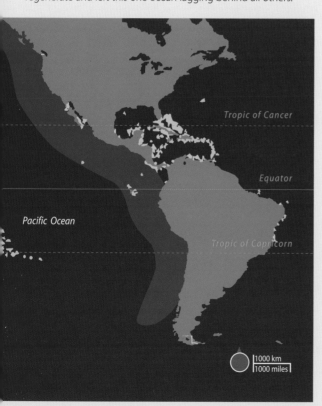

Tropic of Cancer

Equator

Pacific Ocean

Tropic of Capricorn

1000 km
1000 miles

marine
conservation

A few years ago, Jean-Michel Cousteau spoke on Capitol Hill: "The ocean holds 97% of Earth's water, drives climate and weather, generates more than 70% of the oxygen we breathe, absorbs carbon dioxide, supplies our fresh water through rain, provides food, and is a deep source of inspiration to our spirits."

Yet our seas are heavily endangered and coral reefs are one of the most threatened ecosystems on the planet. If destruction continues at its present rate, 70% of the world's coral reefs will disappear in a generation. And where will that leave us?

Most people (divers generally excluded) think nothing of how the fish arrives on their dinner plate, nor what happens to sewerage or the side-effects of many industries. Centuries of bad practices have led to the direct destruction of the world's coral reefs – some figures suggest that up to 30% have been lost already. Over time, few people realized they were literally killing the resource that supported them. Fishing practices, both commercial and small scale, are much to blame for damage to many marine ecosystems. Drag-netting the sea floor, for example, kills indiscriminately, while at the other end of the scale, poor local fishermen have been dropping chemicals to catch fish in greater numbers, never understanding that this kills everything, leaving nothing to sustain either the people or the fish. As a coral reef dies, so do other environments around it. With no reef paralleling the shore, mangrove nursery grounds become eroded and creatures that used these as a safe haven no longer can. A once protected coast becomes open to the ravages of weather and may well collapse into the sea. Other man-made issues, such as pollution, simply aggravate these problems.

Coral reefs

There is a lot of publicity about how climate change is leading to rises in sea levels, but less focus on how this impacts on corals and consequently on the planet as a whole. Corals need a specific temperature range (around 25-29°C) and it only takes an increase of one degree in water temperature for corals to start struggling.

Tiny individual corals feed on *zooxanthellae*, symbiotic yellow-, green- or brown-hued algaes, which live inside the corals, giving them colour and sustaining them via photosynthesis. But, as waters warm, the algae either dies, or the corals expel them, causing them to bleach. Water that is too warm also encourages the growth of harmful algae over the corals. This blocks out the sun; the *zooxanthellae* cannot photosynthesize so they die, taking the corals with them. The marine realm has created an antidote to this problem: the algae are usually eaten by fish, but overfishing means there are insufficient numbers to keep the balance. Other side-effects are seen when corals get ill and predators move in. The Crown of Thorns starfish is a well-known example, as these predate on corals, which causes bleaching. Their natural predators are few, and the ones that do exist are depleted by overfishing as well.

Right around the world, people depend on coral reefs for foods as well as a source of income. Despite their environmental and economic importance, new research indicates that more than half of the world's coral reefs could die in less than 25 years.

Marine predators

A subject that does, fortunately, gain a lot more publicity is anything to do with shark species. It is well-known that shark finning is devastating the worldwide population of the ocean's top predator, but there is less understanding of how that will affect the seas as a whole. It's just basic science: sitting at the top of the food chain, sharks regulate the natural balance of ecosystems in every ocean. By hunting old or sick animals, they help to keep the prey population in good condition.

Mono-filament net dragged over a reef then caught and left there; coral destruction of a hard probably caused by dropping an anchor.

The knock-on effect is that this controls numbers further down the food chain ensuring a healthy supply and demand effect for all marine creatures. For example, when a cow nose ray population wasn't being kept under control by sharks, the ray numbers increased and they destroyed their own food supply. Likewise, sharks regulate the behaviour of species like turtles. Turtles graze on seagrass, but if there is nothing to prey on them, the sea grass habitats they occupy are destroyed by overgrazing and this kills all the smaller creatures that were once there as well.

Several countries are now making notable contributions to creating a balance in these areas. In 2009, the small nation of Palau created the world's first shark sanctuary and continues to fight for economic sanctions against commercial fishing in surrounding waters. In 2014, the Indonesian Government passed legislation to protect all manta rays within their six million square kilometre exclusive economic zone and, in doing so, they created the world's largest sanctuary for both species of manta.

Meanwhile, heated discussions continue over the Western Australia shark cull policy. Despite having no scientific evidence, the government went ahead with this much-maligned policy and did not consider other ways to protect both people and sharks. The answer is simple: you just tow big sharks out to sea and let them go. And unlike the cull policy, this idea is actually backed up by scientific evidence. In Brazil, a trial reduced shark incidents by 97% with minimal environmental impact.

Recently, one rather well-known environmental campaigner said: "Protecting our planet's oceans and the marine species that call them home is one of the most pressing sustainability crises facing humanity today and a moral imperative that we must acknowledge." Leonardo DiCaprio was addressing the US Department of State at the Our Oceans 2014 summit. Here's hoping other governments will take note.

Dead juvenile tiger shark captured inside an African marine park.

◐ Divers and conservation

A diver's role may seem to be a comparatively small one but it is one that is vital. Every individual action adds to the bigger picture and spreads the word at a local level that our reefs are worth saving.

Always remember one of the first rules of diving – look but don't touch. Sadly, there are divers who genuinely don't care, and you have to wonder what it is they are doing if they have only gone down to destroy.

▶▶ Do not touch corals, or any other living organism, as your hands can leave harmful oils and the pressure can damage protective coatings allowing destructive bacteria to penetrate.

▶▶ Don't wear gloves, unless absolutely necessary, as you will be too tempted to put your hands down without thinking about where they are going.

▶▶ If tough conditions dictate that you must touch the reef, a single finger is enough to give you balance, and a carefully placed reef hook does less damage than two hands.

▶▶ Don't bring anything up from the seabed, not even a shell. It may seem to be dead, but you just don't know what tiny creature has crawled inside.

▶▶ Be careful to stay above the reef, good buoyancy is vital.

▶▶ Ensure all your gauges and equipment are either hooked to your BC or tucked in a pocket.

▶▶ Watch what you do with your fins; be aware that your fins are longer than you are tall and it's easy to misjudge what is behind you.

There are many organizations dedicated to looking after our seas and the animals that live within them. Look at WWF (panda.org), Reef Check (reefcheck.org), the Marine Conservation Society (mcsuk.org), the Shark Research Institute (sharks.org) and the International Coral Reef Action Network (icran.org).

Get involved by helping to monitor reefs. Ask your dive operator about PADI's Project AWARE activities (projectaware.org) or, if you have time, sign up for an expedition run by a body like Coral Cay Conservation (coralcay.org) or GlobalVision International (gvi.co.uk).

diver
training

For many, the underwater experience starts on holiday. There you are, snorkelling over some exotic reef but watching the divers far below and wanting to join in. So it's over to the hotel pool for a try-dive session followed by a quick resort course. For others, it can be the influence of friends at home who are so enthusiastic about their chosen pastime, they spend every waking minute talking non-stop about it. Either way, for those who discover that their blood no longer circulates without additional nitrogen in it, it's time to take things seriously and get qualified.

There are several ways to do this, each of which should be assessed carefully: you can train at home, abroad or even online these days, but the most important factor is to ensure that you get the best training possible from one of the world's major diving organizations. This is not a sport in which it pays to cut corners.

Training organizations

By far the largest and best known dive body is **PADI** (Professional Association of Diving Instructors, padi.com). You will see their signs right around the world, from your local dive store to resorts abroad, but they are by no means the only training organization. Other well respected international bodies include the **British Sub-Aqua Club** (BSAC, bsac.com), the **National Association of Underwater Instructors** (NAUI, naui.com) and **Scuba Schools International** (SSI, divessi.com).

Each of these bodies has a range of comparative courses run via weekly club-style meetings, local day courses or residential courses either at home or away. All courses are well-structured, thorough and will cover the relevant concerns for each level. Courses are designed to be completed in a specific number of days, and any training operation will do their best to ensure you meet that target. Before signing on the dotted line, do your research: get some recommendations, ask to meet your potential instructor, then go with the company and person who makes you feel confident and relaxed within the training environment. Bear in mind that you will need a well-recognized certification. If your training is not internationally recognized you may find that another country will not accept your certification card and you will have to start over.

Learning to dive

This should include three straightforward steps. Basic training is often called **Open Water** and builds essential skills to get you safely in the water but limits your depth and may not teach any rescue skills. An **Advanced Open Water** course will expand your knowledge, and further in-water practice ensures competence in deeper water and under differing conditions. Finally, take a **Rescue Diver** course. This may be included in one of the above stages but, if not, ensure you do it. It is important to learn how to save your own life, or someone else's, and is a vital addition to the initial training programme.

Where to learn

One option is, of course, to go on holiday somewhere lovely and, hopefully, qualify in warm waters under sunny skies. The downside of this is that you are giving up precious holiday time to sit in a classroom. There are several Asian hot-spots that regularly attract backpackers, gap-year travellers and those who

A try-dive session for honeymooners in Zanzibar; learning basic skills in the pool.

just want to learn. Lombok's Gili islands and Thailand's Koh Tao are well regarded and popular training destinations. On the other side of the globe, Utila in Honduras ranks as one of the world's busiest and cheapest training islands, but bear in mind that anything too cheap indicates that your operator may be forced to cut corners somewhere. Many rock-bottom courses do not include manuals and fees. Also make sure your dive school has an instructor who can speak your language.

Alternatively, you could book into a school in your home country or join a club. These will have a range of options from more relaxed week-by-week training sessions to intensive long weekend options. If these are all going to put a dent in your schedule, you could learn at your own pace with an online course (padi.com/elearning) then register with a local school for your qualifying open water dives.

When you do choose to kick off your dive training, remember that you need to be in good health and reasonably comfortable in the water – no, you don't need to be an Olympic swimmer, but you should be able to swim further than from the pool edge to the swim-up bar. If you have any known medical conditions, for example asthma or diabetes, get advice from a medical professional before you start.

Continued training

At this point many people stop training, and that's fine, but the half dozen or so dives taken to get you through a course will not make you a competent diver. Practice, as they say, makes perfect, so try to get in some diving on a regular basis and consider doing either some speciality or higher level courses as they will help refine your skills. Some ideas are on the right.

More recently, technical diving has become increasingly popular, and for experienced divers, this can be a challenging step forward, allowing for new and unusual diving experiences. Open circuit diving on mixed gases and rebreather diving can increase no-decompression limits and reduce gas consumption. Rebreathers recycle gases, and as breath is not expelled, there are no bubbles – and that means there is the opportunity for some incomparable marine life encounters because the animals are not scared off by an unfamiliar noise .

Continued safety

Finally, every time you are back in the water remind yourself again never to cut corners. It's important to be healthy when you dive, continually check the state of your equipment and always dive in a buddy pair. Listen to every dive brief carefully: the divemaster is there to ensure his divers come back safely, not just lead them around, so the information he supplies is vital to both an enjoyable dive and a safe one.

🔆 The training ladder

There is a clear route that takes potential divers from novice to qualified, yet diving is a sport where you can, and should, keep learning. Improving your technical skills as time goes by means you will enjoy dives more, as will understanding the environment you are exploring and your impact on it.

One interesting way to keep learning is by taking a few PADI speciality courses. While you are on holiday, take a short course every now and then that matches the dive style you are doing. You will soon build up to the ultimate non-professional accolade, Master Scuba Diver.

▶▶ Progress up through PADI Rescue Diver then concentrate on improving your own skills and levels of confidence in all situations with Deep Diver, Wreck Diver, Night Diver or even Ice Diver.

▶▶ Focus on specific interests like Digital Underwater Photographer and Underwater Videographer which will add to your camera equipment skills and can be combined with a Peak Performance Buoyancy Course which will make shooting, and diving generally, easier.

▶▶ Understanding the marine environment will also enhance your dives. Consider Coral Reef Conservation Diver, National Geographic Diver Project AWARE Specialist and Underwater Naturalist.

In addition to these great options, there are courses tailored for children: Bubblemaker can be taken at eight years old and Junior Open Water from ten. If you have a family, get them involved. Or, if you want to teach, there are several courses that cover instructor qualifications at varying levels, which should be augmented by plenty of in-water experience.

health
and first aid

There are many healthcare issues involved in being a diver and most of the "can I, can't I?" stuff will be covered by your training. The following information is for guidance only. If you are unsure about anything at all to do with how a medical condition may affect your ability to dive safely, make sure you contact a doctor with specialist dive knowledge before you go away.

Before you go

Insurance Never underestimate the necessity of good, diver-specific medical insurance. Ensure that it covers repatriation in an emergency and check depth limitations. Many policies will only cover you up to 30 metres while others confusingly say "covered to the depth you are qualified to."

Check up If you have any pre-existing health issues or conditions, take a trip to your doctor and ensure you have both sufficient medications and information to handle your own healthcare. Most doctors are willing to prescribe in advance if you explain why. Remember to have your teeth checked every now and then, as trapped air in a cavity can be a very painful thing.

Vaccinations With most divers heading off to at least one distant destination every year, it's worth getting a full set of vaccinations then having boosters as and when necessary. Discuss this with your doctor too, allowing plenty of time in advance of your trip.

First aid kit Ask a pharmacist to help you put together items in small quantities that are suitable for use in the tropics:

▸▸ an 'anti-itch' cream for use on insect bites or rashes
▸▸ an analgesic, like paracetamol (acetaminophen) or ibuprofen
▸▸ antihistamine tablets for mild allergic reactions
▸▸ band-aids and a small pack of sterile bandages
▸▸ seasickness remedy   ▸▸ sinus decongestant tablets
▸▸ rehydration sachets   ▸▸ anti-diarrhoea drug
▸▸ ear drying aid   ▸▸ a small Swiss Army style knife

Malaria The best way to avoid getting malaria is not to get bitten. Yes, easier said than done, but the usual advice of a repellent lotion plus covered arms and legs after dusk will help enormously. However, as it's hard to avoid mosquitoes in damp environments such as kitting-up areas, you may need to take an anti-malarial drug. Which one to take is where it gets more complicated; the best advice is to research via a doctor or travel clinic. Make sure you tell them you are diving, as some have side-effects such as nausea, diarrhoea and sun sensitivity. Check cdc.gov/travel and fitfortravel.scot.nhs.uk for up-to-date recommendations.

While you're there

The tropics are beautiful but they do throw up some health issues especially those who arrive from colder climes. Here are some tips on ways to ensure your holiday isn't ruined but if in doubt always visit a local doctor. You may be reluctant to do this in some out-of-the-way village, but many doctors, even in the most remote countries, are highly trained.

Dehydration One of the most common ailments for divers. Being dehydrated can lead to other problems, not least of which is the bends. Drink at least two litres of water a day. Sugary drinks do not aid rehydration, nor, sadly, does beer.

Sunburn and heat-stroke Perhaps the second most common ailment. Use factor 30 sunscreen to prevent sunburn and wear a hat while you are out on the water where there are reflected rays. Heat stroke arrives disguised as the flu (headaches, muscle aches and pains, fatigue) but with some stomach problems thrown in.

Mosquito bites Try not to scratch or they may get infected by all the mini-nasties in seawater. Use an anti-itch cream and keep your hands in your pockets.

Seasickness Some people suffer, the rest are oblivious. If you suffer, stay out in the fresh air and keep your eyes on the horizon. If you suffer badly, there is no doubt about it, drugs work the best. You will need to find a brand that doesn't make you drowsy.

Ear problems Being immersed in salt water for hours at a time can cause a lot of trouble for ears. Remember to clear your ears – gently – before you feel pressure to alleviate potential problems. Those with recurring issues could use a steroid nasal spray, which will cut down on inflammation caused by the normal barotrauma of diving. If your ears get sore, rest them for a day. If you suspect you have an infection, an on-the-spot test is to press the hollow behind your ear lobe. If this is really painful, start antibiotic drops.

Sinus problems, colds and flu Arriving from cooler climates can bring on a cold or flu-like symptoms. Many people swear by nasal decongestants as these often make equalizing easier. However, they can also wear off halfway through a dive causing a reverse ear block, so be careful. Nothing clears sinuses as well as a good salt water sniff if it's just a case of clearing some city pollution. Antibiotics won't help a cold or flu unless you have a specific infection. Go back to mother's remedies – lots of fluid, vitamin C (oranges and lemons), a mild painkiller and keep warm.

Allergies Many people have become intolerant to allergens such as dust mites and pollen or have food intolerances to things like wheat or gluten. These can cause discomfort but are not life threatening so can be easily treated with an oral antihistamine. However, if you have a serious – true – allergy ensure you are carrying any necessary drugs with you. Specific food allergies such as seafood or nuts are extremely dangerous. If you are miles offshore, carry an epi-pen with you at all times and make sure that someone else knows where that is and what to do with it.

❝❞ My travel medicine kit always includes ear drying agent but I make my own. It's heaps cheaper and works just as well. Mix half rubbing alcohol and half vinegar: the vinegar helps change the pH of the ear canal to inhibit the growth of fungi which are responsible for most infections. The alcohol does the drying so if it irritates a little, reduce the quantity – this varies from person to person so it takes a bit of experimenting. The trick though is to prevent rather than treat, so if you are subject to ear problems, try this at the end of every day. And I always like to remind people that for cuts and grazes, even insect bites, there really is no substitute for a daily wash with plain old soap and fresh water.

Doctor Joann Gren, emergency medicine specialist, Australia

Women's issues There are few women who would choose to go diving when they have their period. There are various drugs you can use to delay this but ensure you get good advice on how long you can safely do so. Pregnancy is a little more of an issue. There is no definitive research on how a foetus might be affected by diving. Many women have dived before realizing they were pregnant with no ill effects, but is it worth the risk?

Diving-related conditions

There is no way a travel guide can guide you through the myriad issues related to diving accidents, which is why it's imperative to dive with a recognized and trustworthy dive operation who will ensure your divemaster is able to cope. All the same, it's as well to have basic knowledge of what is going on.

The bends Symptoms of a bend that involve the nervous system include joint or muscle pain, dizziness, difficulty breathing, extreme fatigue, skin rashes, unconsciousness and paralysis. Regardless of how minor or severe the symptoms are, get advice immediately. So-called 'minor' bends (skin and lymphatic) are becoming more common. These are comparatively mild but may resolve after a break from diving, so take the break and always tell a divemaster.

Bruises, sprains and broken ribs It would be an amazing dive trip where someone doesn't drop a tank on their foot, slip on a wet deck or trip en route to the RIB. If you can get to a doctor do, otherwise apply the **RICE** principle… **R**est, use **I**ce on the injured area, use a **C**ompression dressing, and **E**levate it.

Nitrogen narcosis Not an accident as such, except that narked divers often do silly things and can have one. To reverse the effects, ascend to a shallower depth making slow, controlled safety stops.

Severe headaches Again not an accident but may lead to one if ignored. There are many factors that contribute to headaches, but one way to control them is to ensure you breathe constantly and gently. Try not to hold your breath – ever.

Marine creatures

No matter how careful we all are in the water there are times when the marine world takes exception to us being there:

Fish bites It may not happen often, but there is the potential for an unimpressed fish to dash out and bite a diver. Triggerfish are the best known aggressors but even cute little Nemos are known to take a nip. In all cases, clean out the wound with clean water or vinegar then apply an antibiotic ointment. Large bites may get infected so need antibiotics and anti-tetanus treatment.

Venomous animals Not that you would intentionally touch anything dangerous, but should you happen to get too close, use these basic first aid treatments then seek professional advice. The venom of some marine animals is broken down by heat, so the following treatment can be used for sea urchins, crown of thorns starfish and stingrays. It will also aid, but is less effective on, stone, scorpion or lionfish, cone shells and seasnakes.

» clean the wound
» immerse in hot water (50°C) until pain stops (up to two hours)
» apply pressure immobilization: wrap a broad, firm bandage over the bite quite tightly and extend as high as possible over the limb. Keep still, apply a splint and bind so that the limb cannot be moved.
» seek advice on whether an antivenom or injection of long-acting local anaesthetic is needed.

Corals and all the rest Fire corals, hydroids, plankton and other stings, even jellyfish, can all be treated with acetic acid – vinegar or lemon juice – or an anaesthetic cream. Coral cuts are easily infected, so wash the cut well with clean, soapy water or vinegar then apply an antibiotic ointment frequently. These will take a long time to heal unless you stay out of the water, so you should repeat the treatment after each dive. Snorkellers should be very careful and wear swim shoes

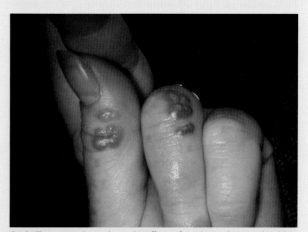

Ouch! The image above shows the effects of touching what you shouldn't. This is the result of brushing against a stinging hydroid while taking a photo; the skin has reacted to the toxins in the hydroid.

marine
nasties

Every time we dive, we descend into a realm where hidden dangers lurk in the form of unrecognized or misunderstood creatures. We are all familiar with more obvious nasties, such as much-maligned sharks, seldom-aggressive barracuda and even mildly stinging anemones. However, it pays to be aware of creatures you may encounter underwater that can be a less obvious threat.

Cephalopods The only nasty cephalopod is the tiny blue-ringed octopus. Rarely aggressive – and rarely seen – this chap spends most of his life hiding from predators. But take heed if those bright blue rings are flashing: these octos harbour tetrodotoxin, one of the most deadly poisons known to man.

Corals and hydroids These very fragile organisms should never be touched as they are easily damaged, but also because some

species will retaliate. Hard coral skeletons are made of calcium carbonate, which is brittle and sharp and can cut or scratch soft skin. Some, like fire coral, also contain stinging nematocysts (a microscopic cell containing a poisoned barb) which can penetrate skin then burn or itch for some time. Hydroids (or seaferns) are seen on many reefs. These swaying, fern-like clusters are often mistaken for harmless plants. However, hydroids have a serious sting in their 'fronds'. They contain hundreds of stinging cells in their tentacles.

Crustacea Cute as a puppy scampering about the reef floor, the mantis shrimp is deceptively dangerous. There are two types, which are fondly described as thumbcrackers or spearchuckers, all depending on the shape of their modified front claws. When hunting or attacked these claws shoot out with enough power to crack a thumb or spear a hand.

Fire or Bristle Worms These small caterpillar-like critters may seem innocuous and fairly uninteresting, but their ultra-fine spines can easily penetrate gloves and wetsuits. Once embedded in the skin, the spines break and cause a burning sensation, swelling or rashes. Scrubbing with pumice may help.

Fish All fish have some form of defence, even if it's just a simple one like the teensy teeth on sweet little 'Nemo' fish. Far more

serious is the razor sharp caudal blade that sits in front of a surgeonfish's tail fin. Triggerfish are perhaps the most dangerous on the reef, as both titan and yellowmargined triggers are incredibly aggressive. They will chase off sea creatures and land lubbers alike when they are nesting and think nothing of nipping at a fin or an ear. Many forms of jellyfish sting, ranging from the deadly Australian box jellyfish to ones that are almost harmless. Balls of lined catfish rolling across the seabed are entertaining but the highly venomous, razor-sharp spines in their fins can inflict serious wounds and the venom has been known to cause death.

The scorpionfish family are one of the reef's most contrasting, with some very beautiful species and some really ugly ones. However, they all employ the same form of defence – a ridge of venomous spines runs along their bodies and these can inject varying strengths of venom into the attacker. Generally, lionfish stings are less serious than those of scorpionfish; more dangerous is the false stonefish, then the devilfish whose venom is almost as potent as the potentially deadly stonefish. Many divers confuse these species so take care to avoid touching them all.

Sea snakes and eels These animals suffer from a reputation they don't really deserve. Many snakes are venomous but they are also mostly just curious. If a sea snake appears to be taking too much interest, offer it your fin to 'taste' and it will soon leave. Likewise, a moray's reputation for aggression is due to poor eyesight and the way they search for food – head poking out of a hole, mouth gaping, teeth bared. If your hand is too close they will snap, thinking it's a fish.

Sea urchins Put an unwary foot down on a sea urchin and you are unlikely to forget it. Their brittle, needle-sharp spines easily penetrate skin and neoprene. The common, long-spined urchin is not toxic but others have potentially fatal poisons. Take care over any that have swollen tips on the spines – these are poison sacs – such as the very beautiful but toxic fire urchin. The notorious Crown of Thorns starfish is part of the same species group as sea urchins but is better known for its ability to destroy large swathes of coral. At up to half a metre across, their thick rigid spines have sharp points. A sting has a similar effect to those of sea urchins but severe cases have been known to cause paralysis.

Shells Only a handful of shells are dangerous. These are mostly within the cone shell group which have a venom-filled, harpoon-like radula dart or tooth. Injected into prey, its venom will paralyse and is toxic enough to kill humans.

Top: blue-ringed octopus; bristleworm; inimicus or devilfish; cone shell.
Bottom: fire coral; titan triggerfish; sea snake; toxic fire urchin.

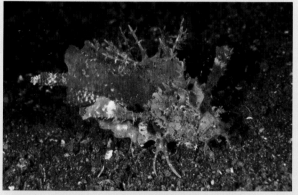

credit where it's due

Every new version of Diving the World becomes a whole new voyage for us. For this third edition, we have been lucky enough to spread our wings yet again, visiting a few unexplored destinations, revisiting some old favourites and – as always – we have had some outstanding experiences along the way. There has been continuing support from many diving professionals and even more from our friends. Without these people, we would never get a project like this done.

So without further ado, our thanks to:

Dominick Macan of Dive Advice Travel for getting us to Saba and St Kitts and, for re-introducing us to Jordan, Teresa Bennett of Dive Worldwide.

There are people who love to tell us tales. In this edition, they were: Suzanne Al Qadi, Carole Bellars, Helen Brunt, Lindy Bucceri,

Roy Calverley, Linda Cash, Gabriel Frankel, Jackie Hutchings, Jill and Sean Keen, Brenda and Duncan Kirkby, Anne-Marie and Matt Kitchen-Wheeler, Sue Laing, Cindi LaRaia, Gavin Macauley, Carol and Mike Metz, Andrew Perkins, Rich Rubin, Vladimir Soto, Phil and Patricia Tobin, Steve and Suzanne Turek, Amy Wheeler and Estelle Zauner-Maughan.

Nothing could make us happier than being able to share some of our travels with the best dive buddies we could ever hope for. A big hand for those who trekked across the planet to the Maldives, Palau, the Philippines, Komodo and the uncharted waters of Halmahera. A standing ovation goes to the various Babes on the Bow teams: this tradition was started more than two decades ago and is one that never fails to keep the crew of any boat amused!

Beneath Sangeang volcano, Indonesia. *Seated*, Roy Calverley, Phil Tobin, Shaun Tierney, Greg Openshaw, Carol Metz, Patricia Tobin; *standing*, Dennise Openshaw, Estelle Zauner-Maughan, Carole Bellars, Beth Tierney, Alison Gibson; *and sleeping*, Mike Metz.

Insets: Joann Gren and David Barr, Sue and Andrew Perkins, Sean and Jill Keen, Susan Laing, Steve and Suzanne Turek.

Top: The Babes on the Bow in Palau.

When they're with us, Jill Keen and Estelle Zauner-Maughan have stepped perfectly into the role of being extra photographic models (go girls!) as did Nick Rogers. A lot of other dive buddies get snapped without always realizing. Thank you all.

We remain fit and healthy because both Joann Gren and Estelle Zauner-Maughan are involved in all things medical.

The following people have been involved in one way or another, sometimes in past editions, sometimes in this. Whether for business or personal reasons, whatever you did for us, we appreciated it (and if we left you out, we're really sorry):
Michèle Abraham, Rosario Afuang, Max Ammer, Vanessa Auge, Trina Baker, Gill Balchin, David Barr, Tim Beard, Rick Belmar, Max Benjamin, Rob Bryning, Mike Caver, Vincent Chew, Jonathan Cross, Richard De

Villa, Dolores Diez, Don Dunlop, Domingo Ramon Enerio, Susie Erbe, Dieter and Karen Gerhard, Simone Gerritsen, Gary Greig, Holly Hawkins, Jane Herbert, Sheldon Hey, Sten Johanssen, Andrew Lok, Clay McCardell, Bruce Moore, George More, Greg and Dennise Openshaw, Sue Perkins, Mike Perun, Alan Raabe, Alberto Reija, Tony Rhodes, William Sawalha, Gerlinde Seupel, Mark Shandur, Paul Shepherd, Andrew Shorten, Diana Standen, Rick Taylor, Annabel Thomas, Peter Wincott and Jim Yanny.

Finally, many thanks as ever to the entire team at Footprint and especially to Patrick Dawson and Liz Taylor.

And always in memory of Larry Smith.

 # Resources

Research and reference
The following were our principal forms of reference, although there were more:
Reefbase (reefbase.org), Earthtrends (earthtrends.wri.org), The CIA World Factbook (cia.gov), Starfish (starfish.ch), The World Atlas of Coral Reefs (Spalding, Ravilious and Green).

Marine identification
The entire Reef Identification series, New World Publications (mainly Humann & DeLoach); World of Water Marine Publications (Neville Coleman); IKAN Reef & Fish guides (Debelius, Kuiter, Norman, Halstead); Fishbase (fishbase.org)

Photography
Cameras Nikon F90/Nikon D200/Nikon D300 SLRs in Sea and Sea housings; Nikonos V; Nikon Coolpix 5200 digital; Fuji Finepix F500/F600 EXR/Canon S120.

Flashes Ikelite Substrobe 50s; Sea and Sea YS90 duos; Sea and Sea D1s, Inon Z240

Lenses Nikkor 17-35 zoom, 10-24 zoom, 60mm micro, 105mm micro, 16mm, 20mm

Film Fujichrome Velvia 50 & 100 and Fujichrome Provia 100F

Suppliers Kevin Reed at Aquaphot (aquaphot.net); Cameras Underwater (camerasunderwater.com); Jon Cohen at Fujifilm UK (fujifilm.co.uk)

Dive kit Amphibian Sports, London

Additional images
Thanks to Seen Keen for the latest great author portrait of us and to anyone – but especially Estelle and Phil – who ever clicked a camera then sent us a picture that has ended up on this page.

66 99 Aaaah. Fish!
Ambon and Banda Tierney, Sherborne, UK

dive travel directory

Daily dive tours
Dive packages
PADI scuba courses

Diving like nowhere else

SCUBA IGUANA

GALÁPAGOS

info@scubaiguana.com
www.scubaiguana.com

Tel. 593-5-252-6296
593-5-252-6497
Cel. 593-9-9702-4031
593-9-9815-1283

Most experienced Galápagos day trip dive operator

Sea the difference with SeaStar
Red Sea diving without the crowds

PADI courses ▪ PADI TecRec
Daily guided dives from boat
and shore ▪ Free transfers from
hotels ▪ Private beach club

SeaStar WaterSports

PADI
5STAR
INSTRUCTOR
DEVELOPMENT
CENTRE

PADI TecRec

www.aqabadivingseastar.com

Image: Phil McIntyre

australia ecuador jordan

There are some diving spots in the world that offer cave diving and vibrant corals, others offer wall diving with excellent visibility and several places offer whalesharks.....

CHRISTMAS ISLAND ▪ TOURISM ASSOCIATION

....but we boast all of these and more

CHRISTMAS ISLAND

www.christmas.net.au
www.facebook.com/ChristmasIslandTourism | @CITourism

DIVE ADVICE TRAVEL

WORLD'S FINEST DIVING DESTINATIONS

www.diveadvice.com

Customized, personalized, diving odysseys
Every voyage is unique
Let our expert team customize your dream trip

www.DiveAdvice.com
Dom@DiveAdvice.com

+33 (0) 492 940 299
skype: adventuredom

worldwide

Siren Fleet

Affordable luxury for
liveaboard diving in
Asia & the Pacific

Deluxe en-suite cabins, outdoor dining
& plush lounges, spacious dive deck,
camera station

Guided dives in small groups,
free Nitrox &
equipment rental

info@sirenfleet.com • www.sirenfleet.com

PUERTO GALERA

Dive. Explore. Repeat

It's more fun in the
Philippines

A famed underwater paradise, Puerto Galera is also
gateway to many unspoilt overland natural attractions

Getting There : Accessible from Manila via Batangas
pier and ferry service in 3 hours

More Things to Do:
• Dive Apo Reef National Marine Park
• Visit Ambulong Island's underwater caves
• See Tamaraw Falls
• Climb Mt. Halcon

🌐 www.itsmorefuninthephilippines.com
f www.facebook.com/itsmorefuninthephilippines

BALI

AquaMarine Diving - Bali only offers Bali's better dive sites:
Nusa Penida - drift-diving
Tulamben - wreck and reef-diving
Padangbai - sharks and pelagics
Menjangan Island - wall-diving

Day Trips, Safaris (dive/accom packages), PADI Courses.

Muck Divers & Macro Photographers: Book an AMD-B dedicated spotter.

Agent for other reputable Indonesian dive resorts and liveaboards.

Info@AquaMarineDiving.com

indonesia

Leave the crowds behind for
Gorontalo Sulawesi, Indonesia

Dense coral growth
New and endemic species
Caverns, muck, pinnacles, walls and wrecks

"Indonesia's best-kept secret"
Asian Diver magazine

www.miguelsdiving.com

Photo: Stephan Wong

MOYODIVE
RESORT

www.moyodiveresort.com

info@moyodiveresort.com

A HIDDEN PARADISE IN
INDONESIA

PRISTINE. BREATHTAKING. PERFECT.
BOTH ABOVE AND BELOW THE INDIAN OCEAN.

Experience some of the world's finest diving at Anantara Medjumbe Island Resort
& Spa in the jewel-like Quirimbas Archipelago, northern Mozambique.
An underwater wonderland with untouched coral reefs and an astounding
diversity of marine species awaits. Where tropical waters seldom drop below 27°,
this exclusive Indian Ocean retreat has earned a reputation for sophisticated
simplicity and unrivalled hospitality.

Anantara
MEDJUMBE ISLAND
RESORT & SPA

For tailormade diving packages and special offers, contact:
info@raniresorts or tel: +27 11 658 0633
www.medjumbe.com

mozambique
micronesia
worldwide

Palau www.SOLITUDE-ONE.com
Liveaboard Diving Redefined

SOLITUDE ONE

DIVE
THE WORLD

• Resorts, courses and
  worldwide liveaboards
• Up-to-date local knowledge
• Prices to suit every budget
• Lowest prices guaranteed

www.dive-the-world.com

Maldives • Galapagos • Indonesia • Fiji
Thailand • Malaysia • Australia • Red Sea
Cocos • Mexico • Belize • Palau & more...

dive DISCOVERY
Complete Dive and Adventure Travel

WWW.DIVEDISCOVERY.COM
WWW.AFRICA-DISCOVERY.COM
INFO2@DIVEDISCOVERY.COM

Unique diving destinations | Exotic African escapes

We go
FURTHER...

We offer over 190 locations
worldwide, handpicked for
the best dive experiences.

ABTOT

DIVE
WORLDWIDE
TRAVEL | EXPERIENCE | CONSERVE

diveworldwide.com
0845 130 6980   sales@diveworldwide.com

Footprint
credits

Proofreader: Sophie Blacksell Jones
Indexer: Leonie Drake
Layout and production: Beth Tierney
Picture editor: Shaun Tierney
Maps: Beth Tierney
Cover design: Beth and Shaun Tierney
Publisher: Patrick Dawson
Managing Editor: Felicity Laughton
Advertising: Elizabeth Taylor
Sales and marketing: Kirsty Holmes

Photography credits
Cover images:
© Shaun Tierney/SeaFocus
Inside images:
© SeaFocus/seafocus.com

Print
Manufactured in India by Thomson Press Ltd

Disclaimer
Every effort has been made to ensure that the facts in this guidebook are accurate. However, travellers should still obtain advice from consulates, airlines, etc, about travel and visa requirements before travelling. In addition, contact the relevant governing bodies with regards to diving operations. The authors and publishers cannot accept responsibility for any loss, injury or inconvenience caused.

Publishing information
Footprint Diving the World 3rd edition
© Footprint Handbooks Ltd
October 2014

ISBN 978 1 910120 05 7
CIP DATA: A catalogue record for this book is available from the British Library

® Footprint Handbooks and the Footprint mark are a registered trademark of Footprint Handbooks Ltd

Published by Footprint
6 Riverside Court, Lower Bristol Road,
Bath BA2 3DZ, UK
T +44 (0)1225 469141
F +44 (0)1225 469461
footprinttravelguides.com

Distributed in the USA by
National Book Network, Inc.

All rights reserved. No part of this publication may be reproduced, stored in a retrieval system, or transmitted, in any form or by any means, electronic, mechanical, photocopying, recording, or otherwise without the prior permission of Footprint Handbooks Ltd.

Join us online...

Follow **@FootprintBooks** on Twitter, like **Footprint Books** on **Facebook** and talk travel with us! Ask us questions, speak to our authors, swap stories and be kept up-to-date with travel news, exclusive discounts and fantastic competitions.

Upload your travel pics to our **Flickr** site and inspire others on where to go next.

And don't forget to visit us at **ʃ footprint**travelguides.com

All dive sites listed in this book are indexed here and highlighted as follows:
Alice in Wonderland (Fij) 246

Country/region abbreviations: Australia = (Aus), Caribbean = (Crb) East Africa = (EAF), Fiji = (Fij), Galápagos = (Glpgs), Central America (CA), Indonesia = (Ind), Malaysia = (Mas), Maldives = (Mald), Mexico = (Mex), Micronesia (Mic), Papua New Guinea = (PNG), Philippines = (Phi), Red Sea = (RS), Solomon Islands = (Solm), Thailand = (Thai)

A

Abu Dabab Bay (RS) 301
Abu Galawa Soraya (RS) 303
acknowledgements 358
Aida, the, Big Brother (RS) 300
air travel 14
airlines 14
Alice in Wonderland (Fij) 113
allergies 354
Alma Jane Wreck (Phi) 272
Alona Beach Sanctuary (Phi) 278
Altún Ha 76
Ambergris Caye 76
Ambon 158
Amet, Nusa Laut (Ind) 159
Amman 309
Anchors Aweigh (Crb) 45
Angel's Window (Ind) 151
Anilao 270
Anker Wreck, Menjangen (Ind) 142
Aqaba 304
Aquarium I & II (CA) 74
Aquarium, the (CA) 67
Aquarium (EAF) 91
Arch, the, Darwin Is. (Glpgs) 128
Arco Point (Phi) 278
Ari Atoll 195
Atmosphere Reef (Phi) 282
Australia 16
    drying out 32

B

Baa Atoll 196
baggage 14
Bali 142
Bali Aga village 161
Bali Barat National Park 161
Balicasag 279
Banda 160
Bangkok 345
Barracuda Caves (Mex) 209
Barracuda Point (Mas) 173
Barracuda Point (Solm) 319
Bartolomé, (Glpgs) 127
Bat Cave, Dos Ojos (Mex) 210

Bedegul 161
Bedouin camp 308
Belize 64
    drying out 76
Belize City 76
bends, the 355
Bev's Reef (PNG) 259
Bianca C (Crb) 51
Big Brother (RS) 299
Big Rock Market (Crb) 43
Black Forest (Ind) 156
Black Forest (Phi) 279
Blackforest (Crb) 51
Black Rock, South Atoll (Phi) 275
Blue Corner (Mic) 235
Blue Hole, the (CA) 69
Blue Ribbon Eel Reef (Fij) 114
Bodhufinolhu Thila (Mald) 195
Bohol 287
Boiler, the (Mex) 216
booking 11
Boon Song Wreck (Thai) 338
Boulders (Phi) 272
Bouma Falls 117
Brisbane 32
British Sub Aqua Club 352
Brothers, the (RS) 299
budgets 12
Burma Banks (Thai) 342

C

Cabilao 280
Cable Canyons (RS) 304
Cabo Pearce (Mex) 219
Cabo San Lucas 223
Cage diving (Mex) 215
Cairns 32
Cairo 308
Calvin's Crack (CA) 70
Cancún 222
Cannibal Rock (Ind) 146
Canyon, the (EAF) 86
Canyon, the (Mex) 216
Canyons II (CA) 64
Cape Marshall (Glpgs) 131
Cape Tribulation 32
Caribbean 34
    drying out 54
Carriacou 48
Castle, the, Kawe (Ind) 154
Cat's Cables, (Aus) 29
Cathedral (CA) 67
Caves, the, Wolf Is. (Glpgs) 128
Cave 20 (EAF) 93
Caye Caulker 76
Cedar Pride (RS) 306
Cenotes, the 210
Central America 56
    drying out 76
Central Zone (Glpgs) 126
Chac-Mool Cenote (Mex) 211

Chandelier Cave (Mic) 237
Chankanaab National Park 222
Channel, Clerke Reef (Aus) 28
Chichén Itzá 222
Christmas Island 30
Christmas Point (Thai) 338
Chuuk 232
Cockscomb Basin Sanctuary 76
Cocoa Thila (Mald) 192
Coconut Point (Aus) 31
Coconut Point, Apo Is. (Phi) 281
Cocos (Keeling) Islands 29
CocoView Bay and wall (CA) 72
Cod Hole, Mermaid Reef (Aus) 28
Cod Hole, the (Aus) 26
colds 354
Cologne Gardens (Aus) 29
conservation 350
Copán Ruinas 77
Coral Gardens, Kenya (EAF) 87
Coral Gardens, Tanzania (EAF) 90
Coral Sea 27
Coral Triangle 349
Corner, the, Rainbow Reef (Fij) 114
Coron 276
costs 12
    Australia 19
    Caribbean 37
    Central America 59
    East Africa 81
    Fiji 103
    Galápagos 119
    Indonesia 137
    Malaysia 167
    Maldives 185
    Mexico 203
    Micronesia 227
    Papua New Guinea 246
    Philippines 265
    Red Sea 291
    Solomons 313
    Thailand 329
Cousins Rock (Glpgs) 127
Cozumel 212
credits 364
Crystal Rock (Ind) 145
Cyclone Reef (PNG) 259
currency 12

D

Daintree Rainforest 32
Darwin 128
Dauin (Phi) 283
Dave's Drop Off (Crb) 44
Dead Palm (Phi) 270
dehydration 354
Devil's Throat, Punta Sur (Mex) 213
Dhonfanu Thila (Mald) 196
Dibutonai Reef (Phi) 277
Dickie's Place (PNG) 254
directory 360

dive brief
    Australia 20
    Caribbean 38
    Central America 60
    East Africa 82
    Fiji 106
    Galapagos 122
    Indonesia 138
    Malaysia 168
    Maldives 186
    Mexico 204
    Micronesia 228
    Papua New Guinea 247
    Philippines 266
    Red Sea 292
    Solomons 314
    Thailand 330
diver training 352
Divers Dream (Phi) 279
Diver's Surprise (Crb) 48
Dogtooth Lair (Mas) 177
Dolphin House (Phi) 284
Dos Ojos (Mex) 210
Double Bommie (Aus) 24
drying out
    Australia 32
    Caribbean 54
    Central America 76
    East Africa 99
    Fiji 116
    Galápagos 132
    Indonesia 161
    Malaysia 180
    Maldives 198
    Mexico 222
    Micronesia 242
    Papua New Guinea 256
    Philippines 286
    Red Sea 307
    Solomons 324
    Thailand 344
Dumaguete 286
Duppy Waters (CA) 73

E

ear problems 354
East Africa 78
    drying out 99
East of Eden (Thai) 337
Edge of Reason (EAF) 97

Egypt 296
    drying out 308
Eiger Wall (Phi) 275
El Gouna 307
Elephant Rock (Thai) 337
Elphinstone Reef (RS) 302
End Bommie (PNG) 256
Entrance, the (Aus) 27
equipment 15
essentials
    Australia 19
    Caribbean 37
    Central America 59
    East Africa 81
    Fiji 105
    Galápagos 121
    Indonesia 137
    Malaysia 167
    Maldives 185
    Mexico 203
    Micronesia 227
    Papua New Guinea 247
    Philippines 265
    Red Sea 291
    Solomons 313
    Thailand 329

F

Far South, Egypt 300
Fathers Reefs 253
fees 12
Fiji 102
    drying out 116
Finger Point, Eriyadu (Mald) 190
first aid 354
fish bites 355
Florida Islands 321
flu 354
Flying Fish Cove (Aus) 31
Forty Foot Point (CA) 71
Froggie Fort (Mas) 178
Fujikawa Maru (Mic) 234

G

Galápagos 118
    drying out 132
Gap, the (EAF) 94
German Channel (Mic) 238
Goldilocks (Fij) 112
Gordon Rocks (Glpgs) 126
Gorgon 1 (RS) 305
Gorgonia Wall (Phi) 280
Great Barrier Reef 24
Great Wall (CA) 73
great whites 214
Great White Wall, the (Fij) 115
Grenada 51
    drying out 55
Gulf of Phuket 334
Gulf of Thailand 330

H

Hairball (Ind) 152
Half Moon Caye National
Monument 76
Half Way Wall (Aus) 27
Halliburton Wreck (CA) 74
Hamata 307
Hanifaru Lagoon (Mald) 197
Hans (Ind) 144
health 354
heat-stroke 354
highlands, the (PNG) 261
Hin Muang (Thai) 335
Hol Chan Marine Reserve (CA) 64
Holbox 222
Honduras 70
    drying out 76
Honiara 325
House Reef/Jetty Wreck (Mas) 178
Hurghada 307

I

Ibo Island 101
Indonesia 134
    drying out 161
insurance 13
Isabela 130
Isla Guadalupe (Mex) 214
Isla Lobos 133
Islas Revillagigedo 216

J

Jack Rock (Mas) 179
Jackfish Spot (EAF) 90
Jahir (Ind) 152
Japanese Gardens (RS) 305
Jayne's Reef (PNG) 253
Jellyfish Lake (Mic) 239
Jerash 309
Jessie Beazley Reef (Phi) 274
Joe's Ridge (EAF) 98
Jolanda (RS) 297
Jordan 304
    drying out 309
Jozani Forest 100

K

Kakani (Mald) 196
Kandooma Corner (Mald) 192
Kani Corner (Mald) 191
Kapalai 174
Kapalai Jetty/House Reef (Mas) 174
Karang Hatta (Ind) 160
Karangasem 161
Kasai Wall (Phi) 284
kava ceremonies 117
Kawe Castle & the Keep (Ind) 155
Kenshu Maru (Mic) 234
Kenya 86
    drying out 99
Kichwani (EAF) 91

Kimbe Bay 252
King Cruiser (Thai) 334
Kintamani 161
Koh Tachai (Thai) 339
Komodo 145
Koroyanitu National Park 117
Kota Kinabalu 180
Kuda Giri (Mald) 193

L

Laha I, II & III, Ambon (Ind) 158
Lake Nakuru 99
Lake Tagimoucia 117
Lama Shoals (PNG) 255
Lankanfinolhu, outside channel
(Mald) 191
Lankayan 178
Larry's Heaven (Ind) 157
Lavena Village 117
Lava Flow (Mex) 217
Layang Layang 176
learning to dive 352
Leeward Islands 42
Lekuan I, II & III (Ind) 149
Lembeh 151
Leru Cut (Solm) 319
Liberty Wreck, the (Ind) 143
Lighthouse Reef 67
Lighthouse, the, Cabilao (Phi) 280
Lionfish Wall (Mic) 241
Little Brother (RS) 299
Little Giftun (RS) 298
Little Komodo (Ind) 157
Loloata Island 256
Lombok 142
Lumahlihe Passage (Solm) 322
Luxor 308
Luzon 270

M

M'll Channel (Mic) 241
M'n'M (Mald) 194
Maaya Thila (Mald) 195
Mabul 175
Magic Garden (Crb) 50
Mainit Point (Phi) 270
Malaysia 164
    drying out 180
Maldives 182
    drying out 198
Malé 199
Malindi 99
Manado 148
Mandarin City, (Ind) 160
Mandarinfish dive, the (Mic) 241
Mandolin (Ind) 150
Manta Alley (Ind) 146
Manta Point, Pemba (EAF) 88
Manta Reef, Jerien Is. (Ind) 154
marine biodiversity 348
marine conservation 350

marine nasties 356
Marovo Lagoon 322
Marsa Alam 307
Masa Plod Sanctuary (Phi) 282
Masai Mara National Park (EAF) 99
Mataram 161
Maya Wall, Phi Phi Lei (Thai) 335
Mayura Water Palace 161
Medjumbe Island 101
Melissa's Garden (Ind) 154
Mentjeng Wall (Ind) 145
Mergui Archipelago 342
Mexico 200
    drying out 222
Micronesia 224
    drying out 242
Mid Reef (Mas) 174
Midway Reef (PNG) 253
Mindoro 272
Moalboal 284
Moc-che (Mex) 209
Molas Wreck (Ind) 149
Molinere Bay (Crb) 52
Mombasa 99
mosquito bites 354
Mount Sinai 308
Mozambique 94
    drying out 101
Mt Rinjani 161
Mtangani, Pemba (EAF) 88
Myanmar 342
Mystery Reef (Fij) 113

N

Nadi 117
Nampele Mangroves (Ind) 155
Namotu Wall (Fij) 110
Negros Oriental 281
New Britain 252
Ngedbus Coral Garden (Mic) 238
Nilandhoo Atoll 194
Nippo Maru (Mic) 233
nitrogen narcosis 355
North Horn (Aus) 27
North Malé 190
North Sulawesi 148
North Twin (Thai) 343
Northern Point (RS) 300
Northern Zone (Glpgs) 128
Nudi Wall (Phi) 273
Nuggets (Fij) 112
Nyulli Reef (EAF) 87

O

Occabali Thila (Mald) 191
Oil Rig, the, Mabul (Mas) 175
Old Road Bay (Crb) 46
Otavalo 133
Ovalau Island 117

P

packing 15
Palancar Caves (Mex) 213
Palau 235
Palawan 274
Panglao, Bohol 278
Panorama (RS) 299
Pantai Parigi (Ind) 152
Papua New Guinea 244
    drying out 260
Paradise 1, Mabul (Mas) 175
Paradise Reef (Crb) 46
Pemba, Mozambique 94
Pemba island, Tanzania 88
Peninsular Malaysia 179
Perpendicular Wall (Aus) 30
Pescador Island (Phi) 285
Petra 309
Philippines 262
    drying out 286
Phuket gulf 334
Pico Bonito Cloud Forest 77
Pinnacle, the, Koh Bon (Thai) 339
Pixie Pinnacle (Aus) 25
planning a trip 10
Plantation Pinnacles (Fij) 111
Playa del Carmen 208
Playground (EAF) 95
Point 8 (EAF) 92
Port Douglas 32
Port Moresby 261
Puerto Ayora 133
Puerto Egas 133
Puerto Galera 272
Punta Tosca (Mex) 218
Punta Tunich (Mex) 212
Punta Vicente Roca (Glpgs) 131
Pura Meru Temple 161
Puri Jati, Siririt Bay (Ind) 142
Purple Rain (Crb) 53

Q

Quirimbas National Park 101
Quito 133

R

Raja Ampat Islands 154
Rakiraki 117
Ranch, the (EAF) 95
Ras Mohammed (RS) 297
Ras Mohammed National Park 308
Red Sea 288
    drying out 307
Red Firefish Reef (EAF) 87
Rendezvous Point (CA) 66
Rest Orf Island (PNG) 252
Restaurant, the (EAF) 25
Ribbon Reefs (Aus) 25
Richelieu Rock (Thai) 341
Roca Partida, North (Mex) 221
Roca Partida, South (Mex) 220

Roatán 70
Roca Rodonda (Glpgs) 130
Rockslide, Wolf Island (Glpgs) 129
Rowley Shoals 28
Russell Islands 318

S

Saba (Carib) 42
Sabah (Mas) 172
Safaga 307
safaris 100
Sahaong, Bangka (Ind) 150
Sailfish Tree/Rivermouth (EAF) 96
Salem Express, the (RS) 299
salt lake kayaking 117
Sambi-Sambi (EAF) 98
Samburu 99
San Benedicto 216
San Diego 223
San Jos, del Cabo 223
Sanctuary (Phi) 281
Sandakan 180
Sandslope (CA) 65
Sankisan Maru (Mic) 232
Santa Cruz 126
Savusavu 117
Sayonara Wreck (CA) 65
seasickness 354
Secret Bay (Ind) 271
Sekolah Desar (Ind) 143
Sepik River 261
Seven Stingrays (Mald) 194
Sha'ab Claudio (RS) 303
Sha'ab Malahi (RS) 303
Shakem (Crb) 53
Shark Airport, Tubbataha (Phi) 275
Shark Point (Thai) 335
Sharky's Hideaway (Crb) 50
Sharm el Sheikh 307
Shimba Hills, Pemba (EAF) 89
Shimba Hills National Reserve 99
Shindano (EAF) 92
Sian Ka'an Biosphere Reserve 222
Sigakota 117
Siladen (Ind) 149
Similans, the 336
Simon's Reef (Ind) 144
Sinai Peninsula 296
sinus problems 354
Sipadan 172
Sipadan Drop-Off (Mas) 172
Sister Rocks (Crb) 48
Socorro 218
Solomon Islands 310
    drying out 324
South coast, the (RS) 298
South Malé 192
South Point (Mas) 172
South Point, Cabilao (Phi) 280
South Point, Surin (Thai) 340
South Twin (Thai) 343

Spice Islands 158
Spice tours 100
Stingray (Ind) 144
St Catherine's Monastery 308
St Kitts 45
Steve's Bommie (Aus) 25
sunburn 354
Surin 340
Susan's Reef (PNG) 252
Suva 117
Suzie's Bommie (PNG) 257
Sydney 32

T

Taj Mahal (Mex) 211
Tanah Lot 161
Tanavula Point (Solm) 321
Tanjung Lain, Pulau Tiga (Ind) 161
Tanzania 88
    drying out 100
Tarpon Cave (CA) 68
Tatawa Besar (Ind) 145
Taveuni 114
Tedran Reef and Wall (Crb) 42
Ted's Point (CA) 75
Tent Wall and Reef (Crb) 43
Teshio Maru (Mic) 237
Thailand 326
    drying out 344
Thistlegorm, the (RS) 297
Thundercliff (Aus) 31
Tiger Reef (Mas) 179
Tikal 76
Tioman 179
tipping 13
Tobia Arba (RS) 298
Tongue Reef (Aus) 24
Tormentos (Mex) 212
Torrens Point (Crb) 42
Tortugas (Mex) 208
Tower, the (RS) 296
training organizations 352
trekking 261
Triton Bay 156
Tsavo East 99
Tubbataha 274
Tubular Barrels (CA) 66
Tufi 258
Tufi Bay (PNG) 259
Tufi Pier (PNG) 258
Tulum 222
Tunuloa Peninsula 117
Twin Tugs (Crb) 49

U

Ubud 161
Ukwele (EAF) 92
Ulong Corner & Channel (Mic) 236
Utila 73
Uvinje Gap, Pemba (EAF) 89

V

vaccinations 354
Valley of the Kings (CA) 70
Valley of the Rays (Mic) 240
Valley, the (Mas) 177
Vanua Levu 112
Velvia (Solm) 321
venomous animals 355
Vilamendhoo House Reef (Mald) 195
Visayas, the 278
Viti Levu 110

W

Waikiri mission 117
Waisali Rainforest Reserve 117
Waivunia Village 117
West Papua 154
Western Australia 28
Western Rocky (Thai) 342
Western Zone (Glpgs) 130
White Beach (Solm) 320
Who Maru 1 & 2 (Solm) 323
Wickham Island (Solm) 322
Wilke's Passage (Fij) 111
Windward Islands 48
Wiray Bay (PNG) 254
Witu Islands 254
Wolf 128
women's issues 355
Wrasse Strip (Mas) 177
wrecks
    Akitsushima (Phi) 277
    Ann (Solm) 318
    Fujikawa Maru (Mic) 234
    Kogyo Maru (Phi) 276
    Kuda Giri (Mald) 193
    Liberty (Ind) 143
    MV Corinthian (Crb) 47
    MV Pacific Gas (PNG) 257
    MV River Taw (Crb) 47
    Nippo Maru (Mic) 233
    Salem Express, the (RS) 299
    Sankisan Maru (Mic) 232
    Taiei Maru (Phi) 276
    Thistlegorm, the (RS) 297
    Who Maru 1 & 2 (Solm) 323

X

Xcaret 222
Xel-hà 222

Y

Yacab (Mex) 212
Yap 240
Yucatán Peninsula 208

Z

Zanzibar 90

Galapagos

Turks & Caicos

Maldives

Saba/St. Kitts

Silver Bank

Unique liveaboard experiences.
Exceptional value.
Dive with us!

Five fantastic destinations worldwide

EXPLORER VENTURES
adventures in liveaboard diving

www.explorerventures.com
info@explorerventures.com
USA/Canada: 1.800.322.3577 / +1.307.235.0683